CW00971890

LIVING ABROAD IN
CANADA

CAROLYN B. HELLER

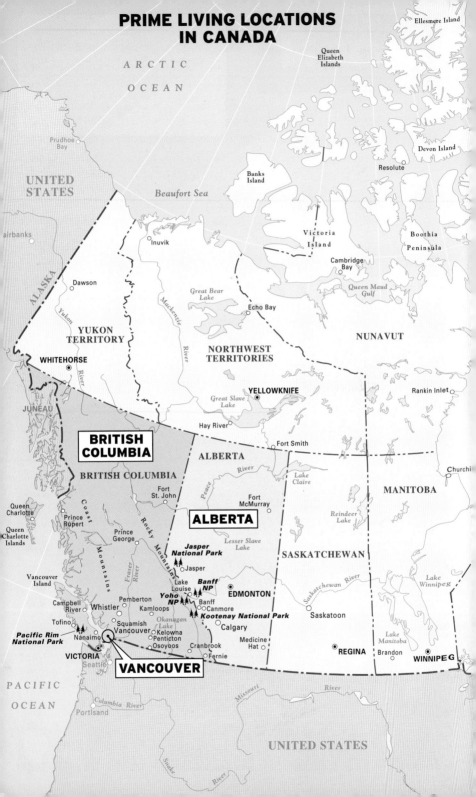

PRIME LIVING LOCATIONS IN CANADA

Contents

At Home in Canada

"You seem familiar, yet somehow strange –
are you by any chance *Canadian?*"

This *New Yorker* cartoon caption sums up the relationship many Americans have with Canada. We know Canada like we might casually know any next-door neighbor. We're cordial, say "hello," and go about our own business.

Sure, most Americans know something about our northern neighbor. We've scanned headlines about universal health care, same-sex marriage, and hockey mania. We've seen photos of majestic mountains, quiet coves, towering evergreens, and vast stretches of arctic wilderness. We're *familiar* with Canada, but we may not really know our Canadian neighbors – until something happens that makes us take notice.

For my family, it was a job offer.

For years, my husband and I had dreams of living abroad – fantasies, really, of lounging in Mediterranean cafés, settling under Caribbean palms, or even exploring a booming Asian city. But relocate to Canada? It's not that we weren't interested in our Canadian neighbor. It just wasn't on our living-abroad radar.

A job offer changed that, triggering an unanticipated move over the border. And as my family and I began figuring out how to manage the transition to our new Canadian home, we quickly discovered that crossing the border on vacation – something we'd done many times – wasn't the same as living and working in a different country.

Because Canada *is* a different country. Of course, that sounds silly, even presumptuous; we knew we were moving to a new nation with its own government and money and laws. Yet because Canada felt so comfortable – so simi-

lar to the United States — we were surprised at how many things we needed to sort out, how many things *were* different.

The paperwork we needed to begin working. The documents we needed to move our car. How to arrange for health insurance and file our tax returns. Unlike many immigrants heading abroad, we didn't need to learn a new language or adapt to exotic customs. We were going to the country right next door. Yet there were still plenty of challenges.

After we sorted out the paperwork, though, we began to adjust to our adopted country. Slowly, we discovered many differences between Canadian and American culture. We became acquainted with timbits. Learned what toques are and why the kids needed them for soccer. Figured out why there's a holiday on the Queen of *England's* birthday.

We came to appreciate the active, outdoor-oriented culture, where people make time to go skiing, ride their bikes, or walk along the waterfront. And we began to slow our hurry-up attitudes to a more laid-back Canadian speed. Sure, plenty of people work hard, spending too much time at their desks and not enough with their families, but many Canadians at least try to live balanced lives.

If you're reading this book, you may be thinking about moving to Canada or you may already be here. Whatever your reason for considering Canada — that neighbor who's familiar yet just a bit different — welcome. I'd like to introduce you to my new Canadian home.

► WHAT I LOVE ABOUT CANADA

- The ocean, downtown high-rises, and snow-topped mountains are all right outside my window.

- People are nice, people are tolerant, and they don't make a big deal about how nice and tolerant they are.

- Toronto has five Chinatowns.

- British Columbia has a desert.

- Montréalers move effortlessly between French and English.

- The United States isn't the center of the political universe.

- Skiing, sailing, hiking, bicycling, kayaking, camping—even when you live in the city, all these activities are close by, and people do them.

- Croissants for breakfast, sushi for lunch, and wild salmon, local greens, and bumbleberry pie for dinner.

- Maple syrup on snow.

- Gravy on french fries.

- Not having to worry about health insurance.

WELCOME TO CANADA

© CAROLYN B. HELLER

INTRODUCTION

Canada is the place all Americans want to live but just don't know it yet.
– Actor Richard Dreyfuss, as quoted in *Vancouver Lifestyles* magazine,
November 2006

Is Canada right for you? In many ways, life in Canada is quite similar to life in the United States. On both sides of the border, you can settle in a city, a suburb, or a small town. You can make your home by the ocean, in the mountains, or on the prairies. In both the United States and Canada, you can watch many of the same movies, listen to the same music, and tune in to the same TV shows. You can shop at the same big-box stores and drive through familiar fast-food windows. Many industries that thrive in the United States—from traditional agriculture and manufacturing to real estate and tourism to up-to-the-minute high technology and biotech—are also major components of the Canadian economy.

For better or worse, many people—in the United States and even abroad—

seem to consider Canada the 51st state. Perhaps because of the historically close relationship between the two countries, and the ease of traveling back and forth across the border, many Americans don't think of Canada as a "foreign" destination. If you're considering settling outside the United States, a move to Canada is one of the simplest possible relocations.

Yet Americans who relocate to Canada are often surprised to find that not everything is just like it was back home. Most importantly, you can't just head across the border and expect to be able to work. Although U.S. citizens can enter Canada as visitors and stay for six

strawberry season at Montréal's Jean-Talon Market

© CAROLYN B. HELLER

months, you can't get a job without a work permit or a permanent resident card (similar to a "green card" in the United States). Similarly, if you're planning to attend a university in Canada, you need to apply for a study permit. And if you're looking to retire to Canada, you also need to apply for permanent residency, unless you can limit your stays in Canada to no more than six months a year.

But beyond the paperwork requirements, and despite the similarities between the two societies, Americans in Canada need to understand that they are in a different country with its own distinctive culture. Canada has its own system of government, banking laws, and unique national health care system. Canada has its own media, film industry, and telecommunications suppliers, musicians and performers, authors and artists, as well as its own local foods and wines. The country has its own attitudes about immigration, multiculturalism, and social welfare, and in recent years, Canada and the United States have diverged on a number of social issues. As Canadian political scientist James Laxer wrote in his book, *The Border,* "The Canada–U.S. border draws a line between two societies with strikingly different views on key contemporary societal questions. On guns and capital punishment, the environment and health care, war and peace, Canada and the United States march to different drummers."

On a day-to-day basis, Americans living in Canada may not have to consider these larger social issues, but you do need to adjust to a host of little things—from a different system of money to local humor to distinctively Canadian language. As one of the British Commonwealth countries, Canada's official head of state is still the Queen of England. And north of the border, the Thanksgiving holiday is in October.

A documentary filmmaker who relocated from California to Canada put it this way: "When you live in the United States, it's as if there's a big mirror along the 49th parallel, reflecting the United States back on itself. And looking into this mirror, many Americans assume that Canada is just the same as the United States. But when you cross the border, you can suddenly see *through* the mirror. You not only see Canada in a new way, but you also look back at the United States through a different set of eyes."

CANADIAN STEREOTYPES – TRUE AND FALSE

Before you can begin seeing Canada more clearly, though, you need to examine the stereotypes that appear frequently in the American media. And there are quite a few:

Canada has more moose than people.

False. Canada's moose population has been estimated at between 500,000 and 1 million, while the country has more than 30 million people. If you're walking down the street in Toronto or Vancouver or any Canadian city, your chances of seeing a moose are slim to none.

Canada is cold.

True. Canada is one of the world's coldest countries, if you average the annual temperatures across the entire nation. Remember, though, that only a minority of Canadians live in the frigid far north. And several Canadian destinations, primarily Vancouver, Victoria, and other locations in British Columbia have a mild, temperate climate.

Canadians are nice.

True. Of course, everyone has bad days, but on the whole, Canadians pride themselves on being polite. Compared to people in many other countries, Canadians are more likely to wait politely in line, yield in traffic, and at least think about helping their neighbor.

Canadians are all politically liberal.

False. But "liberal" isn't a dirty word in Canada either. In fact, the country's Liberal party is actually in the middle of the political spectrum, with the Conservative party on the right, the New Democrats on the left, and several other parties in between.

Lacrosse is Canada's national sport.

True. If you thought that the national sport was hockey, you're not wrong. But Canada actually has two official pastimes: Hockey is the national winter sport, and lacrosse is the official summer sport. Of course, it's hockey that gets the most attention, and scads more Canadian kids grow up playing hockey than lacrosse.

All Canadians speak French.

False. Canada has two official languages: English and French. Any official government communications—tax forms, airport signs, tourism brochures— are in both English and French, and products sold in Canada must contain information in both languages. Outside the province of Québec, however, day-to-day life in most parts of Canada is conducted in English. And with the country's high rate of immigration, in some areas, the major second language isn't French—it might be Mandarin, Cantonese, Punjabi, or one of a host of other tongues.

AN AMERICAN BY ANY OTHER NAME

Throughout this book, the term "American" is used to refer to citizens or residents of the United States. Although the term can, of course, denote residents of other countries in the Americas, including Canada, for purposes of this book, it signifies people from the United States.

In Canada, though, people don't refer to the United States as "America." Most often, it's called either "the U.S." or "the States."

The Lay of the Land

Canada is the world's second-largest country in area, after Russia and just ahead of the United States. From east to west, it stretches more than 7,000 kilometers (4,350 miles). Despite all this space, Canada's population is relatively small. Roughly twice as many people live in France or Italy or the United Kingdom than in Canada, and the U.S. population is nearly 10 times larger.

Canada is divided into 10 provinces and three territories. The provinces are Newfoundland and Labrador, Nova Scotia, Prince Edward Island, New Brunswick, Québec, Ontario, Manitoba, Saskatchewan, Alberta, and British Columbia. The territories are Nunavut, Northwest Territories, and Yukon Territory.

Canadian provinces are analogous to U.S. states, each with its own provincial government. Like the United States, Canada has a federal system of government; some laws and policies apply nationwide, while others vary by province. For example, there's a national sales tax, but some provinces levy a provincial sales tax as well. Likewise, education is federally mandated but controlled at the provincial and local levels. Canada's territories are similar to U.S. territories, too; they have some of the responsibilities, but not all the rights, of the provinces.

THE CITIES

More than one-third of Canada's population lives in the three largest cities: Toronto, Montréal, and Vancouver. All three are modern, multicultural metropolises with thriving downtown districts, sprawling suburbs, several universities, and a variety of job opportunities across

© CAROLYN B. HELLER

Vancouver is the host city for the 2010 Winter Olympics.

a number of industries. Not surprisingly, the majority of expats who come to Canada to work or study settle in one of these metropolitan areas.

After these "Big Three," Ottawa, Canada's national capital, is the next largest city. While the city of Ottawa is part of the province of Ontario, the Ottawa metropolitan region—officially designated Ottawa–Gatineau—straddles the provincial border with Québec. Many of the jobs in this area are related to the national government; about a third of Canada's federal employees are based in the capital region, and government positions account for about one-fifth of Ottawa's total jobs. However, as in other large cities, Ottawa has significant sectors of its workforce engaged in retail, manufacturing, technical and scientific endeavors, education, and tourism-related ventures.

In the province of Alberta, the cities of Calgary and Edmonton, numbers five and six respectively on the population chart, have experienced a boom over the past decade, led by this resource-rich region's mining, oil, and gas industries. Many of the jobs here are in engineering, information technology, and other scientific arenas, as well as skilled labor, transportation, and related manufacturing that support these growing resource industries. Alberta's provincial government has been actively promoting immigration as a way to provide workers to sustain this growth. Canada is the leading foreign supplier of energy to the United States, and much of this energy comes from Alberta.

Officially, Canada's population is about 80 percent urban. Of course, "urban"

CANADA'S TOP 10

The following chart lists the population of Canada's largest metropolitan areas.

City	Population
Toronto (ON)	5.4 million
Montréal (QC)	3.7 million
Vancouver (BC)	2.2 million
Ottawa-Gatineau (ON-QC)	1.2 million
Calgary (AB)	1.1 million
Edmonton (AB)	1 million
Québec City (QC)	720,000
Winnipeg (MB)	707,000
Hamilton (ON)	716,000
London (ON)	465,000

Source: Statistics Canada, 2006

is a relative term, since only six cities in the entire country have a population of more than one million. Compare that to the United States, where at least 50 metropolitan areas are home to more than a million people. In Canada, an "urban area" has 100,000 people or more. If you're a city person, you should be able to narrow down your choice of living locations very quickly.

However, several smaller Canadian cities are also appealing destinations for expats, particularly those seeking a more laid-back lifestyle, those looking for second homes, and those seeking retirement destinations. British Columbia's capital city of Victoria, which rather confusingly is located on Vancouver Island (where the city of Vancouver is *not*), has a significant community of retirees, lured by some of the mildest weather north of the 49th parallel. Even though Victoria formerly had a reputation as a place for the "newly wed and nearly dead," it's experiencing its own mini-boom, as younger people, families, and entrepreneurs are lured here by the natural setting and by some expanding job opportunities.

Farther inland in B.C., the cities of Kelowna and Kamloops—in the region known as the Okanagan—are also appealing destinations. With the huge Okanagan Lake as its centerpiece, and a much drier climate than coastal B.C., this interior region is an increasingly popular vacation destination among both Canadians and Americans. The region has a newly thriving wine industry, as well as an active winter ski season, both of which are fueling the growth in vacation home development and drawing entrepreneurs who want to work in food, tourism, or real estate–related businesses.

While the climate in Ontario can't compete with the more temperate weather in British Columbia, this eastern province still has several smaller cities, including Hamilton, London, and the Kitchener-Waterloo region, centered around universities and emerging information industries. Hamilton, a former steel town, is developing new businesses, especially in health care and the sciences. London, too, is a former manufacturing hub with a growing biotechnology and science sector, and the Kitchener-Waterloo area is actively working to lure tech entrepreneurs from both sides of the border, billing itself as Canada's Technology Triangle.

Québec City, less than three hours' drive north of Montréal, has a much smaller expat population than other major Canadian cities. Most immigrants to Québec City come from Europe—not surprising, perhaps, since historic Québec City is one of Canada's most European-influenced communities. But there are roughly 1,200 U.S. expats who've settled there, and it may be worth considering if you speak French and are interested in francophone culture.

THE OUTDOORS

If you love the outdoors, Canada has more places to visit than you could explore in a lifetime. The country has 41 national parks, hundreds of provincial parks, and wide swaths of undeveloped territory. Canada's first national park, the now-well-known Banff National Park, was established in 1885 in the Rocky Mountains of Alberta, about a dozen years after the United States declared Yellowstone the first official national park in North America. The newest, designated in 2003, is Ukkusiksalik (pronounced "ooooo koo sik' sa lik"), just below the Arctic Circle in the territory of Nunavut. Plans are in the works for a massive new national park, covering more than 8.5 million acres in the Northwest Territories.

These protected natural resources are a wonderful asset, but if you're looking to settle or buy a second home in a recreational area, Canada has lots to offer as well. For skiers and snowboarders, popular destinations include Whistler, North America's largest ski resort, in British Columbia; the Banff, Lake Louise, and Jasper areas in Alberta, along with the fast-growing town of Canmore, which sits just outside the boundaries of Banff National Park; and Mont-Tremblant in the Laurentian Mountains, north of Montréal yet within a day's drive of many cities in the U.S. northeast.

There are also less-known winter-recreation regions that may be worth

© CAROLYN B. HELLER

The Rocky Mountains were voted one of the seven wonders of Canada.

a look, too. Vancouverites flee from Whistler's crowds by heading east to the Okanagan, where smaller, family-friendly resorts like Big White, Silver Star, and Sun Peaks get plenty of fluffy snow. Westerners are also keeping an eye on the developing Rocky Mountain region along the B.C.–Alberta line, checking out more remote resorts like Revelstoke, Kicking Horse, Panorama, Kimberley, and Fernie mountains. In the east, Québec's Eastern Townships—just over the border from Vermont and within a four-hour drive of Boston—have several smaller mountains in stereotypically quaint francophone towns. From Québec City, skiers head to nearby Mont-Sainte-Anne, eastern Canada's second-largest ski area.

If it's island life you're seeking, Canada can oblige as well. Vancouver Island, a 90-minute ferry ride across the Strait of Georgia from the city of Vancouver, is roughly 500 kilometers (300 miles) long. It's home to British Columbia's capital city, Victoria, as well as varied terrain that includes everything from beaches and secluded coves, to an 800-year-old fir tree, to Canada's highest waterfall (it's Della Falls, not the more-famous Niagara).

British Columbia's Gulf Islands—located between Vancouver Island and the mainland—are also appealing destinations for vacation homes or a getaway lifestyle. About a dozen of these islands are settled; the largest include Salt Spring, Galiano, Pender, Mayne, Denman, Hornby, and Quadra. In the east, vacationers seek out Ontario's Thousand Islands, as well as the coastal communities in Nova Scotia and Prince Edward Island. And other long-standing vacation and second-home destinations include Ontario's lakes and the well-known Niagara peninsula.

WEATHER

If you're thinking of moving to Canada, you have to think about the weather. Much of the country has long, cold winters, and if you're not prepared for weeks of sub-freezing temperatures, you won't last in many Canadian locations. That said, Canada's cities cope well with the climate. In urban areas such as Toronto, Montréal, and Calgary, enclosed walkways link many downtown buildings, so you can walk long distances without ever venturing outside. Some cities, notably Québec City, have huge winter festivals to bring cheer to the colder months. And in most locations, residents simply bundle up and go about their business.

Who moves to Canada for the weather?

Looking for the place with the most sunshine in Canada? Among Canada's cities, that honor goes to Saskatoon, Saskatchewan. Environment Canada, the nation's weather service, reports that this prairie metropolis typically gets 2,450 hours of sunshine per year. Of course, some of those sunny days come not in the hot summers, but in mid-winter—when temperatures might average a crisp -16°C (3°F).

So who moves to Canada for the weather?

Don't laugh—not all of Canada has harsh winters. Coastal British Columbia, for example, including Vancouver, Vancouver Island, and the Gulf Islands, has a temperate rainforest climate. The winters are rainy but comparatively short, the springs are long and mild, and summers are sunny and dry. When much of Canada is still shoveling snow, many B.C. residents are strolling on the beach.

Canada even has its own desert, and it's in British Columbia as well. The southern reaches of the B.C. region known as the Okanagan are surrounded by the Great Basin Desert. There's none of the coastal rainforest climate here—the towns of Osoyoos, Oliver, and vicinity get the least amount of rain in Canada. Much of this dry, hot region is farmland for peaches, plums, apricots, cherries, and grapes. North America's first aboriginal-owned and -operated winery, Nk'Mip Cellars, is based here, too, anchoring this developing wine-producing area.

So what can you expect—weather-wise—in Canada? The following chart shows the average annual temperatures in Canada's largest cities. Keep in mind, however, that these are averages, and that temperatures can fluctuate significantly on a given day.

For example, even though Calgary's average July temperature of 16°C (61°F) may seem cool, on a typical July day the temperature might vary from a night-time low of 9°C (48°F) to an agreeable daytime high of 23°C (73°F). In Toronto, that typical July day might range from 18°C (64°F) at night to 26°C (79°F) during the day.

City	January	April	July	October
Toronto (ON)	-4°C, 25°F	7.5°C, 45.5°F	22°C, 71.5°F	10°C, 50°F
Montréal (QC)	-10°C, 14°F	5.5°C, 42°F	21°C, 70°F	8°C, 46.5°F
Vancouver (BC)	3°C, 37°F	9°C, 48°F	17.5°C, 63.5°F	10°C, 50°F
Ottawa (ON)	-11°C, 12°F	5.5°C, 42°F	21°C, 70°F	8°C, 46.5°F
Calgary (AB)	-9°C, 16°F	5°C, 41°F	16°C, 61°F	5°C, 41°F
Edmonton (AB)	-12°C, 10°F	5.5°C, 42°F	17.5°C, 63.5°F	5.5°C, 42°F

Source: Environment Canada

FLORA AND FAUNA

As you'd expect in such a vast country, Canada is made up of many different ecological zones, from the arctic to the prairies, from the maritime regions to the forests to the mountains.

Some of the largest trees in the country grow in the Pacific coastal regions of British Columbia, where the mild maritime climate keeps things green for most of the year. You might not have to mow your lawn much in Vancouver in January, but it will stay pleasingly verdant. Several varieties of fir, spruce, hemlock, and pine trees thrive in the moist environment, and outside the urban areas, bear, beaver, deer, elk, caribou, and moose all make their homes. In Vancouver and other southern B.C. coastal communities, it's not uncommon to see eagles and hawks, and you can occasionally spot whales from the ferries in the Strait of Georgia.

The climate changes as you go east, crossing first the Coast Mountains and then the Rockies. In central and eastern B.C. and along the Alberta border, the Montane Cordillera ecological zone is one of the country's most diverse. As the terrain changes from mountainous to desert, trees and shrubs vary from pine, fir, and spruce to sagebrush and wheatgrass. Animal life, too, ranges from caribou, deer, and bear, to coyote, mink, and rattlesnakes.

East of the Rockies, southern Alberta is prairie land. In the flat, dry fields, wheat, barley, and a variety of grasses grow, and the region is home to pronghorn antelope, elk, coyote, badgers, rabbits, prairie dogs, chipmunks, and squirrels. Central Alberta, in contrast, is an ecological zone called the Boreal Plains, which is colder than the prairies but still relatively flat. Bison still live in some areas, as do elk, caribou, muskrats, and gophers. Plant life ranges from Saskatoon berry bushes to deciduous trees like maples, birches, and alders.

The populous area that extends through southern Ontario and southern Québec, including the cities of Toronto, Ottawa, Montréal, and Québec City, is part of the zone known as the Mixedwood Plains. The most common trees here are deciduous—maple, oak, elm, ash, and poplar—which lose their leaves each year after a blaze of brilliant fall colors. While bears, deer, wolves, and coyotes live in this region, it's smaller creatures like squirrels, raccoons, and skunks that you'll most commonly see, particularly in and around the more urban areas.

Social Climate

Compared to the United States, with its population of nearly 300 million, Canada's population is tiny. With just over 33 million people, Canada's population is a mere 10 percent of the United States'. And Canadian settlement is overwhelmingly clustered in the country's southern tier. Nearly three-quarters of all Canadians live within 150 kilometers (100 miles) of the U.S. border.

Slowly but surely, though, Canada's population is growing. In fact, from 2001 to 2006, the rate of Canada's population growth was more rapid than the growth rate of populations in the United States, Italy, France, the United Kingdom, Japan, Germany, and Russia. But it's not because of a baby boom. In the United States, the average birthrate is roughly two children per woman. In Canada, that figure is only 1.5 children per woman.

With such a low birthrate, what's fueling Canada's population increase? Immigration. According to Statistics Canada, roughly 1.2 million immigrants arrived in Canada between 2001 and 2006, which means that approximately two-thirds of Canada's population growth is due to international migration. In the United States, the pattern is reversed: approximately 60 percent of the population growth is due to births.

In recent years, the fastest-growing Canadian province has been Alberta, due largely to that region's booming natural resources industry, especially oil, gas, and mining. Ontario, British Columbia, and to a lesser extent Québec, are also all growing in population.

Between 2001 and 2006, more than 600,000 immigrants settled in

© CAROLYN B. HELLER

Chinese is Canada's third-most widely spoken language, after English and French.

Ontario—about half of all immigrants who came to Canada during that time—and about 125,000 immigrants came to British Columbia. While some Canadians are migrating west in search of jobs, especially from the Atlantic provinces, international immigration is the main factor that's increasing the population in Alberta and British Columbia.

WHERE CANADIANS COME FROM

According to the Canadian Embassy in Washington, D.C., more than 300,000 people travel between Canada and the United States *every day.* Of course, most of that border traffic is temporary—visitors traveling back and forth for business or vacation, not to settle permanently. Still, based on Canada's most recent complete census (in 2006), roughly 6.2 million Canadian residents—approximately 20 percent of the population—were immigrants. Of these, nearly 60 percent came from Asia and the Middle East, 16 percent from Europe, and more than 10 percent each from Africa and the Americas, including approximately 250,000 from the United States. In the United States, by contrast, roughly 12 percent of the population is foreign-born; more than half of all immigrants to the United States came from Latin America and 25 percent from Asia.

As you might expect, most new immigrants to Canada settle in the cities—in Toronto and surrounding communities in Ontario, in the Vancouver metropolitan area in British Columbia, in and around Montréal in Québec, and in Calgary or Edmonton in Alberta. Immigrants from the United States follow the same pattern: There are roughly 42,000 Americans in Toronto, 25,000

GUNG HAGGIS FAT CHOY!

With its large Asian population, Vancouver celebrates the Lunar New Year in a big way. New Year's greetings of "Gung Hay Fat Choy" (in Cantonese) or "Gong Xi Fa Cai" (in Mandarin) are common on the streets of Chinatown and suburban Richmond, and there are parades, special events, and dinners all over town.

But an imaginative Asian-Canadian artist and entrepreneur has created a distinctive holiday event that recognizes not only the Asian experience but that of the city's Scottish immigrants. In a joint celebration of Chinese New Year and Scottish poet Robert Burns' birthday, Todd Wong – a.k.a. "Tod-dish McWong" – throws a quirky annual dinner and performance event that he dubbed "Gung *Haggis* Fat Choy."

Held every January, it's a multicultural extravaganza that typically draws more than 500 people for a Chinese-style banquet – with such innovations as haggis wontons or haggis lettuce wraps thrown in. Performers have included bagpipers and erdu players, opera singers and Asian-Canadian authors, as well as local radio and TV personalities. Multiculti to the max? Sure, but it's also great fun.

For more information, check out www.gunghaggisfatchoy.com.

in Vancouver, 17,000 in Montréal, and 11,000 in Calgary. So if you're coming to Canada from the United States, you'll find plenty of other Americans in most major cities.

MULTICULTURALISM VS. THE MELTING POT

With its history of immigration, the United States has long considered itself a melting pot—a nation where immigrants come to seek their fortunes and, if they're successful, assimilate into the great melting pot of American society. Canada's tradition of immigration is equally ingrained in the culture. However, Canadians tend to think of their country as a multicultural one—a place where multiple ethnic groups can live side-by-side in multi-ethnic harmony.

Of course, in reality, things haven't always been so cozy, and discrimination against various groups continues to plague parts of Canadian society today. Still, Canadians increasingly celebrate each other's differences and share in each other's celebrations, from parades to fête the Asian Lunar New Year to festivities marking the Indian community's Diwali holiday.

WHAT CANADIANS THINK OF AMERICANS

If you're thinking of relocating to Canada, you may wonder what sort of a welcome you'll receive. Since Canadian society needs immigrants to sustain its population, the government officially encourages people from all over the world to consider settling in Canada—at least if those people are well educated, entrepreneurial, or possessing specialized skills that Canadian businesses need. That welcome extends to Americans as well.

Canadians often make a distinction between the American people and U.S. policies. When a 2008 poll asked Canadians to name the country that stands out as a negative force in the world, the country named most often was the United States. Americans in Canada often say they're asked to explain U.S. government actions—particularly when more conservative administrations are in power. Many expats from the United States, too, are surprised by how much the average Canadian knows about issues and politics south of the border. As Canadian political scientist James Laxer explains, Canada is in the unusual position of having only one border—its border with the United States. He writes:

> Through the ages, Canadians have been taken aback by the Jekyll and Hyde personality of their great neighbour – sunny, effusive, liberal and grandiose for long stretches, followed by startling bursts of isolationism, self-absorption, bellicosity and compulsive patriotism.
>
> – James Laxer, *The Border: Canada, the U.S., and Dispatches from the 49th Parallel*

Yet because the United States is Canada's only neighbor, Canadians feel that they have to co-exist with the nation to the south, whether they agree with its politics or not. While you'll likely meet plenty of Canadians who disagree with U.S. policies, most Canadians have no complaints with U.S. people. And if you can be an asset to Canada, it's likely that Canada will welcome you.

HISTORY, GOVERNMENT, AND ECONOMY

At first glance, Canada's history may seem similar to that of the United States. Both countries were populated by aboriginal peoples who lived undisturbed until European explorers began arriving in the late 1400s and early 1500s. In both countries, the British and French struggled for domination, triggering violent battles in the process. Both countries had periods of significant western expansion in the 1800s, and each nation built railways that connected their eastern and western shores. In modern times, the United States and Canada have remained allies on many important political issues.

For many years, immigration was a basis for both nations' population growth. Both countries also had a "baby boom" following World War II that created the large generation now moving into middle age and retirement.

Yet at several points, the histories of these two nations diverged. Why did Montréal become French-speaking while New York did not? How did the English royals retain their role in Canadian government? What prompted

© CAROLYN B. HELLER

the United States and Canada at various points in time to go to war—against each other?

The United States and Canada took separate paths, and the result today is two countries that share a related past but now maintain a different governmental structure, have a distinctly different linguistic legacy, and are influenced in part by different economic drivers.

History

It's impossible to condense all of Canada's history into a brief summary. What follows is a highly selective collection of historical highlights—a Canadian history cheat sheet.

THE RISE AND FALL OF NEW FRANCE

Why do some Canadians speak French? Here's how it started.

Back in the 1400s and 1500s, European explorers, including the French, English, Spanish, and Portuguese, set out to find trade routes to the Indies. John Cabot—who was born Giovanni Caboto in Genoa, but later settled in England—set sail in 1497, five years after Christopher Columbus' historic voyage. Like Columbus, he didn't reach the Orient. Instead, he landed in eastern Canada, claiming the land for the English crown.

In the 1530s, French explorer Jacques Cartier ventured along the St. Lawrence River into what is now Québec. Cartier and his men claimed the region for France.

Another Frenchman, Samuel de Champlain, returned to the St. Lawrence area in 1608, and established a fur-trading post at the present-day Québec City. Slowly, more French settlers arrived, and Québec City became the capital of the colony known as "New France."

During this same period, the English were building settlements of their own, including Jamestown in 1607 and Plymouth in 1627, and in Newfoundland and Nova Scotia throughout the mid-1600s. Both the French and the English continued to push farther inland on the North American continent into the 1700s and repeatedly clashed—not only with the aboriginal communities they encountered, but also with each other. By 1755, the population of Canada had grown to 60,000, many of whom were French-speaking; the 13 American colonies to the south had more than a million inhabitants.

In 1756, a full-fledged war broke out between England and France—the Seven Years' War (what the United States calls "the French and Indian War"). From the Canadian perspective, one of the most important battles took place

Founded in 1608, Québec City recently celebrated its 400-year anniversary.

CAROLYN B. HELLER

on September 13, 1759, when English and French troops met on the Plains of Abraham outside Québec City. Both the French and British commanding officers, Louis-Joseph de Montcalm and James Wolfe, were killed in the fight, but the British won the battle, and ultimately the war.

So why did eastern Canada, and Québec in particular, retain its French culture—if the French lost? After "the Conquest," as the defeat of the French is known, the former New France became a British colony. However, the British allowed the French-Canadians to remain in their settlements and carry on with daily life. Historians have suggested that the British needed the Québec settlers, both to help retain control of their northern territories and as a buffer against the increasing unrest in the American colonies. This decision was an early step toward securing the francophone language and culture in Canada.

AMERICA INVADES CANADA

Author Will Ferguson wrote, "If the Conquest was the Big Bang of French-Canadian history, the American Revolution was the Big Bang of *English*-Canadian history. America went. Canada stayed."

In 1775, the American colonies invited the Canadians to join them in their emerging struggle against the British. The Canadians declined. Some historians say that, for the Canadians, it was choice of "the devil you know"—the British rulers—over "the devil you don't"—the Americans. The American colonists saw it differently, believing that they needed to liberate Canada from the British crown.

ILANAAQ THE INUKSHUK

How did a pile of stones become the symbol of the 2010 Winter Olympic Games in Vancouver? It's not just any old pile of stones.

Across Canada, you'll see many emblems of aboriginal culture, from towering totem poles, to carvings representing eagles, bears, and other creatures, to traditional native dwellings. One such symbol comes from the Inuit people of Canada's Arctic. The Inuit have long stacked rocks in the shape of a human, using these constructions as guideposts. Each of these stone figures, which marked trails or caches of food, is known as an *inukshuk*.

The Winter Games adopted a stylized version of the *inukshuk* as its emblem. This Olympic *inukshuk* was dubbed "Ilanaaq," which means "friend" in the Inuit's Inuktitut language. Ilanaaq the Inukshuk may become one of recent history's most well-publicized piles of stones.

In September 1775, American troops invaded Canada, with one company marching to Montréal and another heading for Québec City. After the Americans captured Montréal, the British eventually defeated them in Québec City. In July 1776, just before the Continental Congress issued the Declaration of Independence, American soldiers withdrew from Canada and subsequently launched their own war south of the border.

There was no "Canadian Revolution" similar to the Revolutionary War in the United States. During the American Revolution, Canada remained loyal to Britain, and nearly 50,000 American colonists who sympathized with the British moved north to Canada. Known as Tories in the United States, these settlers were called Loyalists in Canada.

The Loyalists became the largest group of English-speaking residents in British North America's Canadian colonies. Some, who had settled in francophone Québec, began pressuring the British to create their own separate English-speaking colony. The Constitutional Act of 1791—also called the Canada Act—divided Britain's Canadian territory into two: Upper Canada (the English-speaking region that would eventually become the province of Ontario) and Lower Canada (French-speaking Québec). The Canada Act signaled the first officially recognized split between the English- and French-speaking populations.

THE AMERICANS ARE COMING (AGAIN)

At the end of the 1700s and early 1800s, Britain and France went to war again, this time in Europe. The British navy set up a blockade, preventing French

WHY IS THANKSGIVING IN OCTOBER?

Canadians celebrate the Thanksgiving holiday roughly six weeks earlier than Americans do. And U.S. expats always ask, "Why?"

While Canada doesn't share the pilgrim legends that infuse U.S. Thanksgiving traditions, the country does have a history of thanksgiving feasts. Throughout the 1800s, Canada declared days of thanksgiving for everything from the end of the War of 1812 to the waning of a cholera epidemic, and simply "for God's mercies."

The Canadian government first proclaimed an official holiday for "the blessings of an abundant harvest" in November 1879. For the next 40-some years, Canada celebrated Thanksgiving on varying dates in either October or November.

In 1936, Parliament issued a proclamation designating the second Monday of October as Thanksgiving Day "for general thanksgiving to Almighty God for the blessings with which the people of Canada have been favoured." Finally, in 1957, Parliament permanently declared that Thanksgiving would be celebrated on the second Monday of October.

But why October? Historians don't agree, although many say it's because October is harvest time in much of Canada. By late November, wide swaths of the country are already covered in snow.

Most Americans will find Canada's Thanksgiving foods familiar. Canadians typically load up their holiday table with turkey, stuffing, mashed or sweet potatoes, cranberry sauce, at least of couple of other vegetables, and some sort of pie. Just don't be surprised when turkeys appear in the market in early October.

ships from reaching the Americas and stopping American ships heading for the Continent.

Fed up with the blockade, in 1812 the United States declared war on Britain. The Americans attacked the closest outpost of the British Empire: Canada.

During the War of 1812, a Canadian woman became the northern equivalent of Paul Revere. Legend has it that settler Laura Secord overheard American officers planning an attack at Beaver Dams, in the Niagara region. Secord went to warn the British commander that the Americans were coming, and the British set up an ambush, taking nearly 500 American prisoners.

The Americans didn't succeed in capturing Canada, and as a result of the War of 1812, Britain and the United States negotiated a clearer division between their territories. In the east, the United States–Canada border returned to its pre-war state, and in the west, the boundary was set along the 49th parallel as far as the Rocky Mountains.

In a precursor to Canada's ultimate national union, Upper and Lower Canada joined together again in 1841 to create the Province of Canada.

During the same period, explorers, traders, and adventurers continued to push across the continent, both in the United States and in British North America. In 1846, the border was extended across the 49th parallel all the way to the Pacific.

WESTWARD HO

In the 1850s, Canada had a gold rush. After gold was discovered in British Columbia, thousands of miners, including many Americans, went west to seek their fortunes. Although the gold rush didn't last long, many settlers remained in B.C. and found work in the emerging fishing and lumber

In 1947, oil was discovered in Leduc, Alberta, launching western Canada's oil boom.

© CAROLYN B. HELLER

industries—businesses that would remain the backbone of the province's economy for years to come.

Around the same time, Canada also struck oil. In 1857, North America's first oil well was drilled not out west, but in Ontario. Within just a few years, the Ontario town that became known as Oil Springs had 400 wells. This oil boom, too, was short-lived—oversupply caused prices to plummet—but exploration continued over the next decades. In 1947, oil was discovered in Leduc, near Edmonton, Alberta. The Leduc strike was the beginning of the Alberta oil boom that continues today.

CONFEDERATION: WHEN CANADA BECAME A COUNTRY

If you're going to live in Canada, you need to know the date July 1, 1867. That's Canada's birthday, or Confederation day, the date the country was established. The four original provinces to join Confederation were Ontario, Québec, New Brunswick, and Nova Scotia.

The official document that established the country of Canada was called the British North America Act. Even though Canada was now a new nation, it remained part of the British Empire, and Canadians were still British citizens.

In creating the United States of America, the country's founders had defined

SING *O CANADA* – BUT ONLY SINCE 1980

How long does it take a song to become a country's national anthem? In Canada, it was 100 years.

The song that eventually became the Canadian anthem was first performed in Québec City in 1880. Calixa Lavallée, a composer and music teacher, wrote the music, and Sir Adolphe-Basile Routhier, a judge, penned the original lyrics – in French. Over the years, several writers created English-language lyrics, but the words that stuck were based on a poem that R. Stanley Weir, another judge, wrote in 1908. By 1914, *O Canada* had become the most widely known patriotic song in the country.

It wasn't until 1980, however, that Parliament declared *O Canada* to be the nation's anthem. The National Anthem Act of 1980 authorized two official sets of lyrics, an English version based on Weir's poem and a French version from Routhier's original.

The English-language lyrics are:

O Canada! Our home and native land!

True patriot love in all thy sons command.

With glowing hearts we see thee rise,

The True North strong and free!

From far and wide,

O Canada, we stand on guard for thee.

God keep our land glorious and free!

O Canada, we stand on guard for thee.

O Canada, we stand on guard for thee.

Canada's national flag – the red and white maple leaf – is also a fairly recent creation. Until the 1960s, the Canadian flag included the British Union Jack. In 1964, however, Prime Minister Lester Pearson led a campaign for a truly Canadian symbol, and the maple leaf banner was born.

the nation's ideals as "life, liberty, and the pursuit of happiness." In Canada, the British North America Act laid out different objectives: "peace, order, and good government." These principles have come to represent Canadian values of reasonableness, tolerance, and harmony.

Sir John A. Macdonald became Canada's first prime minister. The "Father" of Canada has been immortalized on the country's $10 bill, and July 1 is now a national holiday: Canada Day.

The Canadian Confederation continued to grow, adding Manitoba (1870), the Northwest Territories (1870), British Columbia (1871), and Prince Edward Island (1873). They were followed by the Yukon (1898), Alberta and Saskatchewan (both 1905), Newfoundland (1949), and finally Nunavut (1999).

ASIAN IMMIGRATION: THE FIRST CHAPTER

Chinese immigration to Canada began with the gold rush in the 1850s. Many more Chinese came in the 1880s to work on Canada's transcontinental railway. In 1885, workers drove the last spike on the Canadian Pacific Railway line that stretched approximately 5,000 kilometers (3,100 miles). The railway opened up the west to rapid settlement and drew large numbers of immigrants from eastern Canada, the United States, Asia, and Europe, especially from Italy, the Ukraine, Poland, Germany, and Hungary.

Canada didn't always welcome these immigrants, however. Despite the Chinese role in constructing the railroads, the federal government attempted to restrict further immigration from China. They imposed a "head tax" on every Chinese newcomer. In 1885, the tax was $50; by 1903, it had been raised to $500. In 1923, the Parliament passed the Chinese Immigration Act, an exclusionary measure that effectively prevented Chinese immigrants from entering Canada. The Act was finally repealed in 1947 after World War II.

Small numbers of Japanese began arriving in Canada in the late 1800s and early 1900s. The majority settled in British Columbia, where many found work in the fishing industry on boats or in canneries. In World War II, more than a million Canadians fought for the Allies, but at home, one of the blots on Canada's history was the forced resettlement of British Columbia's Japanese residents. More than 22,000 people, three-quarters of whom were Canadian citizens, were sent to relocation camps in remote locations.

QUÉBEC SEPARATISM

Fast forward to the 1960s. Canada celebrated its 100th birthday, welcoming the world to Expo '67, the World's Fair in Montréal. The following year, Pierre Trudeau—the man sometimes called "Canada's J.F.K."—became prime minister. One of Trudeau's first achievements was the passage of the Official Languages Act, the legislation that made Canada a bilingual country.

Despite government support for bilingualism, some Québec francophones had concluded that the only way they could retain their language and culture was for Québec to separate from Canada and become its own sovereign nation. The radical Front de Libération du Québec (FLQ) launched a campaign of violence—including robberies, bombings, and kidnappings—in support of the separatist cause.

To quash the FLQ, Trudeau in 1970 invoked the War Measures Act, which allowed the government to suspend civil liberties, round up potential suspects, and detain them without trial. Within several weeks, federal troops had arrested the FLQ leaders and the organization was effectively disbanded.

Although the violence stopped, separatist sentiment in Québec remained high. In 1980, the province held a referendum on separatism, or rather "sovereignty-association," the idea that Québec would be its own sovereign nation but retain a formal association with the rest of Canada for matters such as currency and national defense. After an acrimonious campaign, the referendum went down to a 60-40 defeat.

Separatism continued to be an issue throughout the 1980s and early 1990s, leading up to another voter referendum in 1995. Again, the pro-separatist measure was defeated.

THE TIMES THEY *AREN'T* A-CHANGIN'

In the 1960s and '70s, Canada was a well-known haven for Americans who opposed the war in Vietnam. Citizenship and Immigration Canada estimates that during this period, 30,000–40,000 U.S. draft resisters were admitted into Canada. Some came through official channels, as legal permanent residents. Others entered as visitors and simply disappeared into Canadian communities.

But well before the Vietnam era, Canada was a refuge for disillusioned and disenfranchised Americans. Back in the 1700s, colonists opposed to the American Revolution made their way north to the Canadian settlements. In the 1800s, Canada was the "promised land" at the end of the Underground Railroad, the network of safe houses that sheltered escaping slaves. In the early 1900s, Mennonite communities settled in Canada's prairie regions, escaping religious persecution and anti-foreign sentiment in the United States. More Americans fled to Canada during the McCarthy era in the 1950s.

More recently, smaller waves of American immigrants have made their way north. Known as the "Bush refugees," some Americans moved to Canada to protest the growing conservatism of the country under President George W. Bush. When Canada made same-sex marriage legal in 2005, American gay and lesbian couples began crossing the border to make their unions official and seek a more tolerant place to live.

Government

Canada has a three-tiered governmental structure, with federal, provincial (or territorial), and municipal governments. The federal government, headquartered in Ottawa, is responsible for foreign policy, national defense, immigration, and other national issues. The provincial governments handle health care, education, policing, and the highways, among other things. Local issues, such as zoning, city police and firefighting, snow removal, garbage, and recycling, are the municipal governments' purview.

As in the United States, Canada's federal government has three branches: executive, legislative, and judicial. However, Canada's British roots are reflected in its executive leadership and its Parliament structure.

WHO'S WHO IN CANADIAN GOVERNMENT

Canada's prime minister is the country's chief executive. Parliament, the national legislature, has two components: the House of Commons and the Senate.

The 308 House of Commons members, known as MPs or members of Parliament, are elected to five-year terms. Each represents a "riding," or district, that's geographically based.

Unlike their counterparts in the United States, Canada's 105 senators aren't elected. The prime minster appoints them. Once they're in office, they can remain on the job until they reach age 75.

How are laws made in Canada? When a bill is introduced in Parliament, it must be approved by majorities in both the House of Commons and the Senate. The governor general, who is officially the Queen of England's representative in Canada, then gives final approval—known as "Royal Assent"—to a bill before it becomes law.

The governmental structure at the provincial level parallels that of the federal government. The head honcho of each provincial government is the premier, a position analogous to a U.S. state governor. Each province and territory has its own legislature.

Canada's judicial system is similar to the judicial system in the United States. The country's highest court is the Supreme Court of Canada. Nine judges sit on the Supreme Court, led by the chief justice. Three of the justices must come from Québec, and by convention, the remainder of the court includes three from Ontario, two from western Canada, and one from the Atlantic provinces. Beneath the Supreme Court are federal and provincial courts.

WHERE LIBERALS ARE MIDDLE OF THE ROAD

Canada has several major political parties: the Liberals, the Conservatives, the New Democrats, and the Bloc Québécois. The New Democrats are on the left of the political spectrum, the Conservatives on the right, and the Liberals occupy the center. The Bloc Québécois runs candidates only in Québec, promoting Québec's sovereignty and interests.

For Americans who think of "liberal" as "left," it can be a surprise to find that Canada's Liberal party is in the middle of the political spectrum. Historically,

Republican administrations in the United States have favored Canadian Conservatives (colloquially known as the Tories), while Democratic administrations have generally supported the Liberals (sometimes called the Grits).

Canada also has an active Green Party, which focuses on environmental issues. In the 2006 federal election, there were 15 registered parties, although only the four majors won any seats. Many of these smaller parties, ranging from the Libertarians to the Communists to the Marijuana Party, represent a variety of special interests.

ELECTIONS ON DEMAND

The process of choosing a prime minister in Canada is very different from the electoral system south of the border. The prime minister is not elected directly. Rather, the prime minister is the leader of the political party with the most elected members of the House of Commons. So unlike the United States, where the executive branch is separate from the legislative branch, Canada's chief executive—the prime minister—is actually a member of Parliament first.

Here's how it works: The party that wins the most seats in the House of Commons becomes the party in power. The leader of that party becomes the prime minister. The rest of the parties become the "opposition." The opposition party with the most members in the House of Commons becomes the "official opposition," and the leader of that party becomes the leader of the opposition.

A "minority government" exists when the leading party (which the prime minister heads) does not have a sufficient majority without aligning itself with at least one other party. Canada has been in a minority government situation a number of times, including the 2006 government led by Conservative Prime Minister Stephen Harper.

According to Canada's Constitution, federal elections must be held at least every five years. Historically, however, the ruling government has had the power to call an election at any time. In addition, when the current government loses a confidence vote in the House of Commons, that vote brings down the government and triggers a new election. Canada's shortest Parliament session lasted just 66 days (in 1979) before the government was brought down. The longest serving government, from 1911 through 1917, retained power for 2,152 days.

In 2007, Parliament passed a bill setting a fixed election date every four years on the third Monday of October. The government can still be brought down between the scheduled election dates, but otherwise, an election must be held on a specific date every four years. The bill is scheduled to take effect in 2009.

Canada's voting age is 18, and most Canadians take their right to vote seriously. Since 1980, an average of nearly 70 percent of registered voters cast a ballot in the federal elections. In the United States, even counting only the presidential election years when the number of people who vote is higher, the voting rate during the same period was just over 50 percent.

THE QUEEN OF CANADA

Until 1947, there was no such thing as a "Canadian citizen." With Canada still part of the British Commonwealth, Canadians were considered British subjects.

That changed when the Canadian Citizenship Act became law, but Canada's government—retaining its British roots—remains a constitutional monarchy. The country's head of state is officially the monarch of the United Kingdom, so the Queen of England is also the Queen of Canada.

Although Canada has preserved many of its British influences and traditions, the monarch's role in Canada has become largely symbolic. You'll find Queen Elizabeth II's portrait on Canadian bills and coins, and there's a May holiday—Victoria Day—in honor of England's Queen Victoria. In the summer, there's a daily Changing of the Guard ceremony in front of the Parliament Buildings in Ottawa, complete with guards in the iconic red uniforms and tall fur hats.

On a day-to-day basis, the British sovereign has little practical effect on the operation of Canada's government. The queen's official representative in Canada is the governor general. This, too, is largely a ceremonial role. The governor general is something of a governmental ambassador, officiating at ceremonies, bestowing awards, and opening and closing Parliament sessions. With the prime minister's advice, the Queen appoints the governor general for a five-year term.

THE CHARTER OF RIGHTS AND FREEDOMS

Canada's Constitution was created at Confederation in 1867, and until 1982, the only way the Constitution could be amended was by the British Parliament. However, the Canada Act of 1982 cut Canada's remaining legislative ties to the United Kingdom.

That same year, the government passed the Constitution Act, creating a new all-Canadian Constitution. A significant component of this new Constitution was the Charter of Rights and Freedoms. Similar in concept to the United States Bill of Rights, the Charter guarantees certain rights to all Canadians. These "Charter rights," as they're often called, include:

CANADA'S FIRST WOMEN

As Canada's official head of state, the Queen of England may be Canada's ultimate "first woman." But others have had the honor of being the first Canadian women to serve in various government positions, including Canada's first – and to date, only – female prime minister.

In 1918, two years before the 19th Amendment to the U.S. Constitution guaranteed women the right to vote in the United States, the Women's Franchise Act gave Canadian women the right to vote in their federal elections. Three years later, in 1921, Canada elected Agnes Campbell Macphail the first woman MP in the House of Commons.

Emily Murphy was appointed a magistrate in the city of Edmonton in 1916, the first female magistrate in the entire British Empire. However, many people protested her appointment, arguing that under the British North America Act of 1867 – Canada's founding document – only a qualified "person" could hold public office, and a woman was not legally a "person." Murphy, along with four other female reformers in Alberta, eventually took the "Persons Case" to Canada's Supreme Court – and lost. They persisted, appealing to the Privy Council in Britain, which finally ruled in 1929 that, yes, women were "persons," too.

A. Kim Campbell, a British Columbia-born lawyer who was elected to the House of Commons in 1988, became Canada's first female Minister of Justice and Attorney General. Then, in June of 1993, Campbell took office as Canada's first female prime minister, after her predecessor Brian Mulroney retired. She retained her title for only 123 days, however, before Jean Chrétian and the Liberal party defeated her government in November of that same year.

- Fundamental freedoms: Freedom of religion, expression, the press, assembly, and association.

- Democratic rights: The right to vote for and be represented by a legislative assembly.

- Mobility rights: The right to live, travel, and work anywhere in the country.

- Legal Rights: The right to life, liberty, "the security of person," to be presumed innocent until proven guilty, to legal representation, to a fair trial, to be protected against unreasonable search and seizure and against cruel and unusual punishment.

- Equality rights: Protection from discrimination based on race, national or ethnic origin, color, religion, sex, age or mental or physical disability.

The Charter also confirmed English and French as the country's two official languages.

Although the Charter of Rights and Freedoms itself is comparatively new, it has become an important symbol to most Canadians.

Economy

How do Canadians earn their loonies (as Canada's dollars are known)? Canada's oldest company, the Hudson's Bay Company, was founded way back in 1670, and its early business was in the fur trade. Nowadays, Canada has a largely services-based economy.

Nearly two-thirds of the country's jobs are service-related, from professional, scientific, or technical services, to education, health care, tourism, finance, insurance, and real estate. About a third of Canada's economy derives from manufacturing, construction, and resource-based production (including mining, oil and gas, forestry, and fishing). Despite Canada's acres of fertile prairie land, agriculture now accounts for just over 2 percent of the economy.

The United States is by far Canada's largest trading partner. The North American Free Trade Agreement (NAFTA), which took effect in 1994, helped solidify the economic ties between the two countries. More than 80 percent of Canada's exports—which include machinery and equipment, automotive and other industrial products, energy, forest products, and agricultural products—go to the United States, and more than 55 percent of its imports come from the United States. Even as Canada looks to expand its markets farther afield, developing economic ties to Asia (especially China and India), Latin America, and Eastern Europe, the Canadian economy remains firmly linked to the United States.

PEOPLE AND CULTURE

"Throughout my childhood," novelist John Irving once wrote, "Canada was always perceived as a more beautiful, unspoiled version of New Hampshire and Maine. We certainly had—I think most Americans had—no sense of any nationalistic differences."

Irving was not the first to assume that Canadians are just like Americans. If you're coming to Canada from the United States, you could be forgiven for thinking that the people you'll meet are pretty much like the people you know back home. And you wouldn't be entirely wrong. The culture and heritage of both nations has many things in common.

On both sides of the border, you can watch many of the same movies, read the same books, and listen to the same music. You can channel-surf through the same TV programs and watch athletes from both countries play side by side on U.S. and Canadian sports teams. Even the food isn't that different; the Golden Arches and their familiar fast-food cousins have populated both countries with the same burgers and fries.

With all these similarities, many Americans are surprised to find that there's a thriving Canadian culture that's quite distinct from its south-of-the-border neighbor's. From the nations' ethnic compositions to their filmmakers, authors, and artists, from their social policies to their social norms, and even to their food traditions, the cultures of Canada and the United States have diverged in fairly significant ways. Even those fries—in Canada, they're as likely to come with gravy and cheese as with the familiar ketchup.

Ethnicity and Class

The Canadian government actively encourages immigration as a way to counterbalance the country's declining birthrate and provide workers for the nation's growing economy. Due to these immigration policies, which began in earnest in the 1970s, Canada's largest cities have become among the most multicultural on the planet.

Canada's 2006 census found that 20 percent of its residents—one out of every five Canadians—were born outside the country. Compare that to the United States, where immigration continues to be a divisive issue: Only about 12 percent of U.S. residents are immigrants.

Where do Canadians come from? Since the country's earliest days, the greatest numbers of immigrants migrated to Canada from the British Isles. Even today, more Canadians claim ancestors from Britain than from any other nation. After Britain, it's France; roughly 20 percent of present-day Canadians have French ancestry. Italians, Germans, and Ukrainians also immigrated to Canada in large numbers, particularly in the late 1800s and early 1900s.

"Smith" may still be the most common surname in the country, but in metropolitan Vancouver, it's a distant fourth to the names Lee, Wong, and Chan. Canada overall, and the West in particular, has seen significant immigration in recent years from Asia, especially China, Taiwan, Hong Kong, and India. Since 2001, more than 60 percent of Canada's immigrants have come from Asia and the Middle East. Immigrants from the Caribbean and parts of Latin America continue to settle in eastern Canada.

Today, only 60 percent of Canadians speak English as their first language, while just under one-quarter are native French speakers. In the United States, in contrast, more than 80 percent of Americans are native English speakers, while about 10 percent consider Spanish their first language.

Twenty percent of Canadians are "allophones"—that is, their native language is neither English nor French. The country's third-most widely spoken

BONJOUR, WINNIPEG?

Québec, of course, is the part of Canada that retains the most visible legacy of the country's French heritage. Yet even outside of Québec, Canada has a number of regions and communities where French is the dominant language.

Wander into the St. Boniface neighborhood in Winnipeg, Manitoba, for example, and you might easily think you were on a street in Montréal. In the post office and local businesses, shopkeepers and clerks greet their customers in French, and street signs are posted in both French and English. Winnipeg is predominantly an English-speaking city, so most St. Boniface residents are bilingual, but it's still a fascinating sliver of francophone culture.

SOIS FIÈRE, WINNIPEG

© CAROLYN B. HELLER

Even outside of Québec, Canada has many francophone communities.

language is Chinese. After that, Italian, German, Punjabi, Spanish, Arabic, Tagalog, and Portuguese round out Canada's linguistic top 10.

WHAT IT MEANS TO BE A "BILINGUAL" COUNTRY

Ever since European explorers first landed on Canada's shores, the country was settled by both English- and French-speaking colonists. It wasn't until 1969, however, that Canada officially became a bilingual nation.

In that year, Canada's Parliament passed the Official Languages Act, designating both English and French the country's official tongues. It declared that all federal institutions must provide their services in both English and French. The act further mandated that federal institutions must hire English- and French-speaking Canadians in numbers that reflect their proportion in the overall Canadian population.

The Official Languages Act didn't just affect federal agencies. It also confirmed that both English and French are equal in Canadian society. As a result, you'll find both languages on all government forms, in all federal offices, and in many public places, from airports to museums. You'll find both English- and French-language labels on packages, including many familiar American brands, in your local market. You can tune into French-language programs

PRESS 1 FOR ENGLISH, 2 FOR MANDARIN...

Even though Canada's two official languages are English and French, you might never know that in West Coast cities like Vancouver. Sure, kids learn French in school, and as in the rest of the country, airport signs, government notices, and product packaging are written in both English and French. However, Canada's West Coast is the gateway to the Pacific Rim, and with the large Asian population, you're much more likely to hear Mandarin or Cantonese on the streets. Even the voicemail systems of some Vancouver-area companies say "Press 1 for service in English, press 2 for service in Mandarin..."

Does this mean you need to learn Mandarin or Cantonese to live and work in Vancouver? No, of course not. You can do everything you need in English. But if you can communicate in Chinese in addition to English, it may open up additional job opportunities. In 2005, Vancouver mayoral candidate Sam Sullivan (a Vancouver-born Caucasian) got great press – and undoubtedly many of the votes that led to his election – because he can speak competent Cantonese.

on the radio, and your kids will have the opportunity to study both English and French in schools.

Many prospective expats wonder whether they have to learn to speak French to live in Canada. The answer is no. Unless you'll be settling in predominantly francophone Québec, you don't need any knowledge of French. But an awareness of francophone culture, and its influence on Canadian society, will give you a richer appreciation of your adopted country.

CANADA'S ABORIGINAL COMMUNITIES

Canada has three "officially recognized" aboriginal groups: the First Nations, the Inuit, and the Métis. "First Nations" is the politically correct term for aboriginal people who are neither Inuit nor Métis. The Inuit people live primarily in Canada's far north, while the Métis—descendents of French settlers and their First Nations' spouses—have historically settled in the Prairies and the West.

Canada's aboriginal peoples—totaling just over one million individuals—make up about 4 percent of the nation's population. Almost 60 percent live in urban areas, with the balance in smaller communities and on reserves (as Canadians call "reservations"). Roughly a quarter of the aboriginal people live in the province of Ontario and 17 percent in British Columbia. About 40 percent are divided equally between the provinces of Québec, Manitoba, and Saskatchewan. Canada's native communities are a significant part of the country's present-day cultural mosaic, and aboriginal issues regularly emerge in both local communities and the national media.

Customs and Etiquette

"To Americans," Canadian humorist Eric Nicol quipped, "Canadians are proof that the rule 'Everything in moderation' can be carried to excess."

Many Canadians pride themselves on being polite, mild-mannered, and yes, moderate. While personal social interactions may not have the same importance as they do in some countries, Canadians do generally believe in civility. Particularly in the more laid-back Western cities and in small towns nationwide, supermarket cashiers are likely to say hello, people smile at each other on the street, and transit riders line up patiently to board an arriving bus. In fact, a 2007 *Reader's Digest* "courtesy test" found that four of the top five most courteous cities in Canada were in the West: Vancouver, Calgary, Edmonton, and Victoria.

Are Canadians *too* nice? Opening a bank account or renewing your car insurance can sometimes seem—to Americans, at least—to involve as much polite chitchat as actual business. Call the customer-service line of a Canadian retailer, and it may take forever to resolve your complaint, but invariably the staff will be cordial. Many U.S. expats, and even some Canadians themselves, grumble that people can be too nice, valuing sociability over efficiency. Some complain, too, that Canadians can be too mild-mannered, hesitating to express opinions that might be controversial.

Yet if you chill out and slow yourself down just a bit, you'll find it easier to get things done in Canada. Many Canadians complain that Americans talk too loudly, express their opinions too forcefully, and don't listen well to alternate views. In fact, if someone is being extremely pushy or aggressive, you may hear the insult, "He's so American."

GENDER ROLES

Approximately 55 percent of Canada's doctors and dentists are female. Canada has nearly 900,000 women entrepeneurs. At Canadian universities, six out of 10 undergraduates, and just over half the graduate students, are women.

Canadian women are firmly established in the country's social fabric. More than 70 percent of Canadian women over the age of 15 are in the workforce, either working, volunteering, or looking for work, roughly the same percentage as in the United States. Although salaries for Canadian women on average are still lower than average salaries for men (as in the United States), it's illegal everywhere in Canada to pay a woman less than a man for doing the same job.

The Canadian Human Rights Act prohibits discrimination on the basis of "race, national or ethnic origin, colour, religion, age, sex, sexual orientation, marital status, family status, disability and conviction for which a pardon has been granted." Discrimination still exists, but most Canadians pride themselves on getting along—an attitude that affects not only gender roles but life in general.

If you're coming to Canada from the United States, you won't see many significant differences in gender roles north of the border. What you will see is a somewhat more tolerant attitude toward various cultures and alternative lifestyles, especially in the larger cities.

Gay and Lesbian Culture

"There's no place for the state in the bedrooms of the nation." Former Prime Minister Pierre Trudeau made this now-famous statement in the late 1960s, while defending a bill he introduced that would make broad changes to Canada's criminal code. Among other things, it decriminalized homosexual acts. This first step made it possible for Canada, 30 years later, to legalize same-sex marriages.

In 2003, the provinces of Ontario and British Columbia recognized same-sex marriages, and several provinces followed suit over the next 18 months. In July 2005, Canada made history when Bill C-38, the federal law enabling same-sex couples to legally marry, became law. Many gay couples tied the knot. Some gay and lesbian couples from the United States moved to Canada to marry, while others began considering emigration.

Canada's three largest cities all have significant gay and lesbian communities. In Vancouver, the West End has the area's largest number of gay residents, while many lesbian couples live on the East Side, in the Commercial Drive area. In Toronto, the Village—centered around Church and Wellesley Streets—is the city's gay hub, and in Montréal, the similarly named Village is the center of gay life.

This official sanctioning of same-sex relationships does not mean that Canada is immune to prejudice, but many Canadian gays and lesbians report that they feel comfortable and well accepted. One U.S. expat, a gay man who relocated to Canada and married his partner here, said that he felt more welcome in Toronto and Vancouver than he ever felt in the States, even in his previous hometowns, the comparatively gay-friendly New York and San Francisco.

Common-Law Marriage

If you're involved in a long-term relationship but you're not married, you should be aware of Canada's definition of common-law partnerships. If you've lived with someone in a "conjugal relationship" for at least one year, then you're officially considered common-law partners. Same-sex common-law couples are treated the same way under Canadian federal law as opposite-sex common-law couples.

While a common-law relationship isn't the same as being legally married, a common-law partner has many of the same rights and obligations as a spouse. For example, if you're entering Canada with a work permit, you can apply for an open work permit for your common-law partner in the same way that you can for a spouse.

Abortion

In 1892, Canada's Parliament enacted the country's first criminal code, which among other things, made it illegal to sell contraceptives or offer abortion services. The no-contraceptives provision was struck down in the 1960s, as was the blanket prohibition against abortion; however, the procedure was allowed only to protect the life of the mother. It wasn't until 1988 that Canada's Supreme Court declared the country's abortion prohibition unconstitutional, saying that it violated a woman's right to "life, liberty, and security of person" that the Charter of Rights and Freedoms guaranteed.

Today, Canada has no law prohibiting abortion, and abortions performed in hospitals are covered by Canadian health insurance.

RELIGION

Christianity is the major religion in Canada. More than 40 percent of Canadians are Catholic and about a quarter are Protestant. In the United States, those percentages are almost reversed: more than

More than 40 percent of Canadians are Catholic.

© CAROLYN B. HELLER

LITTLE MOSQUE ON THE PRAIRIE

In 2007, the Canadian Broadcasting Corporate debuted a TV comedy about a Muslim community in a fictional rural town. Though it's a sitcom, not a serious drama, "Little Mosque on the Prairie" earned nationwide attention for its humorous portrayal of one of Canada's larger religious minorities.

Across Canada, roughly 2 percent of the population is Muslim, which may sound small, but it's the largest non-Christian denomination. By comparison, approximately 1 percent of the population is Jewish and another 1 percent is Buddhist. The Muslim population is concentrated in the larger urban areas in Ontario and Québec, and in the cities of B.C. and Alberta.

Relatively few Muslims live in the prairies, like the characters in "Little Mosque," and some commentators have criticized the stereotypical portrayal of both the Muslim and non-Muslim characters. Yet simply by creating a series focused entirely on the day-to-day life of a Muslim community, rather than portraying Muslims as extremists or terrorists, the creators of "Little Mosque" may have achieved something of a breakthrough in mainstream North American television.

And besides, where but Canada would you find a tagline like, "Jihad on Ice: Amaar challenges Fred Tupper to a curling face-off at this year's bonspiel?"

50 percent of Americans belong to a Protestant affiliation and about a quarter are Catholic.

Although only about 1 percent of Canada's population, or roughly 350,000 people, is Jewish, Canada has the fourth-largest Jewish population in the world, after Israel, the United States, and France. More than half of Canada's Jews live in Toronto and nearly a third in Montréal. Vancouver also has a small but active Jewish community.

Canada's largest non-Christian religious group is Muslim, representing about 2 percent of the population nationwide. North America's oldest mosque is in the city of Edmonton; the Al Rashid Mosque opened there in 1938. Canada's Muslim communities are concentrated in the large urban areas of Toronto, Ottawa, Montréal, and Vancouver.

Recent census figures indicate that more than 15 percent of Canadians claim no religious affiliation at all. Like the United States, Canada officially separates "church and state." The one major policy difference between the two countries is that Canada's constitution guarantees Protestant and Catholic citizens the right to separate religious-based *public* education. Today, several provinces still have these "separate" Catholic public schools.

SPORTS

> I like Canadians. They are so unlike Americans.... They think Art has been exag-
> gerated. But they are wonderful on ice skates.
> – Ernest Hemingway, in his 1923 poem, "I Like Canadians."

If Canadians are excessively polite in social interactions and tolerant in their social policies, you may find that they let loose on the sports field. In many parts of Canada, particularly the outdoorsy Western cities like Calgary and Vancouver, you may meet people who ask, "What sports do you play?" It's not "Do you play any sports?" or "What sports do you like?" The assumption is that of course you're involved in some sort of active pursuit.

Canadians' enthusiasm for sports may have helped the country win Olympic bids three times in the past three decades. Montréal hosted the Summer Games in 1976, and the Winter Games came to Calgary in 1988. The Winter Olympics return to Canada in 2010 with events in and around Vancouver and Whistler.

With so many kids and adults across Canada who are passionate about hockey, it will help you fit into your new Canadian community if you can tell a helmet from a hat trick. The National Hockey League's teams in Montréal, Ottawa, Toronto, Calgary, Edmonton, and Vancouver have legions of loyal fans, and during hockey playoffs, other activities come to a halt as devotees remain glued to their TVs or radios. "Hockey Night in Canada," the Canadian Broadcasting Corporation's regular hockey program, is one of the longest-running sports broadcasts (it got its start in the 1930s) and remains one of the country's most-watched programs. Even junior hockey—the league for age 20-and-under players—is covered extensively in the mainstream media.

Plenty of Canadian girls and woman play hockey, but Canada also has a similar women's-only game, known as ringette. Skating on ice in teams of six, ringette players use straight sticks to pass and carry a rubber ring to the goal. Although ringette is most widely played in Ontario and Québec, there are leagues in all the provinces.

Canadian kids—both girls and boys—have embraced soccer in a big way, and many expats have gotten to know their new communities from the sidelines of the soccer fields. Most Canadian cities have youth leagues and clubs. At the professional and semi-pro level, Vancouver, Montréal, Toronto, Ottawa, and Thunder Bay (ON) have men's teams that play in the United Soccer League, as do the women's teams from Vancouver, Toronto, Ottawa, Hamilton (ON), and London (ON).

THE ARTS
Hollywood North

The U.S. public radio show, *This American Life,* once did a program called "Who's Canadian?" It opened with several contributors to the show marveling incredulously about "American" entertainment icons, who—gasp!—are actually Canadian. William Shatner, who played Captain Kirk on *Star Trek.* Monty Hall, host of the long-running game show, *Let's Make a Deal.* Singer Neil Young, of Crosby, Stills, Nash, and Young. The late Peter Jennings, NBC news anchor. And the list goes on.

Canada's cities all have active local theater scenes.

Back in the 1920s, actress Mary Pickford became known as "America's Sweetheart," yet few knew she was born in Toronto. CBS News correspondent Morley Safer, an integral part of the U.S. television landscape and a contributor to the news show *60 Minutes* since 1970, is Canadian. Actor Lorne Greene, who starred in the all-American wild-west series *Bonanza,* was born in Ottawa.

Comedians Dan Ackroyd, Jim Carrey, and Martin Short are all Canadians, as are the actor Michael J. Fox and *Jeopardy* host Alex Trebek. Singers Joni Mitchell, Diana Krall, k. d. lang, Sarah McLachlan, and Celine Dion all hail from Canada. Once you start looking for Canadians in the entertainment world, you'll find that they're everywhere.

Canadians often say with some regret that actors, musicians, and other media personalities haven't made it unless they've achieved success south of the border. Yet Canada has a thriving film industry of its own. Both Vancouver and Toronto claim the title "Hollywood North," and Vancouver is North America's third-largest film production center, after New York and Los Angeles.

Running Off to Join the Circus

One of Canada's major contributions to the arts world was born outside of Québec City. Cirque du Soleil, arguably the world's most famous circus company, was launched in Canada in the early 1980s.

Cirque founder Guy Laliberté started his performing career as an accordion player, stilt walker, and fire eater. Unlike circuses of the past that highlighted performing animals and "freak" shows, his fledgling troupe mixed street performing, acrobatics, and original music to create what's become known as "new circus." Their earliest show debuted in 1984, and since then, more than 80 million people in Canada, the United States, and around the world have watched a Cirque du Soleil performance, including nearly 10 million in 2007 alone.

If you have a youngster who's an aspiring acrobat, juggler, or clown, you should know that Canada has a national circus training school, located near Cirque du Soleil's Montréal headquarters. L'École Nationale de Cirque is a professional training program for would-be circus artists. Several Canadian cities, including Vancouver, Toronto, and Montréal, have children's circus programs to help the little ones get started. It may not launch their career with Canada's most notable circus, but they'll have some good fun.

Literature

Canadian writer and satirist Douglas Coupland penned this definition of Canadian literature—a.k.a. "CanLit"—in a blog entry for the *New York Times*: "CanLit is when the Canadian government pays you money to write about life in small towns and/or the immigration experience. If the book is written in French, urban life is permitted, but only from a nonbourgeois viewpoint."

All irony aside, listing all the notable Canadian writers, "CanLit" or not, would take pages. If you want to get acquainted with contemporary Canadian literature, a good place to start is with the novels of Margaret Atwood, Alice Munro, and Carol Shields. There's Mordecai Richler's *The Apprenticeship of Duddy Kravitz*, Michael Ondaatje's *The English Patient*, Malcolm Lowry's *Under the Volcano*, Rohinton Mistry's *A Fine Balance*, and Yann Martel's *Life of Pi*. Douglas Coupland himself has weighed in with *The Gum Thief*, *jPod*, *All Families are Psychotic*, *Generation X*, and several others.

Besides these (and many other) Canadian authors, at least one more notable literary figure may have Canadian roots: Winnie the Pooh. Legend has it that, during World War I, a Canadian army veterinarian named Harry Colebourn purchased an orphaned bear cub from an Ontario hunter and named her for his home city of Winnipeg. He brought "Winnie" to England as his regiment's mascot and then gave her to the London Zoo. It was there that writer A. A. Milne and his son Christopher first met the bear that was to inspire Milne's most famous stories.

FOOD

In a 1957 radio interview, Colonel Harlan Sanders—the founder of the KFC fast-food chain—derided Canadian food as "plumb tasteless." But back then, both the United States and Canada were in their pre-gourmet era, when few people in North America ate arugula or falafel or the now-ubiquitous ramen noodles. Thanks in part to waves of immigration from Europe, Asia, the Caribbean, and elsewhere, the major Canadian cities now have thriving food scenes that draw on ingredients from around the world and incorporate traditions from many cultures.

© CAROLYN B. HELLER

Butter tarts are a Canadian classic.

Take Vancouver, for example. If you were dropped there from outer space, you might be forgiven for thinking that Canada's national dish is sushi. The city has hundreds of sushi bars, and you can find *maki* and *nigiri* everywhere from the top Japanese dining rooms to the corner grocery store.

Does Canada have a true national cuisine? In such a vast country, regional specialties predominate more than any specific national dish. Yet there are certain iconic Canadian foods that any newcomer to Canada should know:

- *Poutine:* French fries topped with brown gravy and melted cheese, originally from Québec. You can now find *poutine* in many other parts of the country.

- Back bacon: What Americans call "Canadian" bacon, back bacon is cured, smoked, and cooked pork loin, more like smoked ham than American bacon. One of its most common incarnations is in eggs Benedict.

- Syrup on snow: Canada is well known for its maple syrup, and this Québec winter treat is an entertaining way to enjoy the country's maple bounty. Pour hot syrup in the snow, and let it sit for a minute or two until the syrup sets. Take a lollipop stick, roll up the syrup, and then lick.

- Montréal smoked meat: What pastrami is to Manhattan, smoked meat is to

Montréal. It's a smoked, spiced beef brisket, usually piled high in a sandwich and slathered with mustard.

- Butter tarts: You might picture a pie full of creamy yellow butter, but these petite pastries are filled with a brown sugar, butter, and egg blend that resembles pecan pie without the pecans.

- Bumbleberry pie: No, there's no such thing as a bumbleberry. A bumbleberry pie is what Americans might call a mixed-berry pie, made from some combination of blueberries, blackberries, strawberries, or raspberries.

- Saskatoon berries: Native to the prairie provinces, the Northwest Territories, and the southern Yukon, these sweet fruits—similar to blueberries—turn up in pies, jams, and syrups.

- Nanaimo bars: Reportedly created in the Vancouver Island city of Nanaimo in the 1950s, this chocolately confection is made in layers. There's a mixture of chocolate, graham cracker crumbs, and ground nuts on the bottom, custard filling in the center, and chocolate glaze on top.

- Wine gums: A chewy, fruity candy that resembles a jelly bean or "gummy bear," wine gums contain no actual wine. Still, they have an iconic status among many Canadians, both young and old.

For tips about where to sample regional specialties in each of Canada's Prime Living Locations, see *Planning Your Fact-Finding Trip*.

PLANNING YOUR FACT-FINDING TRIP

What's driving your move to Canada? Are you considering a job offer? Looking for a second home, investment property, or retirement destination? Planning to go to university? Or are you simply scouting out a potential place to relocate? Your objective for your relocation will determine the type of fact-finding trip that you plan.

If you're considering a job in Canada, you'll most likely visit the city or region where you'd eventually live. Simply read on throughout this chapter for the practical information you need to plan your trip.

If your plans are more open-ended and you haven't settled on the location that's best for you, you'll need to give more thought to organizing your trip. Do you want to explore the country's biggest cities, or are you looking for a smaller town? Do you want to live by the ocean, in the mountains, or on a lake? Is school for the kids important, or are you looking for a place to retire? How important is the weather? Do you want a home on a large lot, an urban townhouse, or a condo in a modern tower?

Answers to these questions will help narrow down your search before you embark on your fact-finding trip. After all, Canada's a big country.

Preparing to Leave

Begin preparing for your Canadian fact-finding trip with some preliminary research about cities, neighborhoods, and places to live. Whether you already know which city you'll be settling in or you're looking for the spot that captures your fancy, think about where to start your on-the-ground research.

Even if you're not planning to buy a home right away, scan the Multiple Listing Service website (www.mls.ca) to get an idea of prices in different neighborhoods, or look at rental ads on Craigslist. You may not know till you get to town whether a particular community is as good as it looks on paper or online, but at least you'll have an idea of where to start.

WHAT TO BRING
Documents
In the past, tourists could cross the border between the United States and Canada simply by providing some proof of citizenship—a birth certificate, a driver's license, or an expired passport. In 2008, the rules changed. While there are some exceptions, assume that a valid passport is required for travel between the United States and Canada. U.S. citizens do not need a visa for stays of less than six months.

Clothing and Personal Items
You'll need the same kind of clothes in Canada that you'd wear in similar locations in the United States: business clothes for business meetings, warm outerwear for winter travel, jeans or casual wear for weekends.

It's worth tapping into the style of the city you'll be visiting, though. In Montréal, chic counts, while in laid-back Vancouver, some people go everywhere in yoga pants. Toronto and Ottawa tend to be more conservative in their dress, while the West is more relaxed. Industries such as banking, finance, and insurance are more buttoned-down than high-tech, design, or publishing. Still, business is business everywhere, and if you're going for job interviews or meetings, dress as you would for similar appointments in the United States.

It's helpful to bring a notebook or PDA for keeping notes about the neighborhoods and properties you'll visit. A digital camera will also help you remember what you've seen.

Pack any prescription medication into your carry-on bag, and bring your prescription. Many Canadian pharmacies will refill U.S. prescriptions, although they may require that a Canadian doctor approve the refill. Providing your original prescription will simplify the process.

Otherwise, most everything that you might need, from toothpaste to tampons, is available across Canada.

Money

It's convenient to bring a small amount of Canadian dollars, so you don't have to exchange money the minute you arrive. But the major Canadian airports all have currency exchange facilities, and you can find ATMs throughout the metropolitan areas. MasterCard, Visa, and American Express cards are widely accepted across Canada.

In many parts of Canada, early autumn has lovely weather and fewer tourists.

WHEN TO GO

In planning your fact-finding visit to Canada, you can take one of two strategies: Go when the weather is nicest to see your potential new home in its best light, or go in the worst of winter to prepare for what you're getting into.

Summer is high season for travel in Ontario and Québec. Expect hot, humid weather, plenty of tourists, and peak lodging prices. Late spring and early fall have the best weather. Autumn is busy with foliage tourists, but if you're visiting cities, rather than the countryside, you can avoid the leaf-peeping crowds. The second Monday in October—Columbus Day weekend in the United States—is Canada's Thanksgiving holiday, when businesses and services may be closed.

In Alberta, you'll find the best weather during the warm, dry summers—from June through August. In the Canadian Rockies, that's when you'll also find the region inundated with tourists. Late spring (May–June) or early fall (September–October) usually have pleasant weather and fewer visitors. Snow can begin to fall in October or November and remain on the ground till at least April.

CANADIAN NATIONAL AND PROVINCIAL HOLIDAYS

DATE	HOLIDAY
January 1	New Year's Day
Third Monday in February	Family Day (Alberta)
March/April	Good Friday
March/April	Easter Monday
Monday before May 25	Victoria Day
June 24	St. Jean Baptiste Day/National Day (Québec)
July 1	Canada Day
First Monday in August	BC Day (British Columbia), Civic Holiday (Ontario), Heritage Day (Alberta)
First Monday in September	Labour Day
Second Monday in October	Thanksgiving Day
November 11	Remembrance Day
December 25	Christmas Day
December 26	Boxing Day

In British Columbia, the nicest time to visit is in the sunny, mild summers, but that's when lodging rates are highest. Spring (March–May) in Vancouver, Victoria, and the Gulf Islands means moderate lodging prices and lots of daylight, despite frequent drizzly days. In the cool damp winters, accommodations can cost half what they do in mid-summer.

If you're planning to live or work in a ski destination such as Whistler, Banff, or the Laurentians, early fall is the prime time to visit. You won't find snow, but you will find discounted accommodations; that's also when many ski areas hire for the upcoming winter season.

Arriving in Canada

CUSTOMS REGULATIONS

When you enter Canada as a visitor, you can bring in clothing, cameras, computers, and other items for your personal use. If you have expensive electronics or other similar goods, you are supposed to declare them to the Canada Border Services Agency and demonstrate that the goods are leaving the country with you at the end of your trip; otherwise, you could be charged duty.

Entering Canada from the United States, you can bring a small amount of alcohol and tobacco duty-free. There are additional restrictions on bringing in fruits and vegetables, meats, and firearms. Check the Canada Border Service Agency website (www.cbsa-asfc.gc.ca) for details.

TRANSPORTATION

Should you rent a car for your travels in Canada? It depends. If you're confining your trip to a major city, such as Toronto, Montréal, or Vancouver, you could forgo a rental car and get around by public transportation. Or you could use transit initially and rent a car when you're ready to travel farther afield. When you're exploring suburbs, smaller cities, or the mountains, however, having your own wheels will make it easier to get around.

If you're planning an extended trip covering a large swath of the country and you enjoy the outdoors, you might join the hordes of travelers who journey across Canada by recreational vehicle. Many companies, including Cruise Canada (www.cruisecanada.com), Canada RV Rentals (www.canada-rv-rentals.com), and CanaDream (www.canadream.com), rent RVs nationwide.

Sample Itineraries

ONE WEEK

When you have only one week, confine your trip to one or two cities in one region. We've laid out a week-long sample trip to Vancouver, but you could construct a similar itinerary in other parts of the country. In a week, you could visit Toronto and briefly explore the surrounding communities, or combine time in Montréal with a day or two in the Laurentians or Eastern Townships. Seven days would let you scout out both Calgary and Edmonton, leaving a day to relax in Banff National Park.

Days 1-2

Assuming you've arrived in Vancouver on Friday night, settle into a café on Saturday morning and organize your day. Many homes for sale have open houses on weekend afternoons, so you could combine neighborhood explorations with a few preliminary house-hunting stops. Find open house listings on www.realtylink.org or in the *Vancouver Courier*'s free real estate supplement.

Before you throw yourself into house-hunting, though, take time to walk around. Head for whatever neighborhoods appeal to you and wander. You could cover more ground by car, but unless you're planning to live out in the suburbs, walk or use public transit to get a feel for the community.

Stroll through the West End or Yaletown, walk around Kitsilano or Point

Grey, or meander along funky Main Street or Commercial Drive. See who's out and about. Stop into the community center or library, looking at the bulletin boards for neighborhood happenings. Have lunch in a local bistro, or pick up a picnic at the Granville Island Public Market. If you're feeling more adventurous, go the suburb of Richmond for dim sum and an introduction to Vancouver's Pacific Rim culture.

Continue your neighborhood investigations in the afternoons, but knock off early to relax. People-watch on the beach. Rent a bike and circle Stanley Park. Contemplate the sunset over the water. Much of Vancouver's appeal is its natural setting, and you'll want time to enjoy it.

Days 3-4

Devote Monday and Tuesday to more intensive research. Schedule appointments with a real estate agent who can drive you around different neighborhoods and tour homes for sale. Many Vancouver brokers set aside Tuesday mornings for "brokers' open houses," when homes new to the market are shown to agents; if your agent brings you along, you can get in on these preview showings, too.

Use these days to meet prospective employers or, if you're just starting your job search, to network and begin learning about potential opportunities. If you have children, schedule appointments to visit schools. Private schools are typically better equipped to deal with visitors than public schools are, but you should still be able to meet the principal or assistant principal, talk about the school, and have a look around.

In the evenings, enjoy a leisurely dinner, or pick up the free *Georgia Straight* to see what else is happening around town.

Day 5

You've been working hard, so it's time for a day off. If you're visiting during ski season, head for the slopes at Grouse, Cypress, or Seymour Mountain on the North Shore. Or if you start early, you could do a day trip to Whistler. You can be schussing down the North Shore hills in under an hour, but allow two hours to Whistler.

If it's summer, you could still go to the mountains to hike and enjoy the views, or explore the outdoors in town. Take a dip at Kitsilano pool, wander the serene Nitobe Japanese Garden at the University of British Columbia (stroll around the rest of the campus, too), or hang out with the hardbodies on English Bay Beach. Rent a kayak (at English Bay, Granville Island, or Jericho Beach) and paddle the calm waters beneath the urban skyline.

Days 6-7

Reassess your needs as you near the end of your fact-finding week. Do you want more time to explore neighborhoods or house-hunt? Do more job research or spend time at schools? If so, follow a schedule similar to Days 3 and 4. If you have a lot of ground to cover, these would be good days to rent a car.

Alternatively, use your remaining days to discover the surrounding region. Catch a morning ferry to Victoria, where you can start with a walk around the Inner Harbour. Then, if you're checking out places to live, drive through James Bay, Rockland, Oak Bay, or Victoria West. Another approach would be to arrange a half- or full-day "Relocation Vacation" tour with Victoria-based Kathy McAree, who'll take you to new real estate developments while introducing you to surrounding communities. Either way, you can have an early dinner and get a late ferry back to Vancouver or stay the night, returning to Vancouver for your trip home the next day.

TWO WEEKS

With two weeks, you can cast your exploring net more widely. In the West, you could travel from Vancouver, through the Okanagan wine country and the Rocky Mountains into Alberta, ending your trip in Calgary. Or you could island-hop from Vancouver Island to several of the smaller Gulf Islands, with city time in Vancouver on either end of your trip.

Farther east, you could take in Toronto and still have time to visit Niagara Falls and scout out Ottawa or other smaller cities. Or, as in the following sample, you could concentrate on the metropolitan areas, dividing your time between Toronto, Ottawa, and Montréal.

Days 1-2

For this city-focused trip, suppose you've arrived in Toronto Friday night. In the morning, buy a subway pass and start exploring. Stroll around the University of Toronto campus, check out the Victorian homes in the Annex, or browse the upscale shops in posh Yorkville. Peruse the stalls in Kensington Market and stop for a bowl of dumplings in Chinatown.

If it's a nice day, catch the subway toward the harbor. Admire the views from the CN Tower, stroll along the lakeshore, or take the ferry to the Toronto Islands. Unwind back downtown with dinner in one of the many wine bars.

Continue your explorations into new neighborhoods. Stop for a baklava in Danforth Village (formerly known as Greektown), or visit Riverdale or the Beaches in the East End. Take the streetcar along bohemian Queen Street West, then explore Parkdale, High Park, or Bloor West Village. Head north to the residential communities in Midtown or North Toronto. Depending on where you end your day, you might sup on Caribbean roti, homemade pasta, or grill-your-own Korean barbecue.

Days 3-4

Now that you're more familiar with the city, it's time to get down to business. Use the next couple of days to tour homes with a real estate agent, meet with potential employers, and visit local schools.

Day 5

If you've gotten a good feel for Toronto, take a break today. One option is to rent a car and drive south

CAROLYN B. HELLER

Make time during your fact-finding trip to see the sights.

to Niagara Falls, or tour the wineries along the Niagara peninsula. If it's summer or fall, you could take in a play at the Shaw Festival in Niagara-on-the-Lake; there are matinees on Wednesdays, so you could have lunch, see a show, and return to Toronto by nightfall.

Day 6

The next stop on your fact-finding trip is Ottawa. Whether you drive or take the train, allow about five hours' travel time. Check into your hotel and walk along the Rideau Canal before dinner.

Days 7-8

If you're visiting between June and August, be a tourist in the morning and watch the changing of the guard ceremony in front of the Parliament buildings. It starts at 10 A.M., but arrive at least 15–20 minutes early. Sign up (in advance) for a free Parliament tour, which you can take after the ceremony.

Next up is neighborhood exploration. Check out the refurbished Victorian homes in the Glebe, the estates in Rockcliffe Park (if you have time, tour Rideau Hall, the governor general's residence), or the more diverse areas around the University of Ottawa. Westboro Village and surrounding residential communities are also worth a look. Have supper in the Glebe or the Byward Market.

Day 9

This morning, finish your Ottawa research, or visit the Museum of Civilization or the National Gallery. Both museums are huge, so be selective about the things you want to see.

In the afternoon, you're off to Montréal—about two hours by car or train. If you've driven to Montréal, find a place to park your car; not only is public transportation convenient, but the narrow streets and aggressive drivers can make driving here stressful. For dinner, go traditional with *steak frites* or a smoked meat sandwich, or opt for more contemporary fare.

Days 10-12

Hop on the Métro; it's time to discover Montréal. Even if you don't want to live in the city's oldest neighborhood, you'll want to visit Vieux Montréal. Leave plenty of time for wandering around the artsy Plateau. Check out Mile End and Outremont, walk through gentrifying Rosemont, or go west to Westmount and some of the more anglophone communities. Be sure to visit Jean-Talon Market—ideally around lunchtime.

Take time each day to sightsee. If the weather isn't great, explore downtown's Underground City—a 30-kilometer (20-mile) network of shops, theaters, and offices. If it's nice out, take in the city views atop Mont-Royal Park, or rent a bike and cycle along the Lachine Canal.

Touring with a real estate agent will help you decipher Montréal's disparate neighborhoods. If you're job-hunting, schedule interviews or informational meetings in advance, and organize your touring around these sessions. While you can get by without much French in Montréal, build extra time in your schedule to account for any language difficulties.

Day 13

Today, either continue your Montréal research or do some sightseeing. Visit one of the many museums, tour McGill University's campus, or go shopping. Or take a day trip to the Laurentian Mountains or the rural Eastern Townships—both regions are less than two hours from downtown.

Day 14

If you need to return to Toronto for your flight home, today is your travel day. It's about five hours by car or train; check out flights, too, since you can often get cheap seats between Montréal and Toronto. If you're heading home from Montréal directly, linger over a final café au lait.

FESTIVALS AND SPECIAL EVENTS

If the purpose of your fact-finding trip is as much to learn about Canada as it is to find a place to live, schedule your trip to coincide with one of these special events. Alternatively, if your trip is all about getting settled, plan your travel to avoid these festivities.

Date	City	Event
February	Québec City	Québec Winter Carnival, www.carnaval.qc.ca
February	Ottawa	Winterlude, www.canadascapital.gc.ca/winterlude
May and October	Okanagan region (BC)	Okanagan Wine Festivals, www.owfs.com
May–August	Banff (AB)	Banff Summer Arts Festival, www.banffcentre.ca/bsaf
June/July	Montréal	Festival International de Jazz de Montréal, www.montrealjazzfest.com
July	Ottawa	Canada Day celebrations, www.canadascapital.gc.ca
July	Calgary	Calgary Stampede, www.calgarystampede.com
July/August	Toronto	Caribana Festival, www.caribanafestival.com
July/August	Vancouver	HSBC Celebration of Light fireworks competition, www.hsbccelebrationoflight.com
August	Edmonton	Edmonton International Fringe Theatre Festival, www.fringetheatreadventures.ca
September	Toronto	Toronto International Film Festival, www.torontointernationalfilm-festival.ca
November	Whistler (BC)	Cornucopia Celebration of Wine and Food, www.whistlercornucopia.com

ONE MONTH

A month would give you time for a leisurely trip across the West, with stops in Vancouver, Victoria, and the Gulf Islands, before heading inland to the Okanagan and the Rockies. After visiting Banff, Lake Louise, and Jasper, you could finish your trip in Calgary or Edmonton.

Farther east, you could explore Toronto's many neighborhoods and still visit Ottawa, Montréal, and Québec City. You'd also have time to unwind in the Niagara wine region, Mont-Tremblant, or Québec's Eastern Townships.

Alternatively, you could travel between British Columbia and Ontario or Québec, stopping to see the Rockies en route. We've outlined a sample trip to take in Canada's highlights while still allowing time to explore regions where you might want to live. You'll see lots of different places, but at each stop, be sure to walk around, see what different neighborhoods are like, and assess whether it's a place where you and your family can be happy.

Late spring can be a pleasant time to visit the Rocky Mountains, but expect snow on the ground at higher elevations.

Week 1

You could do this cross-country trip in either direction, but we'd suggest starting in the East; you can look forward to spectacular scenery as you head to the West Coast. Although a month would give you time to do this journey by car, you'll have more time to explore each stop—and less time rolling across the prairies—if you combine flying and driving.

Spend your first week in Toronto and/or Montréal, following an itinerary similar to the two-week schedule outlined earlier in this chapter. You could explore one city in depth with time for side trips or, if you use your time efficiently, you could cover both cities in 7–8 days.

Week 2

In your second week, fly west to Calgary. Budget 3–4 days to get the lay of the land here. Explore downtown and the riverfront (best done on foot, or by hopping on and off the light rail), and then get acquainted with residential areas like funky Kensington and elite Mount Royal, eclectic Bridgeland and Inglewood, and more suburban Elbow Park. Poke around in the shops on 17th Avenue S.W. or rent a bike to explore Nose Hill Park beyond the University of Calgary campus. Both downtown and the Mission neighborhood have interesting dining options.

On your third or fourth day in Calgary, pick up a rental car (you'll return it in Vancouver at the end of your trip). Before you leave town, use the car to check out outlying communities like McKenzie Town in the southeast or any of the northwest suburbs. Then, it's an easy three-hour drive north to Edmonton where you'll spend the rest of the week.

While Edmonton does have a public transit system, the city is fairly spread out, and it's easiest to explore by car. Visit the established residential neighborhoods west of downtown, including Glenora, Crestwood, and Parkview, and cross the river to tour the University of Alberta and the surrounding Strathcona area. Browse the shops along Whyte Avenue and visit the Farmer's Market. If there's a festival going on—there's one nearly every week in summer—be sure to check it out.

Week 3

This week, you'll explore the Rocky Mountains, then make your way to British Columbia's Okanagan region. From Edmonton, drive west to Jasper. Check out the town, and go for a hike in the national park. When you're ready to leave Jasper, you'll drive the scenic Icefields Parkway south to Lake Louise. Stay near the lake or continue on to Banff, where there are more lodging options. Attend a concert or lecture at the Banff Centre, soak in the hot springs, or just spend time hiking the mountains and walking around town.

From Banff, head west into British Columbia. Allow at least two days to work your way through the mountains into the Okanagan Valley. This region is western Canada's wine country, so you can split your time between touring new real estate developments—the Okanagan has been in the midst of building boom—and tasting your way from winery to winery. The city of Kelowna has the largest number of places to stay, but the southern Okanagan towns of Oliver and Osoyoos are more picturesque.

Week 4

From the Okanagan, it's about 4–5 hours' drive to Vancouver, where you'll spend the rest of the week. Follow the one-week itinerary (above), or spend 3–4 days researching places to live in Vancouver, then unwind for a couple of days in the Gulf Islands. If you're considering island life, Salt Spring, which has one of the islands' largest year-round communities, is worth exploring, or you could visit smaller islands, such as Mayne, Pender, and Galiano. Return to Vancouver at least one day before your flight home. That way, you'll have time for a West Coast dinner to celebrate a successful fact-finding trip.

Practicalities

ACCOMMODATIONS

Canada has the same lodging choices you'd see in the United States, from upscale boutique inns, roadside motels, and cozy bed-and-breakfasts to chain hotels of all types. For longer stays, or for a less expensive place to live while you house-hunt, seek out an apartment-hotel, a vacation rental, or university accommodations. You can find short-term rentals on nationwide websites such as Vacation Rentals By Owner (www.vrbo.com), Home Away (www.homeaway.com), and Craigslist (www.craigslist.org).

What follows are more tips for each region covered in this book. Estimated prices shown are based on the average cost of a standard double room, not including taxes, in high season, generally May through October.

Vancouver

At the stylish **Pacific Palisades** (1277 Robson St., tel. 800/663-1815 or 604/688-0461, fax 604/688-4374, www.pacificpalisadeshotel.com, $200–250 doubles), all the brightly hued rooms have kitchenettes, and there's a nice-sized pool.

A contemporary apartment hotel catering to business travelers, the **Meridian at 910 Beach** (910 Beach Ave., tel. 888/609-5100 or 604/609-5100, fax 604/609-5111, www.910beach.com, $200–300 doubles) offers attractive specials, especially in winter; see their website for details.

The **Rosellen Suites** (2030 Barclay St., tel. 888/317-6648 or 604/689-4807, fax 604/684-3327, www.rosellensuites.com, $185–310 doubles), a former apartment building in the West End near Stanley Park, has family-friendly studios, and one- and two-bedroom units with kitchens; discounts are available for weekly and monthly stays.

The **Chocolate Lily B&B** (1353 Maple St., tel. 866/903-9363 or 604/731-9363, www.chocolatelily.com, $140–165 doubles) rents two smartly appointed ground-level apartments near Kitsilano beach.

On the University of British Columbia campus, the **West Coast Suites** (5959 Student Union Blvd., tel. 888/822-1030 or 604/822-1000, www.ubcconferences.com/accommodation, $130 doubles) are comfortable one-bedroom apartments; from May through August, the university also offers dormitory and budget hotel accommodations.

British Columbia

Whistler has a large supply of vacation rental apartments that, while pricey in the winter, can be discounted significantly in the spring or fall. Look for short-term rentals at **Allura Direct** (www.alluradirect.com), **Vacation Rentals by Owner** (www.vrbo.com), and **Craigslist** (www.craigslist.org). If you're planning to work in the Whistler area, check with the **Whistler Housing Authority** (www.whistlerhousing.ca) for less-expensive lodging ideas.

In Victoria, the studio, one-, and two-bedroom units at the **Oswego Hotel** (500 Oswego St., tel. 877/767-9346 or 250/294-7500, fax 250/294-7509, www.oswegovictoria.com, $215–300 doubles) are outfitted in West Coast stone and wood, and all have kitchen facilities; ask about discounts for stays of a week or more.

Many Victoria bed-and-breakfasts offer reduced rates for longer stays between November and April. Try the elegant **Fairholme Manor** (638 Rockland Pl., tel. 877/511-3322 or 250/598-3240, fax 250/598-3299, www.fairholmemanor.com, $155–325 doubles) or the homey **Abbeymore Manor** (1470 Rockland Ave., tel. 888/801-1811 or 250/370-1470, www.abbeymoore.com, $180–240 doubles).

Considering a golf community? Stay at the **Westin Bear Mountain Victoria Golf Resort & Spa** (1999 Country Club Way, tel. 888/533-2327 or 250/391-7160, fax 250/391-3792, www.bearmountain.ca, $250–350 doubles) while exploring the golf and other facilities at this planned community.

The **University of Victoria** (tel. 250/721-8395, fax 250/721-8930, www.housing.uvic.ca/visitor) has seven bed-and-breakfast rooms available year-round ($88 doubles) and dormitory rooms for visitors May–August ($58 doubles). In summer, you can also rent a campus apartment by the night or the month.

The city of Kelowna is a convenient base for scouting out the Okanagan region. **The Cove Lakeside Resort** (4205 Gellatly Rd., Westbank, tel. 877/762-2683 or 250/707-1800, fax 250/707-1809, www.covelakeside.com, $225–335 doubles) combines a resort-like setting on Okanagan Lake with such practicalities as in-suite kitchens, washer/dryers, and Wi-Fi.

Bellasera Tuscan Villas (1795 Country Club Dr., Kelowna, tel. 866/313-7372 or 250/765-5556, www.bellasera.ca, $3,400–4,000 per month), a Mediterranean-themed townhouse community on a golf course, rents spacious units for stays of at least 30 days. Golfers might also like the lodge or townhouses overlooking the links at **Predator Ridge Golf Resort** (301 Village Centre Pl., Vernon, 888/578-6688 or 250/542-9404, fax 250/542-3835, www.predator-ridge.com, $195–350 doubles), a golf-themed development 40-minutes' drive north of downtown Kelowna.

Toronto

In downtown Toronto, the **Suites at 1 King West** (1 King St. West, tel. 866/470-5464 or 416/548-8100, fax 416/548-8101, www.onekingwest.com, $170–390 doubles), a deluxe condominium-hotel, rents sleekly modern apartments for short or extended stays. To sleep downtown without spending big bucks, try the friendly **Hotel Victoria** (56 Yonge St., tel. 800/363-8228 or 416/363-1666, fax 416/363-7327, www.hotelvictoria-toronto.com, $135–160

© CAROLYN B. HELLER

Apartment-hotels, such as Toronto's Lowther Suites, are convenient for longer stays.

doubles), one of Toronto's oldest hotels; the "deluxe" doubles are larger than the standard rooms and have mini-fridges. For something edgier, the **Gladstone Hotel** (1214 Queen St. West, tel. 416/531-4635, fax 416/539-0953, www.gladstonehotel.com, $175–275 doubles) is a combination art gallery and hotel in a restored 1889 building.

In the residential Annex neighborhood, **Lowther Suites** (88 Lowther Ave., tel./fax 416/925-4600, www.lowthersuites.com, $110–195 doubles) has five spacious one- or two-bedroom apartments with full kitchens and washer/dryers in a renovated brick mansion. The property caters to independent travelers, since there's no on-site staff (although a caretaker is on call). In the same neighborhood, the **Annex Quest House** (83 Spadina Rd., tel. 416/922-1934, fax 416/922-6366, www.annexquesthouse.com, $105–120 doubles) is an ascetic but serene bed-and-breakfast where the rooms have fridges, coffee makers, and private baths.

On the University of Toronto campus, the **University Women's Club of Toronto** (162 St. George St., tel. 416/979-2000, fax 416/979-3266, www.uwconbloor.com, $115 doubles) runs a small bed-and-breakfast that's open to the public, males and females alike. The guest rooms have been nicely updated, although the six rooms share three baths.

Designed primarily for relocating businesspeople, **Apartments International** (tel. 888/410-2400 or 416/410-2400, fax 416/210-2410, www.apts-intl.com) represents a number of furnished apartments across the city that are available for short-term rentals. If you'll be in town awhile, they may offer some cost-effective options.

Ontario

In Ottawa, for apartment-style lodging with kitchenettes, laundry facilities, and Wi-Fi, the **Extended Stay Deluxe Ottawa** (141 Cooper St., tel. 613/236-7500, fax 613/563-2836, www.extendedstayhotels.com, $140–165 doubles) has a convenient location within walking distance of downtown. Less spacious but more stylish are **The Arc** (140 Slater St., tel. 800/699-2516 or 613/238-2888, fax 613/238-0053, www.arcthehotel.com, $195–265 doubles), Ottawa's first upscale boutique hotel, and **Hotel Indigo** (123 Metcalfe St., tel. 877/846-3446 or 613/231-6555, fax 613/231-7555, www.hotelindigo.com, $160–200 doubles), which offers boutique style at slightly lower prices.

Québec

Tourism Montréal sometimes offers attractive lodging promotions; check their website (www.tourisme-montreal.org) for details.

Despite its bland chain-style interior, the **Marriott SpringHill Suites** (445 St-Jean-Baptiste, tel. 866/875-4333 or 514/875-4333, fax 514/875-4331, www.marriott.com, $200–225 doubles) in Vieux Montréal has family-friendly studios with kitchenettes. For more style, opt for a loft-like room in the chic **Hôtel Gault** (449 rue Sainte-Hélène, tel. 866/904-1616 or 514/904-1616, fax 866/904-1717 or 514/904-1717, www.hotelgault.com, $235–375 doubles) in a former Old Montréal warehouse, or for the classy **Château Versailles** (1659 rue Sherbrooke Ouest, tel. 888/933-8111 or 514/933-8111, fax 514/933-6867, www.versailleshotels.com, $215–320 doubles) at the foot of Mont-Royal, near downtown.

In the busy Latin Quarter, the basic-but-smart **Auberge Espace Confort** (2050 rue St-Denis, tel. 514/849-0505, fax 514/844-2221, www.montre-alespaceconfort.com, $119–149 doubles) has good-value doubles with kitchenettes. If you don't need frills, the simple rooms at **Hotel Y de Montréal** (1355 Blvd. René-Lévesque Ouest, tel. 514/866-9942, fax 514/861-1603, www.ydesfemmesmtl.org, $85 doubles) downtown are a steal.

In Québec City, many warehouse buildings in the Lower Town have been converted into stylish inns, including **Auberge Saint Pierre** (79 rue St-Pierre, tel. 888/268-1017 or 418/694-7981, fax 418/694-0406, www.auberge.qc.ca, $200–225 doubles) and **Hôtel des Coutellier** (253 rue Saint-Paul, tel. 418/692-9696, fax 418/692-4050, www.hoteldescoutellier.com, $215–285 doubles). In the gentrifying Saint-Roch district, **Appartments-Hôtel Bonséjours** (237 rue St-Joseph Est, tel. 866/892-8080 or 418/681-4375, fax 418/380-8084, www.bonsejours.com, $115–185 doubles) has 14 simple studios and apartments, all with kitchen facilities; ask about discounts on stays of a week or more.

Alberta

Several former apartment buildings in downtown Calgary are now hotels catering to longer-term guests. The most modern is the **International Hotel Suites Calgary** (220 4th Ave., tel. 800/661-8627 or 403/265-9600, fax 403/290-7879, www. internationalhotel.ca, $150–300 doubles), but the older **5 Calgary Downtown Suites Hotel** (618 5th Ave., tel. 888/561-7666 or 403/451-5551, www.5calgary. com, $160–290 doubles) and **Regency Suites Hotel Calgary** (610 4th Ave., tel. 800/468-4044 or 403/231-1000, fax 403/231-1012, www.regencycalgary. com, $155–280) are comfortable alternatives. If boutique is more your style, make tracks to Calgary's trendy **Hotel Arts** (119 12th Ave., tel. 800/661-9378 or 403/266-4611, fax 403/237-0978, www.hotelarts.ca, $350–400 doubles).

In Edmonton, the low-rise **Canterra Suites** (11010 Jasper Ave., tel. 877/421-1212 or 780/421-1212, fax 780/421-1211, www.canterrasuites.com, $170–200) is a friendly spot with large apartment-style units; it's next door to a shopping center with a grocery, pharmacy, and dry cleaner. On the north side of town (you'll want a car here), the **Chateau Nova Hotel & Suites** (159 Airport Rd., tel. 888/919-6682 or 780/424-6682, fax 780/424-6683, www. novahotels.ca, $120–230) has modern rooms and one-bedroom apartments. Near the University of Alberta, the **Metterra Hotel on Whyte** (10454 82 Ave., tel. 866/465-8150 or 780/465-8150, fax 780/465-8174, www.metterra.com, $175–215 doubles) is one of Edmonton's trendiest options.

FOOD

Unless otherwise specified, prices shown are estimated costs for an average main dish at dinner.

Vancouver

For an introduction to contemporary West Coast cuisine, book a table overlooking English Bay at **Raincity Grill** (1193 Denman St., tel. 604/685-7337, www. raincitygrill.com, lunch 11:30 A.M.–2:30 P.M. Mon.–Fri., brunch 10:30 A.M.– 2:30 P.M. Sat.–Sun., dinner 5–11 P.M. daily, entrée $27) or in Kitsilano at trendy **Gastropod** (1938 W. 4th Ave., tel. 604/730-5579, www.gastropod. ca, dinner 5:30–10:30 P.M. daily, lunch entrée $17, dinner entrée $26). Small plates are big in Vancouver, and **CRU Wine Bar-Restaurant** (1459 W. Broadway, 604/677-4111, www.cru.ca, 5–10 P.M. daily, small plates $15) in South Granville serves some of the best.

To sample the flavors of Vancouver's large Asian community, try Japanese tapas at **Guu with Garlic** (1698 Robson St., tel. 604/685-8678, www.guu-izakaya.com, 5:30 P.M.–midnight daily, small plates $6), sushi at **Yoshi** (689

Denman St., tel. 604/738-8226, www.yoshijapaneserestaurant.com, lunch noon–2 P.M. Mon.–Fri., dinner 5:30–10:30 P.M. daily, entrée $20), or dim sum at **Sun Sui Wah** (3888 Main St., tel. 604/872-8822, www. sunsuiwah.com, 10 A.M.–3 P.M. and 5–10:30 P.M. daily, dim sum plates $5, dinner entrée $18).

The **Granville Island Public Market** (1689 Johnson St., tel. 604/666-6477, www.granvilleisland.com, 9 A.M.–7 P.M. daily) is a great place to grab a quick bite.

British Columbia

In Whistler Village, visit **Pasta Lupino** (4368 Main St., tel. 604/905-0400, www.pastalupino.

One of the pleasures of exploring Canada is sampling a variety of foods.

com, 11 A.M.–9 P.M. daily, entrée $15) for simple Italian fare or **Splitz Grill** (4369 Main St., tel. 604/938-9300, 11 A.M.–9 P.M. Sun.–Thurs., till 10 P.M. Fri.–Sat., entrée $10) for the huge selection of burgers (including turkey and veggie varieties).

In Victoria, locals flock to **Zambri's** (911 Yates St., tel. 250/360-1171, www. zambris.ca, 11:30 A.M.–2:30 P.M. and 5–9 P.M. Tues.–Sat., lunch entrée $12, dinner entrée $22), hidden in a strip-mall, for first-rate contemporary Italian fare. Updated French bistro cooking, paired with a huge selection of wines by the glass, is the lure at welcoming **Brasserie L'École** (1715 Government St., tel. 250/475-6260, www.lecole.ca, 5:30–11 P.M. Tues.–Sat., entrée $20).

For vegetarian dishes in a funky, brightly colored room, head for **Rebar Modern Food** (50 Bastion Sq., tel. 250/361-9223, www.rebarmodernfood. com, 8:30 A.M.–9 P.M. Mon.–Wed., till 10 P.M. Thurs.–Sat., till 3:30 P.M. Sun., entrée $12). **Choux Choux Charcuterie** (830 Fort St., tel. 250/382-7572, 10 A.M.–5:30 P.M. Mon.–Fri., till 5 P.M. Sat.) sells homemade pâtés, cured meats, and cheeses—perfect for lunch on the ferry.

The Okanagan is known for its wineries, many of which have first-rate dining rooms; among the best are **The Terrace at Mission Hill Family Estate Winery** (1730 Mission Hill Rd., Westbank, tel. 250/768-6467, www.missionhillwinery.com, 11:30 A.M.–4 P.M. daily May–mid-June and early Sept.–

early Oct., 11:30 A.M.–4 P.M. and 5–8:30 P.M. daily mid-June–early Sept., entrée $22) near Kelowna and **The Sonora Room at Burrowing Owl Estate Winery** (100 Burrowing Owl Pl., Oliver, tel. 250/498-0620, www.bovwine. ca, 11:30 A.M.–2:30 P.M. and 5:30–9:30 P.M. daily, lunch entrée $19, dinner entrée $34), in the south Okanagan hills.

A stylish spot for a light meal and a sampling of local vino is **Waterfront Wines Wine Bar & Restaurant** (1180 Sunset Dr., Kelowna, tel. 250/979-1222, www. waterfrontwines.com, 5–11 P.M. daily, small plates $10); in summer, don't miss the fresh tomato salad. **Okanagan Grocery Artisan Breads** (2355 Golden Dr., Kelowna, tel. 250/862-2811, www.okanagangrocery.com, 9:30 A.M.–5:30 P.M. Tues.–Sat.) sells top-quality breads and locally made cheeses.

Toronto

From gravlax with fennel salad to braised pork belly with green cabbage and fresh scallops, some of Toronto's most creative comfort food is served at the upscale **Jamie Kennedy Wine Bar** (9 Church St., tel. 416/362-1957, www. jamiekennedy.ca, 11:30 A.M.–11 P.M. Mon.–Sat., 11 A.M.–3 P.M. and 4 P.M.– 11 P.M. Sun., small plates $12). Tapas draw inspiration from Spain, the Mediterranean, and Latin America at **Cava** (1560 Yonge St., tel. 416/979-9918, www. cavarestaurant.ca, lunch noon–2 P.M. Mon.–Fri., dinner 5–10 P.M. daily, small plates $10), where intriguing dishes might include lemony chickpea soup or sweetbreads paired with a radicchio and poblano chile salad.

Build your own rice bowl full of organic ingredients at **The Rice Bar** (319 Augusta Ave., tel. 416/922-7423, 11:30 A.M.–10 P.M. Mon.–Fri., 11 A.M.–10 P.M. Sat.–Sun., entrée $9), a vegetarian-friendly spot in the Kensington Market area. No-frills **Mother's Dumplings** (79 Huron St., tel. 416/217-2008, www. mothersdumplings.com, 11 A.M.–midnight daily, entrée $5) in Chinatown, cooks up authentic Chinese dumplings, paired with excellent side dishes; try the bean curd sheets dressed with peppers and fragrant cilantro.

Regroup from West End house-hunting at **Easy Restaurant** (1645 Queen St. West, tel. 416/537-4893, www.easybreakfast.ca, 9 A.M.–5 P.M. daily, entrée $9), a funky diner serving breakfast all day. The only problem with ordering their signature *huevos divorciados*—poached eggs with black beans, tortillas, salsa, guacamole, and ancho-chile jam—is that you'll be hungry again in about three days.

When you get tired of eating out, shop for prepared and fresh foods at **The Big Carrot** (348 Danforth Ave., tel. 416/466-2129, www.thebigcarrot. ca, 9 A.M.–9 P.M. Mon.–Fri., 9 A.M.–8 P.M. Sat., 11 A.M.–6 P.M. Sun.), a well-stocked natural foods market, or at gourmet grocer **Pusateri's** (1539 Avenue Rd., tel. 416/785-9100, www.pusateris.com, 8 A.M.–8 P.M. Mon.–Wed., till

9 P.M. Thurs.–Fri., till 7 P.M. Sat.–Sun.; 57 Yorkville Ave., tel. 416/785-9100, 10 A.M.–8 P.M. Mon.–Wed., 10 A.M.–9 P.M. Thurs.–Fri., 8 A.M.–8 P.M. Sat., 10 A.M.–7 P.M. Sun.).

Ontario

A local favorite in Ottawa's Byward Market, **The Courtyard** (21 George St., tel. 613/ 241-1516, www.courtyardrestaurant.com, 11:30 A.M.–2 P.M. and 5:30–9:30 P.M. Mon.–Sat., 11 A.M.–22 P.M. and 5–9 P.M. Sun., lunch entrée $14, dinner entrée $30) offers contemporary regional dishes, such as juniper-braised quail or locally-raised lamb with lentils, in a historic stone building. Capturing the laid-back yet hip vibe of the Glebe neighborhood, **Urban Pear** (151 Second Ave., tel. 613/569-9305, www.theurbanpear.com, lunch 11:30 A.M.–2 P.M. Tues.–Fri., brunch 11 A.M.–2 P.M. Sun., dinner 5:30–9 P.M. daily, lunch entrée $14, dinner entrée $29) serves creative market-driven fare. Also in the Glebe, **The Wild Oat** (817 Bank St., tel. 613/232-6232, 8 A.M.–8 P.M. Mon.–Sat., 9 A.M.–6 P.M. Sun., entrée $7) caters to vegetarians and their friends with breakfasts, sandwiches, and baked goods.

Québec

Among Montréal's scores of bistros and brasseries that serve French classics (often alongside more contemporary fare) is **La Brasserie Brunoise** (1012 de la Montagne, tel. 514/933-3885, www.brunoise.ca, noon–midnight Mon.–Fri., 5 P.M.–midnight Sat., entrée $17), a casual-chic space downtown that's equally appropriate for a relaxed business meal, a solo dinner, or a get-together with friends. In Old Montréal, **Olive and Gourmando** (351 rue Saint Paul Ouest, tel. 514/350-1083, www.oliveetgourmando.com, 8 A.M.–6 P.M. Tues.–Sat., entrée $10) makes wonderful breads, pastries, and sandwiches.

For a light meal or to pick up picnic fare, don't miss Montréal's **Jean-Talon Market** (7070 rue Henri-Julien, at rue Jean-Talon Est, www.marches-publics-mtl.com, 7 A.M.–6 P.M. Mon.–Wed. and Sat., till 8 P.M. Thurs.–Fri., till 5 P.M. Sun.). Across from the market, graze on Middle Eastern *mezze* at vegetarian-friendly **Le Petit Alep** (191 rue Jean-Talon Est, tel. 514/270-9361, 11 A.M.–11 P.M. Tues.–Sat., entrée $10). And be sure to try such Montréal icons as **Schwartz's** (3895 Blvd. Saint-Laurent, tel. 514/842-4813, www.schwartzs-deli.com, 8 A.M.-12:30 A.M. Sun.–Thurs., till 1:30 A.M. Fri., till 2:30 A.M. Sat., entrée $10), which has had patrons lining up for its smoked meat since 1928, or **Fairmount Bakery** (74 ave. Fairmount Ouest, tel. 514/272-0667, www.fairmountbagel.com, open 24 hours), famous for fresh-baked bagels.

In Québec City's Lower Town, **L'Ardoise** (71 rue Saint-Paul, tel. 418/694-0213, www.lardoiseresto.com, 11:30 A.M.–10 P.M. daily, entrée $20) does a good job with *moules frites* (mussels with french fries) and other bistro classics, while in the Upper Town, petit **Casse-Crêpe Breton** (1136 rue Saint-Jean, tel. 418/692-0438, 7 A.M.–midnight daily, entrée $8) makes savory and sweet crêpes. Outside the Old City, wander Rue Saint-Jean for small, local eateries; one of the best is **Le Moine Échanson** (585 rue Saint-Jean, tel. 418/524-7832, http:// moine.echanson.ifrance.com, 5 P.M.–midnight Wed.–Sun., entrée $14), a welcoming *boîte* that serves sophisticated small plates matched with Québecois and French wines.

© ALAN ALBERT

One of Québec City's best local eateries is Le Moine Échanson.

Alberta

On a summer evening, all of Calgary seems to sip and sup at the outdoor tables along Stephen Avenue downtown, but whatever the weather, the contemporary fare at **Divino Wine and Cheese Bistro** (113 8th Ave. SW, tel. 403/410-5555, www.divinobistro.com, 11 A.M.–10 P.M. Mon.–Wed., 11 A.M.–11 P.M. Thurs.– Fri., 5–11 P.M. Sat., 5–10 P.M. Sun., lunch entrée $21, dinner entrée $29) is worth a stop. At **Mercato** (2224 4th St. SW, tel. 403/263-5535, www.mercatogourmet.com, lunch from 11:30 A.M. daily, dinner from 5 P.M. daily, entrée $18), in the Mission neighborhood, the action is around the dining bar where you can watch the chefs toss pans of pasta and prep first-rate modern Italian creations. Hipsters, vegetarians, and their companions settle into **Café Koi** (1011 1st St. SW, tel. 403/206-1564, www.cafekoi.com, breakfast and lunch 8:30 A.M.–3 P.M. Mon.–Fri., dinner 5–10 P.M. Tues.–Wed. and 5 P.M.–midnight Thurs.–Sat., lunch entrée $10, dinner entrée $14), where the Buddha bowls and Asian-inspired dishes are sometimes served with live music. The **Calgary Farmers' Market** (4421 Quesnay Wood Dr. SW, tel. 403/244-4548, www. calgaryfarmersmarket.ca, 9 A.M.–5 P.M. Fri.–Sat., till 4 P.M. Sun.) sells ready-to-eat meals and decadent pastries, alongside the produce stands.

Some of Edmonton's most eclectic—and delicious—contemporary cuisine is served in the storefront **Culina** (9914 89th Ave., tel. 780/437-5588, www.culinacafe.ca, breakfast and lunch 9 A.M.–3 P.M. Mon.–Fri., brunch 10 A.M.–3 P.M.

PASS THE *POUTINE*

Ask any Québec resident what the region's favorite junk food is, and the answer is likely to be *poutine*.

What's *poutine*? Start with a plate of crisp, hot french fries, sprinkle them with cheese curds, and slather the whole mess with brown gravy. You'll find it across the province – and increasingly across the rest of Canada as well – in fast-food joints, snack bars, and bistros.

It's a popular snack in the wee hours when the bars close, and it will fuel you up on the ski slopes.

You'll even see it in more upscale eateries, where these days, chefs top increasingly decadent *poutine* with bacon, duck confit, even foie gras.

In Montréal, locals recommend **La Banquise** (994 Rachel Est, tel. 514/525-2415), where a wide variety of *poutine* concoctions is served 24/7. The only question, other than which type to try, may be how the chic Montréalers who frequent this joint can fit into their sleek black pants after indulging their *poutine* habit!

Sat., dinner 5–10 P.M. Sun.–Fri., till 11 P.M. Sat., lunch entrée $11, dinner entrée $19). For inventive noodles and other Asian-fusion creations, try **Wild Tangerine** (10383 112th St., tel. 780/429-3131, www.wildtangerine.com, 11:30 A.M.–10 P.M. Mon.–Thurs., 11:30 A.M.–11 P.M. Fri., 5 P.M.–11:30 P.M. Sat., entrée $17). From borscht to pierogies, the traditional Ukrainian fare at **Taste of Ukraine** (12210 Jasper Ave., tel. 708/453-2040, www.tasteofukraine. com, 5–10 P.M. Tues.–Sun., entrée $15) is worth a visit, too.

DAILY LIFE

MAKING THE MOVE

So you've decided to move to Canada. Congratulations! You're joining the nearly 40,000 Americans who immigrated to Canada between 2001 and 2006. Now it's time to take care of the paperwork.

You can't just pick up and head across the border, at least if you plan to work or go to school or stay for more than an extended vacation. You need permission from the Canadian government.

How do you get that permission? How do you figure out the best way to immigrate to Canada—the way with the greatest chance of success—for you and your family?

The factors to consider are:

· Will you be coming to Canada for more or less than six months?

· Do you have a job offer or potential employment in Canada?

• Are you coming to Canada to go to school or university?

• Are you planning to retire to Canada?

• Do you want to move to Canada permanently or for at least several years?

Get comfortable, because even when you've defined your reasons for coming to Canada, the paperwork process is rather lengthy, and you need to understand the various immigration options. Read on…

Immigration and Visas

YOUR IMMIGRATION OPTIONS

First some definitions. Americans coming to live in Canada can enter the country as either temporary or permanent residents.

Citizenship and Immigration Canada, the country's immigration agency, has defined three "classes" of temporary residents in Canada: visitor, worker, and student. Temporary residents are allowed to stay in Canada for a specified time. For U.S. citizens entering as visitors, this period is generally up to six months.

U.S. citizens who are granted work permits are usually authorized to live and work in Canada for anywhere from six months to three years. Before applying for a work permit, *you must have a confirmed job offer.* Similarly, American citizens can typically receive study permits for the duration of their university studies; you must be accepted by a university or other school before submitting your permit application. Most Americans admitted to Canada with work or study permits are eligible for publicly funded health insurance.

In 2006, Canada approved approximately 113,000 work permit applications, 13 percent more than in the previous year. Citizenship and Immigration Canada has a stated goal of "further facilitating the entry of temporary foreign workers into Canada," so if you want to work in Canada, it's a good time to apply.

Besides entering the country in one of these temporary categories, the other alternative is to apply to become a permanent resident. Permanent residents have many of the same benefits that Canadian citizens do. They can work, start a business, or go to school. They can live anywhere in Canada and travel freely in and out of the country. The major restrictions are that permanent residents cannot vote or run for political office, and they can be deported if they're convicted of a serious crime. Having permanent resident status is similar to obtaining a green card in the United States, except that in Canada, permanent residents receive publicly funded health care and other social benefits.

In 2006, Canada admitted about 250,000 people as permanent residents, including approximately 11,000 from the United States. You don't need to have a job offer to apply for permanent resident status, but you will have to demonstrate that you have the means to support yourself (and your family).

Once you become a Canadian permanent resident, it doesn't mean that you must live in Canada permanently. However, to maintain your resident status, you have to live in Canada for at least two of every five years.

Sometimes the road to immigration can seem steep...

When you submit your application to become a Canadian permanent resident, you apply under one of several "classes." See *Becoming a Permanent Resident* for information about how to choose the best class for you.

VISITING OR LIVING PART-TIME IN CANADA

U.S. citizens who'll be in Canada for less than six months, and who aren't going to be working, are considered "visitors" to the country. Visitors from the United States don't need anything more than valid passports to enter Canada.

If you want to live in Canada for less than six months at a time—for example, if you're going to spend summers in Canada and winters elsewhere—you can enter as a visitor. Non-Canadians are allowed to buy property in Canada, so you don't need immigration documents to purchase a home or vacation residence. The only restriction is that, as a visitor, you can live in Canada for a maximum of six months a year.

Can you enter the country as a visitor and then look for work? Yes, you can network and arrange interviews during your visit to Canada. If you're offered a position, however, you'll need to apply for a work permit before you can begin working, as outlined in the following section.

WORKING IN CANADA

When it comes to immigrants working in Canada, Citizenship and Immigration Canada quite bluntly states that "It is illegal to work without a required work permit." You must have a confirmed job offer (in writing) before you can apply for work permit, and in general, you must apply for a work permit *before you arrive in Canada*. The majority of work permit applications from U.S. residents are processed within one month.

A few professions are exempt from the work permit requirement. These include some types of performing artists, athletes and coaches, news reporters, clergy, and emergency service workers, among others. Check the Citizenship and Immigration Canada website (www.cic.gc.ca) to see if your occupation falls into this category. For most jobs, though, a work permit is required.

Applying for a Work Permit

In some cases, your prospective employer will handle your work permit application for you. In others, your employer will give you some of the materials you need, but you must submit your application yourself.

For detailed instructions on applying for a work permit, and to download the application forms, refer to the Citizenship and Immigration Canada website. Along with the completed application, you need to provide your passport, two photos of you and any family members who will accompany you, a copy of your job offer or contract, and a detailed resume or other evidence that you have the experience required to do the job. The application fee for a work permit is $150.

If you're planning to work in healthcare, primary or secondary education, or childcare, you may be required to have a medical exam as part of the application process. For other occupations, a medical evaluation isn't usually necessary.

Canada's official jobs policy is to hire Canadians first. When a business wants to hire a non-Canadian employee, they must provide evidence to the government jobs agency, Human Resources and Social Development Canada (HRSDC), that there is no qualified Canadian candidate for a job. Your employer must get a "labor market opinion" from HRSDC confirming that they're allowed to fill the job with a foreign worker. After receiving this opinion, your employer should provide you with a file number from HRSDC to include on your work permit application.

"Fast-Tracking" Your Work Permit Application

In several special cases, a labor market opinion from HRSDC isn't required. If

© ALAN ALBERT

Before you can work in Canada, you need to have the proper documents.

you fall into one of these categories, be sure to let your prospective employer know, since it can reduce the work permit processing time and increase the likelihood that your application will be approved. These fast-track categories include businesspeople applying "under NAFTA," intra-company transfers, and information technology (IT) workers.

The North American Free Trade Agreement (NAFTA) has made it easier for businesspeople who are U.S. citizens to work in Canada. If you work in one of more than 60 professions defined under NAFTA—including management consulting, accounting, engineering, and many more—your employer doesn't need HRSDC approval. Several U.S. expats have reported that this NAFTA provision has simplified their application process and enabled them to get their Canadian work permits approved rapidly.

Do you work for a U.S. company that wants to transfer you to its Canadian office? That's another NAFTA fast-track category. To qualify as an "intra-company transferee," you must be a manager, executive, or professional with "specialized knowledge," and you must have worked for your employer in the United States for at least one year.

Do you work in IT? The Canadian government has determined that the country has a shortage of certain types of information technology professionals. If your job is in one of these categories, your employer doesn't need HRSDC's OK, so your permit should be approved faster.

You can get more information about these fact-track options, including the professions that are included under the NAFTA provisions as well the eligible IT jobs, from Citizenship and Immigration Canada.

What About the Family?

If your spouse or common-law partner also has a job offer to work in Canada, s/he should apply for a separate work permit through his/her new employer before you arrive in Canada. Otherwise, you can include your spouse or partner, as well as your children, on your own work permit application. As long as your application is approved, your family can accompany you to Canada for the duration of your work permit. (The Canadian government defines a common-law partner—either opposite-sex or same-sex—as "a person who has lived with you in a conjugal relationship for at least one year.")

When you meet certain conditions, your spouse or partner can get an "open" work permit, which will allow him/her to arrive in Canada without a job, look for work, and accept a job with almost any employer. These conditions include: (1) your own work permit is valid for at least six months, and (2) the work you'll be doing meets minimum skill requirements, usually requiring a college degree. Essentially, if you have a professional or managerial job, your spouse can be issued an open permit. Your spouse doesn't have to apply separately for this open permit; when you've included him/her in your own application and it's been approved, your spouse's open permit will generally be issued at the border when you arrive in Canada.

Special Rules for Québec

Do you have an offer for work in Québec? Before you apply for a work permit, you need another form: the Application for Certificate of Acceptance of Temporary Work. Complete this application and submit it to your potential employer, who in turn submits it to the provincial government. The fee for processing this application is $175.

If your application is accepted, your future employer will send you a *Certificat d'acceptation du Québec* (Québec Acceptance Certificate, or CAQ). Then you apply to Citizenship and Immigration Canada for a work permit, enclosing the CAQ as part of your supporting documentation.

Québec Immigration is the best source of information about the province's special rules. They have a helpful English-language website at www.immigration-quebec.gouv.qc.ca.

GOING TO SCHOOL IN CANADA

If you're coming to Canada to attend university, then you need to apply for a study permit before you enter the country. You must receive your school acceptance before you submit your study permit application. Study permit applications from U.S. citizens generally take about a month to process. The study permit fee is $125.

Do you have kids? If you're going to university, and you have school-age kids, they need study permits as well.

If you're entering Canada with a work permit, your children don't need study permits, unless you're planning to live in Québec. Study permits are required for children of temporary foreign workers in Québec, but not in other provinces.

If you enter Canada as a permanent resident, your children don't need study permits either. The *Language and Education* chapter explains when and how to apply for a study permit.

RETIRING TO CANADA

Are you planning to retire to Canada? The major decision for retirees is whether you plan to live in Canada for more than six months a year. If you're a U.S. citizen and you want to stay in Canada for *less than six months* within a one-year period, you can come to Canada as a visitor. No special paperwork is required. Many Americans who summer on Vancouver Island, for example, and winter in Phoenix or Palm Springs, live in Canada as visitors, heading south every year before their six months are up.

To live in Canada permanently or for more than six months a year, you usually must apply for permanent resident status. As a retired person, it can be difficult to qualify for permanent residence, since the government considers your ability to work—and support yourself—an important factor.

The good news is that education counts. If you're well educated, you speak fluent English and French, and your spouse also has a university degree, you're more likely to qualify.

Another factor is the amount of savings you have. Even though you're retired, if you can demonstrate that you have ample financial resources to take care of yourself and your family, Canada will usually look more favorably on your application. And if you have funds to invest in Canada, that's another plus. You can learn more about the process of applying for permanent residence in the following section or from Citizenship and Immigration Canada.

BECOMING A PERMANENT RESIDENT

Have you decided to settle in Canada permanently or for an extended time? Do you want to come to Canada before you have a job lined up? Are you planning to launch a business in Canada? Are you already living in Canada with

© CAROLYN B. HELLER

Are you moving to Canada in search of a sweeter life?

a work permit but you want to remain in the country indefinitely? Then you should apply to become a Canadian permanent resident.

Applying for Permanent Residency

If you're already living in Canada with a work permit, you can apply for permanent resident status from within the country. Otherwise, your application must be submitted and approved before you enter Canada.

Canada has a "point system" for evaluating permanent residence applications. You must have a minimum number of points for your application to be considered, and the more points you have, the more likely that your application will get the green light. You get points for your education, the type and duration of your work experience, your fluency in English and/or French, your age (you get the most points if you're over 21 but under 50), and whether you already have a job or potential job in Canada.

If you have a spouse or common-law partner, you get additional points for his/her education and work experience. In fact, you can decide whether you or your spouse/partner should be the "principal applicant" based on which one of you would have the greater number of points. The Citizenship and Immigration Canada website includes a calculator that can help estimate the number of points you and your spouse/partner would have.

If you don't have a job lined up, you need to demonstrate that you have the financial resources to support yourself and your family once you arrive in Canada. Canada doesn't want you to turn up and go on the dole.

You need to provide proof of everything on your permanent resident

BLOGGING TO THE BORDER

Now that scores of people blog about what they ate for dinner and where they went last Saturday night, it's no surprise that a number of expats who've made the move from the United States to Canada have kept online diaries or built websites about the process. Although blogs come and go, you may want to look for some of the following:

- "American by birth, Canadian by choice," writer Laura Kaminker chronicles her move from New York to Ontario in her blog, "We Move to Canada," www.wmtc.blogspot.com.

- Blog authors Daniel and Alan describe themselves as "a male/male married couple from Seattle," and their blog www.wouldbecanadians. blogspot.com follows their immigration journey north to Vancouver.

- American-born Emily Way, who relocated to Canada in 1992, records her observations about Canadian life at "An American's Guide to Canada," www.americansguide.ca.

application. To document your education level, you need to supply university transcripts and a copy of your diploma. To prove your work experience, you have to list every job you've had as an adult, provide reference letters from former employers, and submit pay stubs or tax returns to verify your salary. You must list the address of every place you've lived since you were 18 years old. You need to supply bank statements or other documents to prove your financial stability.

Be extremely careful filling out your application! Check and double-check everything. Making a mistake or omitting information can significantly delay your application.

Once your application passes the initial screening, you and your family members need to have a medical exam. The purpose of the exam is to make sure that you don't have a communicable disease or condition that "is a danger to public health or safety" or that "would cause excessive demand" on the Canadian health care system. For this exam, you can't see your regular doctor; you must go to a doctor who the Canadian government has authorized to perform immigration medical screenings. The Citizenship and Immigration Canada website has lists of approved doctors worldwide.

The doctor will take a medical history and do a basic exam that includes blood and urine tests, as well as a chest X-ray. If you're over 15, you'll be screened for HIV and syphilis. Note that your medical insurance will normally not cover the costs of this exam and that the doctor may expect you to pay in cash.

Canada also requires that you pass a security check to determine whether you have a criminal record. U.S. citizens need to be fingerprinted (either at your local police station or by a private fingerprinting service) and submit your fingerprints to the F.B.I. The F.B.I. will issue a "police certificate" that is either your criminal record or a statement saying that you have no record. The F.B.I. website (www.fbi.gov) outlines the process, including the required cover letter and details about fingerprinting.

Although it can take 16–18 weeks to receive a reply from the F.B.I., Citizenship and Immigration Canada normally advises you not to begin this process until they specifically instruct you to do so. The police certificate has a limited validity period, so you don't want to apply until the processing of your permanent resident application is well underway. If you've lived outside the United States for six months or more since you turned 18, you must obtain a police certificate from each country where you lived.

Sometimes, as a final step in your application process, you'll have a personal interview with a Canadian immigration officer. Citizenship and Immigration Canada will notify you whether an in-person interview is required.

The process of becoming a permanent resident used to be called becoming a "landed immigrant." Immigration officers may still sometimes ask if "you're landed." They don't want to know whether your plane has touched down— they're asking if you're a permanent resident.

Important Note: When you apply to become a Canadian permanent resident, you choose to apply under one of several categories. Your major choices, which are explained below, are: Provincial Nominees; Skilled Workers and Professionals; or Investors, Entrepreneurs, and the Self-Employed. Make your choice carefully, as the category in which you apply can affect the time required to process your application and potentially the likelihood that it will be approved. The application process for resident status generally takes a minimum of 18 months, and waits of two or three years are not uncommon. However, you might be able to speed up the process if you qualify as a Provincial Nominee.

Provincial Nominees

Canada's Provincial Nominee Program is designed to encourage immigrants who have certain skills that a province needs. As a provincial nominee, you're applying to live and work in a specific province.

The benefit of this program, according to many expats, is that applications are typically approved much more quickly than those in other categories, frequently in under a year. In 2008, Canada was expecting to grant permanent resident status to approximately 20,000 provincial nominees nationwide.

The first step in applying as a provincial nominee is to find a match between the skills you have and the province in which you'd like to live. British Columbia has a wide-ranging provincial nominee program targeting applicants who work in construction, information technology, film and TV production, life sciences, clean energy technologies, aerospace, engineering and environmental services, international financial services, health services, tourism, and several other professions. Alberta is looking for immigrants to fill not only professional and managerial positions, but also a variety of trades and "semi-skilled" jobs.

You then apply for a Certificate of Provincial Nomination, which confirms that the province wants you to come and work. Once you have that certificate, you can proceed with your application for permanent resident status. Get the details about the application process from the immigration department of the province where you'd like to live. Citizenship and Immigration Canada also publishes a helpful "Guide for Provincial Nominees," available online.

To apply for permanent residence as a provincial nominee, there's an application fee of $550 for yourself and $550 for your spouse or partner, plus an additional $150 application fee for each of your children.

Skilled Workers and Professionals

Canada wants to encourage highly trained, well-educated professionals to live and work in the country. If you have experience in a professional, managerial, or technical position, you may be able to apply for permanent resident status in the "Skilled Workers and Professionals" class. In contrast to the Provincial Nominee Program, the Skilled Worker category is a federal program, so you can apply regardless of where you intend to live in Canada.

To find out whether your profession qualifies, look it up on the Canadian National Occupational Classification list, available on Citizenship and Immigration Canada's website. Your job must be Skill Type 0 (managerial occupations), Skill Level A (professional occupations), or Skill Level B (technical occupations and skilled trades).

In 2008, Canada was expecting to grant permanent resident status to approximately 70,000 immigrants from all over the world as skilled workers or professionals—the largest class of applicants.

To apply in the Skilled Worker class, the application fee is $550 for yourself and $550 for your spouse or partner. There's an additional application fee of $150 for each of your children.

Eighty percent of all applications from Americans applying as skilled workers are finalized (either accepted or rejected) within 28 months.

Investors, Entrepreneurs, and the Self-Employed

Canada welcomes well-qualified (and well-financed) businesspeople who want to launch a new business or invest in the Canadian economy. There are three categories of federal "business class" immigrants: investors, entrepreneurs, and the self-employed.

To apply as an investor, you must be willing to invest $400,000 into the Canadian economy. You are essentially giving the Canadian government an interest-free loan for five years. You must also demonstrate that you have high-level business experience (for example, you've owned or managed a business) and that you have a minimum net worth of $800,000. You further need a minimum number of points among the criteria defined above, but the point requirement is lower than it is for the skilled worker class.

You might think that few people would be willing to put up this sum of money to come live in Canada. But you'd be wrong. The immigrant investor program currently has a long waiting list. It can take several years to process your application.

To apply as an entrepreneur, you have to demonstrate a level of business expertise similar to the investor class and show a minimum net worth of $300,000. In this case, though, you're not just investing money. You have to launch or manage a business in Canada that meets several conditions:

- You must control at least one-third of the equity of that business;

- You must be actively involved in managing that business; and

- You must create at least one new full-time job in that business for a Canadian citizen or permanent resident, not including yourself and any members of your family.

When you're granted permanent resident status as an entrepreneur, you have to make periodic reports to the government to demonstrate that you're fulfilling these conditions.

To apply for permanent residence as a self-employed person, you can't be self-employed in just any job. This category is designed for two disparate groups of people: (1) those who can "make a significant contribution to the cultural or athletic life of Canada," and (2) farmers. The first group includes writers, photographers, artists, graphic designers, librarians, athletes, coaches, and referees, among others. Self-employed people need to demonstrate "world-class" experience in their field, have a minimum number of points among the application criteria defined above, and prove that they have enough money to support themselves and their families. Unlike the entrepreneur class, self-employed people who become permanent residents don't have to provide the government with updates on their activities after they're settled in Canada.

According to recent statistics from Canada Citizenship and Immigration, half of all applications for U.S. business class applicants (including investors, entrepreneurs, and the self-employed) were finalized within 46 months—nearly four years. Canada was expecting to admit roughly 12,000 business class immigrants in 2008.

Some provinces have Provincial Nominee programs for business class applicants with different requirements than the federal program—and potentially shorter timelines. For details, check with the immigration department of the province where you'd like to live.

The fee for applying for permanent residence in a federal business class is $1,050. There's an additional fee of $550 for your spouse and $150 for each child. Applicants must document their business experience by including with their application financial statements, corporate and personal income tax returns, bank statements, business licenses, letters of reference, and other relevant material.

Special Rules for Québec

The province of Québec has its own rules for approving permanent residence applications, with a special class called the Québec-selected skilled worker class. Before you apply for permanent residence in Québec, you first apply for a Certificate of Selection (*Certificat de sélection du Québec*) from the Québec government. Once you have received this certificate, you can proceed with your application for permanent residence.

For more details about immigrating to Québec, refer to Québec Immigration.

Your Application is Approved. Now What?

When your application for permanent residence is finally approved, first let out a cheer, then get out your checkbook. You and your spouse/partner each must pay a "Right of Permanent Residence Fee" of $490 per person. Fortunately, there's no additional fee for your kids.

You also have to send your passport to Citizenship and Immigration Canada; they'll paste in a visa and send it back. They'll also mail you a wallet-sized card confirming your permanent resident status. Then you can proceed with your moving plans. You're on your way!

If you ultimately want to become a Canadian citizen, you must keep your permanent resident status for at least three years. Both the United States and Canada allow dual citizenship, so it's possible to maintain your U.S. citizenship and become a citizen of Canada as well. You can also live and work in Canada for many years as a permanent resident without ever applying for citizenship.

CAN AN IMMIGRATION PROFESSIONAL HELP?

Immigration lawyers, immigration consultants, and relocation services assist would-be expats with various aspects of the relocation process. What are the pros and cons of using these various professionals?

If you're coming to Canada with a job already lined up, your employer should help you get a work permit and arrange the logistics of your relocation. Unless you're the first expat they've ever hired, they should be able to advise you about the paperwork you need. An immigration lawyer might not add significant value to what the company's human resources personnel can provide.

If you're coming to Canada without a job, if you're self-employed, or if your immigration status changes shortly after you arrive (if, say, you decide not to stay with the employer that brought you to Canada, but you want to remain in the country), an immigration lawyer may be able to help sort out your options and complete the necessary documents.

Immigration lawyers should be able to provide proof of their legal credentials. Be aware that some people set themselves up as immigration "consultants" without any special background, so check references. Immigration lawyers may tell you that they can speed up the permanent resident application process, but the government insists that all applications are processed equally regardless of whether a lawyer is involved.

Relocation consultants typically follow one of two models. A real estate agent may specialize in relocation, providing advice about purchasing a home and getting settled in the community. Generally, they don't charge a fee for relocation advice; they earn their money from the commission they make when you buy a home. A real estate agent may not be able to walk you through the immigration process, but a good agent who does a lot of business with expats can be a valuable source of information.

A relocation consultant who isn't a realtor will charge fees for the services they provide. Most offer a selection of services that you can pick and choose as you need. The majority of relocation consultants in Canada work for corporations who engage their services on behalf of their employees, but some consultants will work directly for an individual or family who is relocating. If your employer will pay for the service, a qualified relocation consultant can save you time and hassle. If it's your own nickel, it's up to you to determine whether the time you'll save is worth the money you'll pay.

Moving with Children

If you're arriving in Canada with a work permit, your children don't need a study permit or other special permission to enter the country (unless you'll be living in Québec). They'll receive an immigration document that links their stay in Canada to yours and gives them permission to attend school.

If you're entering Canada as a permanent resident, and your family will be coming with you to Canada, you apply as a family. Include yourself, your spouse, and your children on one application.

The *Language and Education* chapter details the cases in which students need study permits and outlines educational options available in Canada.

TRAVELING WITHOUT BOTH PARENTS

Because of incidents in which a divorced parent has attempted to take a child across the U.S.–Canadian border without the consent of the other parent, Canadian immigration officials may question you if you're a single parent traveling with your child. Even if you're happily married, but you're not traveling with your spouse—your spouse has gone ahead to look for a home, for example—you may be asked to prove that the children are traveling with your spouse's consent.

Besides making sure that you have your child's passport, you should carry a letter of consent from the parent who isn't traveling with you, giving permission for that child to travel. It should include the date and travel details, as well as contact information for the non-traveling parent. While the letter doesn't have to be notarized, it might help if there were any reason for the immigration official to question its validity. If you're separated or divorced, border officials may ask for a copy of your separation, divorce, or custody decree. The department of Foreign Affairs and International Trade Canada has more information on their travel website (www.voyage.gc.ca).

Moving with Pets

Bringing your dog or cat from the United States? You may bring dogs and cats younger than three months old into Canada without submitting any documentation. If your pets are older than three months, you must provide a certificate signed by a veterinarian providing proof that the animal is vaccinated against rabies (including the vaccine name and expiration date)

© CAROLYN B. HELLER

DAILY LIFE

When you're moving with children, get them involved in the moving process.

and listing the animal's breed, age, gender, coloring and any distinguishing marks. Refer to the Canada Border Service Agency's website (www.cbsa.gc.ca) for more details.

Other pets, such as turtles, parrots, gerbils, and guinea pigs, are usually allowed as well, but you may have to provide additional documentation. Get more information from the "animals" section of the Canadian Food Inspection Agency website (www.inspection.gc.ca).

What to Bring

You should be able to find almost anything you need in Canada, so it's reasonable to bring just the basics with you and buy the rest once you arrive. However, some things—particularly cars, furniture and other household goods, and clothing—are typically priced higher in Canada than in the United States. Compare the costs of moving your existing belongings with estimates for purchasing new things.

The exchange rate between the U.S. and Canadian dollars at the time of your move may also affect your bring-or-buy decision. If the Canadian dollar is high relative to the U.S. currency, it may be cheaper to bring your things with you. If the loonie is low compared to the greenback, buying in Canada may be more cost-effective.

The Canadian government has specific rules for moving goods from the United States to Canada, so if you're bringing more than a few changes of clothing, read on for the details.

BRINGING MOM AND DAD?

I'm relocating to Canada, and my retired parents are wondering, "Can they come with me?"

If your parents want to live in Canada for only part of the year, they could simply enter the country as visitors. Citizens of the United States (or other countries including the United Kingdom, Australia, and New Zealand) can enter Canada as visitors and remain up to six months. If your parents winter at their condo in Florida and want to spend summers with you in Canada, and they're U.S. citizens, they don't need a visa or other special documents.

If your parents want to relocate to Canada permanently, they can either apply for permanent resident status on their own, or you can "sponsor" them. If they're retired, they're less likely to qualify on their own than they would if they're still working. The exception is if they have the financial resources or experience to apply in the "investor" class (see *Becoming a Permanent Resident*).

Sponsoring a family member is not a responsibility you should take lightly, however, as it could involve a significant financial obligation. If you're a Canadian permanent resident or you become a Canadian citizen, you can sponsor your parents (or certain other family members) who are applying to become Canadian permanent residents. Becoming a sponsor means that you agree to take financial responsibility for the people you sponsor, ensuring that they have housing, food, clothing, and any health care not covered by the government (such as dental services). If you sponsor a parent, you are assuming this responsibility for a period of 10 years.

For more information, refer to the "Sponsoring a Family Member" section of the Citizenship and Immigration Canada website.

© CAROLYN B. HELLER

After you've settled in Canada, you can consider "sponsoring" extended family members who want to join you.

YOUR HOUSEHOLD INVENTORY

Before leaving the United States, take an inventory of everything that you're planning to move with you to Canada. This inventory must list each item with its approximate value, make, model, and serial number (if applicable). Make two copies of this list and bring them when you enter Canada. You can prepare the inventory on your computer—a spreadsheet is useful—or by hand, or you can use the Canadian customs Form B4 "Personal Effects Accounting Document," which is available from the Canada Border Services Agency (CBSA) website.

On your inventory, you can

You'll have to decide what to bring with you and what to purchase when you arrive in Canada.

group items into general categories. For example, you don't have to list each individual fork and spoon, but you do need to specify "kitchen utensils" and their estimated value. If you have jewelry or other expensive items, have them appraised and have the appraiser's report with you.

If you're not moving all your goods at the same time, you must record them on separate lists. For example, if you're driving some of your belongings across the border yourself with the remainder to follow in the moving van, or if you're bringing a few things with you by air and the rest are coming by truck, specify which items are traveling with you and list the remaining items as "goods to follow." Keep copies of both lists with you. If you're using the CBSA forms, use Form B4 for items moving with you and Form B4A for goods to follow.

When you're coming to live in Canada temporarily (with a work or study permit) for less than three years, you can generally bring in any personal or household goods, from clothing and furniture to books and computers, duty- and tax-free. The main restriction is that you must take everything with you when you leave the country. Refer to the Canada Border Service Agency (CBSA) online publication "Entering Canada to Study or Work" for more details.

When you're entering Canada as a permanent resident, your belongings become what the government calls your "settler's effects." To bring in these items duty-free, you must be able to prove that you "owned, possessed, and used" your things before you arrived in Canada. You may have to provide receipts or other documentation if there's any question about the status of your belongings. The CBSA's online publication "Settling in Canada" outlines the rules.

If you have a wine collection, either find it a new home or expect to pay tax—you're allowed to bring in only 1.5 liters (two standard 750-ml bottles) of wine tax-free. If you do decide to transport the contents of your wine cellar, don't just show up at the border with a car full of wine; contact the liquor board authority of the province where you'll be living in advance to pay the applicable charges. Then, when you arrive at the border, present the receipt to the customs officer.

The rules about transporting food products, especially fruits and vegetables, are complex, so if you don't have to cross the border with a crate of apples or a cooler full of cheese, you can save yourself some hassle. Similarly, some houseplants from the United States are OK, but others are not. Check with the CBSA to see what's allowed.

What about money? As long as you're carrying less than $10,000 (in Canadian dollars or the equivalent in U.S. or another currency), you don't have to report it. If you're bringing $10,000 or more into Canada, however, you must report it to the CBSA. When you arrive in Canada, you'll need to complete Form E677, "Cross-Border Currency or Monetary Instruments Report." Details are available on the CBSA website.

When you're taking inventory of your belongings, in addition to listing your physical possessions, you have to record separately the fair market value of stocks, mutual funds, and other investments you have on the date that you arrive in Canada. The fair market value is defined as "the highest dollar value you can get for your property in a normal business transaction." If you sell this property after you settle in Canada, any gain or loss may affect your Canadian tax obligations.

BRINGING A CAR

If you're entering Canada as a temporary resident, you're typically allowed to bring your car from the United States and use it for the time you'll be in Canada, as long as that period is less than three years.

If you're entering the country for more than three years or as a permanent resident, the process is a little more complicated. In general, most cars purchased in the United States in the last 15 years can be imported into Canada with no problem, as long as they're for your own personal use. However, Canada and the United States have different safety and emissions standards, and this creates some surprising exceptions. For example, Canada won't allow Volkswagen's 2008 Jetta GLI, Suburu's 2007 and 2008 Forester 2.5X, Nissan's 2008

© ALAN ALBERT

Check the rules before bringing your car over the border. Most cars from the United States are allowed, but some aren't.

Altima four-door sedan, or Pontiac's 2004–2006 GTO, among others. Check for details about whether your car qualifies from the Registrar of Imported Vehicles (RIV) at www.riv.ca.

In some cases, if your car doesn't qualify, you might be allowed to bring it into Canada and have it modified to meet the Canadian standards. The RIV charges a fee of $207, which is in addition to the cost of the work on the car.

If your car was manufactured outside of the United States, Canada, or Mexico, you'll have to pay a Canadian import duty as well. If your car has air-conditioning, you'll be charged an excise tax of $100. Canada also levies additional excise taxes on big cars—if your vehicle weighs more than 2,007 kilograms (4,425 pounds). To calculate your duty and tax liabilities, see the Canada Border Service Agency publication, "Importing a Vehicle Into Canada," available on the CBSA website.

Make sure you have your car's original title and registration with you when you cross the border.

Most moving companies who deal with cross-border shipments should be able to ship your car if you're not driving it across the border yourself. The moving truck driver will need the car's title and registration as part of the shipment's paperwork. It's a good idea to keep extra copies of these documents separately.

SHIPPING OPTIONS

For a move from the United States to Canada, the basic choice is whether to drive your goods across the border or contract with a moving company to deliver them.

If you're hiring a moving company, make sure that they're authorized to transport goods internationally and that they have experience with cross-border shipping. Many of the large U.S. moving companies should qualify. Get estimates from several different companies, as prices can vary significantly.

As your belongings are being packed, verify that the items you've listed on your inventory are the items that are actually going in the truck. The driver will need to carry the inventory list along with your shipment.

Try to schedule your shipment to arrive in Canada shortly after you yourself arrive. You (or your spouse/partner) will need to meet the truck at a Canada Border Services Agency office to "clear" the goods in person. The shipper can tell you where the closest office is to where you'll be living. Bring a duplicate copy of your inventory, your passport, and your work permit or permanent resident card. You don't have to take possession of the goods at the CBSA office—the truck can continue on to your new home once you've cleared the shipment.

ENTERING CANADA

Whether you're flying to Canada or driving across the border, you can arrive at any time. Canada Border Services offices are open 24/7 at all Canada's major airports and main land crossings. However, a few smaller border crossings keep more limited hours. If you're taking the back roads, check with the Canada Border Services Agency to confirm that the border will be open when you intend to cross.

When you arrive at the border or the airport immigration desk, inform the border agent that you're officially entering Canada—either on a work or study permit or as a permanent resident. You'll need to report to the Canada Immigration Officer on duty to present your passport and immigration documents, as well as the inventory of your goods. Make sure you have a credit card (or cash) with you; you may need it for fees (for example, if your spouse is issued an open work permit at the border, you'll have to pay for it) or for any taxes due on your goods (e.g., if you have more than the allowable amount of alcohol, you'll be charged duty).

After reviewing your documents, and checking your inventory and goods, the agent will stamp your passport and any other relevant documents with your official arrival date. Welcome to Canada!

MOVING CHECKLIST: BEFORE YOU LEAVE

- Make sure you have a current passport.
- Compile a household inventory, outlining everything that's moving with you to Canada.
- Get a record of your driving history – how long you've been a licensed driver – from the state motor vehicle registry.

- Obtain proof of your safe driving record from your car insurance company.
- Make sure you have copies of your immunization records.
- If you already have a place to live, arrange for renter's or homeowner's insurance.
- Forward your mail.

DAILY LIFE

FOR MORE INFORMATION

If you have questions about what you can bring into Canada, what forms you need, or other queries, contact the Canada Border Services Agency. There's lots of information on their website at www.cbsa.gc.ca. They also run a Border Information Service (BIS) phone line. From outside of Canada, call 204/983-3500 (in the Central time zone) or 506/636-5064 (in the Atlantic time zone); from within Canada, it's a toll-free call: 800/461-9999. The BIS line provides general recorded information 24 hours a day, or you can speak with an agent Monday–Friday 8 A.M.–4 P.M. local time.

When You Arrive

After you arrive in Canada, there's still more paperwork to do: applying for a Social Insurance Number, health insurance, car insurance, and a new driver's license.

GETTING A SOCIAL INSURANCE NUMBER

To work in Canada, you need a Social Insurance Number (SIN), a unique nine-digit number similar to a U.S. Social Security Number. To apply for a SIN, newcomers to Canada must have either a work permit or permanent resident status. There's no fee to apply for a SIN.

Apply for your SIN as soon as possible after you arrive in Canada. To apply in person, go to the nearest Service Canada Centre; offices are listed online at www.servicecanada.gc.ca or in the local phone directory. Bring your passport as well as whatever document verifies your immigration status in Canada: your work permit, study permit, or permanent resident card. You should receive your SIN card in the mail within a week.

Alternatively, you can apply for your SIN by mail. Print an application from the Service Canada website, complete it, and mail it along with the required documents. Note that you'll be without your documents during the processing time, which Service Canada estimates to be 15 days, so use the mail procedure only if you can't apply in person.

If you're not a permanent resident when you apply for your SIN, you'll receive a temporary SIN beginning with the number "9." Your SIN card will be valid for as long as your work permit or other immigration document allows you to remain in Canada. If you subsequently become a permanent resident, you'll need to apply for a new, permanent SIN.

HEALTH INSURANCE

Apply for Canadian health insurance as soon as possible after you arrive, too. Most provinces have a three-month waiting period before newcomers are eligible for government-funded health insurance, but you should still apply as soon as you arrive.

You may also want to arrange for supplemental health coverage and for travel health insurance, which cover services that aren't included in Canada's basic health insurance.

Refer to the *Health* chapter for the details you need about Canadian health care and insurance.

DRIVER'S LICENSES AND CAR INSURANCE

If you have a valid U.S. driver's license, you can use that license to drive as you get settled in Canada. Each province sets its own requirements for when a newcomer must apply for a local license. In Ontario, it's 60 days. In B.C., Alberta, and Québec, it's 90 days.

To apply for a driver's license, check the requirements for your province. In general, you need to bring to the licensing office: your current U.S. license, proof of your status in Canada (work or study permit, permanent resident card), at least one other form of ID (passport, birth certificate, credit card), and proof of your Canadian address. You'll have to pass a vision test and, in some provinces, answer basic traffic safety questions.

If your driver's license was issued in the last two years, but you've been driving for a longer period, bring proof of how long you've been driving; otherwise, you may have to take a road test. The easiest way to provide this proof is to contact the motor vehicle registry in the state where you're licensed and ask them to write a letter on their official letterhead indicating when you were first licensed to drive in that state.

MOVING CHECKLIST: WHEN YOU ARRIVE

- Apply for a Social Insurance Number (SIN).
- Apply for Canadian health insurance.
- Apply for supplemental health and travel medical insurance, if necessary.
- Arrange for phone service (land line and cell).
- Arrange for Internet service.
- Open a bank account.

- Apply for a credit card.
- Register the kids for school.
- Arrange for car insurance.
- Get a new driver's license.
- Find a family doctor. If you don't already have copies of your medical records, have your former physician send them to your new doctor.
- Find a dentist.
- Get settled into your new home!

Which comes first—car insurance or a local license? As long as you have a valid U.S. license, you should first arrange for Canadian auto insurance and then apply for a driver's license. Check with the provincial auto registry to find out how soon you must insure your car locally; in most areas, it's within 30 or 60 days of your arrival.

If you can demonstrate that you have years of driving without an insurance claim, you may be eligible for a discount on your auto insurance in Canada. In British Columbia, for example, you may qualify for a discount of up to 40 percent on your basic coverage if you can show at least eight years of claim-free driving.

To qualify for this discount, you need to provide an original letter from your U.S. car insurance company *(not your broker or agent)* that attests to your safe driving record. The letter should be on company letterhead and list:

- The name of the registered owner and principal operator of the vehicle

- The insurance policy number

- The time period that you were covered

- The dates of any at-fault insurance claims

Arrange for this proof-of-safe-driving document before you leave the United States, so you can bring it with you when you apply for insurance in Canada.

CANADIAN EXPERIENCE CLASS

One constant about immigration policies and procedures is change. New requirements may be implemented, and both application fees and processing times may change. For example, the Canadian government announced plans in mid-2008 for a new "Canadian Experience Class," designed to make it easier for people already working or studying in Canada to apply for permanent resident status.

As you're planning your move, check with Citizenship and Immigration Canada for the most up-to-date details. You can also get more information from www.livingabroadincanada.com, the companion website for this book.

The Canadian insurance company may require that this letter be an original—not a fax or a photocopy—so if you don't have this document with you, you'll have to pay for your insurance at the undiscounted rate and then retroactively apply for a discount once the original document arrives.

As in the United States, Canadian auto insurance includes required minimum coverage (which varies by province) and additional optional coverage. In some provinces, you may save money by purchasing the required insurance from one company and optional insurance from another. A licensed insurance broker should be able to outline these options for you.

For example, in B.C., basic car insurance is provided by a government-run company, Insurance Corporation of British Columbia (ICBC). You must buy required minimum coverage through ICBC, but you can contract with a private company for optional insurance. In Québec, too, insurance is provided by a combination of government-run and private companies. In Ontario and Alberta, insurance has been privatized, so private companies compete for insurance business. In all cases, it pays to shop around.

The Insurance Bureau of Canada, an industry trade association, can provide information about insurance in Canada. Although their perspective reflects the needs of the insurance companies, rather than consumers, it's still a useful source of general information.

HOUSING CONSIDERATIONS

Ah, home, sweet home. Finding a place to live may be one of the bigger decisions a new Canadian resident can make. The good news for Americans considering a move to Canada is that housing in Canada overall is quite similar to the United States. You can find a range of housing options—from all types of single-family homes to townhouses, condos, and apartments—in whatever region of Canada you decide to settle.

The process of finding a home, whether you plan to rent or buy, will also be familiar. While it may take time to make the rent/buy decision and to locate the right place in the right neighborhood, you don't have to learn any new skills for house-hunting in Canada.

The major differences between buying a home in Canada and in the United States are related to mortgages and taxes. The process of applying for a mortgage, and some of the mortgage terms, may be somewhat different than what you're used to in the States. Canadian tax laws will present expats with some new challenges as well.

© CAROLYN B. HELLER

BUYING OR RENTING?

Approximately two-thirds of all Canadians own their homes; the remaining one-third are renters. From 2000 to 2007, as housing prices in the United States were falling, prices in Canada continued to rise. Home prices in western Canadian cities such as Vancouver, Victoria, Calgary, and Edmonton have climbed steadily, and in some years, have spiked up significantly. Prices in Toronto and Montréal have risen, too, but at a more moderate rate. Rents, on the other hand, have not gone up as quickly.

Given the current state of the housing markets, a crucial decision many expats face is, "Do we rent or do we buy?"

In a hot housing market, it can be in your interest to buy as soon as you can, even if the place you find isn't ideal and you're planning to move again. If you wait and rent for a year, home prices may have escalated further by the time you're ready to buy. In a slower market, however, the pressure to buy right away might abate.

The relationship of the U.S. and Canadian currencies at the time of your housing search is another major factor in the rent/buy decision. If the Canadian dollar is high relative to the U.S. dollar and you think that the U.S. greenback will gain strength, you might want to delay your home purchase until your U.S. dollars will buy more. On the other hand, if you're looking to buy in Canada when the loonie is low relative to the U.S. dollar, buying quickly will help you take advantage of the U.S. dollar's power. Of course, it's difficult, if not impossible, to predict currency fluctuations, but be aware of the currencies' effect on your decision to rent or buy. Canada's central bank, the Bank of Canada, lists current and historical exchange rates on its website (www.bankofcanada.ca).

In calculating a budget, prospective homeowners need to be aware that, unless you have permanent resident status, you'll be required to make a larger down payment than you would if you were Canadian (see *Canadian Mortgages*, later in this chapter), and that—unlike in the United States—the interest you pay on a residential mortgage in Canada is not tax-deductible.

Many people feel that, regardless of the cost, it's easier to rent for at least a few months or a year in your new community, rather than jumping into a home purchase. Renting lets you get to know a neighborhood in depth before you make a purchase decision. And you may have to rent anyway, if you can't find a house that meets your needs right away.

Canada's Office of Consumer Affairs has a "Rent or Buy" calculator on its website (www.ic.gc.ca) that helps identify the costs and variables of the rent/buy decision. Although it's designed primarily for domestic consumers and doesn't address the currency exchange issue, it can still help with your calculations.

Remember that whether you're buying or renting, you'll need to have access to sufficient *Canadian* funds. You generally cannot pay for deposits, rent, or other housing related expenses in U.S. dollars or with a U.S. check, even a certified or bank check. Perhaps it sounds obvious, but if you're selling a house in the United States to fund a home purchase in Canada, make sure you allow time to transfer the money you need to a Canadian financial institution and to convert the funds into Canadian dollars.

Renting

Finding a place to rent in Canada can take some time. Nationwide, Canada had a rental vacancy rate in 2007 of only 2.6 percent. Recent vacancy rates have been extremely low in the Western cities: a miniscule 0.5 percent in Victoria, 0.7 percent in Vancouver, and 1.5 percent in Calgary and Edmonton. Québec isn't much better, with vacancy rates of 1.2 percent in Québec City and 2.9 percent in Montréal. In Ontario, Ottawa's rental vacancy rate is 2.3 percent and Toronto weighed in at 3.2 percent. As long as vacancy rates remain low, you should allow a longer period to find a rental unit than you might expect.

While rental prices vary significantly by city—and by neighborhood within a city—the following averages may help with your budgeting. In 2007, the five most expensive cities for renters in Canada were Calgary, Vancouver, Toronto, Ottawa, and Edmonton. The average monthly rent for a two-bedroom apartment was just over $1,000 in Calgary, Vancouver, and Toronto, and just under $1,000 in Ottawa and Edmonton.

FINDING THE RIGHT PLACE
Short-Term Rentals

Many mid-range and higher-end hotels across Canada have studio, one-, or two-bedroom suites with kitchen facilities that can be a convenient base while you house-hunt. Often, these hotel suites cost little more than a standard room, particularly in the winter low season. If you'll be staying for a week or more, you can often negotiate a discounted rate; call the hotel directly, rather than booking online. In *Planning Your Fact-Finding Trip* we list apartment-hotel options in all the Prime Living Locations.

If your employer is helping with your relocation expenses, corporate apartments are an excellent short-term rental option. Catering to business people who are in a city either temporarily while working on a project or while looking for a more permanent place to live, most corporate apartments are upscale units with hotel-like amenities, such as business centers and fitness rooms. Some units are actually in hotels that rent out apartment suites for stays of a month or more. Prices for corporate apartments tend to be high, but the quality is usually high as well.

You can often find short-term rentals through vacation rental services, such as Vacation Rentals By Owner (www.vrbo.com) or Home Away (www.homeaway.com). Because these sites target vacationers, rather than prospective residents, they tend to be higher-end properties with more amenities and correspondingly higher prices.

© CAROLYN B. HELLER

Many Montréal apartments are in traditional triple-deckers.

Long-Term Rentals

Websites such as Craigslist (www.craigslist.org) and Kijiji (www.kijiji.ca) or the local newspaper's online classifieds can be good sources of apartment or home rentals, although the quality, price, and location of the properties available on these sites can vary hugely. Check for ads in the major daily newspapers, as well as weeklies and free papers. You can often find news boxes around town, especially at bus stops or subway stations, with free rental publications.

Most Canadian universities have faculty housing websites where you can find rental listings, especially for furnished houses. A faculty family who's going on sabbatical leave for six months or a year may welcome an expat family as tenants in their home. Academics sometimes take extended trips in the summer when school isn't in session, so a university site can be a good way to locate a summer sublet. Some university sites are restricted to university employees, but many are open to the public.

While it may not seem efficient, many locals recommend simply walking or driving around and looking for "For Rent" signs in the neighborhoods where you want to live. Check the bulletin boards in the neighborhood coffee shop or launderette, or around the local university, for rental listings, too. Don't hesitate to ask everyone you know, and see if they can ask their friends and colleagues. The best places often turn up through word-of-mouth.

COMMON CANADIAN HOUSING TERMS

Americans may find a few unfamiliar terms in real estate ads or listings, even in English-speaking Canada. Here's a brief glossary:

- suite: an apartment
- "bach" or bachelor suite: studio (one-room) apartment
- garden level: basement, although it may be at least partly above ground
- strata unit: condominium
- hydro: electricity
- garburator: garbage disposal
- ensuite laundry, ensuite W/D: washer and dryer are in the unit
- master ensuite: a master bedroom with its own bathroom
- parkade: parking garage

© CAROLYN B. HELLER

Canadians call electricity service "hydro" – but it usually comes from more modern sources.

DAILY LIFE

RENTAL AGENTS AND LEASES

It's definitely worth talking with real estate agents when you're looking for a place to rent. While some won't deal with rentals, others will. Particularly if you're planning to buy a home eventually, agents may happily help you find temporary housing, because they expect to earn a commission on a future home sale.

In many Canadian cities, lots of new condominium buildings have gone up in recent years, and many of these buildings have rental units. Though it can be slightly more expensive, renting a condo can offer more amenities and fewer hassles than renting an apartment in an older building. Real estate agents are more likely to deal with condo rentals, since they may already have a relationship with the condo owner.

Canada has strong tenant protection laws in most provinces. In the *Resources* chapter, we provide links to the relevant regulatory body in each province. These websites have detailed information about landlord and tenant rights and responsibilities.

As in the United States, it's customary in Canada to sign a standard lease for an apartment and, in some provinces, for landlords to ask for a security deposit. Sometimes, you'll be asked to pay first and last month's rent upfront, where the last month's rent will be held as a security deposit. However, in Québec, landlords can't require a security deposit. In Ontario, landlords can ask for the last month's rent in advance, but it's illegal to ask for a damage deposit. In British Columbia, the security deposit amount cannot legally be more than a half-month's rent. In Alberta, the maximum security deposit is one month's rent.

When you've found a place and you're working out the details, confirm whether or not utilities are included, and find out about cable TV and Internet access. Make sure the home has working smoke detectors. And read the lease carefully before you sign on the dotted line.

Buying

FINDING THE RIGHT PLACE

Whether your ideal home is a condominium in a downtown high-rise, a duplex in an eclectic urban neighborhood, or a single-family house in a family-friendly community, you should be able to find all these options, and more, in most Canadian cities. You just need to work out your priorities. How close do you need to be to where you'll be working? Do you prefer to commute by public transit or by car? Is proximity to schools, shops, or recreational facilities important? Are you willing to move into a home that needs renovation? Decide what's essential and what you can live without before you begin your house-hunt.

While home prices vary significantly by city and by neighborhood within a city, here are some averages as of late 2007 for Canada's largest metropolitan areas: $577,219 in Vancouver, $408,638 in Calgary, $393,543 in Toronto, $325,060 in Edmonton, $271,867 in Ottawa, and $239,079 in Montréal. Bear in mind that these are averages, and in many of these locations, real estate agents advise budgeting at least $500,000–800,000 for centrally located, well-kept homes. It's not uncommon in any of these cities to find plenty of houses on the market for $1 million or more.

REAL ESTATE AGENTS AND CONTRACTS

Canadian real estate agents work the same way that U.S. agents do—for a commission on the sale price. More than one agent can work on a deal, often one representing the seller and a second representing the buyer. Even if you—as a prospective buyer—work with a buyer's agent who is nominally advocating your interest, remember that the agent is still motivated to close a deal quickly and at a high price.

In a booming real estate market, agents sometimes pressure potential buyers to remove any conditions (sometimes called "subjects") from their offer to purchase a home. For example, they may urge you to waive your right to a home inspection. That's never a good idea. Without a professional home inspection, you may find yourself dealing with all sorts of unpleasant consequences down the road. One Vancouver couple made a subject-free offer to purchase a downtown condominium, waiving their right to an inspection. After they moved in, they discovered that their apartment was infested with bats!

Is your ideal home in the city, like these new residential towers on the Toronto lakefront?

The Canadian term for owning most single-family or semi-detached homes is "freehold ownership." That means simply that you own the land and the house outright. Alternatively, if you purchase a condominium, you own your unit but share ownership of the building's common space; in B.C. and some other parts of Canada, a condo is called a "strata" unit.

In some Canadian cities and recreational areas, "strata hotels" are becoming a popular twist on the condominium theme. In these buildings, which often include a mix of hotel suites and privately owned units, you have all the amenities of a first-class hotel. You can often choose between full ownership—where you're buying a condo unit that you can use or rent out as you prefer—and partial ownership, which is essentially a time-share arrangement where you're buying the right to use the unit for a certain amount of time annually. The building usually has a management agent who can handle renting out your unit when you're not there. Like owners of a condominium, owners of units in a strata hotel pay a monthly management fee to cover maintenance of common areas and other services.

In some areas, you may find "co-op" units for sale. In a co-op, you buy a share in the co-op organization and have the right to use your unit, but you don't own your apartment outright. Don't confuse buying a co-op with a co-op rental. When you rent in a housing co-op, tenants typically share responsibility for managing the building. Most rental housing co-ops include a mix of market rate and below-market, subsidized, units.

HOUSING TERMS IN QUÉBEC

In Québec, buildings generally follow the French convention, where the "ground floor" (or *rez de chaussée*) is what the rest of Canada and the United States calls the first floor. The "first floor" (or *première étage*) would be called the second floor elsewhere. That is, a unit on the *première étage* would be upstairs, one story above the *rez de chaussée*. In a Québec elevator, press the "R" button for the ground floor.

Québec real estate ads often advertise units as "3 1/2" or "4 1/2." The "1/2" refers to the bathroom, so a "3 1/2" is a three-room apartment with a bathroom (typically one bedroom, a living room, a kitchen, and one bathroom).

Other Québec housing words to know:

- *à louer*: for rent
- *à vendre*: for sale
- *ascenseur*: elevator
- *buanderie*: laundry
- *chambres à coucher*: bedrooms
- *chauffé*: heated
- *meublé*: furnished
- *non-fumeur*: non-smoker
- *planchers en bois*: hardwood floors
- *stationnement*: parking

Canadian contracts for home purchases tend to be simpler than similar documents in the United States, so Canadians don't always hire a lawyer to review them. Instead, notaries who specialize in real estate transactions sometimes handle the paperwork, including the title search, purchase contracts, and other legalities, for a flat fee. Of course, if your deal is complex or you have any concerns about the title or terms, don't hesitate to hire a real estate lawyer to assist you.

Ask for recommendations for lawyers or notaries from friends or colleagues. The Canadian Bar Association (www.cba.org) can also direct you to lawyer referral services. Before hiring someone, make sure you understand their fee structure, and ask them for additional references.

CANADIAN MORTGAGES

Canadian banks have much stricter financing requirements for home buyers who are not Canadian citizens or permanent residents. In general, most banks require that you make a down payment of 30–35 percent of the purchase price. So if you come to Canada on a work permit, you'll need to budget for a large down payment.

If you have permanent resident status when you're ready to buy a home, your down payment requirements will be the same as that of Canadian citizens—generally 5–20 percent. Mortgages with a down payment of less than 20 percent are considered "high-ratio mortgages," and lenders will typically require that you purchase mortgage loan insurance.

In calculating how much you can afford to spend on a home, remember that interest you pay on a Canadian residential mortgage is not tax-deductible. Many expats who are used to benefiting from the mortgage deduction in the United States are surprised that this provision doesn't exist in Canada.

It's especially important for expats to arrange for mortgage pre-approval from a bank or mortgage broker *before* launching a house-hunt. Mortgage approval can take longer for U.S. citizens buying property in Canada, so you don't want any delays that might risk losing a house you want—or your deposit. As soon as you decide that you want to buy a home, contact banks or mortgage companies in your new city to ask about their rates and approval process, and to submit your mortgage approval forms. Banks typically guarantee the interest rates on pre-approved mortgages for 60–90 days.

As in the United States, Canadian mortgages can have fixed or variable interest rates. However, unlike the United States, where mortgage terms of 25–30 years are typical, Canadian mortgages generally have a term of six months to 10 years. Terms of five years or less are most common. If you have a five-year fixed-rate mortgage, for example, your interest rate and payment amount won't change during that five-year term. As the end of that five-year period approaches, you'll need to renegotiate your mortgage at the then-current interest rate. You usually have the option of paying off the mortgage, making a lump sum payment toward the principal to reduce your payments, or shopping around and moving to a different lender if you can get a better rate elsewhere.

Note that while the term of the mortgage contract may be only five years, the amortization period—the time over which the payments would pay off the mortgage—is usually 15–25 years. With a longer amortization, your mortgage payments are lower, but you'll pay more interest over the life of the loan.

PURCHASE FEES AND TAXES
Land Transfer Tax

Home buyers in most Canadian provinces must pay a "land transfer tax" that's based on your home's purchase price. This tax can add several thousand dollars to your purchase price, so be prepared. For example, if you purchase a

Looking for a mountain retreat?

$500,000 house in British Columbia, you would owe $8,000 in land transfer tax. Your lawyer or notary can provide the tax forms that must accompany your payment and confirm the tax amount. Here are the land transfer rates in each province we cover in this book:

- In British Columbia, the land transfer tax is called the "property transfer tax." The rate is 1 percent of the first $200,000 of the purchase price and 2 percent of the remainder.

- In Ontario, calculating the land transfer tax is more complicated. The rate is 0.5 percent of the first $55,000 of the purchase price, 1 percent of the amount between $55,000 and $250,000, 1.5 percent of the amount between $250,000 and $400,000, and 2 percent of the amount above $400,000. To make things even more fun, the city of Toronto has implemented its own land transfer tax, which Toronto buyers must pay on top of the provincial tax.

- In Québec, the transfer tax rate is 0.5 percent on the first $50,000, 1 percent of the amount between $50,000 and $250,000, and 1.5 percent of the amount above $250,000.

- If you're buying a home in Alberta, you're lucky. The province has no land transfer tax.

If the home you're buying in Canada is the first home you've ever owned (anywhere in the world), you may be eligible for a land transfer tax refund. The requirements vary by province, and eligibility for a refund may be limited to Canadian citizens or permanent residents, so check with the tax agency in the province where you'll be living.

Property Taxes

Remember that at closing, you'll need to reimburse the seller for any forthcoming property taxes that they've already paid. And you'll need to include future property taxes in your budget. Property tax rates vary by city, so you can get local information from the city where you'll be living or from local real estate agents.

Other Taxes

If you purchase a newly built home, you will usually have to pay G.S.T. (the Federal Goods and Services Tax) of 5 percent of the purchase price. When you buy a new house that costs less than $450,000, you may qualify for a rebate of part of the G.S.T.; get the details from the Canada Revenue Agency. There is no G.S.T. on the purchase of an existing home, unless it has been "substantially renovated," which typically means that it's more than 90 percent new.

BUILDING AND RESTORING

In 2006, Canadians spent a total of nearly $44 billion on home renovations, improvements, repairs, and maintenance, 9 percent more than in the previous year. Clearly, home building and renovation is a big business.

These days, with housing at a premium and prices rising in many Canadian cities, it's not uncommon for buyers to purchase a small, old, or rundown house, and tear it down to build a new home—or to buy an older house with the idea of doing a significant renovation. The challenge, in these hot markets, is to find architects, building contractors, and tradespeople to do the work. If you're going to build or restore a home, make sure you allow plenty of time for the process.

Before undertaking a renovation, you'll want to find an architect or builder who can advise you about any zoning restrictions or other local building codes. There may be limits on the size of a house relative to the size of the lot, rules about adding a rental unit to a home, and other restrictions. But while some of these details may vary, the overall process of building or renovating a home is similar to what you'd find back in the States.

DAILY LIFE

Household Expenses

Most expats from the United States report that in Canada their costs for utilities, such as electricity ("hydro"), gas, phone, cable, and Internet services, are fairly similar to what they paid back home. Insurance costs, too, for homeowner's or renter's insurance, are not significantly different from what you'd find in the United States, although if you're moving to western Canada, you may want to consider earthquake insurance, as Vancouver and the West Coast lie in an earthquake zone. Property tax rates vary by city (and can change every year); the current range is approximately 0.5–3.5 percent.

Household furnishings, from sheets and towels to furniture, tend to be more expensive in Canada than in the United States. If you can bring these goods with you, it may be less expensive than purchasing them north of the border, as you settle into your new Canadian home, sweet home.

LANGUAGE AND EDUCATION

One of the first questions many potential immigrants to Canada ask is, "Do I have to learn French?" Unless you're moving to the province of Québec, where French is the dominant tongue, the answer is no.

Because Canada is officially bilingual, however, you may want to learn more about the French language and francophone culture. Living here may create opportunities for you or your children to learn to speak French. Even in English-speaking provinces, many students study French, and many choose to do so in a distinctively Canadian immersion environment.

Americans in Canada won't have trouble understanding their fellow Canadian English-speakers. But there are some interesting differences between American and Canadian English.

The U.S. and Canadian educational systems also have a lot in common. Both countries have publicly funded universal education, both have private or independent school alternatives to the public system, and both have a range of colleges and universities. Still, as with the linguistic variations, there are a number of small differences between the two countries' educational programs. While none may be significant enough to derail your relocation plans, understanding where the two countries diverge will help smooth your transition to Canadian life.

Canadian English

You shouldn't have trouble communicating in Canada if American English is your mother tongue. Still, you'll find that Canadian English is just a little bit different.

First, there's pronunciation. Canadians have been famously parodied (at least in the United States) for pronouncing the word "about" as "a-boot." And it's true that you'll often hear that pronunciation. You'll also hear "pro-gress" or "pro-cess"—where the first syllable rhymes with "low" or "hoe." The word "again" may sound like "uh-gain", "been" may rhyme with "green," and "decal" may be pronounced "deck-ul." When some Canadians talk about spaghetti, they'll say "past-uh."

Sometimes, Canadians use different words than Americans do for common items. Some of these draw from British English, but others are distinctively Canadian. Canadians typically don't go to the bathroom or restroom; they use the washroom. When they get in line for the cash register in the market, they queue up at the till. Canadian addresses include a postal code, not a zip code. Canadian kitchens have garburators, not garbage disposals.

You won't get far in Canada until you learn that one-dollar coins are called "loonies," and two-dollar coins are dubbed "toonies." Canadians may not shop at a Dollar Store; they hunt for bargains at the Loonie-Toonie shop. To do their banking electronically, Canadians use an ABM (Automated Banking Machine), rather than an ATM (Automatic Teller Machine). When Canadians vote for their MPs (Members of Parliament), they do so in their home "riding" (district). If someone commits an "indictable offence" (what the United States would call a felony), charges are "laid" against them.

Kids are apt to call their mothers "Mum" or "Mummy," and they learn their alphabet from "a" to "zed." When they go out to play, they wear "runners," not sneakers or tennis shoes. Canadian students don't *take* exams—they *write* them.

Perhaps the most important article of clothing that you can buy in Canada is a "toque" (sometimes spelled "tuque") and pronounced "toook" (with an "ooo" sound). It's a knit ski hat. Canadians debate the origin of the word, but it may have its roots in the French "toque" or chef's hat. But no matter where the word came from, thousands of Canadians wear them every winter.

WELCOME TO YOUR COLOURFUL NEIGHBOURHOOD

Think you're a good speller? Americans coming to Canada will have to get used to Canadian spelling conventions – a hybrid of American and British English, with some Canadian variations.

Some words that are spelled with an "or" in the United States – color, neighbor, flavor – have an added "u" in Canada, becoming colour, neighbour, and flavour. The Canadian holiday in September to honor working people is Labour Day. Some nouns ending in "er" – center, theater, kilometer – have "re" endings north of the border – centre, theatre, and kilometre. Canadians double the "l" in words like "traveller" and "modelling," but Canadian students "enrol" in school (with only one "l").

To drive a car in Canada, you need a licence (not a license). A paper financial instrument is a cheque (not a check). Canadians get dolled up in their jewellery (not jewelry), and when it's time for bed, they put on their pyjamas, not pajamas.

If this all seems baffling, pick up a Canadian dictionary, such as the *Canadian Oxford Dictionary* or *Oxford Canadian Spelling*, or just set the dictionary in your word processing program to "Canadian English." And welcome to the neighbourhood!

And of course, you'll hear plenty of Canadians end a rhetorical question with "eh." As in, "How about that Canadian English, eh?"

Learning French

If you're a native English-speaker, you'll pick up the Canadianisms easily enough. But what about French?

Some people wonder whether Canada's Official Languages Act, which made both French and English the country's official languages, means that you *have to* speak both tongues. You do not. In most parts of Canada, you'll hear English, and English alone. Only about a third of Canadians are bilingual in English and French. Note that if you're applying for permanent resident status in Canada, however, you earn additional points on your application if you can communicate in both English and French.

Can you make more money if you speak both French and English? It depends on your line of work and where you live, but in general, you can. The Association for Canadian Studies reported that bilingual Canadians earn approximately 10 percent more on average than Canadians who speak English only.

In British Columbia and Alberta, knowledge of French has little effect on income levels, not surprising since the vast majority of the population speaks

English. But in Montréal, if you're bilingual, you can earn more—nearly 30 percent more on average than if you speak just English. Even in Toronto, in predominantly English-speaking Ontario, people who speak both English and French earn almost 40 percent more than their unilingually English-speaking peers. So depending on where you're headed, it might pay to take a few French lessons or brush up on your high-school *français*.

If you're moving to Québec, French-language ability is much more essential, especially outside of Montréal. Québec's immigration authorities look more favorably on your application for a work permit or for permanent residence if you have some command of the French language. In some

© CAROLYN B. HELLER

If you'll be living in Québec, it's easier to manage if you can speak some French, especially in smaller towns.

cases, they may require that you study French before they'll even consider your application. And once you arrive, you'll find it easier to do just about everything if you speak at least basic French.

FRENCH LANGUAGE SCHOOLS
Adult French Education

Universities or colleges in most Canadian cities have continuing education departments that offer French language courses for adults. In many communities, the public schools offer French classes designed for adult learners; check the school board website for continuing education course listings. Local community centers often offer basic language classes as well.

The Alliance Française, a worldwide network of French-language schools and cultural centers, has schools in Toronto, Ottawa, Calgary, Edmonton, Vancouver, and Victoria, among other locations. They offer classes in many U.S. cities, too, so you could begin your preparation before you cross the border.

In Québec, the Ministry of Immigration and Cultural Communities (*Ministère de l'Immigration et des Communautés Culturelles du Québec*) encourages new residents to study French. In partnership with universities, colleges, community organizations, and public schools, they offer both part-time and intensive full-time language courses. If you meet their requirements, the courses are free. Get more information at www.immigration-quebec.gouv.qc.ca.

FRENCH FRENCH VS. CANADIAN FRENCH

The French that you'll hear in Québec is certainly similar to the language that's spoken in other francophone countries, but there are some distinctive Québecois words and phrases. Here are a few words you might hear in Montréal or Québec City, but not in Paris:

Un dépanneur: a convenience store
Une tuque: a winter hat
Un frigidaire: a refrigerator
Un bécyque: a bicycle
Des vidanges: garbage

Then there's the Québec accent. The French spoken in Québec, particularly in small towns and rural communities, has its roots in the French language of the farmers and pioneers who settled the region in the 17th and 18th centuries. Some Québecois' accents differ from Parisian French in the same way that an English speaker from Boston sounds different from one in Savannah or Chicago. For example, the familiar word oui (yes) may sound almost like "wah." It's still French, but you may have to listen carefully to understand your new Québec neighbors, even if you speak French yourself.

If you're moving to Montréal and looking for rigorous French training, check out McGill University's eight- or nine-week Special Intensive Program in French. Participants attend classes Monday–Thursday 9 A.M.–3 P.M., and students are asked to speak only French while they're on the premises. McGill also offers part-time evening and weekend classes designed for working professionals.

French Education for Kids

Government statistics indicate that approximately two million English-speaking students across Canada are studying at least basic French. In most provinces, elementary or junior high/middle school students are required to have some French language instruction. However, some families encourage their children to build greater competence in French by sending them to French immersion schools.

French immersion programs are offered throughout Canada in the public school system. Begun in 1965 with a pilot program in Québec, French immersion programs became widely available nationwide in the 1970s. They are designed for students who have little or no knowledge of French when they enter the program and who don't come from French-speaking families. Students don't just learn French grammar or spelling—they learn subjects like social studies, science, and music in French.

DAILY LIFE

French immersion education in elementary school usually follows one of two models: early immersion or late immersion. In early immersion, which begins in kindergarten or Grade 1, students are instructed only in French in their first years. In Grade 3 or 4, English is gradually reintroduced, so that in the later elementary grades, students spend half their day in English and half in French. The goal is for students to read, write, and speak both languages fluently by the time they complete their elementary education.

Some parents wonder whether their children will lag behind in English if their early education is entirely in French. Because most French immersion students come from English-speaking homes, they already speak English fluently when they enter school. They pick up English reading simply from being exposed to English everywhere outside of school. In fact, studies have shown that French immersion students often score higher—in English, math, and other subjects—than their counterparts in English-only schools.

Late immersion is an option for kids who decide later on that they'd like to learn French in a more intensive way or for older students who are looking for more of a challenge. It's also an option for expat children who didn't arrive in Canada at a young enough age to enter the early immersion stream. Late immersion programs typically begin in Grades 6 or 7, and for two or three years, students—with no prior French-language experience—have all or most of their classes in French. It's almost as if they were attending school in Paris or Québec City. Some late immersion programs continue to teach math in English, and most offer at least some English-language reading, spelling, and writing instruction.

Some districts offer a "middle immersion" alternative that starts in Grades 3 or 4. Middle immersion programs are similar to late immersion. All instruction for at least two years is entirely in French—they just start at an earlier age.

Immersion students can continue their French studies in high school, where they take some classes in French and some in English. In districts that offer both early and middle or late immersion programs, the students from both streams are usually merged in secondary school.

The demand for French immersion programs in some cities exceeds the schools' ability to accommodate immersion students, so districts implement a lottery or other application process. If you're interested in exploring French immersion for your kids, find out about application deadlines as soon as possible.

How can you send your children to a French immersion program if you don't speak French yourself? Many parents of immersion students don't speak French at all. Teachers give parents tips on how to work with your children even if you have no French experience. Your kids may even teach you a thing or two.

The Canadian Parents for French organization (www.cpf.ca) is a good source of information about French immersion programs. For specifics about French immersion options in a particular city, contact the local school board.

By law, Canada must also offer French-language education for children of French-speaking parents. These Francophone schools are separate from French immersion schools, and they're open only to children whose parents are native French speakers or who come from a French-speaking country.

Some advocates of Canadian French immersion programs insist that they're almost like getting a private school education within the public schools. Parents of immersion students say that their kids work harder than English-only students. Particularly in late immersion programs, the kids who choose immersion may be more motivated than those in regular programs—after all, they're leaving a regular English program for instruction in a second language. In many districts, class sizes are slightly smaller in immersion programs than in regular classrooms.

Interestingly, the families who select French immersion for their children tend to have higher educational and income levels on average than those who enroll their kids in English-only programs. Yet in the more than 40 years since French immersion programs were first offered in Canada, a wide range of students, from all types of backgrounds, have completed these bilingual education programs.

Education in Canada

Canada provides free public education to all Canadian citizens and permanent residents from kindergarten until they complete secondary school, typically at age 18. Each province administers its own education system, so policies and requirements vary from province to province. There is no national educational authority analogous to the Department of Education in the United States. Within each province, individual school districts—often referred to as school boards—manage the schools on the local level.

As in the United States, Canadian public education in most provinces begins in kindergarten and continues through 12th grade (although in Canada, the convention is to say "Grade N" rather than "Nth Grade"). Québec is an exception to the K–12 program.

If you live in Canada but are neither a Canadian citizen nor a permanent resident, it's still possible (and necessary) to send your children to school. When a parent has a valid work permit, Canada immigration should issue your children a permit that will allow them to register in public school for free.

DAILY LIFE

HOW TO APPLY FOR A STUDY PERMIT

Students coming to Canada from the United States don't need a study permit if they are minors (below age 18 or 19, depending on the province) and their parents are Canadian citizens or permanent residents, or a parent has a Canadian work permit. Study permits are also not required for students attending preschool or kindergarten.

Before applying for a study permit, a student must first be accepted by a school, whether a public elementary or secondary school, a private school, a college, or a university.

Study permit applications and instructions are available online from Citizenship and Immigration Canada (www.cic.gc.ca). In addition to a completed study permit application, a student will need the following:

- Proof of acceptance at a school, college, or university

- A passport

- Two photos of themselves and of any accompanying family members

- Proof that the student (if an adult) has sufficient funds to support themselves and any accompanying family.

Students applying to study in Québec need an additional document called the Certificat d'acceptation du Québec (Québec Certificate of Acceptance, or CAQ). For details about how to apply for a CAQ, see the Québec Immigration website at www.immigration-quebec.gouv.qc.ca.

If you arrive in Canada without a permanent resident card or a work permit, you have to apply for a study permit for your children, who would be classified as "international students." Your child could attend public school, but you'd have to pay tuition—and that tuition could be nearly as much as you'd pay at a private school. If you yourself are coming to Canada to go to school, you need to apply for a study permit.

COLLEGES AND UNIVERSITIES

Most of Canada's colleges and universities are public institutions, operated and funded by the provincial governments. Historically, the only private post-secondary educational institutions have been religious ones. Unlike the United States, Canada does not have an extensive network of private colleges and universities. Canada's first private, secular, non-profit university—Quest University in British Columbia—opened in 2007.

Canada has approximately 90 universities and about 150 colleges. In Canada, a "university" is a four-year degree-granting post-secondary institution, while "college" typically refers to a two-year post-secondary school, similar to a U.S.

junior or community college. A student might attend "college" for two years, and then transfer to a university for the remaining two years. Canadian students planning to attend a four-year post-secondary school don't say they're going to college—they're going "to university."

Tuition

Did you say $5,000 *a year*? Besides the terminology, one of the main differences between attending a Canadian university and an American one is the cost. In the United States, annual tuition at state universities, even for in-state residents, can run to US$10,000, while tuition at private universities can easily exceed US$30,000 per

McGill, in Montréal, is one of Canada's top-rated universities.

© CAROLYN B. HELLER

DAILY LIFE

year. Most Canadian university students pay less than $5,000 for their annual tuition. Even for students coming from outside Canada, international tuition is still a relatively reasonable average of $13,200.

Tuition at Canadian universities varies depending on whether you're a resident of the province where the university is located, of another Canadian province, or of another country. For example, the 2007–2008 tuition at McGill University, a top-rated English-language university in Montréal, was only $1,770 per year for students from Québec who are Canadian citizens or permanent residents, approximately $5,140 for students from outside Québec (who are still Canadian citizens or permanent residents), and roughly $15,000 for international students.

How does Canada maintain university tuition at these relatively modest prices? As you might expect, universities are government subsidized. Each province determines the tuition rates of its universities; of all the provinces, Québec subsidizes its educational system most heavily, so tuition at Québec universities is the lowest nationwide.

Although college and university costs are much lower than in the United States, you'll still need to save your loonies for your children's education. If you expect to remain in Canada long enough that your children might pursue post-secondary education here, consider opening a Registered Education Savings Plan (RESP) account for each child. You may contribute up to $4,000 a year to an RESP, up to a maximum of $42,000 per beneficiary, and the money accumulates tax-free. More information about RESPs is available from Human Resources and Social Development Canada at www.hrsdc.gc.ca.

Depending on your income level, the Canadian government may make additional contributions to your child's RESP through the Canada Education Savings Grant (CESG) program. To find out if your family qualifies, visit the Services Canada website (www.servicecanada.gc.ca).

Don't worry if you have already established an Education Savings Account in the United States to help fund your child's university education, but your child is considering studying in Canada. At least under current tax law, the funds from those accounts can be used at most Canadian four-year universities.

PRIMARY AND HIGH SCHOOLS

In Canada, as in the United States, elementary and secondary school students can choose to attend either public or private schools. To find out more about the school options in the city where you'll be living, refer to the Prime Living Locations chapters in this book.

Many Canadian public school districts offer a variety of special programs or magnet schools, particularly at the high-school level. In addition to the popular French immersion programs, you may find arts- or science-magnet schools, programs for accelerated students, Montessori programs, alternative programs for kids who don't fit a standard classroom or curriculum, and programs such as the International Baccalaureate (IB). Check with your local school district for information about these special programs.

Unlike the United States, where religious education is officially prohibited in the public schools, Canada's Constitution gives Protestant and Roman Catholic citizens the right to a separate religious-based public education system. Currently, Ontario and Alberta have these "separate" school boards. In both provinces, most of these separate schools—public schools, supported by education taxes—are Catholic. Search online for "city name" and "separate schools" to find the options in the city where you're planning to live.

To enroll your children in public school, you normally provide their birth certificates and/or passports, their permanent resident cards or other Canadian identity documents, report cards or records from their previous school, and their health records, including their immunization history. The immunization requirements in most Canadian provinces are similar to those in most U.S. states, so if your kids' vaccines are up-to-date, they won't likely need additional shots. If you can't produce an immunization record, though, the schools may insist that the kids be re-vaccinated before they'll be admitted to a classroom.

Contact the local school board to find out whether to register your children at

CAUGHT IN THE CATCHMENT: AN EDUCATION GLOSSARY

If your kids are going to school in Canada, you might hear some of the following terms:

Catchment area: the geographical boundaries for attendance at a particular school (what in the United States might be called a school district)

Separate schools: publicly funded religious schools

French immersion: programs in which non-French speaking kids are immersed in the French language

Francophone education: French-language school programs for children of French-speaking parents

Registered Education Savings Plan (RESP): an account that allows savings for a student's post-secondary education to grow tax-free

Trillium List (Ontario): the list of textbooks approved for use in the Ontario schools

CÉGEP (Québec): a post-secondary program in Québec that begins after Grade 11

Dogwood Diploma (British Columbia): A certificate of graduation from secondary school (a.k.a. a high-school diploma). It's named for the province's official flower, which decorates graduation certificates.

the school they'll attend or at a central office. Many districts require that kids born outside of Canada or those who aren't permanent residents register at a district office. While it's easiest to register your kids before the beginning of the school year, public schools will generally admit students whenever they arrive. In most Canadian cities, school starts after Labour Day in September and finishes in mid- to late-June. As in the United States, there's a winter break of at least two weeks around Christmas/New Year's and at least a week's vacation in the spring.

Some provinces have provincially mandated exams or achievement tests in certain grades or subjects. Secondary school students should be sure to check with the school board about provincial exam requirements, since they can be mandatory for high-school graduation.

Private School

While most major Canadian cities have both public and private school options, the private school culture is not as firmly established as it is in some American regions. If you opt to send your kids to private school, some Canadians may treat your decision with genuine puzzlement.

Most Canadians are proud of their public education system, in the same way that most support the publicly funded national health care system. Warts and all, public education, like public health care, is part of the Canadian social fabric. And in general, those warts are few. Canadian public schools are well regarded, and Canadian students' scores compare favorably with those in other countries on a variety of assessments.

That said, Canada has excellent private schools, too. Some offer challenging college preparatory programs, while others offer a specialized focus on the arts or the sciences. Many Canadian private schools are modeled on the British system, at least in style, with "head boys" and "head girls," houses, and traditional blue-blazer uniforms. While Canada's public schools typically assume that those students who go on to university will study in Canada, many private schools have better resources for students who may be considering college in the United States, which may be an important factor for expat families.

Most Canadian private or independent schools have application processes and deadlines similar to those of U.S. private schools; applications are generally due in December or January for admission the following September. Some private schools require applicants to take standardized tests, such as the Secondary School Admission Test (SSAT), while others may require their own exams. You'll also need to provide the same documents that the public schools require. The website of the Canadian Association of Independent Schools (www.cais.ca) provides contact information for private schools in each province.

The Fraser Institute (www.fraserinstitute.ca), a Canadian think tank, issues annual "report cards" for Canadian schools, both public and private, which may be useful for comparing schools you might consider. But the best source of information is other parents. Even if you don't know many people in the city where you'll be living, don't hesitate to ask real estate agents, business associates, and friends of friends for school recommendations. If you're applying to private school, ask the schools' admissions directors for names of parents—particularly other expats—who can act as references and tell you what their experiences were really like.

HEALTH

Canadians are among the healthiest people in the world. Access to universal health care, comparatively few environmental problems, a relatively low crime rate, and a nationwide enthusiasm for sports and the outdoors all contribute to the population's general good health. In fact, in 2007, the United Nations ranked Canada as one of the top five best places to live worldwide, based on a variety of environmental, health, and economic indicators.

Many people feel that one of the major benefits of living in Canada is the country's highly regarded national health care system. Yet one of the trials for expats relocating to Canada is learning to navigate the ins and outs of the health care bureaucracy.

Although Canada's health care program is routinely described as a *national* health system, it's actually made up of 13 related programs—one in each province and territory. What this means is that when you move to Canada, you need to understand not only the national health system overall but its specific implementation in the province where you'll be living.

© CAROLYN B. HELLER

Toronto General Hospital   150 Gerrard Street Wes

National Health System

Canada's national health insurance system is known as Medicare. Unlike the U.S. system of the same name, Canadian Medicare is a publicly funded program that provides health insurance for *all* Canadian citizens and permanent residents, regardless of whether you're working or whether you can afford to pay. In most cases, Medicare will also cover you if you're living in Canada with a work or study permit. And if you're used to paying the high costs of health insurance in the United States, the price of Medicare coverage will come as a pleasant surprise.

What does Medicare cost? In several Canadian provinces, basic coverage costs nothing. That's right, zero. Even in provinces where there is a charge, the rates are quite low compared to health insurance costs in the United States. In British Columbia, monthly medical premiums in 2007 were $54 for one person, $96 for a family of two, and $108 for a family of three or more. Alberta residents paid $44 per month for individual coverage and $88 per month for a family of two or more; Alberta seniors pay nothing.

In Ontario, a health care premium based on your income is deducted from employee pay. Imposed in 2004, this approach is quite controversial in Canada but still reasonable by U.S. standards. Even the wealthiest individuals, earning more than $200,600 per year, pay just $75 per month. Individuals earning less than $20,000 per year pay nothing.

HOW MEDICARE WORKS

One of the most important things that a newcomer to Canada needs to do is arrange for Medicare coverage. If you're coming to Canada with a job, your employer will normally arrange for your health coverage, and your health care premiums will be deducted from your salary. If you're self-employed or not yet working, you need to apply and pay for your health insurance through your provincial health agency.

In most provinces, newcomers from outside of Canada have a three-month waiting period before they're eligible for Medicare coverage. You need to be sure that, in the interim, your existing health insurance will cover you and your family in Canada. As long as you have coverage for travel outside the United States, and as long as that coverage extends until your Canadian coverage kicks in, you should have no problem. Otherwise, you need to investigate a temporary plan that will provide health insurance during the Canadian waiting period. The Canadian Life and Health Insurance Association (www.clhia.ca) has information about companies that offer temporary medical insurance.

DO CANADIANS LIVE LONGER?

Is living in Canada good for your health? According to the World Health Organization, it is. Canadians, on average, live longer than Americans (and longer than many Europeans and Asians as well). A baby born in Canada in 2005 could expect to live to age 80.5. A baby born in the United States the same year would have an average life expectancy of 77.9 years.

What accounts for this difference? One factor may be Canada's universal health care system, which ensures that everyone has access to basic medical services.

Approximately 47 million Americans do not have health insurance. That's more than the number of people who live in all of Canada.

Another explanation could be that the Canadian health system puts more emphasis on family doctors who provide primary care and less emphasis on specialists, again making basic preventative care more accessible. And some say that, with Canada's more restrictive gun laws and generally less violent society, Canadians are simply less likely to shoot each other!

Applying for Health Insurance

If your employer is not handling your Medicare paperwork, you must apply for yourself and your family through the health department in the province where you'll be living. *All Canadian residents must apply for Medicare.* While the specific application process varies by province, you generally need to provide proof of your identity (such as a passport, driver's license, or student ID), proof of your Canadian address (such as a driver's license, a lease, or a utility bill), and proof of your status in Canada (your permanent resident card, work permit, or study permit).

In British Columbia, Health Insurance BC operates the province's Medicare program, which is known as the Medical Services Plan (MSP). MSP eligibility information and application materials are online at www. health.gov.bc.ca/insurance. As of this writing, applications were taking two months to process, so apply as soon as you arrive in B.C. That way, your application should be approved before the end of the three-month waiting period.

The Alberta Health Care Insurance Plan (AHCIP) also has its applications online. Find them at www.health.gov.ab.ca. If you move to Alberta from outside of Canada, you're eligible for medical coverage from the day you arrive; there is no waiting period. However, you must register with AHCIP within three months from the date you arrive in Canada.

New residents of Ontario have a three-month waiting period before they can

DAILY LIFE

HEALTH CARE HERO

The Canadian Broadcasting Corporation recently conducted a nationwide poll to find out who was the "Greatest Canadian" of all time. The winner? Tommy Douglas, a Depression-era prairie politician, who is considered the father of the Canadian national health care system.

Elected to the House of Commons from Saskatchewan in 1935, Douglas was a member of the Co-operative Commonwealth Federation, a socialist party. In 1944, Douglas became Saskatchewan's premier and the head of North America's first-ever socialist government.

Over his five terms in office, one of his most notable achievements was to introduce, in the province of Saskatchewan, Canada's first universal health care plan. Douglas' program became the inspiration for the Canadian Health Act of 1984, which established Medicare, the federal health insurance system, in its present-day form.

receive coverage under the Ontario Health Insurance Plan (OHIP). Eligibility requirements and application forms are online at www.health.gov.on.ca.

In Québec, new residents must register with Régie de l'Assurance Maladie du Québec (www.ramq.gouv.qc.ca), Québec's health insurance agency. You must call or visit a Régie office to obtain a registration form and submit your application. You cannot apply online. Contact the Régie as soon as you arrive in Québec to begin the registration process. Québec, too, has a three-month waiting period for new residents who arrive from outside of Canada.

Once you're approved for Medicare coverage, you receive a health insurance card, which is sometimes called a "care card." Everyone, from infants to seniors, must have their own health insurance card with a unique Health Insurance Number. Bring this card whenever you see a doctor, go to the hospital, or have any other medical services. Without your card (or at least your number), you may have to pay for service and then apply for reimbursement.

What's Not Covered?

Medicare does not cover prescription drugs, dental services, or the cost of glasses and contact lenses. Some employers provide supplemental health and dental insurance that covers these excluded items, so check what your employer offers before investigating other alternatives. Also in some provinces, dental coverage is provided for children whose families have incomes below certain levels.

In addition, Medicare excludes any services that are not considered "medically necessary," such as cosmetic surgery. If you need to be transported by ambulance, expect to pay—Medicare doesn't cover ambulance services. Planning

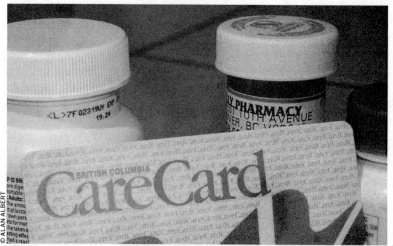

© ALAN ALBERT

Every Canadian resident must apply for provincially funded health insurance.

DAILY LIFE

to take a safari in Africa or a volunteer vacation in India? While routine immunizations are included in basic health care coverage, you generally have to pay out-of-pocket for vaccinations required for international travel.

Even more important, Canadian health insurance may not cover you (or may cover you insufficiently) if you're outside your home province—when you're elsewhere in Canada, in the United States, or abroad. If you live in Vancouver and fall down the steps while you're in Toronto on business, your B.C. health insurance may not cover you. Similarly, if you live in Montréal and break a leg skiing at Vail, you cannot get coverage through your Québec health insurance. It's essential that you purchase supplemental health insurance to cover you and your family outside your home province.

Refer to *International Coverage* later in this chapter for additional important information about travel medical insurance.

Finding a Doctor

In Canada, family doctors provide most basic medical care. If you're used to taking your kids to a pediatrician, seeing an internal medicine specialist for your routine care, or getting your annual exam through an OB-GYN, you'll have to adjust to the Canadian system. Here, family doctors or other primary care providers, such as nurse practitioners, are your first point of contact for medical care. Family doctors provide regular physicals, exams when you're sick or injured, and other routine care. To see a specialist—and pediatricians and OB-GYNs are considered specialists in Canada—you need a referral from your family doctor.

So how do you find a family doctor? Start by asking your colleagues, employer, and friends for recommendations and referrals. If you have a friend or neighbor who is a medical professional, s/he may be able to refer you to a colleague who is accepting new patients. The College of Physicians and Surgeons in most provinces also maintains lists of doctors who are accepting new patients.

What if you need medical help and don't yet have a family doctor? Across Canada, there are walk-in clinics that provide routine medical care, like similar clinics in the United States. Your Canadian Medicare coverage pays for these clinic visits. If the situation is more serious, go to the local hospital's emergency room. Medicare covers visits to the emergency room.

Some medical professionals advertise when they're accepting new patients.

Waiting Lists

The major drawback of Canada's national health system is that you can wait a long time for certain types of medical care. If it's a true emergency, don't worry—go to the hospital emergency room, and you'll generally be examined right away. If your child needs to see your family doctor for a fever, a cough, or a mysterious rash, you can usually get an appointment promptly. But if you need a specialized diagnostic service, such as an MRI, or if you need surgery for a condition that's not life-threatening, you can face a long and sometimes daunting wait.

You can look up information about the waiting lists for various procedures online. Go to the Health Canada website (www.hc-sc.gc.ca) and then to "Wait Times in Canada." From there, find information about your province and the service or procedure you're interested in. Some provinces enable you to see wait times at specific hospitals and even for particular doctors.

The Canadian government has recognized that waiting lists are a significant problem, and several programs are underway to reduce patient wait time. The federal government has been working with each province to establish "patient wait time guarantees" for certain types of services—essentially the maximum

U.S. VS. CANADIAN HEALTH CARE

A 2007 study published in the journal *Open Medicine* surveyed more than 300 Americans living in Canada about their experiences with the Canadian health care system. Respondents said that the significant advantages of the Canadian system were the equality and universality of coverage, as well as the low out-of-pocket costs. The Americans also praised the low cost overall relative to the quality of care in Canada. The negatives? Wait times and, in some areas, shortages of medical personnel.

Fifty percent of respondents rated the Canadian health care system as good or excellent. Overall, 40 percent favored Canadian health care, while 45 percent said that they preferred the U.S. system.

Presumably those who preferred the U.S. system had health insurance there.

DAILY LIFE

time that you'd be expected to wait for a particular test or procedure before you'd be offered some sort of alternative, such as the option to go to another service provider or alternate location. The government's goal is to have these guarantees in place by the year 2010.

In the meantime, if you're waiting for a medical service, be your own advocate. Find out whether the doctor has a "cancellation" list and ask to be put on it; if someone ahead of you can't keep their appointment, you may be able to take their spot. Inquire whether you can have the procedure done at a different location or by a different doctor; the wait may be shorter at a hospital in the next town or with a different practitioner. Or ask if there are any alternative services. Your doctor may be able to suggest other ways to get the services you need—but you have to ask, and you may have to ask more than once.

PUBLIC VS. PRIVATE CARE
Supplemental Medical Insurance

While the publicly funded Medicare program pays for most routine medical services, you can—and in most cases, should—buy supplemental health insurance to cover items that Medicare doesn't include. Supplemental policies cover things like prescription drugs, glasses and contact lenses, ambulance services, semi-private or private hospital rooms, and visits to chiropractors, Physiotherapists, optometrists, and other specialists. Most of these services have a deductible or co-payment.

You can also take out a supplemental policy to cover dental services. Dental plans may cover regular checkups, X-rays, fillings, and more major work, such as root canals, crowns, or dentures.

Shop around for supplemental policies as different providers offer a variety of different options. Figure out, too, what services you and your family are most likely to need. You may find, for example, if you don't have a lot of dental problems, that "self-insuring" for dental services (paying for service as you need it) could be more cost-effective than taking out a dental policy. Or if only one member of your family wears glasses, paying for vision care may not be worth it.

Other types of supplemental insurance that are available in Canada include disability coverage (to provide income if you were disabled and unable to work) and critical illness coverage, which pays you a lump sum if you develop specific life-threatening conditions, such as cancer, heart attack, or stroke. Long-term care policies that are common in the United States are a relatively new concept in Canada, since Medicare provides for basic care in the event of a long-term illness. However, you may want to investigate these additional supplemental insurance products, particularly if you expect to be living in Canada for many years.

Private Health Care Services

In some provinces, private clinics have opened to provide services for which the public system has long waits. If you arrange for service through one of these private clinics, you have to pay for that service yourself; neither Medicare nor supplemental insurance covers these services. However, if you have the money, and you feel your need is more urgent than the government system can deal with, you may want to consider a private clinic.

Private clinics are quite controversial in Canada, since many Canadians feel that these facilities are undermining the country's commitment to universal health care. Others believe that, like private schools, private health care should be an additional option for those who can and want to pay for it.

INTERNATIONAL COVERAGE

Because Canadian health insurance is provided by each province, it covers you *only* while you are in your home province. If you travel elsewhere in Canada, to the United States, or anywhere else in the world, your provincial health plan will generally not cover you. Or if the plan does provide coverage, it may pay only the amount it would pay for the service in your home province, not what you might be billed in the location where you are traveling.

If you travel back to the United States, for example, basic Canadian Medicare coverage would likely pay only a fraction of the cost of a U.S. doctor's visit,

NEED HEALTH CARE HELP?

Health Canada is the federal department responsible for the nation's overall health policy and for administering the health care insurance system. Its website (www.hc-sc.gc.ca) is a good source of general information about health care in Canada.

For insurance questions, the **Canadian Life and Health Insurance Association** can help. Its website (www.clhia.ca) has lots of information about health insurance products, and it runs a Consumer Assistance Centre that dispenses information by phone. Call 800/268-8099 (in Canada) or contact the Toronto headquarters at 416/777-2344.

emergency service, or hospital stay. Say you're an Alberta resident and you're in a car accident while traveling in Los Angeles that puts you in the hospital for several days. Your Alberta medical plan would pay only up to $100 per day, and you'd be personally liable for the rest.

Unless you're planning to remain only in your home province, you should purchase supplemental travel medical insurance. The best policies give you access to a 24/7 emergency hotline, cover foreign hospital costs, and pay for medical evacuation, either back to Canada or to the closest location that can provide medical care. As with any insurance purchase, it's a good idea to get multiple quotes, since coverage and prices may vary.

Travel medical insurance policies cover either a single trip or multiple trips within a year. Remember that if you cross the U.S.–Canada border even for one day—to go shopping, for example—you need medical insurance that covers you outside of the country. Opting for annual coverage is likely the most cost-effective for Americans living in Canada who expect to travel to the United States (or abroad) more than once a year. A multi-trip emergency medical policy covering 30 days out of the country for a 40-year-old would cost around $100–125.

Canadians planning to travel abroad who need vaccinations or advice about other health issues generally visit one of the Travel Health Clinics around the country. You can get a list of these clinics from the Public Health Agency of Canada website (www.phac-aspc.gc.ca). Medicare does not cover most travel-related immunizations, prescriptions, or other medical services, nor do family doctors routinely deal with travel-related issues.

Pharmacies and Prescriptions

Are prescription drugs cheaper in Canada? Yes and no. While you may find that prices are lower for Canadian medications, Canada's Medicare program does not cover prescription drugs. If you previously had a medical plan that paid for prescriptions, your out-of-pocket medication costs may be higher than what you formerly paid in the United States.

A Canadian pharmacist cannot legally fill a prescription that was written by a doctor in the United States (or in any country outside of Canada). Canadian pharmacists can fill only those prescriptions written by medical professionals licensed in Canada.

Bring original copies of any prescriptions with you to Canada, but assume that you'll need a Canadian doctor to approve any refills. Depending on the medication, some health professionals may want to examine you, or at least discuss the prescription with you, before authorizing the refill.

MEDICAL RECORDS

Most family doctors in Canada maintain medical records for their patients, just as doctors do in the United States. Before you leave the United States, request of copy of your records from your current doctor and bring it with you to Canada. Alternatively, wait till you arrive in Canada and then contact your U.S. doctor to have your records sent to your new Canadian physician.

In either case, bring a copy of your immunization records with you when you first arrive in Canada, particularly if you have children. That way, if you step on the proverbial rusty nail and need to know when you last had a tetanus shot, you can easily determine whether your vaccinations are up to date.

Preventative Measures

VACCINATIONS

To enroll in school, children are generally required to have the same vaccines that they need in most U.S. states. The local school board in your new community can provide information about any required vaccines. If your child will attend a private school, ask the school for vaccination details. In either case, bring your child's immunization record with you when registering for school.

Many Canadian schools conduct immunization clinics, so don't be surprised if your child comes home from school with a permission form for a vaccination.

Stay active to stay healthy – like these seniors lawn bowling near Osoyoos Lake.

For example, most provinces vaccinate elementary school students against hepatitis B. The Canadian health system funds these clinics, so there's no charge. You can learn more about the immunizations recommended in Canada and the schedule of publicly funded vaccinations on the Public Health Agency of Canada website (www.phac-aspc.gc.ca/im).

STAYING FIT

The Canadian medical system puts significant emphasis on preventative health care, not only because prevention can ultimately save the government-funded system money but also because it simply makes good sense. An active healthy population loses less time away from work and spends less on medical treatments.

All sorts of government campaigns encourage Canadians to exercise, enjoy the outdoors, and find other ways to keep fit. In many cities, community centers offer good-quality workout facilities and fitness classes at moderate prices.

ALTERNATIVE THERAPIES

Canada's health care system is reasonably accepting of alternative medicine. Perhaps because of the country's large Asian population, practitioners of therapies such as acupuncture, herbal remedies, and traditional Chinese medicine are

© CAROLYN B. HELLER

Canada has many practitioners of traditional Chinese medicine and other alternative treatments.

fairly easy to find. Check with the provincial health agency in your province to find out what types of alternative health services may be covered.

Environmental Factors

If you read the Canadian press, you may come away with the feeling that Canada is in the midst of an environmental crisis. Greenhouse gas emissions are up. Climate change is affecting the country's weather and wildlife population, particularly in the far north. There are concerns about the nation's ability to keep its water supply fresh and pure.

Still, without minimizing these very real environmental challenges, it's also important to realize that Canada's environment is in pretty good shape compared to that of many countries. And Canadians' growing eco-consciousness is leading the country to develop a number of new programs to deal with these environmental issues.

AIR QUALITY

Unlike the United States, Canada signed the 1998 United Nations' Kyoto Protocol, which commits countries to reducing their greenhouse gas emissions. Although Canada has not yet met its Kyoto targets, the country is working toward this goal. Most Canadian cities are actively encouraging residents to get out of their cars—to take public transit, walk, cycle, or carpool—since car use is the country's major source of urban air pollution.

WATER QUALITY

In Canadian cities, as in U.S. metropolitan areas, the municipal or regional government is responsible for maintaining the quality of the public water supply. And in general, Canada's water is judged clean and safe to drink. Bottled water is also readily available across Canada.

There have been isolated incidents when boil-water advisories have been issued, notably in Vancouver in late 2006 when severe winter storms caused abnormally high levels of mud to run off into the local reservoirs. However, these incidents—when the local health agencies recommended that residents boil their tap water before drinking it—have been infrequent.

SMOKING

Canada has one of the lowest rates of smoking in the world. Nationwide, roughly 20 percent of the population, age 12 and up, smokes at least occasionally; the fewest smokers live in the provinces of British Columbia and Ontario. These nationwide statistics may be skewed by smoking rates in Canada's far north, though, where tobacco use remains a serious issue. In the territory of Nunavut, more than 50 percent of adults are smokers, as are over 30 percent of adults in the Yukon and the Northwest Territories.

The federal government is attempting to reduce smoking levels even further—down to 12 percent by 2011. Canada has strict anti-smoking laws that are getting stricter every year. These laws are set at the provincial level, and in some cases by city, so expect some variations. But most provinces, including British Columbia, Ontario, and Québec, have banned smoking in offices, restaurants, and other public places.

Alberta, with its anti-regulatory bent, is a relative Johnny-come-lately to no-smoking laws. However, Calgary, Edmonton, and other cities have enacted public smoking bans, and as this book went to press, the Alberta provincial government was working on legislation that would restrict public smoking province-wide.

Access for People with Disabilities

Perhaps because of the inclusive nature of Canada's national health care system, the country strives to make access to job opportunities, housing, education, and travel available to people with disabilities.

DAILY LIFE

SAM SULLIVAN

In 2005, the city of Vancouver elected Sam Sullivan as the nation's first quadriplegic mayor. Sullivan broke his neck in a skiing accident in 1979 when he was 19. He was later elected to the Vancouver City Council and served as a councilor for 12 years, before being chosen as Vancouver's mayor.

Mayor Sullivan made international headlines in 2006, when he traveled to the Winter Olympics in Turin, Italy, to accept the Olympic flag for Vancouver in anticipation of the 2010 Olympic Games. Closer to home, Sullivan founded several organizations to encourage people with disabilities to become more active and to take greater responsibility for improving their own lives.

One such organization is the Disabled Sailing Association of B.C., which has been operating at Vancouver's Jericho Sailing Centre, providing sailing lessons and support for sailors with disabilities since 1989. The Disabled Sailing Association now has affiliated chapters in 20 locations across North America.

The Canadian government provides a number of benefits to people with disabilities, including tax credits, educational assistance, and a variety of other services. The government website, Persons with Disabilities Online (www.pwd-online.ca), is a good starting point for learning about resources. Access to Travel (www.accesstotravel.gc.ca), also a government site, has details about accessible travel to and around Canada, including information about local public transportation.

The Canadian Abilities Foundation publishes *Abilities Magazine* and provides a wealth of articles and other information online at www.abilities.ca. Another useful information source is the Access Guide Canada, available online at www.enablelink.org/agc.

As with many Canadian government programs, the specific benefits and resources for people with disabilities vary by province, but these umbrella information sites can direct you to regional and local services.

Safety

When many people think about law enforcement in Canada, they think of the "Mounties." Officially known as the Royal Canadian Mounted Police (although these days they go by their acronym), the RCMP is Canada's national police force, which was first established in the 1870s. Not only does the RCMP provide policing services at the federal and provincial levels, in certain areas it's under contract to provide municipal policing. The

RCMP deals with issues such as drug enforcement, terrorism, and organized crime as well.

In 2006, Canada's national crime rate reached its lowest point in more than 25 years, and most Canadians will tell you that their cities are fairly safe. Perhaps they don't walk around alone at 2 A.M. or they avoid certain neighborhoods, but overall, Canadians seem to feel that they live in a pretty safe place.

Statistics Canada reports that the most prevalent crimes nationwide are property crimes, such as car theft, purse snatching, or breaking and entering. In fact, in 2006, the rate of property crimes in Canada was slightly higher than the rate of similar crimes in the United States. However, Canada has far fewer violent crimes than the United States.

The U.S. murder rate is roughly three times that of Canada. And the rate of gun violence in the United States is much higher; statistics show that guns were involved in more than 40 percent of U.S. robberies, compared to 16 percent in Canada. The Canadian Broadcasting Corporation reported recently that there are fewer than one million handguns in Canada—and roughly 76 million handguns in the United States.

EMPLOYMENT

Canada's economy has been expanding briskly since the turn of the 21st century. Whether you're looking for a high-powered job with a high-tech company, an academic position at a large university, work in the booming oil business, a temporary gig in a ski town, or any of a range of other positions, Canada has plenty of opportunities. And with growing industries and a shortage of workers, Canada is looking outside its borders to fill many of the country's jobs.

It used to be that Canadians with the greatest career prospects left the country, many heading for jobs in the United States. And while there are still more Canadians moving south than Americans heading north, the tide is beginning to turn. In 2006, the number of U.S. citizens who relocated to Canada hit a 30-year high.

These days, Canada is welcoming expats, particularly those with skills that the country needs. Well-educated, professional people will find it easiest to get jobs, as will those with technical skills, particularly in information technology, biotech, and resource-based industries, such as oil and gas. The country's

tourism industry is another source of jobs; the 2010 Winter Olympics in the Vancouver area are expected to drive increases in tourism nationwide in the years both before and after the Games.

As an American planning to work in Canada, you'll find that the job search process is similar to the way you'd look for a job back home. You'll need to seek out new sources of job information and deal with some different paperwork, but otherwise, you don't need to master any special skills.

Self-Employment

If you want to come to Canada and work for yourself, in most cases you need to apply for permanent resident status. There's a special permanent resident category for entrepreneurs and certain types of self-employed people, or you may be able to qualify as a provincial nominee. The *Making the Move* chapter has more details.

While this section includes general information about starting and operating a business in Canada, it's not intended to provide legal or business advice. Be sure to seek counsel from the appropriate professionals.

STARTING A BUSINESS

Canada wants you! The Canadian government is actively encouraging immigrants who want to start a business to come to Canada, at least if you have experience, relevant skills, and financial resources. And despite the lingering perception that Canada is a high-tax nation, a 2006 study by KPMG, an international consulting and accounting firm, found that the costs of operating a business, including electricity rates, land and construction costs, and corporate taxes, were lower in Canada than in the other G7 nations (the United States, France, Italy, United Kingdom, Japan, and Germany).

Resources for Entrepreneurs

The Canadian government has a number of resources to offer prospective entrepreneurs. The federal government's Investment, Science, & Technology Branch (www.investincanada.gc.ca) provides a wealth of information designed for non-Canadians who are considering starting a business in Canada. Another good starting point is the government's Canada Business website (www.canadabusiness.ca) for entrepreneurs. Industry Canada (www.ic.gc.ca) publishes "Managing for Business Success," an online guide for small- and medium-sized businesses; it's not tailored to newcomers, but it has links to all sorts of useful data, including sources of financing, Canadian employment laws, and

CANADIAN ENTREPRENEURS

Here are just a few of the Canadian-born entrepreneurs who've made headlines in the business world:

- Scott Abbott and Chris Haney: inventors of the game Trivial Pursuit

- Bonnie Fuller: magazine editor and editorial director, American Media, Inc.

- Nick Graham: founder, Joe Boxer

- Mike Lazaridis: founder, Research in Motion (creator of the Blackberry)

- Jeff Skoll: first employee and founding president of eBay

- Chip Wilson: founder, Lululemon Athletica

- Mortimer Zuckerman: real estate investor, *New York Daily News* publisher, editor-in-chief of *U.S. News & World Report*

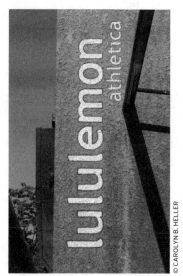

© CAROLYN B. HELLER

Lululemon Athletica is one of Canada's entrepreneurial success stories.

tax issues. Location Canada (www.locationcanada.com) has helpful articles for businesses considering locating in Canada.

The provincial governments also offer extensive resources for entrepreneurs. The British Columbia Ministry of Economic Development and Invest British Columbia; the Alberta Ministry of Employment, Immigration, and Industry; the Ontario Ministry of Economic Development and Trade; and the government of Québec all provide information about launching a business in each of these provinces.

In British Columbia, another source is the "One Stop Business Registry," which has both general information about launching a business in B.C., as well as specific details on how to register your business name or incorporate your company. Investissement Québec has more resources for potential Québec-based entrepreneurs.

If you're making a fact-finding trip to Ontario to research business opportunities, plan to attend a free seminar that the province's Ministry of Economic Development and Trade offers in Toronto twice a month. Designed for businesspeople considering immigrating to Ontario, the seminar gives you an overview of the province, describes the immigration process, and highlights the resources available to business immigrants. You have to pre-register, which you can do from their website (www.2ontario.com). The same agency also offers free seminars on starting a business, Canadian taxes, and the Canadian banking system that you can attend once you've settled in Ontario as a permanent resident.

City and regional economic development organizations are also good sources of information about starting a business in their areas. Refer to the *Resources* chapter for a list of contacts.

Local chambers of commerce may be useful as well. Search online for "city name" and "chamber of commerce" to find the organization in the city where you're planning to relocate.

When you're ready to seek financing, check out the government-run Business Development Bank of Canada. BDC provides long-term financing, venture capital, and business consulting services to small- and medium-sized businesses.

Red Tape

Corporate structures in Canada follow the same general model that they do in the United States, with corporations being the most prevalent form of organization. Corporations can be either public or private, and you can incorporate in Canada as either a federal company (operating nationwide) or a provincial company (operating in one province). Other corporate structures include general or limited partnerships, sole proprietorships, and various types of joint ventures.

Several Canadian law firms publish booklets that address many of the legal issues that entrepreneurs may face in launching or operating a business in Canada, including how to determine the best corporate structure. Look for "Blakes' Guide to Doing Business in Canada" from the firm of Blake, Cassels & Graydon (www.blakes.com), "Doing Business in Canada," from Davies, Ward, Phillips, and Vineberg (www.dwpv.com), and "Establishing a Business in Canada" from Gowling Lafleur Henderson (www.gowlings.com). If you're planning to set up a venture in B.C. or Alberta, check out Lawson Lundell's "Doing Business in Western Canada" (www.lawsonlundell.com).

When you set up your business, you'll need to apply for a nine-digit Business Number (BN) from the Canada Revenue Agency (CRA). You need a BN if you'll be liable for corporate or payroll taxes or if you have to collect G.S.T., the Federal Goods and Services Tax. Most businesses are required to charge G.S.T. on their products or services, and to pass on that tax to the government. This requirement applies to consultants, freelancers, and other individual business people as well, but only if your income is above a minimum threshold. Go to the CRA website (www.cra-arc.gc.ca) for instructions on applying for a BN and to determine whether you have to charge G.S.T.

Once you've settled in Canada, you may want to attend one of the seminars that the CRA offers for small- and medium-sized businesses. These seminars can help you understand your Canadian tax obligations. The seminar schedule is online at www.cra-arc.gc.ca/events.

© CAROLYN B. HELLER

Toronto is Canada's financial hub.

BUSINESS PRACTICES

If you're used to doing business in the United States, doing business in Canada won't be that dissimilar. However, one major difference in Canada is the importance of teamwork and reaching consensus.

Some U.S. expats have reported that Canadian companies place a much higher value on having everyone agree. Canadian employees tend to think of themselves as part of a team who all work together. The aggressive "my way or the highway" approach sometimes found in American businesses is considered inappropriate in many Canadian organizations. Individuals who assertively compete with their team members or toot their own horns may be perceived negatively in some Canadian businesses.

The benefit of this consensus-seeking approach, if done well, is more satisfied employees. When everyone feels part of the team and the decision-making process, they're more likely to be happy with their jobs. The downside, particularly if you're used to a more assertive American style where what the boss says goes, is that it can take longer to get things done. Of course, plenty of U.S. companies in recent years have moved closer to a consensus model, but in Canada, where niceness rules, some Americans have to bite their tongues in order to get along.

The Job Hunt

If you're trying to find out where the best job prospects are in various regions of Canada, check the Canadian government's Labour Market Information site (www.labourmarketinforma-tion.ca). You can search by job or by region; you can also search for which regions have good job opportunities or for which occupations have good opportunities in the region you've chosen.

If you already have permanent resident status in Canada when you're launching your job search, you're in luck—you can apply for most any job. Otherwise, you'll need to apply for a work permit. Remember that you can't submit your work permit application until *after* you have a job offer, and in many cases your prospective employer will need to demonstrate that they were

"salesperson wanted," in Québec City

unable to find a Canadian to fill the position. In general, the better educated and more experienced you are, or the more specialized your skills, the easier it is to convince an employer that it's worth arranging for a work permit on your behalf. The *Making the Move* chapter has more information about the process of applying for work permits.

EMPLOYERS

Canada has a huge range of companies, from small mom-and-pop businesses to multinational corporations, representing many different industries. Canada welcomes many professionals, from business people to professors to consultants, and opportunities in tourism, hospitality, film and TV, sports, recreation, and outdoor activities are also available in many regions. The major Canadian cities are home to numerous non-profit, cultural, and arts organizations as well.

Regulated Occupations

In Canada, certain types of jobs are "regulated occupations," which means that you need a professional license to work in these careers. Regulated occupations fall into two broad categories: professional and trades. Examples of regulated professions include doctors, dentists, nurses, psychologists, and many other healthcare workers; veterinarians; accountants; architects and engineers; lawyers; and teachers. Regulated trades include carpenters, electricians, plumbers, machinists, and cooks. You can get a complete list of regulated occupations on the Work Destinations website (www.workdestinations.org).

If you work in one of these regulated occupations, you need to be licensed in Canada before you can work. Each province is responsible for setting its own licensing requirements; for example, you're not licensed as a nurse nation-wide—you're licensed to work as a nurse in a particular province.

The process of getting licensed depends on your line of work and the province where you intend to live. On the Work Destinations site, you can select a particular occupation, then choose the province, to look up the licensing details. For example, if you're a doctor intending to work in British Columbia, the College of Physicians & Surgeons of B.C. provides licensing information. Or if you're an architect who wants to work in Ontario, you can get licensing details from the Ontario Association of Architects.

Some Canadian professions have reciprocity arrangements with corresponding licensing bodies in the United States. If you're licensed in the United States, it may be easier to become licensed in Canada.

Networking

The most important resource for job seekers is who you know. And that's even more important when you're looking for work in a new country.

Relying on "who you know" doesn't mean you have to be best buddies with the chairman of the board or that your mom's first cousin is the company president. But it does mean networking—and networking widely.

The Canadian job site Workopolis reported that over the last 15 years, more than two-thirds of people who've gotten jobs found those positions either through someone they knew or by contacting a company directly. Only about 15 percent found work through an ad.

What if you don't know anyone in Canada? Start by asking your colleagues and friends in the States. Do they know anyone living or working in Canada? Do their U.S.-based companies have Canadian affiliates? Do they have college classmates or business associates who grew up in Canada? Do you or your colleagues belong to a professional organization that has members in Canada? Sites such as LinkedIn, Facebook, and Plaxo can also be sources of connections. Sometimes, all it takes is one contact who can connect you with someone else, and your networking process is underway.

If you've arrived in Canada without a job, network in your new community. Talk to your neighbors, someone you've met in the local community center, a new acquaintance from the neighborhood coffee shop. Look for local professional associations in your line of work or online groups that share your interests.

For example, Meetup.com (www.meetup.com) has scores of work-related groups across Canada. There's a Vancouver Graphic Design Meetup, a Toronto Marketing Meetup, a Montréal Entrepreneurs Group, and many more.

Doing volunteer work is another worthwhile form of networking. If you can afford to take on one or more volunteer assignments, it can help you make contacts in your new community. And you'll be doing some good at the same time. Volunteer Canada can direct you to local volunteer opportunities nationwide.

Online Job Sites

While networking is crucial, it's still worth searching online, since many jobs in Canada are posted on online job boards. The Canadian government runs a nationwide Job Bank site that lists thousands of jobs in many different industries and regions. Another government-run site, Working in Canada, enables you to search by profession and location to see both specific job postings and general information about the market for the type of job you're seeking.

Other Canadian online job-posting sites include Workopolis, CareerBuilder Canada, AllStarJobs Canada, Brainhunter, Eluta Canada, and JobBoom. CareerClick.com links to newspaper classified ads nationwide. Several of the major job sites that operate in the United States have Canadian affiliates, such as Monster.ca and HotJobs.ca. WorkRights.ca has links to industry-specific job posting sites in education, engineering, finance, healthcare, information technology, media, and the sciences.

Check U.S. job-posting sites as well for positions in Canadian cities. Companies that are recruiting in the U.S will likely be open to hiring U.S. residents and to working with you on the work permit and relocation process.

More Resources for Job Seekers

The provincial governments and related agencies across Canada have plenty of online resources for job seekers, including many that focus on newcomers who are looking for work. While some are geared to non-English-speaking immigrants, they also include information that can be helpful to all newcomers. Some of these sites have links to job sites nationwide and in other provinces, so they're still worth a look regardless of where you're planning to settle:

- WorkBC (www.workbc.ca)

- Immigrant Services Society of BC (www.issbc.org)

- Alberta Immigration Job Search (www.alberta-canada.com/immigration/working/jobs)

- Alberta Learning Information Service (www.alis.gov.ab.ca)

- Ontario Immigration (www.ontarioimmigration.ca)

- Ontario WorkInfo Network (OnWIN) (www.onwin.ca)

- Settlement.org (Ontario) (www.settlement.org)

- Emploi-Québec (www.emploiquebec.net)

CAROLYN B. HELLER

Remember that the library can be a good resource for job hunters.

Don't neglect your local library, either in your U.S. community or in your new Canadian city. Not only can you find directories of Canadian companies and information about Canadian industries, you may be able to access online databases and other sources of information.

Jobs for Students

If you're a full-time university student between the ages of 18 and 35, and you're a U.S. citizen, you should know about a special program called the SWAP Working Holiday.

Through SWAP, you can work in Canada for up to six months. The program doesn't find you a job, but it arranges the paperwork that allows you to come to Canada and look for a position. SWAP has offices in Vancouver, Toronto, and Montréal where you can tap into their job-search resources, including job posting boards, lists of companies that have hired previous SWAP participants, and contacts at area placement agencies.

Once you're approved for the program, you can come to Canada at any time, so you can fit a SWAP break into your school schedule. Graduating seniors are eligible as long as you apply while you're still in school; you could arrange to come to Canada shortly after you graduate.

Many SWAP participants have found jobs in the tourism or hospitality

SKIING FOR YOUR SUPPER

Want to work in a ski town? Canada has lots of jobs in ski resorts large and small.

Whistler-Blackcomb, in British Columbia, is North America's largest ski resort, but there are plenty of other choices. There are several resorts in B.C.'s Okanagan region, including Big White, Sun Peaks, and Silver Star. Still farther east in B.C. are Revelstoke, Kimberley, Kicking Horse, Fernie, and Panorama Mountain, and across the provincial border, Alberta's best-known resorts include Banff and Lake Louise.

Québec's resorts include Mont-Tremblant, northwest of Montréal, and Mont Sainte-Anne and Stoneham, near Québec City. In Québec's Eastern Townships are Mont Orford, Sutton, Brome, and Owl's Head. And there are plenty of other smaller ski destinations across the country.

So how do you find a ski town job and what authorization do you need to work? If you're a student under age 35, the SWAP Working Holidays program (see *Jobs for Students* in this chapter) is a good option. They'll arrange for your work authorization, and then it's up to you to find a job.

If you don't qualify for the SWAP program, you need to arrange for a work permit or apply for permanent resident status, as detailed in *Making the Move*. If you're interested in temporary or seasonal work, it's unlikely that an employer would sponsor your work permit application, unless you have special skills. If you want to relocate to a ski town for long-term, permanent work, you might find an employer willing to arrange for your work permit; alternatively, you may be able to qualify for permanent resident status as a provincial nominee if you have the appropri-

Canada's ski towns are frequently looking for workers.

© CAROLYN B. HELLER

ate skills, since tourism employees are in demand in many regions.

The Whistler Chamber of Commerce website (www.whistlerchamber.com) is full of useful information about living and working in the Whistler area. The town of Banff (www.banff.ca) has similarly helpful information about working there. While some details on these sites are location-specific, much of the advice would also be useful in other ski towns. All the major ski areas list employment opportunities on their websites as well.

Many ski resorts do their winter hiring in the fall, so don't expect to show up in December and find work. But be prepared that if you do arrange a job in October, you may not actually start work till the first snows fall. And remember that many ski towns look for workers in the summer, too, when the areas draw hikers, cyclists, and other outdoor enthusiasts.

industries—on the ski slopes, in hotels, or restaurants. Others have taken retail or clerical work. SWAP participants are not allowed to work in childcare, teaching (in primary or secondary schools), or health services, but are otherwise free to seek out whatever work they can find.

The SWAP program fee is $250. Applicants must also demonstrate that they have at least US$700 to use for living expenses when they first arrive in Canada. To apply or get more information, refer to www.swap.ca.

INTERVIEWS

The process of interviewing for a job in Canada is virtually identical to the interview process in the United States. In larger companies and more traditional industries, the process is typically more formal, while in young organizations or emerging markets, the interview approach may be more laid-back. But overall, you're unlikely to need different skills to interview for a job in Canada.

For expats, one especially important objective of the interview process is to assess how well you'd fit in with the corporate culture. Of course, it's always valuable to determine how you'd fit into an organization—both for you and for your potential employer—but when you'll be working in a new country, your ability to adapt to the company's culture will be even more important.

Informational interviewing—contacting someone to talk about their job, even when they aren't necessarily hiring anyone—is an accepted form of networking, particularly when you have some connection to the person you'd like to meet. Use your network of contacts, asking colleagues and friends of friends who work in the industry or community you're interested in if they'd have time for a brief informational chat. Ask them about their work and request a referral to one of their colleagues or contacts in another organization. And be sure to send a thank-you note afterwards.

LANDING THE JOB

If you don't have permanent resident status when you're offered a job, you'll need to get a work permit before you can start work. The *Making the Move* chapter outlines the work permit application process.

BENEFITS

Canadians are entitled to paid holidays and at least two weeks of paid vacation per year, although the specifics vary by province. Most provinces, including British Columbia, Alberta, Ontario, and Québec, give employees eight or nine paid holidays off. In several provinces, notably British Columbia, Alberta, and

INCOMES IN CANADA

How much money do Canadians earn? In 2005, the median household after-tax income was just under $46,000. As you'd expect, incomes are highest in urban areas.

Among Canada's 10 largest cities, the income levels break down as follows, with Calgary at the top and Montréal at the bottom:

City	Income
Calgary	$56,600
Toronto	$55,400
Edmonton	$55,400
Ottawa	$53,000
Hamilton	$52,300
London	$49,900
Vancouver	$49,200
Winnipeg	$44,900
Québec City	$42,000
Montréal	$40,700

Source: Statistics Canada

DAILY LIFE

Québec, annual paid vacation time increases automatically to three weeks after you've been working for the same employer for five consecutive years.

In most provinces, charges for provincial health insurance will be deducted from your pay. Many employers arrange for supplemental health insurance policies that provide dental coverage and other benefits that aren't covered by the publicly funded health insurance system. Often, the employer and employee share the costs of this supplemental insurance, with your share deducted from your salary. Some employers also provide supplemental disability insurance policies.

Canada has generous leave policies for pregnant employees and new parents. The details vary by province but range from 15 to 18 weeks of unpaid pregnancy leave (for pregnant employees) and between 35 and 37 weeks of unpaid parental leave (for any new parents). A birth mother can take both pregnancy and parental leave time. Québec's parental leave provisions are even more generous, ranging up to a full year off. You have to be working for a minimum amount of time before you're eligible for pregnancy or parental leave.

What the United States calls "unemployment insurance" is known in Canada as "employment insurance" (EI). Most employees must pay into the EI system, with premiums deducted from your salary. As of 2008, the EI premium is $1.73 for every $100 of salary you earn up to a maximum annual salary of $41,100, which makes the maximum annual EI contribution $711.03. (The EI rates are lower in Québec: $1.39 for every $100 of salary up to $41,100, for a maximum annual contribution of $571.29.)

If you lose your job after you've been working a certain length of time (generally at least a year), you're eligible to apply for EI benefits. EI also pays benefits if you have to stop working because you're ill, if you take maternity or parental leave, or if you have to care for a gravely ill family member. The basic EI benefit rate is 55 percent of your earnings (up to an annual maximum insurable amount of $40,000); the maximum EI payment is $423 per week.

Almost everyone in Canada over the age of 18 who earns a salary must pay into the Canada Pension Plan (CPP). Similar to Social Security in the United States, the CPP provides retirement pensions, disability benefits, and survivor benefits to your spouse/partner and children. Your CPP contribution is based on your income; your employer pays half of your contribution, but you pay the balance. (Self-employed people pay both portions.)

Labor Laws and Workers' Rights

Most of Canada's labor laws and protections will seem familiar, at least in their objectives, to Americans coming to work here. Canada has workplace health and safety rules, workers' compensation (for injuries on the job), and anti-discrimination policies. Most Canadians who work full-time officially put in eight hours a day, 40 hours a week.

What is a little different between the two countries is the degree to which the federal government is involved in labor laws. Canada has a federal ministry of Human Resources and Social Development that's responsible for implementing national labor laws and standards, including industrial relations, health and safety, employment standards, and workplace equality. However, these laws cover only federally regulated workers, who comprise just 10 percent of the Canadian workforce.

Federally regulated employees include those working in banking, telecommunications, broadcasting, transportation (including air, interprovincial rail, and road), shipping, uranium mining, and crown corporations. Everyone else is covered by provincial labor laws. Each province sets its own labor laws governing employers and employees within its borders. The Ministry of Labour in each province can provide more details. In general, the labor laws in many provinces, especially B.C. and Québec, tend to be very "pro-employee," particularly regarding issues of discrimination and termination, compared with many U.S. states.

MINIMUM WAGE

Unlike the United States, Canada has no national minimum wage. Each province sets its own minimum wage level. As of 2008, minimum wages ranged from $7–8.75 per hour; in comparison, the U.S. minimum wage that same year was $6.55. Several provinces, including British Columbia, Alberta, and Québec, have a minimum wage of $8 per hour. Ontario's minimum wage is set at $8.75 per hour for 2008, $9.50 for 2009, and $10.25 for 2010.

Some provinces have lower minimum wage requirements for students or new workers. For example, in Ontario, the minimum wage for students under 18 is $8.20. B.C. has a "training wage" of $6 per hour, which is the minimum that can be paid to people working on their first job.

Workers who are not generally covered under minimum wage laws include salespeople who work on commission, real estate agents, and independent contractors. Most provinces also have separate minimum wage provisions for employees who serve alcohol (and get tips) and for farm workers.

DAILY LIFE

FINANCE

It is hard to get rich in Canada. But it is easy to make money.

— Ernest Hemingway, in his 1923 poem, "I Like Canadians"

With Canada's booming economy, at least part of Hemingway's quip might be right. These days, in many parts of the country, there are plenty of jobs to be had. It's a good time to come to Canada to work.

But what about the expense side? Even if you earn a good salary, how far will it go?

According to various economic indexes, the cost of living in Canada's largest cities is less than that of major U.S. metropolitan areas. Your funds should go further in Toronto, Vancouver, or Montréal than they would in New York, Los Angeles, or Chicago.

If you ask most U.S. expats about the cost of living in Canada, however, you'll likely get a mixed message. Depending on where in the States you've come from, you'll find that in Canada some things cost more, while others cost less.

© ALAN ALBERT

When you move across the border, you'll also need to adjust to the Canadian system of banking and investing, which—while similar to the U.S. financial system—has a few important differences. You should be aware of how the exchange rate between the U.S. and Canadian dollars can affect your financial decisions. And of course, there's the always-exasperating issue of taxes.

Cost of Living

In trying to forecast your cost of living in Canada, housing will be a major variable. If you're coming from a U.S. metropolis such as San Francisco, Boston, or Seattle, where housing costs are fairly high, you'll find that the price of housing in Canada's largest cities is similar or slightly less on average than what you paid in the States. However, since the year 2000, housing prices have risen significantly in many Canadian metropolitan areas, particularly in the West, so if you're moving from a smaller U.S. city, housing prices may seem high. Your perception of food costs, too, may depend on where in the States you've come from.

Some things are clearly more expensive in Canada than in the United States, including clothing, books, and gasoline. Expect to pay more tax on day-to-day purchases as well.

The Canadian government will take a chunk of your income at tax time; whether it's more or less than you currently pay in U.S. income taxes will depend on your particular financial situation. On the other hand, your health care costs in Canada will be less—a lot less—than you're likely paying in the United States. Education costs, particularly tuition fees at Canadian universities, are also lower than comparable education expenses in the United States.

Another significant variable in budgeting for life in Canada is the exchange rate between the Canadian and U.S. currencies. If you move to Canada when the U.S. dollar is high relative to the loonie, you'll find that it's less expensive to buy a home, purchase groceries, and go out to eat. If you arrive when Canada's currency is soaring, your U.S. dollars won't go nearly as far.

Whether you're paid in Canadian or U.S. dollars may make a difference, too. When you're paid in Canadian currency, a strong loonie means that your Canadian salary will be higher, relative to the same salary in the United States. Alternatively, if you're paid in U.S. dollars while living in Canada (as you might be for temporary assignments or some consulting projects), you should hope for a weaker Canadian currency so that your greenbacks will buy more north of the border.

WHAT IT COSTS TO LIVE IN CANADA

The following numbers might help in calculating a general budget for life in Canada. They reflect annual household expenditures for the average Canadian family nationwide. Your own costs, naturally, will vary.

Category	Expenditure
Housing	$12,614
Transportation	$9,073
Food	$7,135
Personal insurance payments and pension contributions	$3,921
Recreation	$3,918
Clothing	$2,588
Health care	$1,799
Education	$1,219

Source: Statistics Canada, 2005

HOUSING COSTS

Housing in Canada used to be cheap—at least when compared with similar properties in major U.S. cities. However, in many Canadian markets—particularly the Western cities of Vancouver, Victoria, Calgary, and Edmonton—housing prices have risen significantly since the year 2000, even as the U.S. housing market went into the doldrums. Add that to the exchange rate changes—in 2003, the Canadian dollar was worth roughly U.S.$0.65, but by 2007, the loonie hit parity with the U.S. dollar—and you'll find that the cost of housing in Canada has definitely increased.

However, your housing costs will depend on where in the country you choose to live, since there's significant variation by region. Each of the Prime Living Locations chapters includes information about average rents and home prices.

FOOD COSTS

Statistics Canada reported (as of 2005) that the average Canadian family spends approximately $7,135 per year on food. In general, food costs are slightly higher than this average in the major cities in B.C., Alberta, and Ontario, and slightly below this average in Québec. Overall, food costs in Canada are slightly higher than costs in comparable U.S. cities.

TAXES AND INSURANCE

The average Canadian family pays just under $14,000 per year in personal income taxes, according to Statistics Canada. Your own tax liability will obviously depend on your income level.

Most Americans coming to Canada will be pleasantly surprised by the low costs of health care and other social programs. Comparing out-of-pocket costs for health care in the United States and in Canada, Canadians' expenditures are significantly lower, averaging under $1,800 per year. Canadians also pay much less for insurance of all types than Americans do.

Food costs can be slightly higher in Canada than in the United States.

Purchases in Canada are subject both to a Federal Goods and Services Tax (G.S.T.) and, in most provinces, to an additional provincial sales tax (P.S.T.). As of 2008, the G.S.T. is 5 percent. Canada's P.S.T. rates vary by province, but typically add 7–8 percent to your purchases. The exception is in Alberta, where there's no provincial sales tax.

CLOTHING AND OTHER ESSENTIALS

If your new Canadian home is within driving distance of the U.S. border, you may be surprised to find how often some of your neighbors head across the border to shop. Others plan major shopping excursions for holidays or business trips to the States. Especially when the U.S. dollar is equivalent to or slightly less than the Canadian dollar, it can be much cheaper to buy clothing, books, and housewares in the United States.

Why? A major factor is taxes. Canadian purchases are subject both to the national G.S.T. and to provincial sales taxes. While many U.S. states have a sales tax, there's no corresponding federal sales tax.

Another reason is selection, particularly if you're looking for well-designed, low- to mid-priced goods. Most Canadians—except those in fashionable Montréal, perhaps—will tell you there's simply a better choice of merchandise available in the United States. Target, here we come.

POUNDS, GRAMS, OR BOTH?

You go into a Canadian deli to buy some sliced turkey. Can you ask for a quarter-pound of meat, or do you need to request 100 grams?

Can you buy a pound of fresh peaches from the farmer's market, or is it half a kilo? What about a half-pound of coffee beans from your neighborhood café?

The answer is, "It depends."

Canada converted to the metric system in 1970. Road signs post distances in kilometers, and weather reports give the temperature in Celsius. Your Canadian driver's license will list your height in centimeters and your weight in kilograms. And anything that you buy by weight in the grocery is sold by the gram or the kilo.

In practice, however, anyone who went to school in Canada before the 1970s grew up with the old system. Canadians in their 40s or older often think in pounds and miles, just as most Americans do. Usually, they can go both ways, using metric and imperial units equally well.

It's worth mastering the metric system once you move to Canada. But if you ask for a quarter-pound of turkey, most deli clerks will know what you want – at least if they're over 40.

A third factor is pricing. Go to any clothing retailer that has outlets on both sides of the border—the Gap or Sears, for example. Their base prices in Canada have historically been higher, even taking into account any exchange rate variations.

Most books list two prices, one for the United States and one for Canada. The U.S. price might be $17, the Canadian $24—a far greater disparity than the exchange rate difference would suggest. For one book, it may not matter, but if you're an avid reader or if you're purchasing books for everyone on your holiday gift list, you might want to think about whether buying in the States makes sense.

When the Canadian and U.S. dollars hit roughly equal levels in 2007, Canadians began to be more vocal about these pricing policies. Record numbers of Canadians were shopping in the United States, either by ordering online or by making cross-border shopping excursions. Canadian retailers were beginning to respond with changes to their pricing structures, so by the time you read this, the differences in U.S. and Canadian prices for goods such as books or clothing may have become smaller.

Ordering Online from the United States

If shopping online is part of your regular routine, you may need to alter your shopping patterns once you cross the border. Some U.S. companies won't

Should you shop in Canada or south of the border? It depends.

deliver their products at all outside the 50 states. Others do, including retailers such as Lands' End and L. L. Bean, but you'll face sometimes-hefty taxes and duties on goods coming into Canada from the United States. It's worth calling to ask about your tax liability rather than simply clicking the checkout button.

Some large online shopping sites, notably Amazon, have Canadian affiliates. From Canada, you can shop at Amazon.ca, where goods are priced in Canadian dollars and they're not subject to cross-border duty charges. However, many items sold at Amazon.com in the United States aren't available on Amazon's Canadian site.

Banking

Canada and the United States have parallel but separate banking systems. The structures of both systems are quite similar, but moving between the two systems can be somewhat complicated.

CURRENCY

Canada's currency is called the dollar, and like its U.S. counterpart, it's divided into 100 cents. Canadian bills include five-, ten-, 20-, 50-, 100-, and 1,000-dollar bills. One- and two-dollar currency are coins, which are known as "loonies" (for the picture of the loon on the back of the one-dollar coin) and "toonies" (since they are equal to two loonies). Other coins are in the same denominations as you'd find in the United States: one, five, 10, and 25 cents.

It's easy to exchange U.S. dollars for Canadian currency at commercial banks across Canada. Sometimes, though, you can get a better exchange rate from a currency exchange dealer. You can find dealers in the Yellow Pages or online by searching for your city name and "currency exchange." Shop around for the best rate, especially when you're exchanging large sums. Both banks and currency dealers typically give preferential rates to clients exchanging $10,000 or more.

In major Canadian cities, some businesses will accept U.S. dollars, although the exchange rate may vary from the official rate, and

We can serve you in the following languages:

廣東話
हिन्दी
Italiano
普通话
فارسی
POLSKI
Português

Ⓢ Scotiabank

© CAROLYN B. HELLER

Canada's financial institutions cater to a multicultural population.

you'll get change back in Canadian funds. You're nearly always better off paying in Canadian currency. Most businesses won't accept checks drawn on a U.S. bank.

Over the past 10 years, the exchange rate between U.S. and Canadian dollars has fluctuated significantly. If you had moved to Canada in the late 1990s, it would have cost you only US$0.65 to buy one Canadian dollar. In 2007, the Canada dollar soared in value, at one point hitting US$1.10, its highest level in more than 50 years.

Bank of Canada (www.bankofcanada.ca), the Canadian central bank, publishes the official exchange rate between Canadian dollars and other currencies. Their website also provides historical data about Canadian dollar rates.

OPENING AN ACCOUNT

In Canada, a checking account is known as a "chequing account"; Canadians write cheques, not checks. Canadians frequently refer to Automated Teller Machines (ATMs) as Automated Banking Machines (ABMs).

Except for the slightly different lingo, Canadian banks offer checking and savings accounts that are similar to the products that U.S. banks offer. To open a bank account in Canada, a U.S. citizen needs a passport, as well as at least one of the following Canadian documents: a Canadian driver's license, a

CANADA'S LARGEST BANKS

Canada has 22 domestic banks. The following are the five largest, with offices and ATMs nationwide:

- Royal Bank of Canada
- TD Canada Trust
- Scotiabank
- Bank of Montréal
- CIBC

CAROLYN B. HELLER

TD Canada Trust is one of the country's largest banks.

Canadian Social Insurance Number (SIN), a Canadian permanent residence card, or a Canadian health insurance card.

When you make the initial deposit to your account by check, particularly when you're exchanging and depositing a check from a U.S. financial institution, the bank will usually put a hold on those funds until the check clears. Depending on your bank's policy, the funds may be held for 2–3 weeks.

The Canadian Deposit Insurance Corporation (CDIC) insures deposits of up to $100,000 at commercial banks. CDIC insurance doesn't cover accounts at credit unions, but provincial deposit insurance programs may protect credit union accounts, so be sure to ask.

U.S. Dollar Accounts in Canada

At banks across Canada, you can open Canadian dollar accounts, as you'd expect, but at many financial institutions, you can also open a U.S. dollar account. It's convenient to have a U.S. dollar account locally if you have U.S. dollar income or if you regularly receive or make U.S. dollar payments.

Even when you have a U.S. dollar account at a Canadian bank, however, you can't treat that account the same way that you'd treat a U.S. dollar account in the United States. For example, when you transfer money between that account and a U.S. bank or mutual fund, it's considered an international transfer and subject to potentially high transaction fees—even though it's from one U.S. dollar account to another. Also, these accounts don't offer electronic bill payment services that would allow you to pay U.S. dollar bills. Note, too, that CDIC insurance does not cover U.S. dollar accounts in Canadian banks.

Keeping Accounts in the United States

An alternative (or in addition) to opening a U.S. dollar account in Canada would be to maintain a U.S. bank account in the States. If you have U.S. income, you could send payments to your U.S. bank for deposit, or—even easier—have those payments made electronically. If you expect to have bills to pay regularly in the United States, maintaining a bank account there with an electronic bill payment service will be very convenient. While many Canadian banks offer online bill payment services, these services are for Canadian dollar payments only, so they won't help if you need to pay bills in the United States.

You may find that keeping an account at your existing U.S. bank, but changing the account type to reflect your less-regular access to that account, will be a cost-effective option. For example, if you previously had an account that required a high minimum balance but allowed you to do unlimited transactions at no extra charge, you may find it more cost-effective to change to an account with lower balance requirements that you access occasionally.

CREDIT CARDS

If you have a credit card from one of the major card-issuers based in the United States—Visa, MasterCard, American Express—you can use that card throughout Canada. However, because the card is a U.S.-dollar one, you'll be charged an exchange fee when your Canadian-dollar transactions are converted to U.S. dollars. Before you use your U.S. card in Canada, check with your card issuer to find out what those fees will be.

Using a U.S. credit card in Canada can make sense for a short time—while you're on your fact-finding trip or when you first move over the border. And if you're one of the handful of people who use credit cards only rarely, it may not be a big deal to keep using your U.S. card after you relocate. For most people, however, it's worth applying for a Canadian-dollar credit card as soon as you've settled in Canada.

As in the United States, you can get a Visa or MasterCard at any number of banks. Shop around to compare annual fees, interest rates, and any special benefits, such as annual rebates, credit for airline miles, or insurance for car rentals. Most banks offer credit cards with no annual fee to customers who keep a large balance in their checking or savings accounts.

An alternative to these bank credit cards would be an American Express card. American Express Canada offers a number of credit card options that are denominated in Canadian dollars.

Many expats are surprised to learn that Canadian financial institutions don't consider your U.S. credit history when you're applying for a credit card. The bank may set a very low limit on your credit card or reject your application outright until you have established a credit history in Canada. If you have your salary directly deposited into your checking account and you apply for a credit card from the same bank, they may be willing to increase your credit limit based on your salary amount. Or if you keep a large amount on deposit with that bank, they may be more willing to approve your credit card application.

DEBIT CARDS

According to the Canadian Bankers' Association, more Canadians use automated banking machines and debit card services than anywhere else in the world. Canada has more than 15,000 bank-owned, and more than 35,000 non-bank-owned, ATMs.

The Canadian debit card network is called Interac, and all the major Canadian banks belong to this network. Canadians use debit cards frequently for shopping, dining out, and other purchases for which you might otherwise use cash—it's fast and convenient. Debit cards (which also function as ATM cards) are accepted in over half a million locations across Canada, from local markets to department stores to restaurants.

Canadian banks charge varying fees for ATM and debit card use, depending on the type of account you have and the balances you maintain. For Interac transactions, there's often no fee if you keep a high balance in your checking account, but otherwise fees vary; get details from your bank when you're shopping for the best account. For ATM withdrawals, if you use an ATM that your financial institution doesn't own, you'll typically pay a network access fee of $0.50–1.50 per transaction. And if you use an ATM or cash dispenser in a convenience store, gas station, or other non-bank location, you may be charged an additional "convenience fee" of $1–3 for each transaction. Make sure you clearly understand the potential charges before you begin using your Canadian ATM card.

You can use your ATM card to make deposits to and withdrawals from your Canadian dollar account. Unfortunately, if you have a U.S. dollar account at a Canadian bank, you can't access that account with your Canadian ATM card.

The major Canadian banks belong to either the Cirrus or Plus networks, so when you arrive in Canada, you can continue to use the ATM card from your U.S. bank to withdraw funds (in Canadian dollars) from that U.S. account. Ask your U.S. bank about the fees you'll be charged for using Canadian ATMs.

Taxes

Ah, taxes. The bane of any expat's existence. And unfortunately, the tax situation for U.S. expats in Canada is not a simple one. The bottom line is that as an American citizen living in Canada, you must file income tax returns in both countries.

On the plus side, Canada and the United States have a tax treaty that's designed to prevent double taxation. While you still have to file both U.S. and Canadian tax returns, this treaty means that you can claim a credit on each country's return for the tax you pay in the other country. That is, on your U.S. return, you can claim a credit for income tax you pay in Canada; on your Canadian return, you can claim credit for taxes you pay in the United States.

Canada's version of the Internal Revenue Service (IRS) is the Canada Revenue Agency (CRA). Their website (www.cra-arc.gc.ca) has all the details about Canadian tax obligations. They also publish a useful online tax guide for newcomers to Canada.

CANADIAN TAXES

Anyone working in Canada—or with "residential ties" to Canada—must file Canadian income tax returns, both federal and provincial. Among the factors that give you "residential ties" are having a home in Canada, a Canadian driver's license, a Canadian bank account or credit card, or Canadian health insurance. You may have to file a Canadian tax return even if you live in Canada for only part of the year; refer to the Canada Revenue Agency website for details.

On your Canadian income tax returns, you have to report your "world income"—your income from all sources both inside and outside of Canada.

As in the United States, the rate of income tax that you pay depends on your income. For Canadian federal taxes, there are four tax brackets, which (for 2008) range from 15 percent on the first $37,885 of taxable income up to 29 percent on taxable income over $123,184. (For comparison, the top tax rates in the United States are 33 percent on incomes above $150,000 and 35 percent on incomes over $326,000.)

In addition to federal income tax, you have to pay provincial income tax. Provincial tax rates vary, from about 5 percent up to 18 percent, and in most cases, the rate you pay depends on your income. You can get specific details for each province from the Canada Revenue Agency.

There's no such thing as a "joint return" for married people in Canada. Each person must file his/her own individual tax returns.

Canadian tax returns must be filed annually before April 30. You must include your Canadian social insurance number (SIN) on your tax return. If you've applied for a SIN but haven't received it when the tax deadline is approaching, file your return without a SIN and include a note explaining the situation. Otherwise, you may be charged a penalty for late filing as well as interest on any taxes due.

Canadian employers deduct taxes from your paycheck, just like they do in the United States. You must also pay estimated taxes during the year if your expected tax liability is greater than the amount deducted from your pay.

U.S. TAXES

U.S. citizens who live outside the United States must continue to file U.S. federal tax returns, and Americans living in Canada are no exception.

During the year that you move to Canada, you must in most cases file both U.S. federal and state tax returns, as well as Canadian federal and provincial returns. Fortunately, in subsequent years, you don't have to file a U.S. state tax return unless you continue to have earned income in the state where you previously lived.

GETTING TAX ADVICE

The easiest way to sort out your tax obligations is to work with an accountant who specializes in cross-border tax situations and who can prepare, or advise you about, your tax returns for both countries. Even if you haven't worked with an accountant or tax preparer in the past, it may be helpful to consult a professional for at least your first year in Canada. You'll find them in most major Canadian cities. Refer to the *Resources* chapter or ask colleagues or friends for referrals once you arrive in Canada.

To authorize an accountant, tax preparer, or other professional to prepare your tax returns, you must complete Form T1013 and return it to the Canada Revenue Agency. Your accountant can provide you with this form; it's also available online from the CRA.

Whether or not you work with an accountant, get familiar with the Canada Revenue Agency website. While it may not be the most scintillating reading, it has lots of helpful details about the tax obligations of newcomers to Canada.

Investing

Between 1999 and 2005, the net worth of the average Canadian household increased roughly 30 percent, fueled by a growing economy and a thriving real estate market. So where do Canadians invest their money?

Canadians' investment options parallel the choices available in the United

States. Some put their money in the bank or in money market accounts. Many invest in real estate or in Canada's stock market, either directly or through mutual funds, or in bonds. Canada also has a retirement account program that's similar to the U.S. Individual Retirement Accounts (IRAs).

As an American living in Canada, you'll need to consider whether to invest in Canadian financial products, keep your funds in the United States, or both.

© CAROLYN B. HELLER

CANADIAN MARKETS

Canada's major equities market is the Toronto Stock Exchange (TSX). Established in 1861, the TSX (www. tsx.com) has grown to become the world's seventh-largest exchange group. The TSX lists a diversified range of businesses, including a significant number of mining, oil, and gas companies.

the former Stock Exchange building in downtown Toronto

Types of Investments

You can buy stocks in the TSX through Canadian brokerage firms. You can also invest in Canadian mutual funds. Compared to U.S. mutual funds, however, many Canadian mutual funds have high management expense ratios (MERs)— the percent of a fund's assets that cover the maintenance of the fund. High MERs can reduce your overall profit, so do your research before you invest.

Canadian banks offer interest-bearing accounts, including savings accounts and various time deposits. Canadian money market funds typically offer higher interest rates than the banks, but they aren't covered by Canadian Deposit Insurance Corporation (CDIC) insurance.

Canadian government savings bonds are yet another option. Details about the program are online at www.csb.gc.ca.

Retirement Savings

Canada has a Registered Retirement Savings Plan (RRSP) program that's similar to Individual Retirement Accounts (IRAs) in the United States. Any income you

THE RICHEST CANADIANS

Are Americans richer than Canadians? Statistics Canada reported that the top 5 percent of tax-filing families in 2004 had an income of at least $154,000. In the U.S., the 5 percent threshold was only slightly higher at $165,000.

However, when you compare average income for the two countries' wealthiest individuals, the differences are pretty huge. The richest Americans are much wealthier than the richest Canadians. In Canada, the average income for the top 5 percent of families was $296,000; in the United States, it was 40 percent higher at $416,000.

Still, there are plenty of moneyed folks in Canada. Here are the 10 richest:

Rank	Name	Net Worth	Industry/Business
1	The Thompson Family	$25.35 billion	Media/Thompson-Reuters
2	Edward (Ted) Rogers Jr.	$7.6 billion	Telecom/Rogers Communications
3	Galen Weston	$7.27 billion	Groceries/Loblaw
4	Paul Desmarais Sr.	$5.64 billion	Utilities/The Power Corp.
5	The Irving Family	$5.3 billion	Multiple (Media, Forestry, Retail, Trucking, Energy)
6	James (Jimmy) Pattison	$4.52 billion	Multiple/The Jim Pattison Group
7	Jeff Skoll	$4.48 billion	Technology/eBay's first employee
8	Michael Lazaridis	$4.36 billion	Technology/Research in Motion
9	James Balsillie	$4.09 billion	Technology/Research in Motion
10	Bernard (Barry) Sherman	$3.61 billion	Pharmaceuticals/Apotex Inc.

Source: Canadian Business, *November 30, 2007*

earn from your RRSP is tax-exempt until you withdraw from or cash in the plan. The amount that you can contribute to an RRSP in a given year is based on your income. You can make contributions to an RRSP until you reach age 71.

You can maintain your existing IRA or 401K accounts in the United States after you move to Canada, and you can open an RRSP in addition.

Banks, brokerages, and other financial institutions offer RRSPs. You can get more details about the RRSP program from the Canada Revenue Agency. Before opening an RRSP, it's also a good idea to consult an accountant or other tax adviser who specializes in cross-border investment and taxation issues.

THE 10 MOST PROFITABLE CANADIAN COMPANIES

The 10 most profitable Canadian companies in 2007 were all in one of two industries – oil and gas or financial services:

Rank	Company	Industry	Head office
1	EnCana Corp.	Oil, gas & consumable fuels	Calgary
2	Royal Bank of Canada	Commercial banking	Toronto
3	Toronto-Dominion Bank	Commercial banking	Toronto
4	Manulife Financial Corp.	Insurance	Toronto
5	Bank of Nova Scotia	Commercial banking	Toronto
6	Imperial Oil Ltd.	Oil, gas & consumable fuels	Calgary
7	Suncor Energy Inc.	Oil, gas & consumable fuels	Calgary
8	Husky Energy Inc.	Oil, gas & consumable fuels	Calgary
9	Bank of Montréal	Commercial banking	Toronto
10	Canadian Natural Resources, Ltd.	Oil, gas & consumable fuels	Calgary

Source: Canadian Business, 2007

CANADIAN COMPANIES AND INDUSTRIES

To learn more about Canadian businesses, good sources of information include the business sections of the *Globe and Mail* and *National Post* newspapers, *Canadian Business* magazine, the Business News Network (www.bnn.ca), and *Enterprise* magazine (www.enterprisemag.com) focusing on small and mid-sized companies. There are also publications covering particular regions and industries, including *BC Business* (www.bcbusinessmagazine.com) and *Alberta Venture* (www.albertaventure.com).

KEEPING YOUR U.S. INVESTMENTS

If you have U.S.-based mutual fund investments, you need to find out how a move to Canada could affect those holdings. Some U.S. mutual funds require that investors have a U.S. address; in some cases, you can meet this requirement by maintaining a U.S. post office box. Some U.S. mutual funds don't allow you to log in electronically to your account from a location outside the United States, but you may be able to deal with them over the phone. Contact your mutual fund companies for details, and seek advice from an accountant or tax advisor.

COMMUNICATIONS

When you head north to Canada, it will be easy to stay connected to family, friends, and colleagues back home.

The Canadian phone system—both landline and cell service—is similar in structure to U.S. phone services. The providers may be different, and the service options a bit baffling (as they can be in the United States), but you'll have ready access to just about any type of telephone service you might need.

Similarly, Internet and postal mail services resemble the services you'll leave behind across the border. While you'll need to get acquainted with some new providers, new rates, and of course, new stamps, the services overall will be familiar.

One of the biggest communications changes for U.S. expats in Canada may be the Canadian media. It's possible to get many U.S. TV shows, newspapers, and magazines in Canada, but you'll quickly get to know the Canadian media, too. From national and local newspapers, magazines, radio stations, and TV networks, to the publicly funded Canadian Broadcasting

Corporation, which operates TV and radio stations nationwide, Canada has its own thriving media scene.

Telephone Service

Americans moving to Canada will find phone service quite similar to service in the United States. Just a few things you should know:

To make a local phone call in many major Canadian cities, including Vancouver, Montréal, and Toronto, dial the complete 10-digit number—with the area code.

Canada has 911 emergency services from all major cities and most smaller municipalities. Dial 911 to reach police, fire, or other emergency services.

Dial 411 for local directory assistance or 1-(Area Code)-555-1212 for long-distance information. Many Canadian cities have online phone directories, too.

In Toronto, Calgary, and Edmonton, you can dial 211 for access to non-emergency community, social, health and government services. The 211 project is hoping to make 211 information services available nationwide over the next several years.

Canadian toll-free numbers begin with 1-800, 1-888, 1-877, or 1-866, just as they do in the United States. However, a U.S. toll-free number may not work from Canada, and vice versa.

LAND LINES

Although an increasing number of Canadians use cell phones when they're out and about, few have given up their landline service at home.

When you sign up for residential telephone service, the phone company may ask for a deposit equal to several months' charges if you don't have a credit history in Canada. After that period has elapsed—and assuming you pay your bills—the company will return your deposit or credit it toward future charges.

Bring your home telephones with you from the United States. You can plug them into your new Canadian residence and use them once your phone service is activated.

Phone Companies

Not all Canadian phone companies operate in every province, so you'll need to figure out who to call in the province where you'll be living. Major companies offering residential phone services include Bell Canada (BC, AB, ON, QC), Rogers Communications (BC, AB, ON, QC), Shaw (BC, AB, ON), and Telus (ON, QC). Smaller providers operate in local markets as well.

© CAROLYN B. HELLER

Getting your phone connected doesn't usually take too long.

Domestic Rates

For residential landline service, expect to pay a monthly charge of about $25–40, including unlimited local calling. Some companies bundle in services such as voicemail or call waiting. A typical residential package might offer domestic long-distance calling for an extra $0.04–0.07 per minute.

Alternatively, for domestic long-distance calls, you can buy a monthly plan that includes a certain number of long-distance minutes. For unlimited domestic long-distance, expect to pay around $20–25.

Some phone companies also offer Internet and/or cable TV service. Look for bundles that include one or more of these services at a discounted rate.

U.S. Rates

Remember that calling from Canada to the United States is not a domestic call. But because it's quite common for Canadians to phone the States, many companies offer special long-distance rates to the United States, as well as "North America" rate plans that let you call anywhere in Canada or the United States. A North America plan is cost-effective when you'll frequently be making calls to the United States.

Other International Rates

If you regularly call a particular international location—say, China or the U.K.—shop around to find the best prices to that destination. Sometimes, you simply pay a per-minute rate, while sometimes you might be offered a small monthly fee plus a lower per-minute rate on calls to a specified country or region.

You can also buy pre-paid calling cards for certain international destinations, which are sometimes cheaper than the rate you can get from your landline provider. You can buy calling cards at convenience stores, supermarkets, and many other locations. Again, it's worth shopping around for the best rate if you'll be calling a particular country frequently.

Internet-based phone services, including Skype and Vonage, operate in Canada. You can often save a significant amount of money on international calls by using one of these services.

CELLULAR PHONES

Cellular phone service is firmly established in Canada. The Canadian Wireless Telecommunications Association reported in 2007 that 80 percent of the population in Canada's largest cities was using wireless phones. Nearly half of all Canadian phone calls nationwide are wireless.

Some Canadian cellular companies offer CDMA technology, while others use GSM. If you intend to use your phone extensively for overseas travel, you might consider a GSM phone in Canada. Otherwise, for domestic or North American usage, either technology is fine; choose a service based on the other options that best meet your calling needs.

The challenge is figuring out which service will match your calling patterns. Canadian cell companies offer an absurdly complicated set of plans that seem designed to thwart comparison shopping.

As in the United States, you can choose from contract or pre-paid usage options. For limited usage, a pre-paid plan may be less expensive, but for average to high usage, a monthly contract will likely be cheaper. Contract terms typically run 1–3 years.

In 2007, Canada became the second country in the world (after the United States) to support "wireless number portability." That is, once you have a cell phone number in Canada, you can keep that number even if you change wireless service providers, as long as you stay in the same metropolitan area. If you start out with service from one carrier, and later determine that another provider has a better plan for your needs, you won't have to worry about changing your cell number.

Phone Companies

Canada has several national cell phone brands, plus regional providers that operate in particular areas. Although there may be new options by the time you read this, the major brands include Bell Canada, Rogers Wireless, Telus, Virgin Mobile, and Fido. Other companies, such as 7-Eleven, also sell phones

© CAROLYN B. HELLER

checking for phone messages in Toronto's Distillery District

with pre-paid calling cards. Ask colleagues or your new neighbors what services they recommend in your area.

Domestic Rates

A 2007 study by the SeaBoard Group, a Canadian technology strategy company, found that heavy users of cell phone services in Canada—defined as those using an average of 1,200 minutes a month—pay roughly 50 percent more than users pay for equivalent services in the United States. Average cell users pay about a third more than they'd pay for similar services in the United States. On the other hand, light users—Canadians who use their cell phones minimally, primarily for emergencies or to speak briefly with family members—pay about 25 percent less than they'd pay for comparable service in the United States.

In 2008, basic monthly plans in Canada started at about $20 a month, which typically includes 150–200 minutes that you can use anytime within your local calling area. For around $50 a month, you might get 500 minutes, plus unlimited night and weekend calling, and of course, there are plans that include far more time for high-volume users.

Other plans might give you fewer minutes to use during the day, but lots of talk time at night and on weekends, or unlimited incoming calls but fewer outgoing minutes. Most carriers also offer shared plans where two or more family members split a pool of minutes. If you'll be traveling frequently across Canada, look at national plans that provide unlimited service nationwide without roaming charges. You'll need to set aside some time to figure out all the options.

On top of the regular monthly fee, cell phone carriers charge a monthly "system access fee" of $7–9. You'll usually pay a monthly charge ($0.50–0.75) for 911 access as well. Federal and provincial taxes add another 7–14 percent to your bill, depending on where you live.

For low-volume users, pre-paid minutes may be a less expensive way to go. You pay a relatively high per-minute charge—usually $0.20–0.30—but there's no monthly fee. Check the expiration date on the minutes you buy, since with some companies, the unused time expires within a few months.

Mobile phone companies frequently run promotions, so watch for specials. Always ask for a better rate, extra minutes, or other discounts, too.

U.S. Rates

If you expect to use your cell phone regularly to call the United States, or if you'll be traveling frequently to the United States and want to make calls while you're there, your choice of a phone plan becomes somewhat more complex. On most standard Canadian plans, calling the United States from your Canadian home region will incur long-distance charges, and calling from the United States will mean large roaming bills.

Some carriers offer North American rate plans, which allow you to use your phone anywhere in the United States and Canada without roaming or long-distance fees. You pay a larger monthly charge, but you don't have to worry about getting slapped with an unexpectedly large long-distance or roaming bill. For example, in several provinces, Telus offers a "Talk North America" plan that in 2008 included up to 400 minutes anywhere in Canada or the United States for a base fee of $100 a month. For comparison, Telus' similar 400-minute plan— for nationwide calls within Canada only—started at $50 a month.

Alternatively, if you'll be spending a lot of time in the United States and need to use your cell phone extensively, you may find that it's cheaper to keep a separate U.S. phone. With some plans, you may be able to forward your Canadian number to your U.S. phone when you're south of the border. But be sure you won't pay expensive long-distance charges for the forwarded calls, and calculate whether having two separate phones is worth the expense and the hassle.

Other International Rates

The international wireless market is changing rapidly, so talk to various providers about their options if international calling is important to you. For international travel, GSM phones may give you more options, if you can replace your Canadian SIM card with local ones in the countries you'll be visiting. International calling cards are also worth investigating.

Internet and Postal Service

INTERNET

Many of the same national companies that provide telephone services also offer Internet service. Numerous local companies deliver Internet services in particular provinces as well. Ask around for recommendations once you arrive in Canada.

High-speed cable and DSL services are available across Canada. You can usually get Internet service installed within a few days, particularly if you're moving into a house or apartment that's already wired for access.

An average high-speed Internet service will cost around $30–50 a month, depending on the speed, number of email addresses included, your location, and many other variables. Expect to pay a one-time installation charge as well. Many providers offer sign-up incentives, such as a lower price for the first three months, or bundle Internet and cable TV service for a reduced rate, so always ask about promotions or other discounts.

If you need to get online before your own service is installed, you can find Internet cafés and hotel business centers with Internet access in all major Canadian cities. Wireless access is increasingly common nationwide, and many coffee shops offer free access. Many public libraries offer free Internet connections as well, although you may have to apply for a library card before you get online.

POSTAL SERVICE AND COURIERS
Canada Post

Canada's answer to the U.S. Postal Service is Canada Post. Regular mail between the United States and Canada takes anywhere from a few days to more than a week, depending on its origin and destination.

In Canada, there's no such thing as a zip code; the Canadian equivalent is a postal code. Canadian addresses have a six-character postal code that's an alternating combination of letters and numbers. You can look up postal codes online on the Canada Post website.

Canada Post sells three types of stamps: one for letters to destinations within Canada, another for letters from Canada to the United States, and a third for international mail (from Canada to other countries). As of 2008, domestic stamps cost $0.52, stamps for U.S. letters were $0.96, and other international letters cost $1.60.

For domestic mail, you can also buy "permanent" stamps. They're sold at whatever the current domestic rate is, and you can continue to use them even when postal rates rise.

MY POST OFFICE IS IN THE 7-ELEVEN

Canada Post maintains offices across Canada. Sometimes, they're stand-alone facilities, similar to the post offices you find throughout the United States. But there are also postal outlets in a variety of retail locations, from convenience stores to stationery shops to local markets.

The advantage to using these retail stations is that they keep longer hours than the regular post offices. If you want to buy stamps on Sunday afternoon or send a package on Wednesday at 10 P.M., head for a convenience store postal outlet.

Canada Post's website lists addresses and hours for both standard post offices and retail postal stations. You can search by postal code or street address to find the outlet nearest you.

Forwarding Your Mail

The U.S. postal service will forward mail to Canadian addresses. Fill out a Change of Address form at your local U.S. post office before you move. You cannot use their online Change of Address form to have your mail redirected to Canada.

If you'll have a temporary address when you first relocate to Canada, or if you expect to be moving more than once within the same city, consider renting a post office box in your new Canadian community and having your mail forwarded there. That way, you won't have to keep changing your forwarding address. You can rent a small P.O. box for three, six, or 12 months for $45, $81, or $121 respectively; prices are slightly higher in central Toronto and downtown Vancouver.

If you do move and need to forward your mail within Canada, fill out a forwarding form on Canada Post's website or in your local Canadian post office. Canada Post charges a fee for forwarding mail within the same province of $36 for six months or $65 for a year. There's also a fee to have the post office hold your mail while you're out of town ($6.50 per week, with a two-week minimum).

Keeping a U.S. Post Office Box

Some U.S. expats find it convenient to keep a mailing address in the United States. If you'll be living relatively close to the U.S. border, one way to maintain a U.S. address is to rent a post office box just south of the border. South of Vancouver, for example, the tiny town of Blaine, Washington, has several mailbox outlets. These companies typically receive packages, which can be convenient for receiving orders from U.S. companies, since some shippers won't deliver, or charge significantly more for, goods to Canada. Just remember that you're liable for duties on those goods when you bring them across the border.

You can also use a U.S. P.O. box as the mailing address for a U.S. credit card, which can be handy to have if you travel frequently in the States or do a lot of online shopping. Some U.S. mutual fund companies also require that you have a U.S. mailing address to maintain your investments there.

If you do opt to keep a U.S. P.O. box, remember that you'll have to cross the border to pick up the mail, so use the box only for items that aren't time-critical. For example, if your credit card statements go to this address, arrange to get your bills online, too.

Shipping Options

Canada Post ships parcels within Canada, to the United States, and internationally. Their website lets you calculate the cost and delivery times for different shipping methods. Other familiar international carriers operate in Canada as well, including FedEx, UPS, DHL, and Purolator.

When you ship packages between Canada and the United States, you must fill out a customs form, noting the contents of the shipment and its approximate value.

When your family or friends send you gifts from the United States, they also have to complete a customs form. Beware: You may have to pay duty on the declared value of the items. Similarly, if business associates send packages of documents or computer media, make sure they specify that the goods have a nominal value of $1 and that they're not for resale; otherwise, you may be surprised at the duties you're charged when those packages arrive at your Canadian door.

Media

NEWSPAPERS

Canada has two newspapers that consider themselves national publications. The *Globe and Mail,* which styles itself as the country's *New York Times,* is published in Toronto and distributed nationwide. The more conservative *National Post* is also available across Canada.

Besides these two national papers, Toronto has two other dailies: the *Toronto Star,* which bills itself as Canada's largest daily, and the tabloid *Toronto Sun.* A single company, CanWest Global Communications, which owns the *National Post,* also controls the daily papers in many Canadian metropolises, including Vancouver's two dailies—the *Vancouver Sun* and the tabloid-style *Province,* the English-language *Montréal Gazette,* the *Ottawa Citizen,* the *Calgary Herald,* and the *Edmonton Journal.*

All the major Canadian cities have alternative papers that cover the arts and entertainment scene and offer alternative political coverage. In Toronto, look for *Eye Weekly* and *NOW,* and in Vancouver the *Georgia Straight.* Montréal has two English-language alt-papers: the *Mirror* and *Hour.* You'll also find the *Ottawa XPress, FFWD (Fast Forward Weekly)* in Calgary, and *Vue Weekly* in Edmonton.

© CAROLYN B. HELLER

All the major Canadian cities have alternative papers covering arts and entertainment.

All these newspapers have Internet versions, so you can begin reading up on your new community before you leave the United States. And if you're afraid you'll have to give up your *New York Times* fix north of the border, don't worry—the *Times* has home-delivery service in most Canadian cities. It's available online and on the newsstand as well.

MAGAZINES

Popular Canadian general-interest magazines include *Macleans,* a news magazine in the *Time/Newsweek* mold, and *The Walrus,* which some consider to be a Canadian version of *The Atlantic* or perhaps the *New Yorker.* For an introduction to your new community, pick up one of Canada's glossy city and regional magazines: *Toronto Life, Ottawa Magazine, Vancouver Magazine, Avenue* (Calgary), or *Western Living.*

Where Magazine is oriented to tourists—you'll find its city-specific editions in hotel rooms nationwide—but it's useful for getting to know what's happening in your new community. *Canadian Geographic* and *Canadian Geographic Travel* can acquaint you with the Canadian outdoors. For a more extensive list of magazines, refer to the Canadian Magazine Publishers website (www.cmpa.ca).

Many U.S. publications, including *Time, Newsweek,* and *Consumer Reports,* produce Canadian editions. You can also buy most U.S. magazines in any Canadian city. If you subscribe to lots of U.S. magazines, however, you may have to increase your budget. Magazines that offer a year's subscription in the United States for $10 or $15 typically charge $25 or $30 in Canada.

TELEVISION

In Canada, you'll still be able to tune in to most of your favorite TV programs. Canadian channels broadcast U.S. shows, and with cable TV service, you can pick up many specialty programs from the United States, from food to science to reality TV. But you'll get a heavy dose of Canadian programming as well.

The Canadian Broadcasting Corporation's CBC TV is the country's national public television network, analogous to PBS in the United States. CBC TV broadcasts news, sports, and entertainment programs, with a significant Canadian focus.

CTV, which describes itself as Canada's largest private broadcaster, and Global TV both offer local and national news, sports, and entertainment programming, too. And as in the United States, there are many other specialty networks.

RADIO

Canada's equivalent of National Public Radio is CBC Radio, a publicly funded national radio service that was launched in the 1930s. You can pick up CBC stations across Canada or listen on the Internet.

CBC Radio One broadcasts primarily news and talk programs, with a mix of local, regional, and national content. CBC Radio 2 is Canada's national music network; it has a strong classical emphasis but has increasingly been adding more jazz and contemporary music. CBC Radio 3, available as an Internet podcast and via satellite, plays exclusively Canadian music, from rock and pop to electronica and hip-hop, from new and emerging artists.

CBC also has a French-language service available across the country. And beyond the CBC, Canada has a large spectrum of commercial radio stations that broadcast music, talk, and news.

CANADIAN CONTENT LAWS

Canada's broadcasting laws require that a certain percentage of each TV network's or radio station's programming be devoted to "Canadian" content.

Television networks must ensure that at least 60 percent of its programs are Canadian. On the radio, at least 35 percent of the popular music that all stations play each week must be Canadian as well.

DAILY LIFE

CAN I LISTEN TO NPR?

Is listening to National Public Radio (NPR) part of your regular commuting routine? You'll have to adapt to a different radio culture once you move to Canada. You may be able to pick up an NPR station close to the U.S. border, but in most cities, you can't get NPR.

The good news is that you can listen to NPR and other U.S. stations over the Internet or via podcast. Some expats download podcasts from U.S. radio stations to their MP3 players to listen on the go. While it's not as easy as tuning your car radio to "Morning Edition" or "All Things Considered," you can still stay connected to U.S. news and commentary.

For basic cable TV service, the government mandates that certain Canadian programming be included—CBC's English and French network services, local and regional stations, provincial educational services, and a community channel. Cable companies typically provide access to other Canadian services and to the major U.S. networks.

What does it mean for a TV show to be "Canadian?" The government defines a program as Canadian if the producer and key creative personnel are Canadian and at least 75 percent of "service costs and post-production lab costs" are paid to Canadians.

For music, the government has a system called MAPL. To qualify as Canadian, a recording must meet at least two of the MAPL criteria: the M (music) is composed entirely by a Canadian, the performing A (artist) is Canadian, the P (production) is Canadian (that is, the music was recorded in Canada), or the L (lyrics) were written entirely by a Canadian.

Despite these regulations, you'll find plenty of American TV shows as you click through the channels, and U.S. performers get lots of air time in Canada. But at least you'll have a chance to get to know some Canadian programming as well.

TRAVEL AND TRANSPORTATION

Remember that old story, set in rural Maine, called "Which Way to Millinocket?" Maybe you know it by its punch line: You can't get there from here.

If that story were set in today's Canada, however, the end of the tale would be different. Canada has a modern, well-developed transportation network that includes air, rail, bus, and ferry services. Canadian, U.S., and international airlines connect Canadian cities to destinations in the United States and around world, and from the United States, if you prefer, you can travel to Canada by train or bus.

Once you've arrived in Canada, what's the major challenge in getting around? It's a big country, and distances between many locations are vast. Plenty of rural places remain hard to reach, but it's easy to get between the major Canadian cities.

Public transportation has long been a civic priority in Canadian urban areas, and the country's prime living locations generally have excellent transit options. Many Toronto, Montréal, and Vancouver residents don't own cars

© CAROLYN B. HELLER

TRANSPORTATION

(or rarely use them to commute to work), and in more car-centric cities, such as Ottawa, Calgary, and Edmonton, it's still possible to get around by public transit. Even in smaller cities, such as Victoria or Québec City, plenty of people take the bus.

If you need a car, you'll be happy to know that Canadian driving laws, with minor exceptions, are quite similar to those in the United States. You'll need to adjust to measuring your speed in kilometers and buying gas by the liter, but most traffic rules will be familiar. The main challenge may come if you're headed for Québec, where you'll need to learn enough French to decipher the road signs. But overall, you can get there from here.

Air Travel

Air Canada is Canada's national airline. It provides service throughout the country, to many U.S. cities, and to destinations around the world. Air Canada Jazz, a regional subsidiary owned by Air Canada, also flies between many Canadian cities and between Canada and several U.S. destinations.

Toronto is a hub for scores of flights between Canada and international cities in the United States, the Caribbean, Latin America, Europe, and, to a lesser degree, in Asia. Montréal is a similar hub city, with more flight options to France and other francophone destinations. Vancouver is a base for travel to the Pacific Rim, with direct flights to cities across Asia, including Beijing, Shanghai, Hong Kong, Tokyo, and Seoul, among others. All three cities have plenty of flights to the United States as well, as do cities such as Ottawa and Calgary.

Most of the major U.S. airlines provide service to Canada, including Alaska, American, Delta, Continental, Northwest, United, and U.S. Airways. Unlike the United States, however, Canada does not have numerous "legacy" airlines, besides Air Canada. Nor are there many discount or alternative carriers.

WestJet, which is headquartered in Calgary, has service between many Canadian cities and offers fares that are competitive with, and often cheaper than, Air Canada on many routes. They also fly between Canadian cities and "sun" destinations, including Hawaii, Florida, Los Angeles, Palm Springs, Las Vegas, and Phoenix. WestJet flights do not show up on all the Internet booking sites, so go to their website directly to make your travel plans.

Zoom Airlines, based in Ottawa, flies to London, Paris, and several U.K. destinations, from major Canadian cities.

Montréal-based Air Transat, which bills itself as "the Vacation Airline," has regular and charter service between Canada and Mexico, the Caribbean, and some European destinations.

AIR TRAVEL BETWEEN MAJOR CANADIAN CITIES

Prices for airline tickets can vary widely, and the prices shown here (in Canadian dollars) should be considered very rough guidelines as airline prices are constantly changing. Times, too, are approximate.

Cities	Flight time	Round-trip price
Toronto-Montréal	1.25 hours	$150-250
Vancouver-Calgary	1.25 to 1.5 hours	$200-450
Toronto-Edmonton	3.5 to 4 hours	$500-800
Ottawa-Calgary	4 to 4.5 hours	$475-900
Vancouver-Toronto	4.5 to 5 hours	$475-950
Montréal-Vancouver	4.5 to 5 hours	$475-950

Founded in 2006 and catering to the business traveler, Porter Airlines flies from Toronto City Centre Airport to Montréal, Ottawa, Québec City, Halifax, and Newark, New Jersey.

ONLINE BOOKING SERVICES

Many of the same online booking services that operate in the United States also operate in Canada, either directly or through a Canadian affiliate. Both Travelocity and Expedia have Canadian affiliates. If you type "Travelocity" or "Expedia" into your browser from a location within Canada, the sites will either default to the Canadian site or ask you to confirm whether you are in Canada. Prices on the Canadian affiliate sites are quoted in Canadian dollars. These sites also expect that you have a Canadian billing address.

You can access other airline search and booking sites, such as Orbitz, Kayak, and ITA Software, from either the United States or Canada. When you are price-shopping, just be aware that these sites quote prices in U.S. dollars.

Online booking sites that are based in Canada, including Flight Centre and Flight Network, are also worth checking. The meta-search engine Booking Buddy provides links to both U.S. and Canadian options, which can be useful when you are comparing prices.

For sites such as Travelocity that have both U.S. and Canadian affiliates, you might want to check both versions to see if there are differences in fares. One area in which the two versions of these sites diverge can be in their last-minute air-hotel packages. Sometimes a package may be offered on the U.S. site that's not available on the Canadian version, and vice versa.

However, you have to have a credit card with a U.S. billing address to book from the U.S.-based sites.

Because there are fewer airlines within Canada than in the United States, airfares can be higher north of the border than flights of comparable distance in the United States. For example, it's difficult to find fares between New York and Vancouver for less than $500–600, while New York to Seattle fares frequently dip under US$350. If you're flying to a Canadian city that's near a U.S. gateway, you can often find cheaper fares by flying within the United States. Try flights to Seattle if you're headed for Vancouver, to Buffalo if your destination is Toronto, or to Burlington, Vermont, if you're going to Montréal. However, it's not a short drive from any of these cities, and you have to allow extra time for crossing the border. It may be worth it only if several people are traveling together or if you're flying at a peak time when fares are unusually high.

SECURITY AND CUSTOMS REGULATIONS

Most of the air travel security procedures and restrictions that are in effect in the United States also apply in Canada. The limits on traveling with liquids that the United States imposed in 2006 affect Canadians as well, although they are expressed in metric terms (100 milliliters or 100 grams), rather than the three-ounce U.S. rule.

If you're flying from the United States to Canada, you have to clear Canadian Customs and Immigration at the first point where you land in Canada. If you have a connecting flight, say from New York to Vancouver via Toronto, you have to clear customs in Toronto before you board your Vancouver-bound connection. When you're booking a flight with a connection, be sure to allow sufficient time to pass through immigration; online booking systems may permit you to book a tighter connection than is reasonable, given potential immigration delays.

Flying to the United States from most Canadian cities, in contrast, you must pass through U.S. Customs and Immigration *at your departure airport in Canada,* not when you arrive back in the United States. So if you're flying from Montréal to Boston, you have to clear U.S. customs at the Montréal Airport before boarding your flight to Boston. Again, be sure to arrive at the airport early enough for immigration proceedings. Because the time required can vary with the current security situation, check with your airline before departure for up-to-date guidelines.

Once you are living in Canada, you have to abide by Canadian Customs' rules on what you can bring back to the country. If you leave Canada for 24

HOLIDAY IN HAVANA?

Walk past the window of most Canadian travel agents, and next to the promotions for sun-and-fun holidays in Cancun, Jamaica, and the Dominican Republic, you'll likely see ads for trips to Cuba. And if you're from the United States, these ads may cause you to do a double-take.

Unlike the United States, which severely limits its citizens' ability to travel to Cuba, Canada has no such travel restrictions. If you have a Canadian passport, you can holiday in Havana (or tour other nations, such as North Korea, that are off-limits to U.S. citizens). If you're a U.S. citizen living in Canada, however, you are still subject to the U.S. travel restrictions.

Cuban products are legal in Canada, so if you travel abroad, you can bring back Cuban cigars. You'll also find Cuban cigars and other products for sale in Canadian cities. Just remember – if you're bringing gifts for U.S.-based friends – that these items are not legal in the United States.

hours or less, any goods you buy and bring back to Canada can be taxed. If you are out of the country for 24–48 hours, you may bring back goods worth up to CAD$50. Any more than $50, and you'll be subject to duties—something to keep in mind if you're making a quick shopping trip across the border. If you're out of Canada for at least 48 hours, you can bring back items worth up to CAD$400 without paying duties or taxes. And if you leave Canada for at least seven days, you may bring back up to CAD$750 of stuff duty-free. The CAD$50 limit does not include alcohol or tobacco, but the longer stays do; you're allowed to bring back to Canada up to 1.14 liters (40 ounces) of liquor, 1.5 liters (two standard 750-milliliter bottles) of wine, or a case of 24 bottles or cans of beer. Smokers can bring back up to 200 cigarettes or 50 cigars. These rules do change, however, so get the latest information from the Canada Border Services Agency.

Trains

Crossing Canada by rail, particularly through the Canadian Rockies, is an iconic train journey that lures thousands of tourists every year. Yet it's also possible to travel by train to and around Canada more for transportation than for the landscapes.

Via Rail is Canada's national passenger rail service, which runs railroads across the country.

If your goal is speed, rather than scenery, rail travel makes more sense in the East—between Toronto and Ottawa, or between Montréal and Québec

City, for example—where distances between major cities are shorter, than it does in the wide-open West. You can travel from Toronto to Ottawa by train in 4–4.5 hours and between Toronto and Montréal in 4.5–5 hours. Montréal to Ottawa is under two hours, and Montréal–Québec City takes about three hours. By contrast, the rail journey from Vancouver to Edmonton takes about 23 hours. Fares on the shorter Eastern routes are also cheaper than, or at least competitive with, flights, but in the West, you may pay a premium to take the train.

You can buy Via Rail tickets online, where you can also look up schedule and routing information.

Via Rail, Canada's national passenger railroad, crosses the country.

© CAROLYN B. HELLER

Discounts are available for advance purchases, children, students, and seniors. If you'll be taking the train a lot, look into commuter passes or other rail pass options.

U.S.-based Amtrak provides rail services between several Canadian and U.S. cities. You can take the train between New York and Montréal, Buffalo and Toronto, or between Seattle and Vancouver, with connections to other cities on both sides of the border. Except for short trips, however, rail travel is not cheaper than flying, and it may not save you time.

Buses and Public Transportation

BUSES

Greyhound runs buses between many U.S. and Canadian destinations and also between cities small and large across Canada. As with train travel, the bus may make sense on shorter routes, particularly between the major Eastern cities. Otherwise, the bus caters to those with more time than money.

While Greyhound covers most major routes, there are smaller regional bus companies across Canada as well. In Québec, Orléans Express runs buses between Montréal and Québec City and to many of the province's smaller towns. Autobus Galland has service between Montréal and Mont-Tremblant,

DAILY LIFE

© CAROLYN B. HELLER

Taking Vancouver's Aquabus is a fun way to get downtown.

with stops in other Laurentian towns. Limocar operates buses from Montréal to the Eastern Townships.

Coach Canada runs buses across southern Ontario from Windsor to Toronto to Montréal. They occasionally offer extremely low-priced online-only deals on routes such as Toronto–Montréal. Ontario Northland connects Toronto with towns in the northern reaches of the province.

Many regional buses provide service from the big-city airports to smaller communities. For example, in British Columbia, Perimeter Transportation runs buses from the Vancouver airport to the ski town of Whistler. From the Toronto airport, Niagara Airbus operates buses to the Niagara Falls region, and Airways Transit takes passengers to Hamilton and to Kitchener-Waterloo.

PUBLIC TRANSPORTATION

The major Canadian cities all have convenient, modern public transportation networks. Refer to the *Prime Living Locations* chapters for details about public transit in each major city and to the *Resources* chapter for links to transit system websites.

Similarly, taxis are readily available in the larger Canadian cities. Canadian taxi service is quite similar to taxi service in the United States, and drivers expect tips of about 15 percent. Some drivers accept credit cards.

Driving

For long-distance travel, Canada has a network of well-maintained highways similar to the U.S. Interstate Highway System. The Trans-Canada Highway (Highway 1) is the world's longest national highway, stretching 7,821 kilometers (4,860 miles) from Victoria, British Columbia across all 10 provinces to the city of St. John's in Newfoundland and Labrador. If you're wondering how a highway can cross to these island cities, ferries at both ends link the mainland with the Vancouver Island and Newfoundland stretches of road. The Trans-Canada first opened in 1962, and most of the current-day highway was completed by 1971.

Within each province, highways connect the major cities and venture into more remote areas as well. The best source of information about provincial roadways is the Canadian Automobile Association or the province's department of transportation.

If you have a valid driver's license from a U.S. state, you can generally exchange it for a new driver's license in the province where you'll be living. Most provinces do not require you to take a road test if you're already licensed in the United States.

Throughout most of Canada, road signs are in English or in both English and French. However, in the province of Québec, many road signs are in French only. If you're going to be doing much driving in Québec, you'd do well to pick up at least a minimal French driving vocabulary.

PROS AND CONS OF DRIVING IN CANADA

Do you need a car in Canada? It depends. If you're living in one of the country's major cities, and you can live close enough to your job that you can commute by public transit, bike, or on foot, you may not want a car (or you may not need a car right away). If you live in farther-flung suburbs or in a smaller town, if you're planning frequent weekend or holiday trips out of town, or if you have to shuttle the kids from school to soccer practice to music lessons, you may find that having a car is essential.

In weighing the pros and cons of car ownership, keep in mind that the cost of gasoline is significantly higher in Canada than in the United States. Part of the reason for these higher fuel prices is that gas taxes in Canada are much higher than those in the United States.

What about car theft? Though the overall crime rate in Canada is relatively low when compared with other major industrialized nations, the rate of car thefts is comparatively high. And it's not just the big cities that are prone to

DAILY LIFE

ATTENTION! BROUILLARD!

Do you need to read French to drive in Québec?

One winter evening, we were driving back to Québec City after a day of skiing at Mont Sainte-Anne. All of a sudden, a yellow warning sign with flashing lights announced, *"Attention! Brouillard!"*

My husband Alan pointed to the sign and asked, "What's *brouillard?*"

Before I could think of the answer, we were enveloped in some of the thickest fog we had ever seen. It was as if we had driven directly into a bowl of the proverbial pea soup. Alan slowed the car as quickly as he could, since we couldn't see more than a few feet in front of us. Then just as quickly, we passed through the fog and back into the crisp, clear night.

I turned to Alan and said, "Uh, fog. *Brouillard* means fog."

He rolled his eyes. "Now you tell me."

motor vehicle crime; based on 2006 statistics, the province of Manitoba has the highest rate of auto theft in the country. Overall, in 2006, there were 160,000 stolen vehicles reported across Canada. That translates to a rate of 487 stolen cars per every 100,000 people, similar to the per-capita rate in the United States. However, the actual number of cars stolen in the United States is significantly higher than in Canada. In the state of California alone (in 2005), 242,693 cars were stolen!

The good news is that the rate of vehicle thefts in Canada has declined about 20 percent since the mid-1990s. Still, it's worth exercising caution: Always lock your car. Make sure you have an alarm or other anti-theft device. And don't leave valuables lying around in plain sight.

RENTING, LEASING, AND BUYING A CAR

If you arrive in Canada without wheels, there are plenty of ways to get yourself out on the road.

The major car rental agencies—Alamo, Avis, Budget, Dollar, Enterprise, Hertz, National, Thrifty—all have offices across Canada. Smaller local companies also operate in each province; searching sites such as Kayak.com frequently turns up local rental agents. Renting from an in-town office can sometimes be cheaper than renting a car at the airport, so if you don't need a car when you first land, shop around for rates at different locations. If you'll need a car for an extended time, ask about discounts for long-term rentals.

Car-sharing networks have set up shop in several Canadian cities. If you need a car only occasionally, or if you want to evaluate whether you'll need a car in your new Canadian home, it's worth considering one of these networks. Companies to contact include the Co-operative Auto Network in Vancouver, AutoShare in Toronto, Zipcar in Toronto and Vancouver, VRTUCAR in Ottawa, the Calgary Alternative Transportation Co-operative, and Communauto, which operates in Montréal, Québec City, and Gatineau/Ottawa. For car-sharing companies in other cities, or for more information about car-sharing in general, see www.carsharing.net.

© CAROLYN B. HELLER

Joining a car-sharing network can be an alternative to owning a car.

The process of leasing or buying a car in Canada is similar to the process in the United States (complete with the same buyer-beware warnings about unscrupulous used-car salespeople). Most of the same car companies that operate in the United States sell their cars in Canada, although not all models or options may be available. Cars manufactured for sale in Canada will have metric gauges (although some have dual scales), and you may find more winter-driving features—tires, heated seats, ski bags—than you might find on cars sold in, say, Florida.

Is it more expensive to buy a car in Canada than in the United States? In general, it is. Although the exchange rate is a major factor, Canadian base prices are typically higher than base prices for similar vehicles in the United States. Taxes on new cars, too, are higher in Canada.

You can bring a car you already own from the United States to Canada when you first arrive, but if you buy a brand-new car in the United States and bring it into Canada, it will be subject to significant Canadian taxes and duties. It might still be less expensive to buy in the United States, but it might not be, so do your research before you sign on the dotted line. Also note that some manufacturers do not honor U.S. warranties on cars that cross the border, so you may not be able to get warranty service in Canada.

When you compare cars in Canada, you'll need to learn the Canadian standard for fuel efficiency. If you're used to thinking about "miles per gallon," you'll have to get used to comparing "liters per 100 kilometer." A Canadian government agency, Natural Resources Canada's Office of Energy Efficiency, publishes a useful fuel consumption guide that enables you to compare scores of cars sold in Canada. You may be able to pick up a copy at a car dealership, or you can get it online at www.oee.nrcan.gc.ca.

In 2007, the Canadian government established the ecoAUTO Rebate Program to encourage Canadians to buy or lease fuel-efficient vehicles. If you purchase or lease a car that's on the "approved" list for this program, you may be eligible for a rebate of $1,000–2,000. It's definitely worth a look if you're in the market for a car. Get the scoop from Transport Canada at www.tc.gc.ca/programs/environment/ecotransport/ecoauto.htm.

Canada and the United States have similar, but not identical, safety, emissions, and insurance standards. Insurance in Canada is provincially regulated, so you'll need to contact local companies in your new community to find out about minimum insurance requirements, optional insurance, and estimated costs. The provincial governments maintain lists of licensed insurance brokers and agents. The Canadian Automobile Association sells insurance as well, or you can ask your colleagues or friends for the names of their insurance companies.

See *Making the Move* for more information about how to apply for a driver's license and arrange for car insurance when you arrive in Canada, and for details about bringing your own car into Canada.

RULES OF THE ROAD

U.S. drivers will find that Canadian rules of the road are similar to those back home. One major difference is that, because Canada operates on the metric system, road signs give distances in kilometers and speed limits in kilometers per hour. A speed limit of 100 kilometers per hour is roughly equal to 60 miles per hour. Canadians sometimes refer to "kilometers" as "clicks," so people might complain that they have to drive 25 clicks to get to work.

Gas in Canada is sold by the liter. There are 3.8 liters to a U.S. gallon. If you want a rough estimate of how the price of gas in Canada compares with the cost in the United States, you can multiple the Canadian price by four, and then adjust for the current exchange rate. Or you can just assume that the answer is "Gas in Canada costs more."

Although Canadian seatbelt laws vary by province, it's safe to assume that all passengers are required to wear seatbelts and children must be in appropriate car seats.

Have a radar detector? Leave it at home. They're illegal in Canada, and in some provinces—notably Ontario and Québec—it's illegal simply to have them in your car, even if you're not using them.

The Canadian government has been promoting "turn off your engine" campaigns to reduce auto emissions, and several cities, including Vancouver and Toronto, have adopted "anti-idling" by-laws. These rules mean that if you stop for more than three minutes—if you're waiting for someone, for instance—you should shut off your engine or risk being fined.

OTHER RESOURCES FOR DRIVERS

If you're a member of the American Automobile Association (AAA) in the United States, you have reciprocal privileges with the Canadian Automobile Association (CAA). You can request maps and other travel information from either AAA or CAA offices. Once you have relocated to Canada, you can transfer your AAA membership to a CAA membership simply by contacting the CAA office in your new community. CAA office locations are listed on their website.

If you expect to be traveling frequently back and forth across the border between the United States and Canada, look into getting a Nexus card. Nexus is a program run jointly by the U.S. and Canadian governments that pre-approves travelers for expedited border crossings. At Canada's largest airports, the program uses iris-recognition technology to verify your identity. At land crossings (which currently include selected border points in B.C., Ontario, and Québec), you drive through a dedicated Nexus lane and hold up your Nexus card to be scanned. You must also follow special procedures if you have goods to declare.

To apply for a Nexus card, you have to fill out an application, provide identity documents, pay a fee, and be interviewed by a border services officer. U.S. Customs and Border Protection officers interview people who reside in Canada; Canada Border Services Agency officers interview U.S. residents. You also have to be fingerprinted, photographed, and iris-scanned. For frequent travelers, Nexus can save you a significant amount of time at the borders. However, some people have privacy concerns about the U.S. and Canadian governments' use of technology to monitor your travels, so read up on the program and make your own decision.

PRIME LIVING LOCATIONS

© CAROLYN B. HELLER

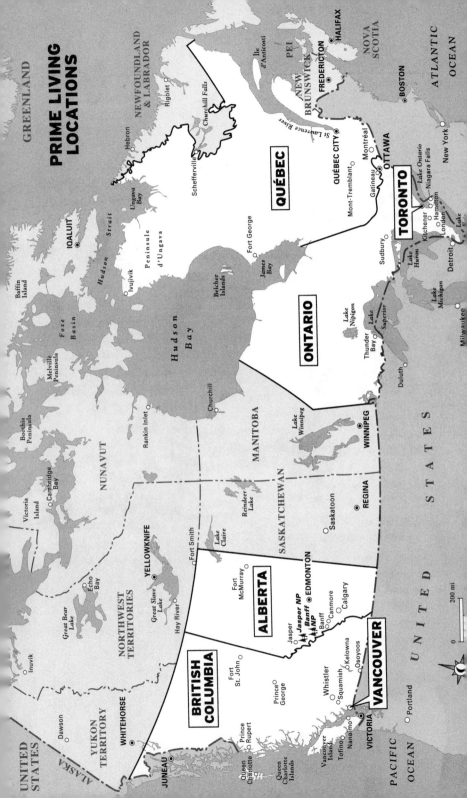

PRIME LIVING LOCATIONS

OVERVIEW

Once you've elected to move to Canada, you still have a big decision to make: what part of this vast country will be your new home. Of course, if you have a job offer, the choice may be made for you. If you do have the freedom to decide where to settle, however, you'll have to narrow down your options.

Since Canada is the second-largest country in the world, we've had to make some choices in this book, too. We've concentrated on the major metropolitan areas of Vancouver, Toronto, and Montréal, which have the largest expat communities, as well as the next tier of cities, including Ottawa, Calgary, Edmonton, Québec City, and Victoria. We've also covered Ontario's "Golden Horseshoe" region, since there are an increasing number of jobs, especially in the technology sector, in the cities of Hamilton, London, and Kitchener-Waterloo.

Beyond the urban areas, we've highlighted places that are simply lovely spots to live. In British Columbia, there are many. Vancouver Island and the Gulf Islands appeal to those who want to settle near the water. Squamish and Whistler draw outdoor adventurers, from skiers and snowboarders to rock-climbers

© CAROLYN B. HELLER

and hikers. Inland, the Okanagan Valley has a surprisingly mild climate, a growing wine industry, and a peaceful lifestyle. And beyond B.C., there's the Niagara region in Ontario, Québec's Laurentian Mountains and quaint Eastern Townships, and the magnificent Rockies in the province of Alberta.

Canada has many other wonderful places to live, so if you're heading for the Atlantic Provinces, the prairies, or the far north, don't worry. Even though we haven't covered these destinations in detail, the information we've provided throughout this book will still help you settle into your new Canadian home.

VANCOUVER

Vancouver, on Canada's west coast, is frequently named one of the best places in the world to live. If you're lucky enough to spend some time here, you'll see why. It starts with a gorgeous physical setting, with the downtown high-rises perched between the water and the snowcapped mountains. Beaches ring the city, and you can be on the ski slopes in under an hour. The temperate climate, similar to Seattle's or Portland's, means that you can enjoy the outdoors virtually year-round.

Vancouver is a vibrant, international city. As Canada's gateway to the Pacific Rim, Vancouver has a large Asian community with food, festivals, and other cultural activities that all residents can enjoy. There's an active restaurant scene, and the laid-back locals line the sidewalk cafés whenever the sun shines.

So what's the downside? All this beauty doesn't come cheap. The major drawback to living in Vancouver is the cost. It's Canada's most expensive housing market, and while it may seem reasonable compared to New York or San Francisco, you'll spend a lot more to live here than you would in Toronto or Montréal.

Even though Vancouver has one of the mildest climates in Canada, the weather can still be a negative. Summer is gorgeous, spring and fall are mild, but winter is unquestionably wet. Freezing temperatures and snow are rare, but if you're headed to Vancouver, you may want to invest in some Gore-Tex.

BRITISH COLUMBIA

If you like the idea of the relaxed, West Coast life, but you prefer a less urban environment than Vancouver, look at some of British Columbia's other regions. The provincial capital, Victoria, located on Vancouver Island across the Strait of Georgia from the city of Vancouver, is an up-and-coming community. It's large enough to have plenty of restaurants, pubs, and cultural activities, but small enough to be neighborly. The climate is mild, and golfing, sailing, hiking, and cycling are just a few of the activities that residents enjoy.

©CAROLYN B. HELLER

enjoying the active life on Vancouver's English Bay Beach

Elsewhere on Vancouver Island, you'll find smaller cities, beach towns, and logging communities. And between Vancouver Island and the mainland, the waters are dotted with islands: the Gulf Island chain. In these island spots, tourism is a big business, but so is telecommuting. Many artists and entrepreneurs have settled on B.C.'s islands, adding a vibrant cultural dimension to life here. And when the surf's up or the sun shines, island residents can get outdoors fast.

Within commuting distance of Vancouver but far enough away to feel like an outdoor outpost, Squamish is one of B.C.'s most active communities. Hiking, mountain biking, rock-climbing, windsurfing, scuba diving, cross-country skiing, and more—in Squamish, you can do them all.

Squamish is located midway between Vancouver and the mega-resort town of Whistler, home to North America's largest ski area. If you live for the snow, look no further than Whistler, a small town with a big mountain. Whistler attracts an international crowd to its snow-covered slopes, and in the sunny summertime, the area still hums with tourists, creating job opportunities year-round. If you're looking for investment property, Whistler has a huge market in second homes as well.

Don't fancy the damp coastal climate? Head east to the Okanagan Valley, the region local boosters call "Napa North." In central British Columbia, the Okanagan is milder, drier, and sunnier than the coast, which has given rise to a burgeoning wine industry. While the Okanagan has neither the number of wineries nor the extensive tourist infrastructure of its south-of-the-border idol— yet—there's good wine made here, plenty to do, and scads of opportunities in tourism, real estate, and other industries. With a chain of lakes and the mountains nearby, the Okanagan's natural setting earns kudos, too.

TORONTO

Canada's largest city is the country's financial and business heart, its most multicultural metropolis, and a vibrant artistic center. Many Toronto residents consider their city the hub of the universe—or at least the universe north of the 49th parallel. If you'd feel at home in Chicago or perhaps Manhattan, you might consider living in Toronto.

Toronto's Bay Street is Canada's Wall Street, headquarters for scores of banks and financial services com-

© CAROLYN B. HELLER

New condos rise amidst historic buildings in Toronto's Distillery District.

panies. Whether you work in high-tech or high finance, in science or health care, real estate, education, tourism, or the arts, Toronto has plenty of opportunities.

With a population of 2.5 million in the city proper, and roughly five million in the metropolitan area, Greater Toronto may not be huge by world standards, but it still ranks among the largest cities in the U.S. and Canada. It's also one of the most ethnically diverse cities in the world. Nearly 50 percent of Toronto area residents were born outside of Canada, and thousands of new immigrants arrive every year.

This diversity has made Toronto a great dining city. You can have Indian food today, Italian tomorrow, Greek the next, Caribbean cuisine another day, and dishes from many regions of China for days after that. Cultural festivals go on nearly all the time.

Toronto may not have an oceanfront, but it is right on Lake Ontario. When the weather's fine, residents make the most of their lakeside location, walking or biking along the shore or ferrying across to one of Toronto's nearby islands.

Of course, climate may not be Toronto's main selling point, since winters are long, and summers are hot and humid. Toronto's ever-increasing traffic, too, gets low marks from locals. Still, if living in a major international city with a wealth of cultural and recreational opportunities appeals to you, Toronto may lure you here.

ONTARIO

Outside of Toronto, the province of Ontario is home to Canada's national capital: Ottawa. The center of the federal government, Ottawa has grand public buildings—the Parliament, the Supreme Court, the governor general's residence, the Museum of Civilization, the National Gallery of Canada—as well as comfortable residential neighborhoods. While the government is the major employer, education and high-tech provide lots of jobs here. Perhaps because the federal government is officially bilingual, Ottawa is one of Canada's most bilingual cities, with many residents moving easily between English and French.

Surrounding the city of Toronto is the region sometimes called the "Golden Horseshoe." From Toronto's sprawling suburbs, this area extends north, west, and south to the cities of Kitchener-Waterloo, London, and Hamilton. Formerly industrial towns—Hamilton, in particular, was known as Canada's Steel City—they're working to reinvent themselves as high-tech meccas. Several major universities are also in this area. Despite its evocative name, the Golden Horseshoe may not be Canada's prettiest region, and it won't win any prizes for its climate, but work may draw you here.

The Niagara peninsula is well-known for the famous Falls that are on every tourist's must-see list. Beyond the Falls and their honky-tonk surroundings, however, Niagara has picturesque villages, an active wine-making industry, and plenty of options for tourism-related jobs.

QUÉBEC

If you want to feel like you've gone overseas when you've simply crossed the border, Québec may be your choice. The province's francophone heritage and culture means that, unlike the rest of Canada, in Québec it's French first and English second.

Fashionable, fast-paced Montréal is fairly bilingual, but you'll be better able to enjoy the city's *joie de vivre* if you speak at least basic *français*. The high-tech, aerospace, and scientific research industries draw the more engineering-minded, while jobs in fashion and the arts bring in the culturally conscious. Finance, real estate, tourism, and the non-profit sector are all major components of Montréal's economy.

For such a big, bustling city—the metropolitan area is home to about 3.5 million people—Montréal is inexpensive. Rents and home prices are relatively low, and the many entertainment options, from festivals to concerts to wine bars, range from free to moderately priced. If you have Paris dreams but a Pensacola budget, consider Montréal.

Québec City, the provincial capital, is much smaller than Montréal and much more francophone. You really need to speak competent French to live and work here. The picturesque Old City—one of the oldest settlements in North America—mixes tourist services with galleries, restaurants, and shops that serve locals as well. Outside the Old City walls, the surrounding neighborhoods, many lined with narrow lanes and tiny shops that would be right at home in a French village, are gentrifying as real estate prices rise.

Québec is a major recreational destination, too, with two prime areas an easy drive from Montréal. Eastern Canada's major ski resort, Mont-Tremblant, is in the Laurentian Mountains northwest of Montréal, while the Eastern Townships—with smaller ski hills surrounded by cute villages—are to the east, just over the Vermont border. Mont-Tremblant feels international, drawing visitors (and second-home owners) from around the globe. The Eastern Townships seem more like New England—with a French accent.

ALBERTA

In recent years, Canada's strongest provincial economy has been Alberta's, driven by the oil and gas industry. Alberta is home to some of the largest oil reserves on the planet, second only to those in Saudi Arabia. The cities of Calgary and Edmonton have each grown to over a million inhabitants, drawing migrants from across Canada and abroad to fuel the oil boom.

But there's more to Alberta than oil. Like many diversified cities, Edmonton has jobs in government and education, engineering and medicine, finance, real estate, and construction. And despite the area's rapid growth, Edmonton still feels homey and welcoming.

Calgary has a developing high-technology sector, as well as solid construction, real estate, and transportation industries. Calgary, a work-hard play-hard city, takes full advantage of its location just east of the Rocky Mountains. Not only are many tourism-related ventures based here, but locals seem to head for the mountains as soon as they close their office doors—skiing, snowboarding, and snowshoeing in winter, and hiking, mountain biking, and camping in the warmer months.

If you want to be in the mountains on a more regular basis, consider settling in Banff, Canmore, Jasper, or one of Alberta's other communities in the Rockies. Whether you spend summers and holidays or live in the region full-time, Alberta's Rocky Mountains have some of Canada's most spectacular scenery. When you wake up to a backdrop of steep mountain peaks, their snowcapped tops sparkling in the sunlight, you'll know that it was a good idea to live abroad—in Canada.

VANCOUVER

Forgive Vancouverites for being smug. In survey after survey, their city is repeatedly ranked as one of the best places in the world to live. With its spectacular setting nestled between the mountains and the harbor, its vibrant multicultural population, and its temperate climate, Vancouver offers its residents a relatively laid-back lifestyle. It may not have the buzz of New York or Toronto, but it's a comfortable, relaxed place, often nicknamed "Lotusland." If you'd feel at home settling in Seattle, Portland, or perhaps the San Francisco area, Vancouver may be an attractive Canadian alternative.

Why Vancouver? Vancouver draws its residents from all over the world. This Pacific-coast city of 600,000—part of a metropolitan area that's home to more than two million—has long been a magnet for people from eastern Canada, the United Kingdom, Australia, and New Zealand who come for the mild weather, job opportunities, and a more hassle-free lifestyle. The city also draws people from across the Pacific Rim, with waves of immigrants in recent

© ALAN ALBERT

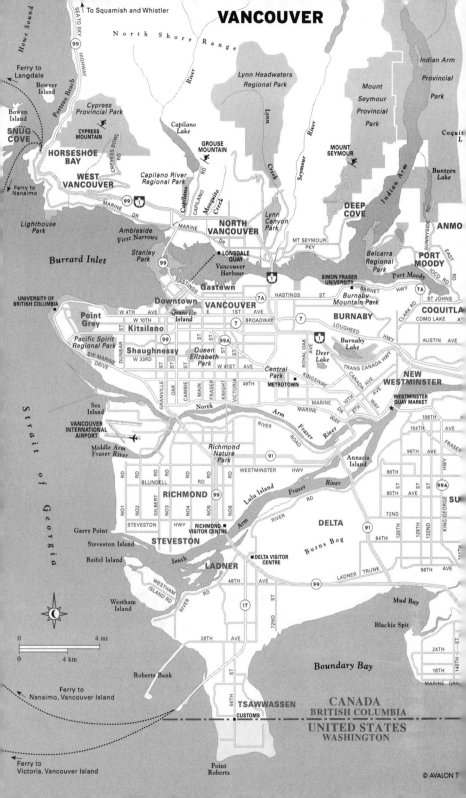

years coming from Hong Kong, Taiwan, China, and India. Today, more than 30 percent of the city's population is of Asian descent.

Vancouver has a fairly large community of U.S. expats. According to recent census figures, approximately 25,000 people in metropolitan Vancouver were born in the United States. The University of British Columbia (UBC), with a striking water-view location on the city's West Side, often lures academics from south of the border, as do companies in the region's growing high-tech sector.

Many Americans are surprised to learn that Vancouver is North America's third-largest film-production center (after New York and Los Angeles), and U.S. expats come to work in film or TV. Tourism is also a major source of jobs, with particular growth in the years before and after the 2010 Winter Olympic Games, held in Vancouver and the ski town of Whistler. Some Americans, whether full- or part-time residents, have taken advantage of the city's strong tourism industry and thriving market for vacation and short-term rental apartments by investing in condos or rental properties.

Vancouverites embrace the city's natural setting, spending as much time as possible outdoors. Even on damp winter days, you can find locals playing soccer, heading for the mountains to ski or snowshoe, or strolling along the beach. When the sun is shining, it seems that the entire city is outside. Even if you're not the athletic type, it's hard to avoid being active in Vancouver—even if that activity is more about hoisting a glass in a sidewalk café than training for a triathlon or cycling to work.

Vancouver is a relatively young city—not only its population, but the city itself. Although aboriginal people settled in the region for thousands of years, Vancouver did not begin its urban development till the late 1800s, incorporating in 1886. Few architectural remains document the city's early days; while you can still find some Victorian-era homes and Craftsman-style bungalows, modern glass-and-steel towers dominate the city skyline. Vancouver has its face turned firmly toward the future.

The Lay of the Land

Downtown Vancouver is on a peninsula, ringed with beaches and surrounded by the waters of the Burrard Inlet. At one end of the peninsula is Stanley Park, a rainforest green space that's larger than New York's Central Park. With its forest of office and condo towers, downtown is connected to other parts of the city by several bridges.

Across False Creek, the remainder of Vancouver proper extends south to

PRIME LIVING LOCATIONS

WHICH WEST?

The West End? The West Side? West Vancouver? Newcomers to Vancouver are frequently puzzled by the similar names of these Vancouver-area communities.

The West End is a downtown neighborhood, bordering Stanley Park and English Bay. It's one of downtown's more established residential communities, with a range of apartment and condo buildings.

The West Side is the part of Vancouver that's bounded by the University of British Columbia on the west, Ontario Street on the east, False Creek on the north, and the Fraser River to the south. This area includes many of Vancouver's prime residential neighborhoods. (Its counterpart — the East Side — runs east from Ontario Street to Boundary Road on the Burnaby line.)

West Vancouver, on the North Shore, is a separate municipality, with its own local government. It has the distinction of being one of the most affluent communities in Canada.

the Fraser River and is divided into the East Side and the West Side. Ontario Street is the dividing line between east and west. Jutting into False Creek is Granville Island, which is home to a wildly popular public market, as well as theaters, galleries, and artists' workshops.

On the other side of downtown, across the Burrard Inlet, is the area known as the North Shore. The communities of North Vancouver and West Vancouver are here, beneath Cypress, Grouse, and Seymour Mountains. In the south, across the Fraser River, is the suburb of Richmond. As you continue south, suburbs and exurbs extend about 40 kilometers (25 miles) to the U.S. border. East of Vancouver, suburban Burnaby is home to a number of high-technology companies, and more suburbs sprawl east from there.

CLIMATE

Although Vancouver's natural setting is undeniably gorgeous, the winters are undeniably wet, so make sure you can tolerate plenty of rainy days if you're thinking of settling here. The rainiest months are November through February, although frequently the rain will fall as a gentle drizzle and the temperatures rarely dip below freezing. Vancouver remains green throughout the year, and while the city does receive occasional light snowfalls, it's unusual for the snow to stick around more than a few days. Plenty of people jog along the beach paths, play golf, or go bicycling year-round.

Spring comes early in Vancouver with the first flowers typically blooming in February. The rainy days begin to alternate with sunny mild ones. When

Summers in Vancouver are glorious.

© CAROLYN B. HELLER

Vancouverites boast of skiing in the morning and sailing in the afternoon, they're often talking about those spring days when it's warming up in the city, while the North Shore mountains are still topped with snow.

So, why do Vancouverites tolerate all the rain? Because the summers are so spectacular.

Most summer days average around 20–25°C (68–75°F), and the sun will shine for day after day. If temperatures occasionally creep a bit higher, everyone grumbles about the heat. It's unusual for homes to be air-conditioned, but it's the rare day when you'd need it. The days are long, too; in June, the sun rises around 4:30 A.M. and doesn't set till after 10 P.M. Vancouverites make the most of these long summer days, picnicking on the beaches after work, going for evening walks, and jamming the sidewalk cafés. The sunshine generally continues into September and October, although temperatures begin to dip and the leaves on many trees turn red, yellow, and gold.

Vancouver has different micro-climates, with cooler, damper weather on the North Shore and somewhat drier, sunnier weather in the southern suburbs. Even in the city, neighborhoods at higher elevations, such as Point Grey, may get an inch or two of snow when just down the hill has none.

CULTURE

Vancouver is an outdoorsy place, and much of the city's social life centers around active pursuits. The harbor is lined with sailing clubs, you can golf year-round, and plenty of people ski, snowshoe, or hike in the nearby mountains. The city has a network of well-maintained public community centers that house gyms and fitness facilities, pools, and skating rinks; the fees are modest, with discounts for families. One of Vancouver's big spring events is the annual 10-kilometer Sun Run—more than 50,000 people, from walkers to nationally ranked competitive runners, join in the fun, and the community centers offer learn-to-run clinics for those who want to get fit and socialize at the same time.

Some expats complain that with all this emphasis on outdoor life, the city's art scene suffers. It's true that Vancouver's cultural life may pale in comparison to arts-focused cities like New York, San Francisco, or Toronto, but there's still plenty for culture vultures to do.

The Commodore, a long-standing nightclub, is in the Granville Street Entertainment District downtown.

Vancouver has several professional theater companies, notably the Vancouver Playhouse and the Arts Club, and more avant garde groups stage works in the performance spaces on Granville Island. The Vancouver East Cultural Centre, off Commercial Drive on the East Side, hosts eclectic theater, dance, and music events, as well as a popular performance series for kids. Ballet BC, Vancouver's resident professional ballet company, is well regarded for its contemporary productions. And like any large city, Vancouver has concert halls and nightclubs that stage everything from Handel to hip-hop.

Vancouver also has a vibrant restaurant culture, with much emphasis on locally sourced, regionally inspired fare. With its large Asian population, the city has some of the best Asian restaurants in North America—from neighborhood noodle shops to elaborate Hong Kong–style banquet halls. And despite the recent proliferation of Starbucks outlets, Vancouver has a long-established café culture; residents love to meet over an espresso or a latte, especially at a sidewalk table on a sunny summer day.

Where to Live

If you're coming to Vancouver to work, you should consider your job location when looking for a place to live, but compared to many North American cities, commuting distances in Vancouver are relatively short. According to Statistics Canada, nearly 75 percent of Vancouver-area commuters travel 15 kilometers (nine miles) or less to work. However, as housing prices within the city increase, more residents are finding that they have to choose between smaller, more centrally located living quarters, and more space out in the suburbs.

Vancouver is surrounded by water, so if you live on the North Shore, in Richmond, or in many suburbs, you'll need to cross that water to get downtown. The bridges and tunnels that bring commuters into the city can become bottlenecks during rush hours. Vancouver does have a well-developed public transit system, so living near a bus stop, a SkyTrain station, or a ferry terminal can simplify your commute. Some Vancouverites who live in town commute to work by bicycle or on foot.

THE HOUSING MARKET

The major downside to Vancouver's appeal is that housing prices are high— the highest in Canada. In the first quarter of 2008, the Real Estate Board of Greater Vancouver reported that the average price of a single-family detached home had increased nearly 100 percent over the previous five years, with homes on Vancouver's East Side averaging $665,000 and average prices for houses on the West Side topping $1.4 million. In prime neighborhoods, even teardowns go for over $1 million.

The condo market is booming as well, with new buildings under construction on seemingly every downtown block. Unlike those in some North American cities, Vancouver's city planners are attempting to rein in urban sprawl, and "eco-density" is a buzzword for urban development. The city is encouraging condominiums, townhouses, and other multi-unit dwellings and relaxing restrictions on adding apartments to single-family homes. In neighborhoods near the University of British Columbia, for example, many homes have a basement apartment that provides rental income for their owners and a less expensive rental alternative for those who want to live in this otherwise pricy area.

If you'd rather rent than buy, be aware that Vancouver is one of Canada's tightest rental markets, with a vacancy rate of only 0.7 percent. Average monthly rents for a one-bedroom apartment range from $800–900, and for a two-bedroom apartment around $1,100–1,200, but rents in popular neighborhoods can run much higher.

You may also be able to find a house—either furnished or unfurnished— for short-term rental, a reasonable option for families who are relocating or who may want temporary accommodations while looking for a place to buy. House rents start at around $2,000 per month.

2010 IN LOTUSLAND

If you spend much time in Vancouver, you'll hear a lot about 2010. That's the year the Vancouver area hosts the Winter Olympic Games. The announcement that the Games would be held in the region launched a bevy of construction projects – from the development of a rapid transit line linking the airport with downtown, the widening of the Sea-to-Sky highway between Vancouver and Whistler (where most of the ski and snowboard events are taking place), and the construction of an Olympic Village, to countless new residential development projects, spurred by the hope that millions of fans will need a place to stay during the Olympics and, potentially, a place to live afterwards.

Not all Vancouverites were in favor of the Games. A vocal minority was concerned that hosting the Games would be a drain on city resources, a burden on taxpayers, and an excuse to ignore the city's homeless and otherwise disenfranchised residents. Anti-Olympics protests were held, but most Vancouverites seem excited about the Olympics, while acknowledging its pros and cons. And most, at least those who've invested in the red-hot real estate market, are eagerly watching to see the effect that the Olympics will have on those investments.

One strategy for short-term housing is to rent from a university faculty family who is going on sabbatical leave. You can often find faculty-owned houses on the West Side to rent for four-month, six-month, or one-year terms. A good source of short-term rental listings is the website of the University of British Columbia Faculty Association (www.facultyassociation.ubc.ca).

DOWNTOWN

If you prefer to be in the center of the urban action, and you don't need a lot of living space, look at one of Vancouver's city-center neighborhoods, which include the West End, Yaletown, and Gastown. Nearly all properties in these areas are rental apartments or condominiums, and many units are small. It's not unusual to find units of only 45–55 square meters (500–600 square feet); apartments over 110 square meters (1,200 square feet) are uncommon. Despite the relatively small spaces, the average purchase price of a downtown Vancouver condominium in early 2008 was approaching $500,000, and more spacious units with mountain or water views easily top $1 million.

The West End

In the West End, there's a mix of older low-rise buildings and newer towers just a short walk from the waterfronts along English Bay or Coal Harbour. Many buildings sit on leafy residential streets or have views of the water, the mountains, or Stanley Park.

A diverse urban neighborhood with a significant percentage of its residents between the ages of 20 and 34, the West End is also the center of Vancouver's sizeable gay community. Lined with bars, pubs, and casual eateries, Davie Street is the hub of this gay district and buzzes until the wee hours. Denman Street, which runs from English Bay across to Coal Harbour, has many of the neighborhood's shops and services, as well as lots of ethnic restaurants. Most West End homes are a short walk from many downtown offices, so it's a convenient place to live if you work downtown.

The Burrard Bridge is one of three spans connecting downtown Vancouver with the rest of the city.

Many buildings on the English Bay side of the West End were built in the 1950s, '60s, and '70s, when many old Victorian homes were torn down and replaced with low-rise apartments. A handful of these Victorian houses remain throughout the West End, often in the shadow of newer buildings; most are now either multi-family residences or bed-and-breakfast inns. Along Coal Harbour are more luxurious condo towers, most constructed since the early 1990s, with more towers under construction seemingly all the time.

Yaletown

Formerly an industrial district lined with warehouses on the north side of False Creek, Yaletown has been become one of the city's trendiest neighborhoods. Many of these former warehouses now house restaurants, bars, and boutiques, and some have been converted to loft-style condos, retaining the historic brick exteriors but completely reconstructed inside. Surrounding these Victorian-era buildings are glass-and-steel residential towers, a mix of condos and rental apartments that make up the bulk of the neighborhood's housing stock.

Nearly 80 percent of Yaletown's residences have been built since 1991. Many have water views or sit within a short walk of the False Creek waterfront. The rapid transit line under construction between downtown and the suburb of

PRIME LIVING LOCATIONS

© CAROLYN B. HELLER

Richmond, slated for completion in late 2009, will have a Yaletown stop, which will help connect Yaletown to other parts of the city.

When Yaletown's towers first began going up, they attracted primarily young singles and couples, particularly since large apartments are relatively rare. However, an increasing number of families are now choosing to live in Yaletown, opting for small, centrally located living spaces over pricey single-family homes. An elementary school that opened in 2005 to serve the neighborhood's growing population is already over-subscribed.

Steam Clock in Gastown, one of Vancouver's oldest neighborhoods

Gastown

Gastown, one of the city's oldest neighborhoods, is emerging as one of its newest real estate sensations, as developers rush to convert the brick-front Victorian-era buildings into lofts and apartments. The area bustles with clubs and restaurants, hip boutiques, and galleries.

Unfortunately, Gastown also borders on the city's most down-and-out area—the Downtown Eastside—which has the greatest concentration of homeless people and a thriving drug trade. That said, if you're coming from a major U.S. city, you may find this "rough" area to be nothing out of the ordinary, and Gastown's edgy vibe may be appealing.

THE WEST SIDE

Whether you're looking for a traditional single-family home in a family-friendly community, a bungalow near an organic market, a townhouse or apartment within walking distance of the beach, or a mansion with inspiring ocean views, you'll find it on Vancouver's West Side. From old-money Shaughnessy to old-hippie Kitsilano, from the waterfront estates and student enclaves around the University of British Columbia to the almost-suburban homes in Point Grey, Kerrisdale, and Dunbar, this established residential area with a variety of housing options has long been one of the region's most desirable places to live.

Many West Side neighborhoods are particularly family-oriented, with some

GREEN, GREEN, AND MORE GREEN

Part of Vancouver's appeal is the many green spaces that dot the city. Within the city limits, there are at least 200 parks.

Vancouver's Stanley Park has an unquestionably gorgeous setting, perched on the end of the downtown peninsula. But while 400-hectare (1,000-acre) Stanley Park is frequently lauded as Vancouver's largest urban green space, that honor actually belongs to Pacific Spirit Regional Park.

Located in the University Endowment Lands on Vancouver's West Side, Pacific Spirit Park rambles across 763 hectares (1,885 acres), with trails for walking, hiking, and horseback riding meandering through the rainforest. You can hike through the park down to the beach, look for the Camosun Bog, or simply wander. Even though the park is surrounded by the university, residential neighborhoods, and busy streets, you can venture just a short distance down the trails and you'd never know you were in the city. In fact, although the trails are marked, it's surprisingly easy to get disoriented in this large forest. Take a map and a friend when you go exploring.

of the area's top-rated public and independent schools. Most of these neighborhoods are filled with single-family homes; the oldest (and increasingly hard to find) date to the early 1900s and often retain their Arts-and-Crafts-style woodwork and stained glass. Many "heritage homes" on the West Side were built in the 1940s, and these, too, often have original wood floors, fireplaces, and other historic details. However, as prices climb, more buyers are tearing down older homes—particularly small houses on larger lots—and replacing them with much bigger, ultra-modern residences.

Apartments, condos, and townhouses are also available on the West Side, particularly in the Kitsilano, False Creek, and South Granville neighborhoods. A number of single-family homes have been converted to duplexes in these areas and farther east near City Hall, along the Cambie Street corridor. Many West Side houses also have basement "suites" that are available as rentals.

The University of British Columbia occupies the far western expanse of Vancouver's West Side. The area that includes the university, part of the surrounding residential community, and the massive Pacific Spirit Regional Park is known as the University Endowment Lands (UEL). Through a governmental quirk, the Endowment Lands, which were created by British Columbia's provincial government in the 1920s, are technically separate from the city of Vancouver. An administrator appointed by the province has day-to-day responsibility for the UEL.

If you're working or studying at UBC, you may be able to find housing in

PRIME LIVING LOCATIONS

and around the campus. New residential communities are under construction around the university, but high prices and limited availability mean that plenty of students and faculty have to live elsewhere in the city.

THE EAST SIDE

Much of Vancouver's East Side, a historically working-class district, has a funky feel. Walk down Main Street in the Mt. Pleasant neighborhood with its one-of-a-kind boutiques, antiques stores, and eclectic eateries, or among the coffee houses, ethnic markets, and idiosyncratic shops along Commercial Drive, and you might think you were in Berkeley, California, or Cambridge, Massachusetts.

Like the West Side, the East Side has a mix of older homes, modern construction, and multi-family dwellings, although lot sizes tend to be smaller. Several East Side neighborhoods are gentrifying, and an influx of both young professionals and immigrants has changed the character of many older communities. Some families live on the East Side to get more space for the money than on the pricier West Side. The SkyTrain travels between downtown and the East Side, which can simplify commuting for residents here.

If you're looking for an older "character" home, check out the areas around Main Street, Commercial Drive, and in the pocket north of East Hastings Street that's bounded by Nanaimo and Renfrew Streets. The Strathcona area, near Chinatown, is one of Vancouver's oldest residential neighborhoods and has some small but attractive older homes; its drawback is that, like Gastown, it borders on the rough-and-tumble Downtown Eastside.

For a bit more space, look in the Trout Lake neighborhood around Victoria Drive, where a large park and community center, with a bustling summer farmers market, draws residents from near and far. Many newer houses are going up in the neighborhoods to the south, closer to the Fraser River.

THE NORTH SHORE

The area known as the North Shore includes the communities of North Vancouver and West Vancouver, across the Burrard Inlet from downtown. Because of its location beneath the area's three major mountains, the North Shore is a popular choice for skiers and snowboarders, hikers, and other outdoor enthusiasts. Also in this area is Bowen Island, a small island community that's a 20-minute ferry ride from West Vancouver's Horseshoe Bay terminal.

North Vancouver

Home to just under 50,000 residents, North Vancouver (known locally as North Van) is a suburban community with a mix of apartments, condominiums, and

WHAT'S SO SPECIAL ABOUT THE VANCOUVER SPECIAL?

If you're house-hunting in Vancouver, you'll likely hear some houses called "Vancouver Specials."

Built in the 1960s and '70s, these flat-fronted two-story homes were constructed quickly, when baby boomers and new immigrants were all seeking housing. The house generally incorporated one living space on each level, which appealed to extended families living together or to homeowners who wanted to rent out a secondary suite.

Unfortunately, they were widely panned as ugly, particularly when they were built in neighborhoods of historic homes. You'll still see plenty of Vancouver Specials around the city and its suburbs, although in pricier neighborhoods, they're considered "teardowns" or as canvases for contemporary renovations.

single- and multi-family homes. Nearly half of North Vancouver's residents work somewhere on the North Shore; of the rest, the majority commute into Vancouver. North Vancouver has its own school district, with 29 elementary and seven secondary schools.

North Van has a significant Iranian population, which makes Farsi the second most-widely spoken language (after English). You can find Iranian markets, bakeries, and shops throughout the community, especially in the commercial district along Lonsdale Avenue.

The price of a home in North Vancouver is generally more than a house on Vancouver's East Side but quite a bit less than homes on the West Side or in West Vancouver. In the first quarter of 2008, the average single-family home in North Van sold for about $900,000, while the average condo went for $380,000.

West Vancouver

Looking for an estate overlooking the water? A cottage tucked into the woods? A comfortable home in an affluent suburban community? If so, look in West Vancouver. This North Shore suburb of 44,000 across the Lions Gate Bridge from downtown Vancouver is one of Canada's most expensive places to live, but many of the homes here are drop-dead gorgeous. West Vancouver's 14 elementary and three secondary schools are among the top-rated public schools in the province, and the city has well-regarded private schools as well. While the average annual income of residents within the city of Vancouver is roughly $50,000, in West Van, it's closer to $90,000.

Although West Van is primarily residential, Canada's first shopping mall,

© CAROLYN B. HELLER

floating homes along False Creek

the Park Royal Shopping Centre, was built here in 1950. Also in West Van, the Cypress Mountain Ski Area will host several Olympic events in 2010, but mere mortals can ski here, too; on a clear day, the mountaintop views of downtown and across to Vancouver Island are magnificent.

What does it cost to take up residence in this pricy enclave? In early 2008, single-family homes here were *averaging* nearly $1.5 million. There are a limited number of condo units available, with average prices over $600,000.

Bowen Island

If you fantasize about living on an island but still want to be within commuting distance of Vancouver, Bowen Island may be the answer. Six kilometers (3.7 miles) wide by 12 kilometers (7.5 miles) long, this hilly patch of land in Howe Sound is home to approximately 3,500 people.

Although the island has a creative community of writers, artists, and other self-employed types who work at home, about 40 percent of island residents commute by ferry to the "mainland" for work. Some residents keep homes here as vacation cottages or retirement properties. The island has a public elementary school and a private middle school, but older students have to go off-island. Small houses start around $500,000, but expect to pay double (or more) if you want to be near the water.

RICHMOND

Home to Vancouver's international airport, this booming suburb about 30 minutes' drive south of downtown has seemed like a permanent construction

A QUICK TRIP TO ASIA

Even if you don't end up living in Richmond, it's worth a visit. While all of the Vancouver area has a significant Asian influence, parts of Richmond could easily be mistaken for Shanghai, Taipei, or Hong Kong. Many of the area's best Asian restaurants are here, and since they cater to a fairly affluent population, you can dine in style. Even the casual dim sum spots and family-run noodle shops serve excellent food.

In the summer, Richmond hosts a weekend night market that looks just like a night market in Asia. It's a whirl of vendors selling everything from socks to vacuum cleaners, and the intriguing food stalls are a grazer's heaven.

site in recent years. A rapid transit line is being built to link Richmond with downtown Vancouver, and apartment buildings, condos, and homes are going up at a breakneck pace. In this relatively young community of 180,000, more than 60 percent of the residents are under age 45. Historically a fishing and farming town, Richmond is now primarily a bedroom community, although the city does have jobs in aviation, high-tech, retail, and tourism.

Forty years ago, nearly 85 percent of Richmond's residents were native English speakers; today, that figure is roughly 45 percent. More than half of Richmond's population was born outside of Canada, and nearly 60 percent of residents are of Asian descent, primarily from China, Hong Kong, or Taiwan. Of the city's six large shopping centers, three cater to the upscale Asian population, as do its many Asian restaurants. Some Richmond residents say that if you speak Cantonese or Mandarin, you could live here for years without having to master English.

Average Richmond single-family homes cost $720,000 in early 2008, while condos were a comparative bargain at $307,000.

OTHER SUBURBS

Because of Vancouver's waterfront location, the only place for the metropolitan area to expand is inland—to the east and south. The closest suburban community east of Vancouver is Burnaby, which, like Richmond, has a mix of residential and commercial development (including B.C.'s largest shopping area, the 500-store Metrotown complex). Burnaby home prices are similar to those in Richmond, too, averaging $736,000 in 2008, with condos costing an average of $338,000.

A spread-out metropolitan area of more than 410,000 people, Surrey is B.C.'s second-largest city. Its northern boundary is the Fraser River; in the south,

PRIME LIVING LOCATIONS

it extends to the U.S. border. Some neighborhoods are quite urban, others are fairly typical suburbs, while still others (notably White Rock just north of the border) are filled with waterfront homes. More than a third of Surrey's residents were born outside Canada, and the city is home to the Vancouver area's largest Indo-Canadian community.

Daily Life

Vancouver is a sociable city, where supermarket cashiers greet you with a "Hi, how are you?" and neighbors frequently stop to chat. The best way to get to know your new neighbors may be through activities you enjoy—whether joining a soccer league, working out at the local fitness center, or simply hanging out at the beach. If you're more of a spectator, join the legions of NHL fans at a Canucks hockey game, or check out the Vancouver Whitecaps' men's or women's soccer teams.

The local community centers offer inexpensive courses ranging from yoga to languages to art, which are good ways to meet like-minded individuals. Volunteer Vancouver (www.govolunteer.ca) compiles an extensive online directory of volunteer opportunities across the metropolitan area.

Vancouver has an active network of "Meetup" groups (www.meetup.com), connecting locals who share common interests, whether playing ping-pong or learning to speak Mandarin or ballroom dancing. There's even an "expat American" group that occasionally organizes get-togethers.

RESOURCES

The City of Vancouver publishes a "Newcomer's Guide" that's an excellent introduction to the city and local services. It's online at www.city.vancouver. bc.ca. Another useful resource is Inform Vancouver, a 24/7 telephone service that provides newcomers (and longer-term residents) with information about social, community, and government services across Greater Vancouver. They can also answer questions and provide referrals about immigration, housing, and jobs. Learn more online at www.vcn.bc.ca/isv/infrm.htm.

Vancouver has two daily newspapers: the *Sun* and the *Province*. The *Georgia Straight* is the main alternative weekly, with extensive arts and entertainment listings. The *Vancouver Courier* is a community paper that publishes twice a week, and the weekly *West Ender* focuses on the downtown area.

The upscale monthly *Vancouver Magazine* covers urban lifestyle, shopping, and restaurants, while the monthly *Western Living* from the same publisher covers home, garden, food, and shops across western Canada. The online

Active Vancouverites make good use of the city's community centers.

publication, *The Tyee,* reports on Vancouver and B.C. issues from an investigative, socially conscious perspective. Oriented toward visitors to the city, *Where Magazine* features the arts and local events. For foodies, the city has several food-focused publications, including *City Food, Eat Magazine,* and the online *Urban Diner.*

HEALTH CARE

Residents of British Columbia receive health insurance coverage through the province's Medical Services Plan (MSP). All B.C. residents must register with Health Insurance BC, the agency that administers the MSP; newcomers should register as soon as they arrive, although health insurance coverage will not begin until you have been in the province for three months.

To register, complete the MSP application form, available at www.health. gov.bc.ca/insurance. Along with your application, you must provide photocopies of each family member's work permit, study permit, or permanent resident card (front and back).

British Columbia also has a prescription drug benefit program called Pharmacare. Pharmacare will reimburse you for prescription drug costs if your drug expenses exceed an annual deductible level. The deductible amount is based on your income. You must register for Pharmacare separately from your standard MSP registration. For details, see www.healthservices.gov.bc.ca/pharme.

To find a doctor in B.C., one useful resource is the College of Physicians & Surgeons of British Columbia, which has a "Find a Physician" function on its website (www.cpsbc.ca).

PRIME LIVING LOCATIONS

SCHOOLS

The Vancouver School Board (VSB) is the governing body for the city's public schools. The city eliminated "middle schools" or "junior highs," so elementary schools teach students from kindergarten through Grade 7, and secondary schools encompass Grades 8–12.

The VSB offers two types of French immersion programs that are very popular with area families, even though Vancouver itself has little francophone heritage. The early immersion program begins in kindergarten, and the late immersion program is an intensive two-year option for students in Grades 6 and 7. Students in either program can continue French immersion studies through high school. The district also offers a Mandarin immersion program that begins in Grade 4. There's a public Montessori elementary school as well.

At the high school level, the VSB offers a number of "magnet" programs, drawing students from across the city. These offerings range from arts to outdoor education to academic challenge programs. Get details about these programs and their application procedures on the VSB website (www.vsb.bc.ca).

For a directory of Vancouver-area private and religious schools, contact the B.C. Federation of Independent School Associations (www.fisabc.ca).

Getting Around

To navigate around Vancouver, remember that the mountains are north of the city. Outside of downtown, most east–west streets are numbered avenues, from 1st Avenue in the north to 70th Avenue in the south. Broadway is actually 9th Avenue; King Edward is 25th Avenue.

PUBLIC TRANSPORTATION

Vancouver's public transit network, Translink, operates a system that includes buses, the elevated SkyTrain, the SeaBus (a ferry that runs between downtown Vancouver and North Vancouver's Lonsdale Quay), and the West Coast Express, a weekday-only commuter train that connects downtown with several eastern suburbs. A new rapid transit line, expected to open in 2009, will link Richmond, the airport, and downtown.

In addition to regular buses, Translink runs express buses, called "B-line" services, on several routes. Make a beeline for a B-line if you can—they're much faster than regular buses that travel the same routes.

Vancouver's waterfront location means that there are other water-based commuting options are well. The Aquabus ferry shuttles passengers across False Creek between Yaletown and Granville Island. Popular with tourists,

DOUBLE, DOUBLE: VANCOUVER'S HOUSING BUBBLE

From 2003 through 2008, Vancouver real estate prices soared. Across all communities in the Greater Vancouver area, prices climbed an average of nearly 100 percent. In general, the cost of housing decreases as you go farther from downtown, with lower prices in such communities as Coquitlam, New Westminster, and Maple Ridge.

The following chart shows average prices (in Canadian dollars) for single-family detached homes and the rates at which those prices have changed.

Area	Average Price	1-year change (percent)	5-year change (percent)
West Vancouver	$1,489,071	30.9	115.6
Vancouver West Side	$1,405,945	24.4	109.3
North Vancouver	$903,240	21.0	86.9
Burnaby	$736,003	13.3	92.3
Richmond	$721,193	10.7	86.0
Vancouver East Side	$665,328	14.6	99.4
Coquitlam	$659,601	14.8	89.9
South Delta	$649,266	11.6	90.8
New Westminster	$539,985	12.4	100.3
Maple Ridge	$457,522	11.9	80.1

Source: Real Estate Board of Greater Vancouver, February 2008

PRIME LIVING LOCATIONS

these cute little ferries can be used by commuters, too; ask about a monthly pass or discounts for regular riders.

From Bowen Island, BC Ferries runs regular boat service. The Bowen Island car ferries travel to Horseshoe Bay (in West Vancouver, about a half-hour's drive from downtown) in about 20 minutes.

CAR

There are no freeways or highways within the city of Vancouver. Sure, there are highways that come into town—Highway 1 that links the North Shore with Burnaby, Surrey, and points east; Highway 99 that runs from the U.S. border through Richmond to the Vancouver line; and Highway 7 that comes in from the east—but within the city proper, traffic moves along a web of local streets.

To keep traffic flowing, both parking and making left turns are restricted on many streets during rush hour. Watch the signs, whether you're driving or trying to park. Rush-hour parking can be prohibited even in metered spaces, so be sure to check before you drop your loonies into the meter.

Vancouverites complain about the challenges of finding parking, but compared to cities like Boston, New York, or San Francisco, it's relatively easy to park in Vancouver, at least if you're willing to pay. Meters line the streets downtown and in business districts, as do parking lots and garages. Parking meters are in effect seven days a week, 9 A.M.–8 P.M., and they're rigorously patrolled; overstay your meter by even a few minutes, and you can expect to find a ticket on your windshield. If you're not sure how long you'll be, pull into a garage instead.

BIKE AND ON FOOT

Vancouver is one of North America's most bicycle-friendly cities. Bike paths crisscross the region, and some streets are designated as "bicycle priority" thoroughfares; cars are supposed to yield to cyclists on these roads.

Vancouver's city government promotes bicycle commuting, and cycling in general, with the objective of having at least 10 percent of trips around town made by bike by 2010. That goal may seem modest, but in the United States, there's no city where more than 3 percent of the population commutes by bike.

Of course, with Vancouver's mild weather, it's often a pleasure to go about by bike or on foot. If you're walking, note that jaywalking (crossing the street in the middle of a block) is against the law in Vancouver. And at intersections, Vancouver pedestrians generally wait patiently for a green light before crossing the street. Perhaps that's more evidence of the laid-back life in this West Coast Lotusland.

PRIME LIVING LOCATIONS

BRITISH COLUMBIA

"Lifestyle." That's the reason many people choose to live in British Columbia, Canada's westernmost province.

Beyond the city of Vancouver, British Columbia is home to Canada's only desert and its premier ski resorts. It has an old-school capital, a newly developing wine region, and a network of islands dotted with laid-back communities. While the province stretches across a vast area north to the Yukon and Alaska, occupying 10 percent of Canada's land, most of the population is concentrated in the southern tier.

B.C. has historically earned its living through farming, fishing, forestry, and mining. While these industries remain important, newer businesses—including high-technology, film and TV, and tourism—are contributing significantly to the provincial economy.

A recent Forbes.com report noted that young, well-educated individuals are increasingly choosing to settle in a place that they like, regardless of the local job prospects. With Canada's mildest climate and a plethora of year-round

© CAROLYN B. HELLER

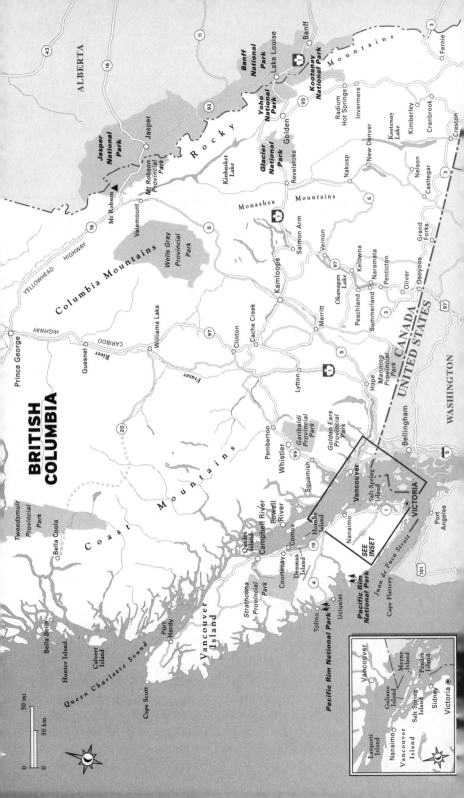

recreation options that range from sailing to skiing to golf, British Columbia is drawing people to its active, outdoorsy communities, where they might work locally or telecommute to jobs farther afield.

In 2007, British Columbia's population topped 4.4 million. Nearly 60 percent of the province's population growth is driven by immigration from outside of Canada. Whether you're coming to B.C. to work, invest, vacation, or retire, you're picking one of Canada's most popular regions for expats.

Vancouver Island

Vancouver may be British Columbia's largest city, but Victoria—across the Strait of Georgia on Vancouver Island—is the province's capital. The rest of Vancouver Island, which is nearly 500 kilometers (300 miles) long and roughly 100 kilometers (60 miles) wide, is dotted with smaller cities, beach towns, fishing villages, and logging communities.

Off the east coast of Vancouver Island, the Gulf Islands stretch north from the Washington State border. Popular as vacation destinations, most of the Gulf Islands have small year-round communities as well.

Who retires to Canada? Plenty of people do, and their destination is frequently Vancouver Island or the Gulf Islands. Drawn by the comparatively mild climate, many retirees come to coastal British Columbia from elsewhere in Canada and from the United States. Some stay year-round, while others winter in drier climes to the south.

But it's not only retirees who settle in this region. About 700,000 people live on Vancouver Island, and of those, roughly 300,000 make their home in Greater Victoria. The provincial government is Victoria's largest employer, providing nearly 12,000 jobs. The University of Victoria employs roughly 5,000 people, and other growing sectors are tourism, financial services, high-tech, and telecommunications. Tourism, in particular, is a major industry, not just in Victoria but across Vancouver Island and on the Gulf Islands as well.

THE LAY OF THE LAND

Victoria is located on the southern end of Vancouver Island. A fairly traditional city that's long been a popular retirement destination, Victoria is attracting a growing number of younger residents.

With a population of just over 90,000, Nanaimo, the island's second-largest city, is about 100 kilometers (60 miles) north of Victoria on the island's east coast. Other communities on the eastern shore include Comox, Courtenay, and Campbell River. At the island's northern tip is the town of Port Hardy, the jumping-off point for ferry service to the province's far north.

An important region for tourism is the west coast, fronting the Pacific Ocean. Outdoor adventurers come to hike the rainforest trails, kayak the bays, and surf the waves in and around Pacific Rim National Park. This area has some of Canada's best beaches, particularly near the easy-going town of Tofino.

The largest of the Gulf Islands is Salt Spring, with a year-round population of about 10,000. It's best known for its established arts community. The second-largest island, Pender, is actually two—North Pender and South Pender—connected by a bridge and home to about 2,000 residents. Nearby are Mayne, Galiano, and Saturna Islands. Farther north, the major islands include Denman, Hornby, Quadra, and Cortes.

Climate

Boasting the mildest climate in Canada, Victoria has early springs, warm and dry summers, mild autumns, and damp but temperate winters. While you won't be basking on the beach in January, it might be mild enough to golf or even sail. Though it does rain frequently in winter, Victoria boosters assert that the city gets one-third less rain than Vancouver or Seattle.

Elsewhere on the island, the coastal regions are fairly mild, with a climate similar to that of Victoria, but the higher elevations do see snow. The Gulf Islands have the same temperate rainforest climate, with short, damp winters and mild, sunny summers.

Culture

Victoria is large enough to support its own symphony and opera company, an early music society, a ballet troupe, and several small theaters. The restaurant scene is heating up, with a growing emphasis on locally sourced food, and plenty of bars and pubs draw both visitors and locals. Just outside Victoria, a small wine-producing region is becoming a weekend getaway for oenophiles.

It's easy to get outdoors in Victoria, whether your preferred activity is a stroll along the waterfront, a bike ride along a rail trail, or a long hike through the rain forest. Across Vancouver Island, residents favor outdoor activities, from beach-going to kayaking to skiing. Yes, you can ski—on Mt. Washington, which rises to 1,588 meters (5,215 feet).

Salt Spring and several other islands have communities of artists, which means art galleries, art shows, and festivals are popular activities, especially in summer. Many islanders are avid sailors or kayakers, too.

© ALAN ALBERT

the Pacific coast near Tofino, British Columbia

WHERE TO LIVE

British Columbia's real estate boom has been going full force in Victoria. In the second half of 2007, prices for single-family homes in Greater Victoria averaged $581,419, condos averaged $319,980, and townhouses $415,648. Victoria real estate agents say that an especially active segment of home-buyers is the "pre-retirees"—45- to 55-year-olds who are purchasing second homes that they may eventually use as retirement residences. Younger families are relocating from bigger cities to Victoria as well.

Tofino, on the west coast, is one of the region's priciest areas, with homes averaging more than $600,000, although the average in the nearby town of Ucluelet is still under $400,000. Elsewhere on Vancouver Island, average prices are lower: $343,168 in Nanaimo, $329,280 in the Comox Valley, and $297,046 in Campbell River. On the Gulf Islands, 2007 prices averaged $568,830, but there's a big range of property available, from modest cottages to waterfront estates.

Greater Victoria

Downtown Victoria, which radiates out from the Inner Harbour, is the hub of the city's tourism industry—with hotels, restaurants, museums, and shops catering largely to visitors—but it's becoming progressively more residential. Many new condominium towers are under construction, and older buildings are being converted to loft apartments and condos, especially near the small Chinatown.

South of the Inner Harbour, the James Bay neighborhood is on a point,

TAKING A RELOCATION VACATION

The best way to get to know an area is through its food. That's according to Kathy McAree, who runs Travel with Taste, a Victoria-based culinary tour company. Not only does McAree lead food-focused tours of Victoria and points farther afield on Vancouver Island, she also offers a unique service – the Victoria Relocation Vacation.

If you're thinking about relocating to the Victoria area, McAree can help. Working with local developers, McAree can create a customized tour of several real estate developments in Greater Victoria. But since a new home is much more than just a place to sleep, McAree will also introduce you to the restaurants, bakeries, and food shops near these developments. You might follow a visit to a sustainable community with lunch at a local vegetarian restaurant, check out the local gelato shop after touring a new condominium hotel, or visit the local farmers' market after visiting a golf resort.

To help you plan your Relocation Vacation, McAree will ask about your interests, your lifestyle, your budget, and any food preferences. A Relocation Vacation tour typically lasts a full day, but customized tours of different lengths can be arranged. A private one-day tour for two will run about $500.

For more information, contact Kathy McAree at 250/385-1527 or www. travelwithtaste.com.

bounded by water. It's a mixed residential/commercial area, with hotels and bed-and-breakfasts in between older homes and newer apartment, townhouse, and condo developments.

Many of Victoria's residential neighborhoods are east of downtown. The Fairfield area has a mix of apartments and single-family homes, with a cute shopping strip along Cook Street. Farther west is posh Rockland, where Victorian-era mansions, newer stately homes, and more modest bungalows coexist, and Oak Bay, an established waterfront community with British roots. More residential neighborhoods stretch north from Oak Bay toward the University of Victoria campus.

West of Chinatown, over the Johnson Street Bridge, is Victoria West. Apartment and condo buildings line the harbor here, many boasting lovely views of downtown and the waterfront. Among several new developments, Dockside Green (www.docksidegreen.com), built on reclaimed industrial land, aims to be one of Canada's most environmentally friendly communities.

Farther west, the communities of Esquimalt, View Royal, Colwood, and Metchosin—collectively known as the West Shore—are all rapidly growing. Although the West Shore towns initially sprawled from Victoria like typical suburbs, more urban-style planned developments are cropping up. Aquattro, a new residential community in Colwood, will include a mix of sleek townhouses and condos. Up in the hills is Bear Mountain, a golf-oriented development encompassing single-family homes, townhouses, and a resort hotel.

North of Victoria, many visitors know the Saanich Peninsula primarily for the road to the B.C. Ferries terminal at Swartz Bay. But the towns along the peninsula include everything from high-end residences, workaday neighborhoods, and suburban-style malls, to rural homes and farms.

Nanaimo and the East Coast

While Victoria alternates between its old-fashioned British heritage and newly hip future, the city of Nanaimo is more down-to-earth. Construction and forestry still provide many Nanaimo-area jobs, although tourism and high-tech are developing components of the economy.

North of Nanaimo, the Comox Valley has a population of about 65,000, encompassing the towns of Courtenay and Comox. Many jobs here are in forestry, construction, and agriculture, or at the nearby Mt. Washington Ski Resort. Increasingly, small businesses and tourism ventures are providing new opportunities.

Billing itself as the "Salmon Capital of the World," the town of Campbell River caters to both commercial and recreational fishing. A short drive from rustic Strathcona Provincial Park, Campbell River is also a base for north-island tourism and outdoor recreation.

The West Coast

The Tofino-Ucluelet area on the island's Pacific Coast feels like the end of the road—and it is, literally, at the end of Highway 4. The peninsula juts into the sea, with Ucluelet to the south and Tofino to the north. Pacific Rim National Park lies midway between the two communities.

Tofino-Ucluelet has a year-round population of about 5,000, but the numbers swell in summer with part-time residents and vacationers. Ucluelet used to be home to fishermen, loggers, and factory workers, while Tofino was a free-spirited, crunchy-granola place. As real estate prices have increased, Ucluelet is shedding its working-class reputation, while in Tofino, hippies share the sidewalks with vacationing tycoons. The region's housing stock ranges from humble homes to waterfront mansions, as well as newer townhouses and condos.

The Gulf Islands

Arty Salt Spring Island's eclectic population includes artists, entrepreneurs, and back-to-nature types. The largest town, Ganges, has most of its

Pacific Rim National Park, near Tofino, on Vancouver Island

services—grocery stores, banks, gas stations, and other businesses. Ganges hosts a popular Saturday Market from April through October, offering local produce, cheeses, baked goods, and a wide selection of arts and crafts.

The other southern Gulf Islands have smaller year-round communities: approximately 2,000 people on Pender, 1,000 on Galiano, and 900 on Mayne. Farther north, Denman and Hornby Island residents include artists, retired people, and part-timers who enjoy the beach as well as the peace and quiet. Denman's population is about 1,200, and nearby Hornby has roughly 1,000 residents.

Some of the 2,700 year-rounders on Quadra Island, a 10-minute ferry hop from Campbell River, make their living through fishing or forestry. Others are small-business people, artists, or writers. Part of the island is residential, while some is wild rainforest.

DAILY LIFE

What Victoria, Vancouver Island, and the Gulf Islands have in common is a fairly relaxed lifestyle. Sure, Victoria is increasingly urban, but compared to Vancouver or Toronto—or to New York or Chicago—it's still pretty hassle-free.

Resources

Tourism Vancouver Island and Tourism Victoria provide information to introduce the region's attractions. Victoria's daily newspaper, the *Times-Colonist,* is the island's largest. *Monday Magazine,* a Victoria-based alternative weekly, provides political, community, and arts coverage. The University of Victoria

© BEAR MOUNTAIN RESORT

You can golf year-round at Bear Mountain, on Vancouver Island.

publishes a relocation guide (www.opportunities.uvic.ca) designed for incoming faculty but useful for anyone relocating to the area.

Schools

In Greater Victoria, elementary schools include Grades K–5, middle schools Grades 6–8, and secondary schools Grades 9–12. School District #61 (www.sd61.bc.ca) manages the nearly 50 public schools in the region.

Nanaimo, the Comox Valley, and Campbell River each have several elementary and secondary schools. There's an elementary school in Tofino, and elementary and secondary schools in Ucluelet.

School District #64 (www.sd64.bc.ca) runs the 10 public schools in the southern Gulf Islands. Salt Spring has several elementary schools, a middle school, and a secondary school. Galiano, Mayne, and Pender have small community schools, but most secondary students go off-island. There are private schools of all stripes on Vancouver Island, plus a private elementary school on Salt Spring.

Denman and Hornby each have a public elementary school. Secondary students attend school in Courtenay. Quadra also has a public elementary school, but students go to Campbell River for high school. Home-schooling is popular, especially in more remote locations.

GETTING AROUND

Victoria's airport has flights to Vancouver, Kelowna, Calgary, Edmonton, Toronto, and Seattle. Floatplanes buzz between Vancouver and Victoria, Nanaimo, and the Gulf Islands; they're faster, but more expensive, than the ferries.

On Vancouver Island, Highway 1 runs from Victoria north to Parksville (north of Nanaimo); from there, Highway 19 continues along the eastern shore to Port Hardy. Highway 4 heads west mid-island to Ucluelet and Tofino. Highway 14 follows the southern shore, traveling west from Victoria.

Public Transportation, Bike, and On Foot

Both Victoria and Nanaimo have regional bus systems, and Salt Spring launched a new public bus service in 2008. Detailed information about services in these and other island communities is online at www.bctransit.com.

Within Victoria, and in many island communities, you can reach many destinations on foot or by bike. The Galloping Goose Trail, Victoria's main commuter bikeway, begins west of downtown and links to bike paths extending up the Saanich Peninsula.

Boat

B.C. Ferries runs a well-developed network of boats that connects Vancouver with Victoria, Nanaimo, the Gulf Islands, and the northern coast. Most ferries transport cars and bicycles as well as walk-on passengers. In summer, on busy weekends, and on holidays year-round, it's a good idea to book ahead when you're taking your car.

Ferries to Victoria and the southern Gulf Islands leave from Tsawwassen, about 30 kilometers (20 miles) south of downtown Vancouver. The B.C. Ferries terminal closest to Victoria is Swartz Bay, north of the city. Ferries to Nanaimo leave from Horseshoe Bay in West Vancouver.

Salt Spring, Galiano, Pender, and Mayne Islands have direct ferry service from the mainland. To reach Denman, Hornby, and Quadra, you cross first to Vancouver Island and then make connections. Detailed route maps and schedules are on the B.C. Ferries website, where you can also book car reservations.

Pacific Coach Lines runs a bus-ferry-bus service from downtown Vancouver to downtown Victoria. It's convenient for short trips between the two cities when you don't have a car.

From Washington State, there are several options for traveling to Victoria. The Clipper Ferry provides passenger-only service between Seattle and Victoria. The Coho Ferry takes both cars and walk-on passengers between Port Angeles (on the Olympic Peninsula) and Victoria. The Victoria Express ferry also travels between Port Angeles and Victoria from May through September. Washington State Ferries runs seasonal service from Anacortes to Sidney (north of Victoria).

© ALAN ALBERT

The Gulf Islands are a sailor's paradise.

Squamish and Whistler

Back on the mainland, traveling north from Vancouver, the aptly named Sea-to-Sky Highway winds between the cliffs and the sea to the towns of Squamish and Whistler.

Billing itself as "the outdoor recreation capital of Canada," Squamish is a mecca for windsurfing, rock-climbing, mountain biking, scuba diving, kayaking, rafting, and hiking. Many of the town's 15,000 residents enjoy an active lifestyle. As real estate prices in the region have climbed, Squamish is also becoming a bedroom community. More than a quarter of Squamish residents commute to Vancouver or head north to work in Whistler.

Squamish is a relatively young community, with more than 80 percent of the population under age 55. Nearly a third of Squamish residents work in service or sales jobs, particularly in accommodations, food, and retail. Transportation, warehousing, construction, and manufacturing provide more local jobs. Quest University, Canada's first private university, opened in Squamish in 2007.

In the resort town of Whistler, it's all about the skiing and snowboarding. Skiers and riders come to Whistler-Blackcomb, North America's largest winter resort, from around the world. With Vancouver, Whistler is co-hosting the 2010 Winter Olympic Games. Summers are busy, too, when the town draws hikers, mountain bikers, and other outdoor enthusiasts.

Nearly 90 percent of Whistler's population is under age 55. In addition to the approximately 9,000 year-round residents, Whistler has a sizeable seasonal population of younger people who work on the slopes and in the restaurants, bars, hotels, and services businesses. Nearly three-quarters of Whistler's jobs are in services and retail, most of which are related to skiing, recreation, and the tourism infrastructure.

Local realtors estimate that, in addition to the permanent population, the area has more than 9,000 second-home owners. Some homeowners live in town part-time, while others use their properties primarily for rental income or investment purposes.

THE LAY OF THE LAND

Squamish is about 60 kilometers (40 miles), or an hour's drive, north of Vancouver along Highway 99, the Sea-to-Sky Highway. Whistler is 60 kilometers—or about 45–60 minutes—beyond Squamish. While it's beautiful, the Sea-to-Sky Highway isn't a fast road.

Climate

Squamish and Whistler have a slightly colder climate than Vancouver, especially at higher elevations. The summers are warm and dry; spring and fall are temperate. In the mountains, you can expect heavy snow in winter. At Whistler, it's not uncommon for rain to fall in the village while it's snowing hard up on the ski slopes.

Culture

In Squamish, the outdoors rules, so if you're looking for fine dining or the latest art flick, you'll have to head to Vancouver or Whistler. Unlike many Canadian cities, Squamish's population is more than 98 percent English-speaking, although there's a small Punjabi community as well.

Drawing workers and visitors from all over the world, Whistler feels quite international. Since many seasonal employees come from Australia and New Zealand, you'll hear plenty of Aussie and Kiwi accents on the slopes and in the pubs. And speaking of pubs, Whistler has a hopping bar scene, especially on winter weekends. The town also has 80-some restaurants, including many high-end dining rooms catering to the moneyed ski crowd.

WHERE TO LIVE
Squamish

Most Squamish residents live in single-family homes, townhouses, or low-rise apartment buildings. While many residential areas rise into the hills on either side of Highway 99, some newer high-end communities dot the Howe Sound waterfront. From 2006 to 2007, the median price for a single-family detached home in Squamish rose 22 percent, from $386,500 to $470,500.

Whistler

Because Whistler has so many temporary workers—estimates of the town's winter workforce top 14,000—low-cost housing is at a premium. Seasonal staffers often end up bunking on their pals' living room couches, at least temporarily, while searching for affordable places to live.

Whistler has scores of townhouses and condo developments, particularly in and around the Village core. Some are available for fractional ownership. Standalone homes and chalets tend to be slightly farther from the town center. While there's a huge price range, you might not want to look at single-family homes if your budget can't handle multimillion dollar price tags.

Toward the south end of town, Whistler Creekside is the site of the original ski area and where much new development is taking place. South of Creekside is the Whistler Olympic Athlete Village, which will be converted to residential housing after the 2010 Games.

The Alta Vista, Blueberry Hill, and Whistler Cay neighborhoods are near Alta Lake, and just north of town, Alpine Meadows has a more local vibe. About 35 kilometers (20 miles) farther north is the small town of Pemberton, a lower-cost alternative that's still within relatively easy driving distance of Whistler.

If you're buying property in Whistler, get familiar with the town's zoning code. Properties that are zoned for "tourist accommodation" can be rented short term (less than 28 days). If the zoning is "residential," the minimum rental period is 28 days.

Some Whistler condominiums restrict the amount of time that the owner can be in residence. A "Phase 1" property allows owners to use their units whenever they want, but some buildings require that you make your unit available to the common rental pool when you're not on-site. A "Phase 2" property allows owners to be at home 56 days a year; the rest of the time, the unit must be rented. Talk with local real estate agents to learn more about these restrictions.

DAILY LIFE

If you don't like to be outdoors, you probably won't be happy living in Squamish or Whistler, since many residents' daily lives—at least when they're not working—revolve around active pursuits. However, if you love the outdoors and you settle in this part of B.C., you might think you've died and gone to heaven.

The best way to get to know your Squamish or Whistler neighbors may be to join them on the ski slopes or on the trails. The Squamish area has eight provincial parks where you can hike, snowshoe, cross-country ski, or camp. In town, the Brennan Park Recreation Centre has a pool, skating rink, tennis courts, and a variety of fitness programs.

In Whistler, of course, there are the slopes, but you can cross-country ski and snowshoe as well. Both residents and visitors make good use of the Meadow Park Sports Centre, with its fitness center, pool, squash courts, and ice rink.

Resources

You can get acquainted with Squamish at the Squamish Adventure Centre, which houses the town's visitors center, as well as its tourism and business development departments. Newspapers include the daily *Squamish Today,* the weekly *Squamish Chief* (www.squamishchief.com), and the weekly *Sea-to-Sky News* (www.stsnews.ca).

Tourism Whistler gives you the lowdown on tourist activities around town, while the Whistler Chamber of Commerce provides helpful information about finding work and housing. Another good resource is the Whistler Employment Resource Centre, which operates a job board and helps job seekers with free Internet access and local phone services.

In Whistler, *Pique NewsMagazine* (www.piquenewsmagazine.com) is a locally owned weekly paper with an extensive classified ad section. They also publish *FAQ: The Insider's Guide to Whistler* (www.faqwhistler.com), which is a mix of ads and attitude. The *Whistler Question* is another free weekly.

Schools

There are six public elementary schools in Squamish and two in Whistler, covering grades K–7. For Grades 8–12, Squamish has two secondary schools, Whistler has one. Each community also has a private Waldorf elementary school.

GETTING AROUND

If you live and work in Whistler, you may be able to manage without a car, since the town is fairly compact and the local shuttle bus system is extensive. The Sea-to-Sky transit program provides bus service for Squamish residents who commute into Whistler. Within Squamish itself, it would help to have your own wheels, although three bus routes do link various neighborhoods.

The Whistler and Valley Express—known as the WAVE—runs buses every day, nearly 'round the clock (5:30 A.M.–3 A.M.), so it's easy to get around

Whistler's various neighborhoods car-free. Whistler Village also has a free shuttle bus system.

The Whistler Village core is a pedestrian-only zone, which makes getting around on foot not only easy but essential. The 35-kilometer (22-mile) Valley Trail, a paved multi-use trail, runs through Whistler, from the Emerald Estates neighborhood south to Creekside.

The Okanagan Valley

About 400 kilometers (250 miles) east of Vancouver is the Okanagan Valley. With a drier climate than the B.C. coast, the Okanagan has historically been an agricultural area. Known for "beaches and peaches," it's long been a summer vacation spot for families who come to swim in the lakes and hike in the hills, and a winter getaway for "snowbirds" from other parts of Canada. Now one of the fastest-growing regions in British Columbia, the Okanagan is popular year-round with retirees, second-home owners, and younger families seeking to escape from urban life.

© ALAN ALBERT

The Okanagan Valley now has more than 130 wineries.

The rapidly expanding Okanagan wine industry—at last count, there were more than 130 wineries—has triggered a boom in restaurants, hotels, and related tourism businesses. The real estate market, both resale and new construction, has also been on a roll.

More than half the Okanagan's jobs are in the services sector. Other important industries include finance, real estate, construction, manufacturing, and transportation. The University of British Columbia's satellite campus, U.B.C. Okanagan, currently enrolls about 5,000 students.

THE LAY OF THE LAND

The Okanagan is centered along a chain of lakes that run north–south from the U.S. border. The largest, Okanagan Lake, is 110 kilometers (68 miles) long. Part of the lakeshore is developed, with small cities, hotels, and vacation homes, but much of the lakefront remains in its natural state.

With a metropolitan-area population of just over 160,000, the city of Kelowna is the hub of the Central Okanagan. Okanagan Lake splits the Kelowna region in two. Downtown Kelowna is on the lake's east side. The U.B.C. Okanagan campus is north of downtown, and to the south is the Mission district where several wineries are located. Across the lake is the aptly named community of Westbank. South of Westbank are the smaller towns of Peachland and Summerland.

Continuing into the South Okanagan, the next major town is Penticton, about 60 kilometers (40 miles) from Kelowna. From Penticton, it's a short hop to the village of Naramata, a burgeoning wine-producing area. Farther south, Oliver and Osoyoos are home to a growing number of wineries and draw entrepreneurs, vacationers, and retirees.

Climate

The Okanagan Valley is sunny and dry for much of the year. In December and January, temperatures hover around the freezing mark, but by March, it's spring-like and summers are hot. In Kelowna, 28°C (82°F) days are common in July and August, and it's usually several degrees warmer in more desert-like Osoyoos.

Culture

Wine tourism highlights Okanagan summers, with tastings and wine dinners attracting visitors and locals alike. Otherwise, the Okanagan's cultural vibe is more laid-back than cutting edge, although Kelowna has a nascent art scene. The art museum is housed in a snazzy modern building, galleries are popping up, and Prospera Place arena hosts bands and touring shows. And if the cultural scene doesn't cut it, at least there's first-rate skiing and snowboarding nearby, and milder weather brings swimming, boating, fishing, golfing, hiking, and bicycling.

WHERE TO LIVE
The Central Okanagan

Kelowna has been in the midst of a building boom, with hotels and condo buildings under construction downtown, and strip malls and subdivisions sprouting everywhere else. If you're looking for an idyllic wine-country getaway, Kelowna isn't it—it's much too suburban. Yet despite all this development, Kelowna remains manageable. You won't find scores of big-city amenities yet, but you won't find too many big-city problems either.

Across Okanagan Lake from downtown Kelowna, the community of

NAPA NORTH

Back in the 1970s, no one was talking about British Columbia's wine – at least no one who was serious about what they put in their glass.

These days, the B.C. wine industry has plenty of buzz. In the mid-'80s, B.C. had 13 wineries. By 2007, there were more than 10 times that number. Much of the excitement is coming out of the Okanagan, the region that's becoming known as "Napa North."

The Okanagan lies in a rain shadow, with a ridge of mountains shielding the region from the dampness of the coast. Summer days are long and hot, which gives grapes plenty of time to grow. As grape quality has improved, so, too, has the expertise of the Okanagan's wine makers. The region's production is still tiny compared to the giant Napa Valley, but the wines are increasingly worth the trip.

Accompanying the development of the Okanagan's wine industry is a parallel growth in tourism. Wine tourists want to dine in upscale restaurants – where the regional food is paired with local wines, of course – and lay their heads in comfortable hotels. Not only has it been a good time to be in the wine business here, but more entrepreneurs have been responding to the demands for dining, lodging, and other services to support the wine tourism market. The wine industry has also helped fuel demand for second homes in the region.

To learn more about the B.C. wine industry in general, and the Okanagan wines in particular, visit www.winebc.com, the website for the British Columbia Wine Institute.

PRIME LIVING LOCATIONS

Westbank is part suburban sprawl and part bucolic wine region. Subdivisions rise into the hills on both sides of Highway 97, so even many modest homes have lake views. Continuing south, tiny Peachland is tucked into a bend between Highway 97 and the lake. Many homes here are within a short walk of the lakeshore.

Highway 97 bisects the town of Summerland, which has a year-round population of just over 10,000. There are residential neighborhoods between the highway and the lake, while the town center and other residential options are on the west side of the highway.

The average price of a home in the Central Okanagan was $497,000 in late 2007. About half of all recent home sales were single-family detached houses. Most of the remainder were condominiums.

The South Okanagan

If you were dropped into the South Okanagan, it would be hard to guess that you were in Canada. The dry, sun-baked hills dotted alternately with scrubby brush, verdant farms, and vineyards look more like southern California—or even Tuscany—than Canada. This region is home to Canada's only desert, and the climate is almost Mediterranean. Agriculture, especially fruit-growing, remains an important part of the regional economy.

Set between Okanagan and Skaha Lakes, Penticton is the South Okanagan's largest city, with 45,000 residents. Penticton's population is part working people and part retirees (a quarter of Penticton citizens are over 65), but several high-end developments are marketing to an affluent crowd. Just east of Penticton, the village of Naramata (population 2,000) is a fast-developing wine region. More than 20 wineries now have a Naramata address.

About 40 kilometers (25 miles) south of Penticton is the town of Oliver. Oliver is transforming from sleepy country village to major tourist destination. The roads around town are lined with wineries and vineyards, and new wineries seem to open every year.

Osoyoos, just north of the U.S. border, has a population of 4,500, and nearly half the residents are over 55. However, Osoyoos, too, is changing. Upscale hotels and condominiums are under construction, and while there are still plenty of farm stands hawking just-picked peaches, cherries, and freshly baked pies, you can also drop $100 per person on an elegant dinner with regional wines.

Real estate prices in the South Okanagan vary significantly by community. Average sales prices in 2007 for single-family homes ranged from $326,202 in Oliver, to the low $400,000s in Osoyoos and Penticton, up to $778,000 in Naramata.

DAILY LIFE
Resources
The Thompson Okanagan Tourism Association (www.totabc.com) can give you the lowdown on the region from a visitor's perspective. More details about living and working in the Okanagan are available from the City of Kelowna (www.kelowna.ca). The City of Penticton (www.penticton.ca) publishes a useful guide for people relocating to the area.

The *Kelowna Daily Courier* (www.kelownadailycourier.ca) is the region's major daily newspaper. The *Penticton Herald* (www.pentictonherald.ca), another daily, serves the South Okanagan.

Schools
In most Central Okanagan communities, elementary school runs K–6, middle school Grades 7–9, and high school Grades 10–12; however, some elementary schools continue through Grade 7, feeding secondary schools that encompass

© ALAN ALBERT

Summer lunch at the Mission Hill Family Estate winery, in Westbank, B.C.

Grades 8–12. The Kelowna-based Central Okanagan School District (www. sd23.bc.ca) can give you the details.

In Penticton/Naramata (www.sd67.bc.ca), elementary school is K–5, middle school is 6–8, and high school is 9–12. The Okanagan Similkameen School District (www.sd53.bc.ca) runs elementary schools (K–7) and secondary schools (8–12) in Oliver and Osoyoos.

Private schools exist in Kelowna and several Okanagan communities; many have a religious affiliation.

GETTING AROUND

The main airport serving the Okanagan region is in Kelowna, with daily flights to Seattle and to several Canadian cities, including Vancouver, Calgary, Edmonton, and Toronto. The small Penticton airport has service to Vancouver and Calgary.

By car, it's about a 4.5-hour drive between Vancouver and Kelowna or about six hours from Seattle. Be prepared for winter driving conditions between November and March in the mountains between the coast and the Okanagan. It can be rainy in Vancouver, sunny in Kelowna, and snowing heavily in the mountains, all on the same day.

Highway 97 is the main north–south route within the Okanagan region.

It takes about two hours to drive the 125 kilometers (75 miles) between Kelowna and Osoyoos along this sometimes-meandering route.

The Kelowna Regional Transit System operates buses in and around Kelowna, with service across the lake to Westbank and other west side communities. Otherwise, it's not that easy to travel the Okanagan without your own transportation.

TORONTO

Canada may not be a country prone to superlatives, yet those that do exist, exist in Toronto.

Toronto is Canada's largest city and the capital of Ontario. It's home to the world's longest street and its second-tallest tower. It's also Canada's most ethnically diverse metropolitan area and one of the most multicultural cities on the planet.

Toronto is a city of immigrants. Roughly half of the metropolitan area's residents were born outside Canada, and approximately 100,000 new immigrants move to the city every year. While the majority of Toronto's early settlers were of British origin, over the past dozen years Toronto's Chinese community has increased by more than 15 percent, the Indian community by 25 percent, and the Filipino community by over 30 percent. The city also has a large Afro-Canadian and Caribbean community. If you're coming to Toronto from the United States, you won't be alone either, since nearly 42,000 people now living in Toronto were born in the United States.

MULTICULTURAL TORONTO

In this city there are Bulgarian mechanics, there are Eritrean accountants, Colombian café owners, Latvian book publishers, Welsh roofers, Afghani dancers, Iranian mathematicians, Tamil cooks in Thai restaurants, Calabrese boys with Jamaican accents, Fushen deejays, Filipina-Saudi beauticians, Russian doctors changing tires; there are Romanian bill collectors, Cape Croker fishmongers, Japanese grocery clerks, French gas meter readers, German bakers, Haitian and Bengali taxi drivers with Irish dispatchers.

Toronto writer Dionne Brand in her novel, *What We All Long For*

Toronto is Canada's financial capital, with the city's Bay Street known as Canada's Wall Street. Not only is Canada's major equities market, the Toronto Stock Exchange, based here, but so are the headquarters of scores of banks and financial services companies. Greater Toronto has also become a major high-tech center, actively welcoming entrepreneurs and technology professionals.

Finance, insurance, health care, real estate, sciences, high-tech, and the arts employ thousands of Toronto residents. With all the new construction going on, there are plenty of jobs in the building trades. Drawing roughly 20 million visitors every year, Toronto is one of Canada's top tourist destinations, which translates into significant employment opportunities in the tourism and hospitality sectors.

Education is also a major employer in metropolitan Toronto. With more than 70,000 students and nearly 12,000 faculty and staff, the University of Toronto is Canada's largest university. York University, Ryerson University, and the Ontario College of Art and Design are based in Toronto as well.

Originally founded as the settlement of York in 1793, the city survived an attack by American troops during the War of 1812 and was renamed Toronto in 1834. Although Toronto continued to grow throughout the 1800s, many downtown buildings were lost when a huge fire in 1904 leveled nearly eight hectares (20 acres) of land. The 1844 St. Lawrence Market, now a popular food and snack stop, is one of the dwindling number of structures remaining from these early days.

Toronto's architecture today mixes the historic and the contemporary. One of the best examples of this mélange of old and new may be the Royal Ontario Museum. It's an elegant, British-inspired building that now sports a wild modern addition, a quirkily shaped glass pyramid that seems to dangle precariously off the edge.

The traditional and the modern coexist not just in architecture but in the city's whole esthetic. Toronto is a place where financial district suits share the sidewalks with downtown hipsters, where you can settle in a historic city-center community or on a quiet suburban cul-de-sac. Glittering glass-and-steel towers line the downtown streets and the lakeshore, while many neighborhoods are filled with rehabbed brick row houses or stately Victorian-era homes. Districts like Queen Street West and Leslieville draw trend-seekers to their galleries, hip cafés, and funky boutiques, while the suburbs have the same malls you find across North America.

Why live in Toronto? With its many financial and cultural institutions, Toronto might be considered a kinder, gentler New York or the Canadian counterpart to Chicago. Many residents say that Toronto manages to balance fast-paced urban life with enough services and amenities to smooth the rough edges of city living. It's a big city of small neighborhoods, where immigrants seeking new opportunities come from every corner of the globe.

The Lay of the Land

Toronto is built on the shore of Lake Ontario. Beginning at the lake and heading north, downtown Toronto includes the financial district, the harbor, and a mix of residential and commercial neighborhoods. Yonge Street bisects the city's east and west sides. Many locals consider "downtown" to extend as far north as Bloor Street, a main east–west artery that also borders the University of Toronto (U of T) campus.

North of Bloor Street is Midtown, where you'll find many of Toronto's most popular residential neighborhoods, alternating with commercial developments. The Annex neighborhood around U of T, posh Yorkville, and high-end residential enclaves like Rosedale and Forest Hill are all part of Midtown. The area around Yonge and Eglinton Streets not only has high-rise apartment towers and leafy residential streets, but it's also become a well-developed business district.

One thing that often surprises newcomers to Toronto is how many upscale homes are set on very small lots. The many older homes in the Downtown and Midtown communities simply weren't built on large plots of land. Not only do single-family homes often have diminutive yards, Toronto also has a large number of "semi-detached" homes, which share a common wall, as well as a small yard or garden.

The current-day boundaries of the city of Toronto incorporate several formerly independent communities, including York, East York, and North York, which are all more or less north of Midtown, as well as Scarborough to the east and Etobicoke (pronounced "a-TOE-ba-coe") to the west. Locals still use those community names, even though these areas are now part of the City of Toronto municipal structure.

Downtown, Midtown, and the rest of Toronto's larger districts are further subdivided into well over 100 smaller neighborhoods. Toronto residents tend to define where they live by these neighborhood designations, which may cover an area of only a few blocks.

When the weather is mild, Toronto residents enjoy the waterfront.

© CAROLYN B. HELLER

Beyond the Toronto city limits, suburbs sprawl out in a horseshoe, where Markham, Richmond Hill, Vaughan, Mississauga, and Oakville, among others, are primarily bedroom communities. City residents sometimes refer to suburbanites as "905-ers," since 905 is the area code for the districts surrounding Toronto. The region sometimes known as the Golden Horseshoe extends farther beyond Greater Toronto to cities such as Kitchener-Waterloo and Hamilton; we've covered the Golden Horseshoe in the *Ontario* chapter.

CLIMATE

Although Toronto is northwest of Buffalo, Torontonians are quick to point out that the "lake effect" that dumps piles of snow on their New York State neighbors has a different result in their city. Toronto's position on Lake Ontario's northern shore moderates the winter weather, and the city averages 115 centimeters (45 inches) of snow per year, less than Buffalo can get on a single day. Winter is still cold—January's average temperatures range from -10°C (14°F) to -2°C (28°F)—but at least you usually won't be shoveling out from blizzards for weeks on end.

Spring is fairly short, beginning in late April or May, and summers can turn hot and humid. In July, the average temperatures range from a low of 15°C

TOUR TORONTO WITH A LOCAL

One of the best ways to get acquainted with a city is to ask a local. Yet when you move to a new community, it's not always easy to find a local to help you out.

It's different in Toronto. Through Toronto Tourism's "greeter" program, called "TAP into TO!," you can take a free tour of a Toronto neighborhood, led by a local "greeter" – an enthusiastic resident who has volunteered to be a tour guide.

You can choose which neighborhood you'd like to visit or let the greeter select a favorite area. If you have a particular interest, whether it's history, culture, architecture, or food, you can request a guide who's knowledgeable in that subject. Each tour typically lasts two or three hours.

One of the program's most animated greeters is Toronto native Ted Genova, who lives and runs a small business near the St. Lawrence Market. A tour with Genova is not just a spin through the city's tourist sites; he'll introduce you to his neighborhood, tell you how it has grown and changed, and share his thoughts on the community's future. And he's great fun.

Sign up for a greeter visit at least a week in advance at www.toronto.ca/tapto.

(59°F) to a high of 27°C (81°F). Fall is a lovely time of year, particularly in October when the leaves begin to change.

CULTURE

Toronto is home to many of Canada's premier cultural institutions. The Toronto Symphony Orchestra, the National Ballet of Canada, the Canadian Opera Company, the Canadian Stage Company, the Royal Ontario Museum, and the Art Gallery of Ontario are all based here. The Toronto International Film Festival is a major event on the fall social calendar.

But the city has a more contemporary side, too. Toronto hosts an annual fringe festival in July and an international writers' fest in October. One of the liveliest summer events is the popular Caribana carnival that celebrates Caribbean culture. There's a Museum of Contemporary Art, dozens of art galleries, and even a museum devoted to shoes.

The acclaimed Second City comedy company has a Toronto branch, and the city has a range of professional and local theater groups. And don't forget the nightclubs, the jazz bars, and the sports pubs broadcasting all hockey all the time.

In multi-culti Toronto, eating out can be a major cultural event, with choices ranging from Vietnamese, Thai, Japanese, Korean, and all manner of regional Chinese restaurants to Indian, Latino, Portuguese, Italian, Polish, Ukrainian,

Caribbean, and more. The city and its suburbs have five neighborhoods that are considered "Chinatown." You can find everything from simple noodle shops to roti stands to Indian buffets, often within a single neighborhood. And it's not all mom-and-pop ethnic joints either. Toronto has some of Canada's top restaurants, as well as innovative dining rooms serving creative cuisine for every budget.

Where to Live

Roughly a third of all jobs in Toronto are based downtown. If you'll be working in the city center, you can simplify your commute by living near a subway stop, streetcar line, or commuter rail station. Other major concentrations of offices and businesses are near Yonge and Eglinton in midtown Toronto and in North York, both of which are on the subway lines as well.

According to 2007 figures from the City of Toronto, the average monthly rent for a one-bedroom apartment was $890 and an average two-bedroom went for $1,050. Of course, these are averages across the region, and rents in prime neighborhoods can go much higher.

In 2007, the average purchase price of a home in metropolitan Toronto was $370,000. However, real estate agents will tell you that to buy a single-family or semi-detached home in a "nice" neighborhood in downtown or midtown Toronto, your budget should be a minimum of $600,000–700,000. In some areas, prices exceeding $1 million are not uncommon.

Because Toronto has so many different neighborhoods, any overview can only scratch the surface. Use this section as a general guide to Toronto's residential communities, but do your own exploring. Finding a good real estate agent can be especially helpful in sorting out the myriad options. See the *Resources* chapter for recommended agents who specialize in relocation to Toronto.

DOWNTOWN
The Harbourfront, Islands, and St. Lawrence District

Downtown Toronto used to be a place where people came to work but not necessarily to live. The lakeshore was an industrial zone, full of warehouses and factories. The Gardner Expressway, which slices an east–west swath through the city, further isolated downtown from the lake.

While the Expressway is still there, Toronto is reclaiming its waterfront, and residential condominium and apartment towers have gone up in the neighborhood now known as the Harbourfront. In early 2008, sales prices for

The Indian Bazaar is one of many Toronto neighborhoods that reflect the city's multicultural population.

Harbourfront condos were averaging $350,000. Many of these "average" units are small one-bedroom apartments, but some boast lovely lake or city views.

From the Harbourfront, you can take a ferry to several small islands in Lake Ontario. Originally developed in the early 1900s as a summer resort, the Islands now have a year-round residential community of about 650 people. Islanders own their homes but lease the land from the government.

St. Lawrence is one of Toronto's oldest downtown communities. Surrounding the landmark St. Lawrence Market, the area is home to a multi-income mix of apartment dwellers and townhouse denizens. Development is extending east of the St. Lawrence neighborhood, too, into the restored Distillery District. In the 1800s, the 40 buildings here housed the largest distillery in the British Empire. Now, they're being revamped into artist studios and galleries, restaurants, bars, lofts, and condos, with a few modern residential towers thrown in. Expect lots of change in this district over the next several years.

Kensington Market, Church-Wellesley, and Cabbagetown

Moving north from the harbor through downtown, the financial district towers give way to urban residential neighborhoods and to the main campus of the University of Toronto.

On the south side of the U of T campus is Kensington Market. It's not a market building, but rather a market neighborhood, filled with vendors' stalls and ethnic eateries that span the globe. There's a Chilean empanada place near a funky Asian-fusion spot, an Indian spice vendor opposite a Latino meat market, and a plethora of fruit sellers, bakeries, nut vendors, cheese shops, and inexpensive clothing outlets. The side streets are lined with rental houses and apartments, some occupied by U of T students and others housing residents as diverse as the Market's stores.

The center of Toronto's large gay and lesbian community is the downtown district known as Church-Wellesley. Housing in this neighborhood, which is east of the U of T campus around the intersection of Church and Wellesley Streets, includes both apartments and restored semi-detached homes. Plenty of clubs and restaurants keep the area lively.

Old and new stand side by side in the Financial District.

Farther east is the neighborhood known as Cabbagetown. According to legend, the immigrants from Italy and Macedonia who settled here in the 1800s could afford to eat only the cabbage they grew themselves—giving rise to the Cabbagetown name. Nowadays, the cost of the meticulously preserved Victorian homes in this now-chic corner of town is so high that you might have to eat cabbage to pay your mortgage, but you'll join a well-to-do collection of professionals and artistic types who appreciate gracious living in an urban setting. And urban it is—Cabbagetown borders Toronto's largest public housing project.

MIDTOWN AND NORTH TORONTO

Surrounding the University of Toronto, the Annex neighborhood is considered prime residential territory. Some Annex homes are rentals for students, and faculty (at least those who can afford it) live in the district's elegantly restored brick Victorians. Both the Bloor and Yonge subway lines have stations in this area, making commuting a snap.

Northeast of U of T, Yorkville is one of Toronto's most posh central districts. Some Victorian townhouses have been converted into upscale boutiques, while others are stylish residences. Newer buildings include many high-end condominiums and hotels. Lots of gourmet markets and designer shops make Yorkville a major shopping destination.

MUTUAL DRIVEWAYS

Many Toronto houses are built close together on small lots divided by a narrow driveway. These "mutual driveways" – some so tight that they can barely accommodate a modern-day car – are typically shared between the adjacent houses. In the rear, the parking area widens enough for residents to park behind their own homes.

If you drive an oversized SUV or other large car, beware: It may be too wide to fit in a mutual driveway. If your car is average-sized, just be prepared to share the driveway with your neighbor.

Wander the tree-lined streets of stately Rosedale, east of Yorkville, and you'd hardly know you were in the city. Lots are much larger than in many Toronto neighborhoods, and the older brick or stone houses are among the city's priciest. Expect to pay well over $1.5 million for homes in Rosedale and surrounding areas. Most homes here are within walking distance of the Yonge subway line.

Mercedes and BMWs fill the driveways in exclusive Forest Hill, which begins north of St. Clair Avenue. Many Tudor-style homes here could easily be called estates—with multimillion-dollar price tags to match. Two of Toronto's top private schools—the boys-only Upper Canada College and the all-girls Bishop Strachan School—are in Forest Hill.

Plenty of other family-friendly communities exist in North Toronto, and they don't all require trust funds to purchase a home. Although it's sometimes known as "Young and Eligible" for the high percentage of single professionals who live nearby, the neighborhood around the Yonge and Eglinton intersection is also home to many families. There are high-rise apartment towers, semi-detached houses, bungalows, and other single-family homes, as well as dozens of shops, restaurants, and offices that provide services and jobs for local residents.

More North Toronto options include the Allenby neighborhood with its older brick single-family houses on quiet streets, Bedford Park with a mix of detached and semi-detached homes near the Lawrence subway station, and Champlin Estates with comfortable homes that date to the 1920s and '30s. The area around Bathurst Street at Lawrence has a large Jewish community, with religious schools, synagogues, and kosher markets.

THE EAST END

Along Danforth Avenue east of the Don River, Danforth Village is sometimes known as Greektown, since it was the center of Toronto's Greek community.

© CAROLYN B. HELLER

Queen Street West is one of Toronto's hipper neighborhoods.

You'll still find souvlaki shops and baklava-filled bakeries, but the Danforth is becoming a trendy community popular with hip young families who shop in the organic market and frequent the local yoga studio. Homes range from restored brick Victorians around Playter Boulevard to more modest houses and bungalows throughout the district. Several subway stops on Danforth Avenue provide handy transit connections.

Riverdale, south of Danforth Avenue, is also growing in popularity with young families. This community has a mix of Victorian townhouses and semi-detached homes, and smaller residences. Around Broadview Avenue and Gerrard Street is one of Toronto's smaller "Chinatowns," which actually has a significant Vietnamese population. Farther east along Gerrard are the sari shops and curry-scented dining rooms of Little India.

Take the Queen Street streetcar east from downtown, and you'll reach the gentrifying neighborhood of Leslieville, which is drawing the artistically inclined to its galleries, cafés, and increasingly hip restaurants and shops. Continuing east is the neighborhood known as The Beaches. Bordering Lake Ontario, with lakefront walkways and, yes, beaches, this residential community mixes single-family and multi-unit dwellings. It's not posh-looking, but its combination of urban convenience and lake access keeps housing prices fairly high.

THE WEST END

Head west from downtown to find the neighborhood known as Queen Street West. Though it still has a grunge feel, this emerging arts district is increasingly "in" for its eclectic shops, galleries, funky hotels, and hip bars.

CANADA'S FIRST SUBURB

In the 1950s, both Canadians and Americans were settling down in record numbers to have the families that would become the baby boom. But where were these families going to live?

Seven miles northeast of downtown Toronto, in what was then a rural area, the first houses went up in the new community of Don Mills. When construction began in 1953, Don Mills became Canada's first suburb.

Many features of Don Mills became standard in North American suburban developments. The curved roads were designed to foster a sense of community and discourage outsiders from passing through. Plenty of green space separated the homes and provided places for kids to play. Unlike Levittown, New York, where the houses hewed to a common plan, Don Mills' designers wanted more variety. While single-family homes predominated, the community also included row houses and apartments. Within a few years, similar developments were under construction on the outskirts of many Canadian cities.

Today, as Toronto's suburbs have extended miles beyond this former outlying area, Don Mills retains its classic suburban layout. It remains a testament to the post-war era when families lived, grew, and dreamed their suburban dreams.

Continuing west, Parkdale is a formerly down-and-out district that's being rediscovered, as young professionals and families have begun to restore its turn-of-the-19th-century homes. The western boundary of Parkdale is Roncesvalles Avenue, where an older Polish community now shares the neighborhood with young families.

The area around High Park is a popular residential neighborhood, where the diverse housing stock ranges from elegant Victorians to new condominiums. Nearby Bloor West Village also draws families who appreciate the 1920s homes, despite small lot sizes. There's a convenient shopping district along Bloor Street, as well as two stations on the Bloor subway line.

Daily Life

In a city as large as Toronto, you can probably meet like-minded people, whether your interests are athletic or intellectual, cultural or culinary, classic or au courant.

You can join one of Toronto's "Meetup" groups (www.meetup.com) to find locals who share your interests. There are groups for film buffs, vegetarians, and wine connoisseurs, kayaking aficionados and business entrepreneurs, a "stitch and bitch" group for knitting hobbyists, and all varieties of singles get-togethers.

Many Toronto families meet through their children—at school, on the soccer field, or at the community centers. The Toronto Parks, Forestry and Recreation department publishes a semi-annual *Fun Guide* (www.toronto.ca/parks/torontofun) that lists arts, culture, recreation, and fitness programs and classes for adults and kids, as well as special events in the city's museums and parks.

To get acquainted with Toronto through volunteer work, check out Volunteer Toronto (www.volunteertoronto.on.ca). If you're between the ages of 23 and 35, another good resource is Toronto Volunteer Bridge (www.volunteerbridge.ca), which promotes volunteerism among young professionals.

Like most Canadian cities, Toronto is wild about hockey; the Maple Leafs are the local NHL team. Toronto is a baseball city, too, home to the major league Blue Jays. The Jays play at the Rogers Centre, formerly known as the SkyDome, notable for having the world's first fully retractable roof. Basketball fans cheer for the Raptors, Toronto's NBA team.

While Toronto may not be as outdoor-oriented as Canada's Western cities, residents do take advantage of its lakeshore location. On mild days, you can walk, run, or bike along the waterfront, sail on the lake, or explore the islands that are just a quick ferry ride from downtown.

RESOURCES

The City of Toronto offers a wealth of information for newcomers at www.toronto.ca/immigration. Another useful resource for getting settled in Ontario is www.settlement.org.

To get a handle on Toronto's myriad neighborhood divisions, take a look at the Toronto Real Estate Board's interactive neighborhood map (www.toronto-realestateboard.com). Click on a district, and you can display an overview and brief history of the area. The city of Toronto publishes demographic profiles of its many neighborhoods online (www.toronto.ca) as well.

In addition, try to get your hands on the now out-of-print book, *Your Guide to Toronto Neighbourhoods,* by David Dunkelman, which profiles more than 150 Toronto-area neighborhoods. While some data, particularly housing prices, is out of date, it's still a hugely useful overview. You may find copies in Toronto libraries or from local real estate agents.

While it's designed for prospective faculty members, any newcomer can benefit from the University of Toronto's online relocation information (www.facultyrelocation.utoronto.ca), which includes resources for buying and renting homes and otherwise getting settled in the city. If you're looking for temporary housing or short-term rentals, check the classified

DINING FROM A TO Z

When he was a University of Toronto student, Jason Taniguchi organized a group of friends to go out to eat. When the gang couldn't decide where to go, they turned to the Yellow Pages and went to the first restaurant listed. The Toronto Serial Diners group was born.

That was back in 1989. Since then, the group has been eating its way through the Toronto phone directory – in alphabetical order. They meet every Friday night at 6 P.M., and they aim to dine in every restaurant from A to Z. They might eat at a Caribbean roti shop, an Irish pub, a French bistro, or a burger joint. Plain or fancy, large or small, it doesn't matter – whatever is next in the Yellow Pages is where they'll go.

A core group of diners has been with the project since the beginning, and new people come and go. More than 50 people showed up for the group's 15th anniversary party.

By mid-2008, they were up to "J," so if you're moving to Toronto in the first half of the 21st century, you'll likely be able to join them. They estimate that they'll finish sometime in the mid-2030s.

To find out where the Serial Diners will be, check www.probability.ca/diners. Everyone is welcome. Just show up, bring your appetite, and a sense of adventure.

ads in the University of Toronto Bulletin. Most rentals don't require a university affiliation. Follow the "online classifieds" link at www.news-andevents.utoronto.ca.

Entrepreneurs and small-business owners can find plenty of support through the city-sponsored Enterprise Toronto (www.enterprisetoronto.com), which hosts networking events, offers seminars, and provides a variety of business resources.

If you're a newspaper junkie, there's lots to read in Toronto. The *Globe and Mail* and the *National Post,* Canada's two national newspapers, are headquartered here, and the city has two other dailies: the *Toronto Star* and the *Toronto Sun.* Alternative weeklies, pairing politics with extensive arts and entertainment coverage, include *NOW* and *Eye Weekly.*

The monthly *Toronto Life* magazine (www.torontolife.com) reviews restaurants and shops and produces an online real estate guide. *Where Toronto* keeps tabs on events around town.

For foodies, *City Bites* reports on the Toronto restaurant scene, while *Edible Toronto* covers local markets, growers, and other food resources. For details about Toronto's many farmers' markets, check the online market directory from FoodShare (www.foodshare.ca). TasteTO (www.tasteto.com) has links to everything food-related around town.

HEALTH CARE

New Ontario residents are eligible for provincial health benefits three months after they arrive in the province. You need to arrange for temporary private health insurance for your first three months, and you must buy this temporary insurance within five days of arriving in Ontario. The *Resources* chapter lists companies that provide this private insurance.

You should also apply for your regular health insurance through the Ontario Health Insurance Plan as soon as you arrive. The Ministry of Health and Long Term care has the details about health insurance (www.health.gov. on.ca), and the government-run "Healthy Ontario" site (www.healthyontario. com) provides links to many health-related resources.

To find a doctor, ask colleagues and friends for recommendations, or try the "Doctor Search" function on the website of the College of Physicians and Surgeons of Ontario (www.cpso.on.ca).

SCHOOLS

The Toronto District School Board (www.tdsb.on.ca) and the Toronto Catholic District School Board (www.tcdsb.org) oversee the city's public English-language schools.

Toronto schools are neighborhood-based. Some elementary schools begin in junior kindergarten and continue through Grade 5 or 6, while others include Grades 7 and 8 as well. Some areas have middle schools for Grades 6–8 and high schools for Grades 9–12, while others have a junior high structure covering Grades 7–9 and high school for Grades 10–12. The district also has a variety of special offerings, from arts magnet schools to French immersion to International Baccalaureate programs. The school boards provide program details as well as a search function to find which schools serve which neighborhoods.

Toronto has a large number of

the Ontario College of Design's eclectic home in Toronto

© CAROLYN B. HELLER

private schools, including many with strong university preparatory programs. The Ontario Ministry of Education has a school search function on its website (www.edu.gov.on.ca/eng/general/elemsec/privsch/index.html) that lists Toronto independent schools.

Getting Around

Toronto's Lester B. Pearson International Airport is the largest in Canada. It's west of the city center, bordering the suburb of Mississauga.

The small Toronto City Centre Airport is located in the Toronto islands. Porter Airlines caters to business travelers with flights from here to Newark, Montréal, Ottawa, Québec City, and Halifax.

Toronto's Union Station is a hub for passenger trains from across Ontario and throughout Canada.

PUBLIC TRANSPORTATION

Toronto residents will tell you that there's no stigma about taking public transit as there is in some U.S. cities, and real estate prices reflect this regional embrace of public transportation. Homes with ready access to transit fetch premium prices.

The Toronto Transit Commission (TTC) runs the city's public transportation network that includes the subway, streetcars, buses, and commuter trains. Of the four subway lines, the two major routes include the east–west Bloor–Danforth line and the U-shaped Yonge line that connects the northern neighborhoods with downtown.

Supplementing the subway is an extensive network of streetcars and buses. Pick up a TTC map (or check their website at www.toronto.ca/ttc) for streetcar and bus routes.

To ride the subway, streetcars, or buses, it's cheapest to buy a pass—either daily, weekly, or monthly. For individual rides, you can either pay cash or buy a ticket or token. Tickets and tokens are sold at a discount, so paying cash is the most expensive option. You can transfer between these various transportation modes for free, but only if you get off one and directly on the other. If you come out of the subway, walk a couple of blocks, and then try to board a streetcar, you'll have to pay another fare.

GO Transit (www.gotransit.com) operates commuter trains and buses that serve many Toronto suburbs. Fares are based on the distance you're traveling, and various pass options give you a discount. Take the rush-hour express trains if you can to reduce your ride time.

CAR

Several major highways run in and around the Toronto area. The Gardiner Expressway follows the lakeshore into downtown Toronto. West of the city it connects with Queen Elizabeth Way (known as the QEW), which despite its rather noble-sounding name, is actually a traffic-clogged multi-lane highway. East of downtown, the Gardiner meets the Don Valley Parkway, a main route from the eastern and northeastern suburbs. Highway 401 crosses the region north of Toronto proper, and Highway 407, which is an electronic tollway, parallels the 401 farther north.

Driving in downtown Toronto is not for the faint of heart. Drivers may be less aggressive than their Québec brethren, but many downtown streets are one-way, and both left and right turns are often restricted. Watch out—and stop—for the frequent streetcars.

Outside downtown, driving is somewhat easier, although traffic on area streets, parkways, and highways is often snarled. Commuting into the city from suburban areas can be a long slow slog. They don't call the Don Valley Parkway the "Don Valley Parking Lot" for nothing.

There's metered on-street parking throughout Toronto, but the rate varies by location, so be sure to check the meter or ticket dispenser. The city also operates 160 parking lots containing about 20,000 spaces. The Toronto Parking Authority website (www.greenp.com) has a useful parking lot finder, showing the location and rates at all municipal parking lots.

BIKE AND ON FOOT

Even when Toronto's weather is uncooperative, it's easy to get around downtown on foot. An extensive network of underground walkways called the PATH links more than 50 downtown buildings. You can walk from building to building and to the subway without venturing outside. The PATH is also one of the largest underground shopping complexes in the world, with 27 kilometers (16 miles) of shopping arcades.

To keep your bearings as you wind through the PATH, note that each letter in the color-coded PATH signs represents a direction. The P is red and directs you to the south. The orange A leads west, the blue T goes north, and the yellow H goes east. If that's as clear as mud, print a PATH map at www.toronto.ca/path.

Toronto may not be as bicycle-friendly as other Canadian communities, but the city is working to make bike commuting safer and more convenient. There are more than 120 kilometers (75 miles) of off-road pathways and about 90 kilometers (55 miles) of bike lanes on city streets. The city is planning

A TOLL ROAD WITHOUT TOLL BOOTHS

Running across Toronto's northern suburbs is the "407 ETR." First opened in 1997, the 407 ETR – the "ETR" stands for "Express Toll Route" – bills itself as the world's first all-electronic, barrier-free toll highway. It's a toll road without toll booths.

Drivers don't stop to pay tolls. Instead, electronic sensors record where they enter and exit the highway. To travel the 407 regularly, drivers lease a transponder that logs their use of the road and generates a bill.

If you enter the highway without a transponder – if you're driving a rental car, for example – the system's video technology will take a picture of your license plate and use the license information to bill you. Many rental car agencies don't want you to take the 407, since the company will get the bill. They'll pass along the charge to you and add a surcharge for their trouble, so you'd best avoid the road unless you're driving your own vehicle.

eventually to extend this network to 1,000 kilometers (620 miles). You can get more information about cycling in Toronto, as well as a bike route map, at www.toronto.ca/cycling.

ONTARIO

As Canada's largest city, Toronto may get all the glory, but beyond Toronto, the province of Ontario has much to offer prospective expats. Forty percent of all Canadians—more than 12 million people—make their homes in Ontario, the country's most populous province.

If you think that Ontario is landlocked in the middle of the country, think again. Canada's second-largest province in area (after Québec) borders four of the five Great Lakes, along more than 3,000 kilometers (2,300 miles) of shoreline. Ontario even has over 1,000 kilometers (680 miles) of saltwater shores on its northern boundary with Hudson Bay.

Ottawa, Canada's national capital, is in Ontario. The capital region not only has many government-related jobs, but it has been working to become "Silicon Valley North"—a major high-tech center. Since several million visitors tour Ottawa every year, the region has many tourism jobs as well.

Ontario is home to many of Canada's major universities. The university towns of Hamilton, London, and Kitchener-Waterloo are also former

© CAROLYN B. HELLER

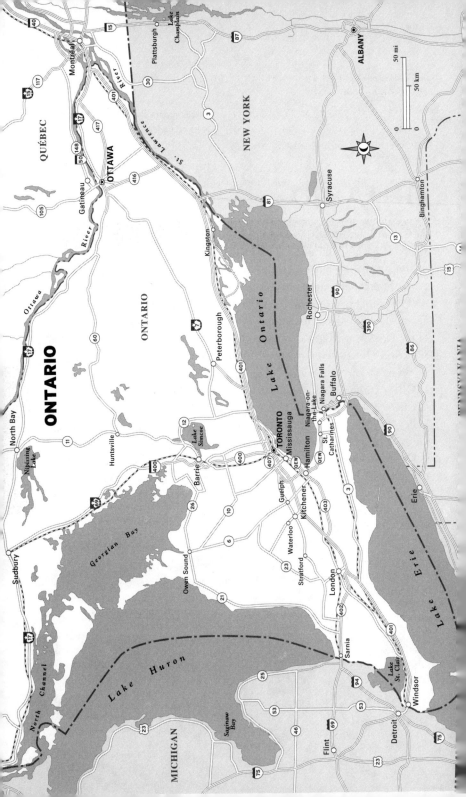

industrial areas that are ambitiously reinventing themselves as high-technology regions.

But Ontario isn't all work and no play. One of Canada's largest tourist attractions—Niagara Falls—is in Ontario, and beyond the Falls, the Niagara region is dotted with vineyards. Ontario is a significant wine-producing area, with more than 50 wineries on the Niagara peninsula alone. If you're looking for small-town life or a vacation home, the lakeside communities in Niagara and around the province may bring you to Ontario as well.

Ottawa

Canada's national capital, a city of about a million people, is full of grand buildings, museums, and monuments. The nation's Parliament, the Supreme Court, and the Royal Canadian Mint are all here, as are numerous federal offices. Ottawa's many cultural institutions include the massive Canadian Museum of Civilization, the National Gallery of Canada, the Canadian Museum of Nature, and the Canada Science and Technology Museum. Just as Washington, D.C. lures tourists from across the United States and abroad, Ottawa, too, is a major attraction for Canadian and international visitors.

As the capital of bilingual Canada, Ottawa is itself a bilingual city, closer in linguistic mindset—and physical proximity—to Montréal than to Toronto. The Ottawa metropolitan area spans two provinces, Ontario and Québec. The city of Ottawa is on the Ontario side of the Ottawa River, but on the opposite riverbank is the community of Gatineau in French-speaking Québec. Residents easily go back and forth across the bridges between the two provinces, many living on one side and working on the other.

Reflecting this linguistic diversity, nearly half the population of the Ottawa region is fully bilingual. The government operates in both languages, as do many businesses. While you can certainly manage in Ottawa speaking only English, having some knowledge of French will increase your professional and social opportunities.

Ottawa is not only a governmental center; it's also a hub for education. The University of Ottawa, with nearly 35,000 students, and Carleton University, with more than 23,000, are Ottawa's major post-secondary educational institutions.

Why choose Ottawa? First of all, your dollar will go far here. Ottawa's cost of living consistently ranks as the least expensive of any Canadian metropolitan area.

Ottawa is a livable, family-oriented city. While Canada's capital is full of

SAFELY DISTANT FROM THE AMERICAN BORDER

How did Ottawa become Canada's capital city?

From 1791 to 1841, there were two Canadas: Upper Canada with Toronto as its capital, and Lower Canada with its capital at Québec City. When the two provinces were united in 1841, neither would accept the other's capital as the seat of government. By 1857, still no agreement had been reached, so the legislature referred the problem to Queen Victoria.

The cities contending to be the new Canadian capital included not only Toronto and Québec City, but also Montréal, Kingston, and Ottawa. In a surprise decision, the Queen and her advisors chose Ottawa.

What made Ottawa, a relatively remote outpost, the winner? Ottawa had location – it was in between English Upper Canada and French Lower Canada. But another important factor was Canada's relationship with her American neighbors – a relationship that hadn't entirely healed from American attacks on Canada during the War of 1812. As the Queen reportedly said, unlike the other potential capitals, Ottawa was "safely distant from the American border."

ceremony and pomp, just a short distance from the Parliament buildings are comfortable residential neighborhoods, and in less than an hour's drive, you can be out in the wilderness.

Ottawa has an active arts scene, with theater, music, and other cultural events on the calendar. Residents also embrace the outdoors, even in the icy winters, heading out with their cross-country skis, snowshoes, and skates.

THE LAY OF THE LAND

Ottawa is 200 kilometers (125 miles) west of Montréal and 450 kilometers (280 miles) northeast of Toronto. The city's central core is bounded by water—by the Ottawa River on the north, the Rideau River to the east, and the Rideau Canal on the west.

In downtown Ottawa, Parliament, the Supreme Court, and the national Library and Archives front the Ottawa River. To the east are the popular Byward Market and the University of Ottawa, and farther east is the elegant suburb of Rockcliffe Park and the more workaday district of Vanier. South of downtown are the comfortable residential district known as the Glebe and the Carleton University campus. To the west are many more residential suburbs.

Across the Ottawa River is the district of Gatineau. Several bridges connect this Québec region, known as the Outaouais, with the rest of metropolitan Ottawa.

Climate

Ottawa residents will claim, with a certain perverse pride, that their city is the coldest capital in the world. Moscow may also claim that honor, but there's no disputing that winter in Ottawa—320 kilometers (200 miles) north of Syracuse, New York—can be frigid. While Ottawa may not get the heavy snows that towns like Syracuse do, it's definitely in the snow belt, averaging 235 centimeters (nearly eight feet) of snow per year.

Though spring can be short, it does eventually warm up, and by July average highs are around 27°C (81°F). And like much of Ontario, Ottawa has beautiful, crisp fall days when the leaves turn brilliant colors.

Culture

Not only does Ottawa house numerous museums, it also puts on a good show. More than 600 music, dance, and theatrical performances play at the National Arts Centre every year. The professional Great Canadian Theatre Company has been producing Canadian works for Ottawa audiences since the 1970s.

The city hosts jazz, blues, and classical music festivals, and the annual Canada Dance Festival showcases top contemporary performers. There's a fringe fest and a dragon boat fest, a Greek fest, a tulip fest, and a pride fest. One of the biggest events is Winterlude, the annual winter carnival. Ottawa may not be as hip as of Montréal or as multicultural as Toronto, but there's still a lot going on.

WHERE TO LIVE

Unlike Toronto, where city-center homes are on tiny lots, Ottawa has many centrally located neighborhoods where the leafy yards and gardens around the renovated brick Victorian homes make them feel almost suburban. In early 2008, the average sales price for an Ottawa home (including both single-family houses and condominiums) was $285,000.

Downtown and the City Center

While government and commercial offices dominate downtown, some residential apartment and condo buildings are also available. Immediately south of downtown, the Centretown neighborhood has more residential options, including townhouses, low-rise apartments, and even some classy Victorians. It's an easy walk to downtown.

Ottawa's small Chinatown, west of Centretown in Somerset Heights, is no longer exclusively Chinese. In this multiethnic community, a Korean restaurant sits next to a Middle Eastern grocery down the street from a Chinese dumpling shop, an Indian market, a sushi bar, and several Vietnamese *pho* joints.

Considered Ottawa's oldest suburb, the Glebe is located between the Queensway and the Rideau Canal. Many homes in this family-friendly neighborhood are Victorian-era brick houses with big porches. Bank Street is the district's commercial center, lined with restaurants and shops. The Glebe is convenient to both downtown and the Carleton campus.

© CAROLYN B. HELLER

restored Victorians in Ottawa's Glebe neighborhood

East of Downtown

One of Canada's oldest public markets, Byward Market was established in 1826 in the neighborhood known as Lowertown, across the Rideau Canal east of downtown. The area still includes fruit and vegetable stands, but it's also a popular restaurant and nightclub district. The nearby residential community of Sandy Hill includes a mix of student apartments and restored older family homes.

The driveways in front of the sprawling mansions are filled with BMWs and Lexuses in the elite enclave of Rockcliffe Park, across the Rideau River east of downtown. Among the neighborhood's distinguished denizens is Canada's governor general, whose official residence here is known as Rideau Hall. As you'd expect, Rockcliffe is among Ottawa's most expensive districts. The New Edinburgh neighborhood, to the east, is still pretty posh, with many restored older homes on tree-lined streets, but prices are slightly lower than in Rockcliffe.

West of Downtown

When Starbucks and Lululemon (the Vancouver-based yogawear company) set up shop in a neighborhood, you can assume that it's an up-and-coming one. That's the case in Ottawa's Westboro Village. Centered around an eclectic commercial strip along Richmond Road west of downtown, Westboro Village and its surrounding neighborhoods include a mix of housing. Apartment towers overlook the river, while the streets farther south are lined with single-family homes.

JOIN THE LOPPET

Ottawans have an "if you can't beat 'em, join 'em" attitude about the long, cold winters, so when the snow falls, Ottawa takes out its skis.

The Gatineau Hills, on the Québec side of metropolitan Ottawa, are an international center for cross-country ski training. Every year, the area hosts the Gatineau Loppet, the largest cross-country ski event in Canada. Part of an international series of ski marathons, the Gatineau event, also known as the Keskinada Loppet, draws more than 2,500 skiers from around the world, who participate in races of 28 and 53 kilometers (approximately 17 and 33 miles).

Even if you're not up for marathon ski racing, you can join one of the Gatineau Loppet's recreational events, including a "mini" two-kilometer (1.2-mile) course for kids and their parents, complete with stops for cookies and hot chocolate. Get more details online at www.keskinada.com.

Gatineau

Some anglophone Ottawans consider Gatineau, on the Québec side of the river, to be something of a down-at-the-heels relation. While Gatineau does have some less-than-grand districts, some areas, particularly up in the hills, are quite comfortable. Housing prices, and the cost of living overall, tend to be lower in Gatineau than in Ottawa proper.

DAILY LIFE

Ottawa is an outdoors-oriented city, with trails for walking, biking, and cross-country skiing across the region. Surrounding the city center is a 500-square-kilometer (200-square-mile) "emerald necklace" of federally owned parks, forests, and green spaces. Across the river, the massive Gatineau Park is a popular outdoor destination.

In Ottawa, the Senators aren't just members of Parliament—that's also the name of the city's National Hockey League team. Gung ho for hockey and for skating in general, many residents take to the ice at rinks around town and along the Rideau Canal.

Ottawa has an emerging restaurant scene, including both ethnic and fine-dining options. The city has a branch of Le Cordon Bleu cooking school, which has upped its foodie credentials.

Resources

The "Live in Ottawa" section of the city's website (www.ottawa.com) provides a useful introduction to living and working in the capital region. For

PRIME LIVING LOCATIONS

THE WORLD'S LARGEST SKATING RINK

You might say that war between the United States and Canada led to the construction of the world's largest skating rink.

After the War of 1812, Canadians were concerned that the St. Lawrence River – a vital shipping channel between Montréal and the Great Lakes – would be vulnerable to another U.S. attack, since the Americans controlled the river's southern banks. In the late 1820s, when Ottawa was still an isolated pioneer outpost, construction began on a canal that would link the region to Lake Ontario.

The Rideau Canal opened in 1832, running 200 kilometers (125 miles) with 47 locks and 52 dams between Ottawa and Kingston. In just a few years, the canal became a busy shipping channel.

Today, it's the oldest continuously operated canal in North America and a UNESCO World Heritage Site. It's popular with boaters in the summer, and in winter, when the canal freezes, the Ottawa section becomes a skating surface that extends for 7.8 kilometers (nearly five miles). Ottawa residents can commute to work – on skates – along the world's largest rink.

entrepreneurs, high-technology folks, and other businesspeople, the Ottawa Centre for Research and Innovation (www.ocri.ca) hosts seminars and networking events and provides other business resources.

The capital region's major daily newspaper is the *Ottawa Citizen*. The city also reads the tabloid *Ottawa Sun* and the alternative weekly *Ottawa XPress*. *Ottawa Magazine* and *Where* magazine cover arts, restaurants, and things to do.

Schools

The Ottawa-Carleton District School Board (www.ocdsb.edu.on.ca) and the Ottawa-Carleton Catholic School Board (www.occdsb.on.ca) manage Ottawa's English-language public schools.

The Western Québec School Board (www.wqsb.qc.ca) provides English-language education to eligible students in Gatineau. However, because of Québec's complex language laws, locals generally recommend living on the Ontario side of the river if you want your children educated in English.

Ottawa also has a number of private schools. You can get the complete list from the Ontario Ministry of Education.

GETTING AROUND

The Ottawa International Airport has flights across Canada, to major U.S. cities, and to several European destinations. Via Rail runs trains from Ottawa east to Montréal and west to Toronto.

© CAROLYN B. HELLER

In posh Rockcliffe Park, Rideau Hall is home to the governor general, the Queen's representative in Canada.

Ottawa residents say that despite stated support for public transit, the city is steeped in "car culture." Highway 417, also known as the Queensway, is the region's main east–west highway. A network of parkways winds along the rivers and the canal.

Ottawa has been planning to develop a light rail system, but so far, the O-Train, as it's known, has only five stations. Unless you live near one of these stations, taking transit means riding the bus. To reduce travel time, Ottawa has a bus "transitway," a dedicated express bus lane that crosses the city.

OC Transpo (www.octranspo.com) runs Ottawa's transit network. The Société de transport de l'Outaouais (www.sto.ca) operates buses in Gatineau, including transport to downtown Ottawa.

The Golden Horseshoe

Extending from Toronto around the western end of Lake Ontario is the region known as the Golden Horseshoe. With cities such as Hamilton, London, and Kitchener-Waterloo, this part of the province may not be on many Americans' radar, but the Golden Horseshoe is the fastest-growing urban region in Canada.

A recent study by Britain's *Financial Times* named several cities here among North America's top "Small Cities of the Future." Why? Business is booming in southern Ontario. It's an exciting time for the Golden Horseshoe, with new industry moving in, new jobs being created, and new developments under construction all across the region.

THE LAY OF THE LAND

The largest city in the Golden Horseshoe region is Hamilton, set on Lake Ontario about 65 kilometers (40 miles) southeast of Toronto. Although Hamilton could almost be considered an outlying Toronto suburb, it's Ontario's third-largest city and the ninth largest in Canada, with more than 700,000 people in the metropolitan area.

West of Hamilton, roughly equidistant between Toronto and Detroit, the city of London feels much less urban. Ranking just behind Hamilton as the country's 10th-largest city, with nearly half a million residents, London still seems less like a major metropolis and more like a college town. London is home to the University of Western Ontario, a large research university with more than 25,000 students.

The twin cities of Kitchener and Waterloo, about 100 kilometers (60 miles) west of Toronto, are another rapidly growing Golden Horseshoe area. Several universities, as well as a booming information technology industry, are helping redefine these former manufacturing towns.

Climate

The Golden Horseshoe's climate is similar to that of Toronto—cold winters, humid summers, short but pleasant springs, and gorgeous autumns.

Culture

A major cultural event in the Golden Horseshoe is the annual Stratford Shakespeare Festival in the town of Stratford (between London and Kitchener-Waterloo). From April though mid-November, theater fans come to Stratford for plays by the Bard and by more contemporary playwrights. The universities in Hamilton, London, and Kitchener-Waterloo also present a variety of arts and cultural events throughout the year.

Kitchener's annual Oktoberfest, which claims to be the largest Bavarian festival outside of Munich, celebrates the region's German heritage. In the early 1800s, communities of Pennsylvania "Dutch" (actually settlers from Germany) moved north to southern Ontario to escape religious persecution in the United States. One of Ontario's original Mennonite settlements, the town of St. Jacobs outside Waterloo still has a significant Mennonite population, including bonnet-clad women and bearded men who sell vegetables, meats, and jams at the local farmers markets.

homemade pickles at the Mennonite farmers market in St. Jacobs, near Waterloo

© CAROLYN B. HELLER

WHERE TO LIVE
Hamilton

In the early 1900s, Hamilton, a former steel town midway between Toronto and Niagara Falls, was known as "the Pittsburgh of Canada." Many American heavy industries set up shop here, including Westinghouse, International Harvester, and Firestone Tire, and by the 1920s, nearly 100 American plants were located in Hamilton. Manufacturing still accounts for many jobs, but the region has a growing health sciences and biotechnology sector, concentrated around McMaster University and its hospitals.

Hamilton's east end remains largely industrial, filled with steel plants and other factories. With nearly 20,000 students, the McMaster campus dominates the city's west end. In between, downtown serves both populations—it's part aging factory town and part gentrifying urban district.

Hamilton's housing options range from older bungalows to new suburban homes. In early 2008, the average price of a single-family house was roughly $295,000, and the average condo was $207,000.

London

Around the green expanse of Victoria Park in the center of London, the city is a mix of old and new. Stately St. Paul's Cathedral was built in the 1840s, while the boxy modern city hall up the street opened in 1971. The leafy campus of the University of Western Ontario is northwest of downtown, with surrounding residential areas housing both students and faculty.

In early 2008, the average sales price of a London-area single-family home

PRIME LIVING LOCATIONS

Students warm up for an informal soccer game at the University of Western Ontario in London.

was $225,000; the average condo sold for $155,000. Housing options include elegant two-story Victorians with big front porches, modest bungalows, student apartments, and everything in between.

Kitchener-Waterloo

While few Americans know much about Kitchener-Waterloo, most are familiar with the region's most famous product—the BlackBerry. Research in Motion (RIM), the maker of this widely used handheld device, is headquartered in Waterloo.

Perhaps because it's home to two universities—University of Waterloo and Wilfrid Laurier University—the city of Waterloo has a reputation for its "thinkers and drinkers." Many of these "thinkers" are helping drive the region's high-tech growth. Besides RIM, other high-tech companies with offices here include Open Text, Electrohome, NCR, and Raytheon.

Due largely to high-tech, Kitchener-Waterloo's population is growing, increasing more than 10 percent between 2001 and 2006, as people from other parts of Canada and from outside the country relocate here for jobs.

Downtown Kitchener is in the midst of a revitalization. There's a spiffy new city hall and new loft-style condos, but they're interspersed with down-at-the-heels blocks where a trendy coffee joint might sit next to a pawnshop. Waterloo is going through similar redevelopment, and in both towns, new subdivisions are going up as fast as they can be built. In early 2008, single-family homes in Kitchener-Waterloo were selling for an average of $250,000.

DAILY LIFE

The universities are a major source of activities and entertainment in the Golden Horseshoe towns, and around the campuses you'll find plenty of pubs and casual eateries. For more high-end dining and urban culture, residents sometimes head for Toronto, although the town of Stratford has numerous upscale restaurants catering to the theater crowd.

high-tech City Hall in increasingly high-tech Kitchener

Resources

You can get lots of information about Hamilton from the community's "My Hamilton" website (www.myhamilton.ca). The Hamilton Economic Development Office (www.investinhamilton.ca) is a good resource for details about living and working in the region.

The City of London (www.london.ca) provides pages of information about the town, and London's Economic Development Corporation (www.ledc.com) offers a variety of business resources. The London Arts Council (www.londonarts.ca) publishes an online directory of local arts events.

The City of Kitchener (www.kitchener.ca) and City of Waterloo (www.city.waterloo.on.ca) can help you research these communities. Canada's Technology Triangle (www.techtriangle.com), an organization promoting business and entrepreneurship in Kitchener-Waterloo, has information about economic opportunities.

Newspapers in the region include the *Hamilton Spectator,* the *London Free Press* and the *Record* in Kitchener-Waterloo. Many residents also read the Toronto papers.

Schools

The Golden Horseshoe has both secular and Catholic public schools. The schools' governing bodies include the Hamilton-Wentworth District School Board, Hamilton-Wentworth Catholic District School Board, London's Thames Valley District School Board, London District Catholic School Board, Waterloo Region District School Board, and Waterloo Catholic District School Board.

The Ontario Ministry of Education can provide a list of private schools in the region.

GETTING AROUND

Hamilton, Waterloo, and London all have small airports with service to Canadian cities and some U.S. destinations. Toronto's Pearson International Airport offers more flight options to and from the region.

The Golden Horseshoe towns all have bus systems that provide local transportation. If you work at one of the universities and live just off campus, you could easily walk or cycle to work. However, few people in these communities seem to manage entirely without a car.

The GO Trains run from the suburbs and outlying towns into Toronto.

The Niagara Region

If you're thinking about a part-time or retirement destination, or if you fancy yourself an innkeeper, wine-maker, or restaurateur, the Niagara region has a lot to offer. Everyone knows Niagara for the eponymous Falls that draw throngs of honeymooners and tourists. But more upscale attractions bring visitors to the region, too, creating opportunities for food-, wine-, and tourism-related businesses and establishing vibrant communities for part-time residents.

The 12 communities on the Niagara Peninsula have a combined population of about 425,000, but the ambiance is more small town than major metropolis. The region's largest city is St. Catharines, a workaday town of 130,000 people. General Motors has a plant here, and the shipping industry also provides jobs.

In Niagara Falls, with about 80,000 residents, the major employers, not surprisingly, are the casinos, hotels, and attractions that serve the more than 10 million annual visitors. The far smaller town of Niagara-on-the-Lake (population 14,000) has a different sort of tourism industry. The largest employer here is the Shaw Festival, the world's only theater specializing in plays by British playwright George Bernard Shaw and his early-20th-century contemporaries.

© CAROLYN B. HELLER

Niagara Falls draws hordes of tourists to southern Ontario.

Bed-and-breakfasts, restaurants, and shops cater to the theater's approximately 250,000 annual patrons.

Although the Niagara Peninsula may be known more for manufacturing and mass tourism, it's become one of Canada's major wine-producing regions. With its hot summers and freezing winters, Ontario is the world's largest producer of ice wine, a sweet, intensely flavorful dessert wine. Not only are the region's more than 50 wineries putting out increasingly high-quality products, the area is attracting more and more wine tourists.

THE LAY OF THE LAND

The Niagara Peninsula is on the south side of Lake Ontario, between Toronto and Buffalo, New York. The Queen Elizabeth Way (known as the QEW), the highway connecting Toronto with Niagara, is the main travel route across the Niagara region.

The communities of Grimsby, Lincoln, St. Catharines, and Niagara-on-the-Lake hug the lakeshore, while Niagara Falls is on the east end of the peninsula, bordering New York State. The wineries are concentrated in Niagara-on-the-Lake and in the Jordan-Vineland area between Grimsby and St. Catharines.

Climate

The Niagara wineries claim that the region's climate is similar to that of France's Burgundy and Loire Valley, with Lake Ontario moderating the more extreme winter weather found in nearby New York State. The warm summers and temperate autumns are the busiest times, when tourism is in full swing. Winters are

PRIME LIVING LOCATIONS

cold and quiet, with many businesses closing or scaling back their operations until spring—and the tourists—return.

Culture

Niagara's major cultural event is the Shaw Festival, where plays take to the stage between April and November. Niagara-on-the-Lake has many upscale restaurants, as do several of the wineries. In Niagara Falls, neon reigns as businesses court the almighty tourist dollar with honky-tonk attractions and the same chains—Hard Rock Cafe, Planet Hollywood, Tony Roma's—you might find in any U.S. city. Fortunately, the Falls themselves remain spectacular, no matter how many visitors crowd in to see them.

© CAROLYN B. HELLER

Theater buffs come to Niagara-on-the-Lake for the annual Shaw Festival.

WHERE TO LIVE

A long-established destination for cultural tourists is the pretty town of Niagara-on-the-Lake. As quaint as Niagara Falls is garish, Niagara-on-the-Lake is home to the Shaw Festival, many wineries and restaurants, and loads of small inns and B&Bs. While the town center is somewhat touristy, the community has a mixture of historic and modern houses, and on the outskirts of town, many of the homes can only be described as estates.

You might think no one actually lives in the town of Niagara Falls, with its scads of hotels and tourist attractions. However, there are plenty of residential districts, where housing includes bungalows, ranch houses, and more distinguished Victorians.

While much of St. Catharines is architecturally uninspiring, the Port Dalhousie district near the lakeshore has many attractive homes. The Jordan-Vineland region, where many wineries are located, remains fairly rural.

DAILY LIFE

Communities such as Niagara Falls and Niagara-on-the-Lake run on a tourist timetable, with quiet winters followed by a frenzy of activity from late spring through early fall. In high season, roads are crowded, shops are busy, and restaurants are full, but even in peak times, you can slip away for a walk along the lake or unwind over a glass of local wine.

Resources

The Niagara Economic Development Corporation (www.niagaracanada.com) is an excellent source of information about communities and businesses in the region, while Tourism Niagara (www.tourismniagara.com) gives you the scoop on visitor attractions. You can learn more about the Niagara wine industry from the Wine Council of Ontario (www.winesofontario.org).

With so many newspapers in nearby Toronto, many Niagara residents read one of the Toronto rags. For local news, there's the daily *Niagara Falls Review* and *St. Catharines Standard.* The weekly *Niagara Advance* reports the goings-on in Niagara-on-the-Lake.

Schools

The District School Board of Niagara (www.dsbn.edu.on.ca) administers schools in Niagara Falls, Niagara-on-the-Lake, St. Catharines, and nine other nearby towns. The Niagara Catholic District School Board (www.niagararc.com) manages the public Catholic schools in the same area.

GETTING AROUND

If you're flying to the Niagara Peninsula, the closest major airports are in Toronto, Hamilton, and Buffalo, New York.

Between stop-and-go tour buses and lost tourists in rental cars, traffic easily gets snarled around Niagara Falls. Niagara Transit runs bus services around the region, and St. Catharines has citywide bus service as well. However, it's difficult to manage here long-term without your own vehicle.

PRIME LIVING LOCATIONS

QUÉBEC

For expats from the United States, Québec may be Canada's most exotic destination. With its predominantly francophone population, Québec seems to have more in common with France than with other parts of Canada. Montréal is arguably as chic as Paris, Québec City may be the most European city in North America, and even the province's smaller communities can feel like towns in the French countryside.

Montréal is the largest city in Québec and the second largest—after Toronto—in Canada. It's a stylish, happening place, with festivals, concerts, theater, sports, and other events to occupy residents, at least when they're not unwinding in one of the scores of bistros, restaurants, and cafés.

Québec City is much smaller than Montréal and far more Old World. While Montréal feels as if it has one foot in France and the other firmly planted in North America, Québec City draws more inspiration from its European roots. Behind the walls of its Old City, and in many of the lanes and byways around town, you might feel like you're in a village in France. Yet as the province's

© ALAN ALBERT

capital, and as a growing technology center, Québec City has a modern side, too—just one that almost always speaks French.

If you settle in one of Québec's urban centers, you may not realize that geographically Québec is Canada's largest province, sprawling from the U.S. border to the Arctic Ocean. The province's 750,000 lakes and 130,000 rivers comprise 3 percent of the earth's water supply, and half the land is covered with forests. An extensive network of bicycle trails, known as La Route Verte (the Green Route), extends 4,000 kilometers (2,500 miles) across several Québec regions.

If you're looking for a vacation home, or if you'd simply like to put down roots in a smaller town, Québec has many options. It's home to a huge international ski resort—Mont-Tremblant, in the Laurentian Mountains northwest of Montréal—but the Laurentians (called Les Laurentides in French) have many lesser-known but intriguing communities as well.

Another alternative is the Eastern Townships. East of Montréal, along the border with Vermont, the Eastern Townships (Les Cantons de l'Est) feel like New England, with their rolling hills, quaint villages, dairy farms, and family-friendly ski resorts, but they're definitely francophone. And if you're partial to good wines, hearty bistro cooking, and local cheeses, this francophone influence is a good thing.

GETTING SETTLED IN QUÉBEC

Moving to Québec from the United States is a little more complicated than settling in other Canadian provinces. There are additional procedures to apply for a work or study permit or for permanent resident status. If you have children, you'll need to learn how Québec's language laws affect schooling and what to do if you prefer that your children attend an English-language program. The process of applying for provincial health insurance is slightly different than it is in other provinces. And of course, the most important issue may be dealing with the language.

Two government agencies offer resources to help newcomers settling in Québec. The provincial Ministry of Immigration and Cultural Communities (Ministère de l'Immigration et des Communautés Culturelles du Québec) has information about all things immigration-related at www.immigration-quebec.gouv.qc.ca, and Services Québec (www.gouv.qc.c) can direct you to a variety of other resources.

Refer to the *Making the Move* chapter for more details about immigration paperwork, and to the *Language and Education* chapter for instructions on applying for study permits for children relocating to Québec.

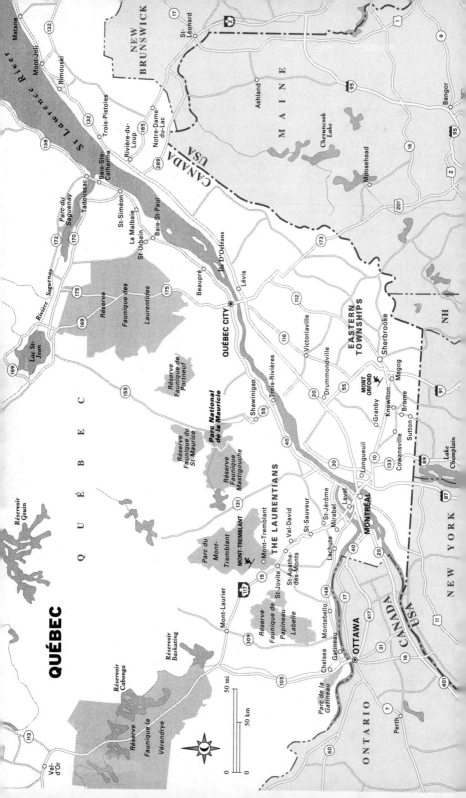

Designed by Buckminster Fuller for Expo '67, the Biosphere is now a Montréal landmark and a museum of the environment.

Do I Have to Speak French?

If you plan to live and work in Canada's most heavily francophone province, speaking French is definitely an asset. Across the province of Québec, roughly 55 percent of the population speaks only French, while about 40 percent speak both French and English. Five percent of Québec residents get by speaking only English.

Montréal, the second-largest French-speaking city in the world (after Paris), is also the most bilingual. More than half of Montréal's residents can communicate in both French and English, and among businesspeople, that number goes up to a whopping 80 percent. Even if you address Montréalers in French, they'll often switch into English if they recognize that you're not a native French speaker. About 8 percent of Montréal's resident speak English only, and it's possible, but not easy, to live here with no French at all.

In areas such as Mont-Tremblant that attract visitors from all over the world, many residents, particularly those who work in tourism, speak both French and English. In Québec City, which also draws many international tourists, you'll find English speakers working in tourism-related businesses. Yet in Québec City overall, only about a third of residents are fully bilingual, while two-thirds speak only French. The number of Québec City residents who get by with English only is negligible. And as you venture into smaller towns, French is definitely the language of choice.

The Québec government wants newcomers to master more than "*Bonjour.*" In partnership with universities, colleges, community organizations, and

QUÉBEC'S "NATIONAL HOLIDAY"

Although Québec celebrates all of Canada's national holidays, the province also has its own Fête Nationale. This "national holiday," also known as Saint-Jean-Baptiste Day, is held on June 24 and is part summer solstice celebration and part Québec pride day.

Saint-Jean-Baptiste (St. John the Baptist) is the patron saint of French Canadians, and the day in his honor takes on a significant flavor of Québec nationalism. Residents wave Québec flags and hang banners from their balconies, while free concerts and events highlight traditional Québécois music and culture. Montréal celebrates with a big parade and huge street parties across the city. Many smaller communities make merry with gusto as well.

Québec essentially shuts down for La Fête – banks, offices, and other services are all closed – so join in the festivities, even if you don't speak much French. The language of celebration is universal.

schools, the provincial Ministry of Immigration offers both part-time and intensive full-time French-language courses for new residents. If you meet their requirements, the courses are free. Their website (www.immigration-quebec.gouv.qc.ca) can direct you to language programs in the community where you'll be living.

Education

Québec has both French- and English-language schools. However, to ensure that they master the province's dominant tongue, children of immigrants to Québec are usually required to attend French-language schools. This requirement applies whether your kids go to public or private schools. The schools have support programs in place to assist students whose first language is not French.

What if you don't want your kids educated in French? There are exceptions to the law. If you're living in Québec temporarily (with a work or study permit), your child may be allowed to attend an English-language school. Children with serious learning disabilities may receive special authorization to be educated in English. If at least one parent is a Canadian citizen who did most of his or her elementary studies in English in Canada, a child may also be allowed to attend an English school.

To apply for permission for your child to attend an English-language school, contact the English-language school board for the district where you'd like to enroll your child (or contact the private school you'd like your child to attend). You'll need to complete an application, provide proof of your status in Canada, and bring your child's birth certificate. For more information, contact the Ministère de l'Éducation, du Loisir et du Sport (Ministry of Education, Leisure, and Sports) at www.meq.gouv.qc.ca.

School programs in Québec begin in kindergarten, and elementary school continues through Grade 6. However, the secondary school structure is different in Québec than it is in other Canadian provinces.

Québec secondary school includes Secondary I through V, which are approximately equivalent to Grades 7 through 11 elsewhere. Then, after completing Secondary V, students attend a two-year post-secondary program called CÉGEP, which stands for Collège d'Enseignement Général et Professionnel, or College of General and Professional Education. A pre-university CÉGEP program lasts for two years—it's essentially a college preparatory course—at which point students transfer to university for three years. There are also three-year CÉGEP technical programs for students intending to pursue a trade. Québec currently has 43 French-language and five English-language CÉGEPs around the province, with the largest concentration in Montréal. More information about the CÉGEP program is available online at www.fedecegeps.qc.ca, although the English-language pages are more limited than those in French.

The Montréal Economic Institute, a Québec-based think tank, publishes an annual "report card" for public and independent secondary schools across the province. The results are online at www.iedm.org.

If you're interested in English-language private schools for your children, a good resource is the Québec Association of Independent Schools (www.qais.qc.ca).

Health Care

The Régie de l'Assurance Maladie du Québec (www.ramq.gouv.qc.ca) is Québec's health insurance agency. Newcomers to Québec are eligible for provincial health insurance after they've been in the province three months. Contact the Régie, by phone or in person, as soon as you arrive in Québec to register and submit your health insurance application. You cannot apply online. The Régie has offices in Montréal and Québec City.

Québec has a Public Prescription Drug Insurance Plan for residents whose employers don't provide prescription coverage. Contact the Régie to register.

Climate

Unless you love icy winters and humid summers, climate isn't a major benefit of settling in Québec. Most years, there's snow on the ground from November through March or April, and mid-winter temperatures average only around -9°C (15°F). Québec City gets noticeably more snow than Montréal (and a bit more rain as well).

As long as you're prepared for the cold, however, the province has some of the best skiing in eastern North America. And on a sunny day in the short but pleasant spring or a crisp autumn afternoon as the leaves turn brilliant golds and reds, Québec residents will all be outside, lingering in cafés, cycling one of many bike trails, or simply enjoying the day.

Montréal

Writer Norman Mailer once called Montréal "a living example of how we can overcome the uniformity of global capitalism that is seeking to turn the world into one vast hotel system with McDonald's on the ground floor." It's not that you won't find McDonald's here—you will—but with the city's strong bilingual culture, you're more likely to find bistros serving *poutine* and *steak frites*.

With its significant francophone community and its fashionable vibe, Montréal doesn't feel like any generic North American city. Montréal is only 75 kilometers (45 miles) from the U.S. border, but the minute you step onto the sidewalk, you'll know that you're not in Kansas (or rather, Vermont) anymore.

Metropolitan Montréal is home to more than 3.5 million people. Although Montréal doesn't have the huge percentage of immigrants that Toronto and Vancouver do, more than one out of every four Montréalers was born outside of Canada. Italians remain the largest non-French-speaking ethnic group, but more recently, many immigrants have arrived from Algeria, China, France, and Haiti. Montréal is also home to Canada's largest Arab community, numbering just under 60,000 people.

Although it sometimes seems that Montréal denizens spend more time in the café than at the office, the metropolitan area is a major high-technology region, with companies specializing in telecommunications, multimedia, and other information technologies. Ericsson, SAP, Motorola, Electronic Arts, and Ubisoft are among the IT companies that have Montréal operations. A hub for scientific research, Montréal has lots of jobs in the pharmaceutical and biotechnology industries. The aerospace industry claims that Greater Montréal is one of the few places in the world where you could buy most parts of an airplane within a 30-kilometer (20-mile) radius.

The fashion industry employs nearly 50,000 Montréalers—perhaps not surprising in a city that prides itself on its style. More than 60 international organizations, from the International Air Transport Association to the International Federation on Aging, have their headquarters in Montréal, as do more than a dozen international banks.

Canada's top-rated English-language university, McGill University, is located in downtown Montréal, and Concordia University, another English-language institution, has two Montréal-area campuses.

Why choose Montréal? It's a cool, stylish city, where francophone joie de vivre meets Canadian practicality. From the bakeries serving up fresh baguettes to the creative bistros drawing inspiration from around the world, it's a gourmet's paradise. The cost of living is surprisingly low, too, so your dollars will go much further than they would in Paris. Montréal may be more "foreign" for Americans than other Canadian destinations, but you'll be rewarded with a rich cross-cultural experience.

THE LAY OF THE LAND

If you fly into Montréal on a clear day, you can see that the city is surrounded by water. Montréal is on an island, bounded by the St. Lawrence River, Rivière des Prairies, and the Ottawa River.

Montréal proper includes 19 boroughs or *arrondissements,* plus another 15 municipalities that are independently governed. Metro Montréal sprawls across the rivers into a ring of suburban communities.

At Montréal's heart is the 200-hectare (nearly 500-acre) Mont Royal Park, designed by Frederick Law Olmsted (who also designed New York's Central Park). Montréalers head for the park—high on the hill that gave the city its name—to walk, cycle, cross-country ski, or simply enjoy the skyline views.

Boulevard Saint-Laurent, often known as "The Main," is the major north–south artery that divides the city's east and west sides. Historically, the west side had a larger English-speaking population, while the east side was home to a francophone majority. These days, this linguistic divide is less clear cut, but in some west-side neighborhoods, particularly in the suburban West Island districts, you're still likely to hear more English.

WHERE TO LIVE

Nearly half of all Montréal residents rent their homes, perhaps because rents are comparatively low. In 2007, the average rent for a two-bedroom apartment was just under $650 a month—the lowest rate of the major Canadian cities.

Most Montréal leases expire on June 30, which make that a big moving day. It also means that the best time to look for an apartment is between March and May.

Home prices in Montréal are relatively reasonable as well. In late 2007, the average price for a single-family home in metropolitan Montréal was $357,000, and the average condominium was $241,000. Plenty of properties are above this average price, however, so your budget will depend on what part of the city you choose to make your home.

Downtown

The city's central district is officially known as the Borough of Ville-Marie. The downtown business district is here, as is the city's small Chinatown, Vieux Montréal (Old Montréal), the Quartier Latin, and the gay-friendly neighborhood known as The Village.

Downtown Montréal is a mix of office towers, hotels, and modern residential buildings. Underneath the downtown streets is Montréal's famous "Underground City"—a below-ground network that extends over 30 kilometers (20 miles), con-

© CAROLYN B. HELLER

Renters occupy about half of Montréal's households.

necting more than 60 buildings, 1,600 apartments, 200 restaurants, nearly 40 movie theaters, and 10 Métro stations. The city estimates that more than a half-million people pass through these underground passageways every day. If you live in a building that's connected to the Underground City, you might be able to go from home to your office without ever venturing outdoors.

Northeast of the downtown core, tourists throng the narrow lanes of Vieux Montréal, trolling the souvenir shops and packing the bars till all hours. If you want to be in the middle of the action, and don't mind constantly being asked for directions, you might consider a trendy loft or condo in a historic Old Montréal building.

Although officially outside the old city, the Quartier Latin is still one of Montréal's oldest neighborhoods. Home to the Université du Québec à Montréal, the district is another lively one, known for its nightlife, but the quieter side streets house residential buildings.

The Village, a.k.a. the Gay Village, is the center of Montréal's large gay community. The area surrounding the Beaudry Métro station is full of gay-friendly bars, nightclubs, restaurants, and shops.

The Plateau, Outremont, and Côte-des-Neiges

As you move northwest of downtown, the neighborhoods become more

MONTRÉAL MERGER MANIA

When you're looking for a place to live in Montréal, you may hear talk of mergers and "demergers." Here's the scoop.

Metropolitan Montréal is made up of many municipalities. Geographically, communities like Westmount and Mont-Royal look like city neighborhoods, but before 2002, they were separate towns with their own local governments.

In 2002, the province merged these municipalities into the city of Montréal, with government and services controlled at the metropolitan level. Although the merger was enacted as a cost-saving measure, many communities saw the restructuring as a loss of control over their local governments – accompanied by an increase in taxes. Vigorous debate erupted across the region.

Only two years later, some of the merged communities voted to "demerge," and by 2006, this demerger had reintroduced local government to a number of Montréal towns.

"Demerged" communities are responsible for services such as snow removal and garbage collection, so residents generally pay a separate local tax bill. Local realtors can explain the structure of particular communities, and you can find out more on the City of Montréal's website (www.ville.montreal.qc.ca).

residential. Many homes in these urban communities are triplexes—three-unit row houses with balconies and distinctive outdoor staircases.

One extremely popular district here is the Plateau. About 8 percent of the Plateau's employed residents are artists, earning it the designation of Canada's "most creative neighborhood." Rue St.-Denis, the Plateau's main street, is lined with eclectic bistros, cafés, and shops. Several Métro stops serve the Plateau, making it well located for commuters.

West of the Plateau is Outremont, where the row houses give way to stately residences on verdant streets. Outremont has historically been home to the francophone elite, and it's still among the city's most upscale communities.

At the foot of Mont-Royal is Côte-des-Neiges, one of Montréal's most ethnically diverse boroughs. Along Chemin de la Côte-des-Neiges, you'll see Muslim women in headscarves, hip young Asians, older hat-clad Jewish men, Afro-Caribbeans in colorful garb, and plenty of students. The side streets have lots of apartment buildings, as well as duplexes and triplexes.

Rosemont, Villeray/Parc Extension, and Mont-Royal

As the Plateau continues to gentrify, surrounding communities are becoming more upmarket. In Rosemont, young couples and families are settling into

Montréal residents are inveterate jaywalkers, as this fellow demonstrates in the Plateau neighborhood.

triplexes along the tree-lined streets and frequenting the foodie-friendly shops and restaurants on Rue Beaubien.

Foodies from all over town flock to the Jean-Talon Market, where the residential streets of the Villeray/Parc Extension neighborhood are more workaday than artsy. With good Métro connections, this neighborhood also seems ripe for gentrification.

West of the Jean-Talon market, the working-class streets give way to the town of Mont-Royal. Here, the solid two-story houses with large yards make the area feel almost suburban.

Westmount, Hampstead, and Montréal West

Set on the side of Mont-Royal (the mountain) and home to about 20,000 people, Westmount is Montréal's anglophone power community, where regal brick and stone homes with expansive yards perch on hilly avenues. Westmount isn't all mansions, though; you'll find smaller homes, duplexes, and apartments on some of the lower roads and around Sherbrooke Street, the neighborhood's main shopping thoroughfare. As you go higher on the hill, the houses become grander and the views more spectacular.

Like Westmount, several other communities on Montréal's west side have traditionally been home to English-speaking families. In Hampstead and Montréal West, suburbs with English roots, you could live on streets like Fleet, Queen Mary, MacDonald, or Granville. You'll still be more comfortable if you can speak French, but there's definitely an anglo influence here.

SAY IT IN YIDDISH

For years, Montréal's multiethnic Mile End neighborhood has had a large Jewish community, initially immigrants from Eastern Europe. Mile End native Mordecai Richler set his 1959 novel about an ambitious young Jewish man, *The Apprenticeship of Duddy Kravitz*, in the neighborhood, and the perpetual rivals for the title of Montréal's best bagel shop – Fairmount Bagel and St.-Viateur – are long-time Mile End denizens.

These days, parts of Mile End are newly hip, yet others recall 19th-century Europe, home to a community of Orthodox Hasidic Jews. Along some Mile End streets, you'll see men with long beards and side curls, wearing traditional black coats and broad-brimmed hats. Women dress in ankle-length skirts and cover their heads with scarves or wigs. There are traditional Jewish bakeries, kosher butchers and restaurants, and Yiddish bookstores. Listen closely, and you'll hear conversations in Yiddish, too, in this slice of Old Europe in contemporary Montréal.

© CAROLYN B. HELLER

Fairmount Bagel cooks up bagels 24/7 in Montréal's Mile End neighborhood.

DAILY LIFE

There's always something happening in Montréal. Every year, the city hosts 90-some cultural festivals, from the Juste Pour Rire comedy fest to the Winter Carnival to the wildly popular Montréal International Jazz Festival, a summer extravaganza showcasing top-name and up-and-coming musicians. Even when there isn't a festival in town, Montréal denizens will likely be out and about—supping in their local bistro, shopping for the latest fashions, or listening to hot tunes in one of the many clubs.

Montréalers are rabid hockey fans, supporting their local NHL team, the Canadiens, with passion. Montréal residents frequently take to the ice themselves on one of 900 outdoor and 100 indoor skating rinks.

To meet Montréalers who share your hobbies and interests, you can join a "Meetup" group (www.meetup.com). If you'd like to get acquainted with people through volunteer work, contact Volunteering in Québec (www.benevolat.gouv.qc.ca).

Resources

The city's Accès Montréal website (www.ville.montreal.qc.ca) has all kinds of useful details about living and working in Montréal. Also helpful, particularly if you're considering settling in a West Island community, is the "Lifestyle Kit" (www.cldwi.com/english/all/lifestyle) that the West Island's business development council produces for new residents.

Montréal's English-language newspaper is the daily *Gazette;* the city also has three French-language dailies. Two of Montréal's alternative weeklies publish in English: the *Mirror* and *Hour.* Several Montréal communities have English-language weekly papers, including the *Westmount Examiner* and the *Chronicle* (covering West Island towns). *Maisonneuve* is a Montréal-based cultural quarterly.

Schools

The city of Montréal has five school boards: three French and two English. The English Montréal School Board (www.emsb.qc.ca) manages the English-language schools in central Montréal, and the Lester B. Pearson School Board (www.lbpsb.qc.ca) is responsible for West Island English-language schools. Even in English schools, elementary students typically receive at least 90 minutes a day of French instruction, and many schools offer French immersion streams as well.

GETTING AROUND

Montréal–Pierre Elliott Trudeau International Airport is in the suburb of Dorval west of downtown. Montréal also has train service to Toronto, Ottawa, Québec City, and south to Vermont and New York.

Public Transportation

Montréal's extensive public transportation system includes the Métro (subway), buses, and commuter trains. La Société de Transport de Montréal (STM) runs the transit network.

Montréal's Métro, which opened in 1966 in anticipation of the Expo '67 World's Fair, is fast and convenient. There's also an extensive bus network, with more than 160 routes. The STM website (www.stm.info) has Métro and bus maps and schedules.

If you'll be taking public transit regularly, it's worth buying multiple tickets or a pass. You can buy a strip of six discounted tickets (ask for "*une lisière*"), or purchase passes for monthly (*une carte autobus-métro* or CAM), weekly (*une CAM hebdo*), or daily (a tourist card, or *une carte touristique*) travel.

Five commuter train routes link Montréal with the suburbs. You can get commuter train details from Agence Métropolitaine de Transport (www.amt.qc.ca).

© CAROLYN B. HELLER

Montréal's Métro system can take you all over the city.

PRIME LIVING LOCATIONS

Car

Driving in Montréal can be more hassle than it's worth. Traffic gets frequently snarled, and Montréal drivers are quite aggressive. They tailgate and lay on the horn if you hesitate even briefly when the light turns green. If you've driven in Boston, Paris, or Cairo, you may feel at home behind the wheel in Montréal. More laid-back motorists will need to adjust to Montréal's driving style.

Although they are legal elsewhere in the province, right turns on red are prohibited within the city of Montréal. Many traffic and parking signs are in French only.

Parking can be a challenge in many Montréal neighborhoods, and on some streets, parking is prohibited on certain days or between certain times. Always check the signs before dropping your loonies in the meter. "*Stationnement interdit*" means "no parking."

Bike and On Foot

Despite the city's harsh winters and steamy summers, Montréal is among North America's top bicycling cities. Many Montréalers commute by bike on the more than 350 kilometers (215 miles) of bikeways.

Montréalers are inveterate jaywalkers. Walk to the end of the block before crossing? Wait for a "Walk" signal? No way. Any Montréaler worth his or her salt is darting across the street before you can say, *"Zut alors!"* If you're driving, be aware that pedestrians may run into the street from almost anywhere. And if you're walking, well, you can do as the locals do or wait for the light to turn green.

Québec City

Many Americans know Québec City primarily as a tourist destination, and in fact, it draws more than six million visitors every year. The only fortified city in North America whose walls are still standing, Old Québec is preserved as a UNESCO World Heritage Site. A recent Canadian Broadcasting Corporation contest named Québec's Old City one of the seven wonders of Canada.

Tourism accounts for many jobs, but if you're thinking of living in Québec City, you'll find employment options beyond the tourism business. More than 40,000 people work in government—Québec City is the provincial capital—and the region has increasing opportunities in technology, including software, lasers, robotics, biomedical sciences and pharmaceuticals, environmental technology, and telecommunications.

With a population of about 720,000, Québec isn't a big city, but it's one of Canada's least expensive. Housing prices are among the lowest of Canada's metropolitan regions.

If you could see yourself living in a mid-sized city in France, you might consider Québec City. Like Montréal, Québec City blends a French-inspired lifestyle with the practicality of Canadian services. Life in Québec City has a certain peaceful quality absent from larger metropolises. And if you enjoy skiing, snowshoeing, hiking, or cycling, there are plenty of opportunities to get outdoors just outside of town.

THE LAY OF THE LAND

Québec City is set along the St. Lawrence River, about 250 kilometers (155 miles) northeast of Montréal. The city is segmented into eight districts. The central area, known simply as *La Cité,* is not only the tourist hub, it's also where you'll find most government buildings.

The heart of La Cité is the walled Old City, which is divided into the Upper Town *(Haute Ville),* high on the hill, and the Lower Town *(Basse Ville),* fronting the river. Outside the walls, to the west, the St. Jean-Baptiste neighborhood is an established urban community, and to the east, within walking distance of the Lower Town, is the gentrifying St. Roch neighborhood.

The remaining seven city districts, including Sainte-Foy-Sillery, Laurentien (where the airport is located), Les Rivières, La Haute-Saint-Charles, Charlesbourg, Limoilou, and Beauport, cluster around La Cité like a horseshoe. Across the river but connected to Québec City by ferry is the separate municipality of Lévis. To the northeast is Île d'Orléans, a bucolic island that is not only a popular weekend getaway but a residential alternative for those seeking a more rural life.

WHERE TO LIVE

The good news for Québec City renters is that rents are quite reasonable. In 2007, the average monthly rent for a two-bedroom apartment was about $640. The bad news is that apartments can be challenging to find, with a city-wide vacancy rate of only 1.2 percent. Renting a condominium can be slightly easier, since about 10 percent of the city's 18,000 condominium units are rentals. Monthly rents approaching $1,000 for two-bedroom centrally located condos are fairly typical.

Housing prices are comparatively low as well. In late 2007, the average purchase price for a Québec City home was under $175,000.

La Cité

Much of the Old City caters to tourists, but there are places to live within the walls. In the Lower Town, in particular, many brick buildings and former warehouses have been converted into gorgeous condos and lofts (as well as boutique hotels and galleries).

Québec City visitors who want to know where "real people" live should head for the Quartier St. Jean-Baptiste. Along Rue St. Jean are many interesting small restaurants and shops catering to local residents. Farther west, Rue St. Jean intersects Avenue Cartier, another shopping district with a popular market building. You won't find large homes here, but there are plenty of apartments and townhouses on the narrow side streets.

South of Rue St. Jean, along the boulevard known as Grand Allée, cafés and nightclubs draw the bar-hopping crowd. Many of the stately Victorian structures here are now offices or other public buildings, but some are elegant residences.

Trendy restaurants, bars, and shops are opening in artsy, gentrifying St. Roch, although many residential streets still seem like French village lanes. To encourage more 21st-century businesses—primarily information technology and multimedia ventures—to locate in St. Roch, the government established the Centre National des Nouvelles Technologies de Québec (Québec National Center for New Technology) here.

PRIME LIVING LOCATIONS

Other Québec City Districts

Along the river west of Old Québec, Sainte-Foy-Sillery is part residential and part commercial. L'Université Laval, Québec City's largest post-secondary institution, with more than 35,000 students, is here, as are several industrial parks. Many families live in Ste.-Foy, attracted by the parks and access to the riverfront.

Charlesbourg, north of the Old City, is primarily residential. Many historic structures—now residences—are concentrated in the Trait Carré area, but the district has many newer homes as well. Re-

biking on Île d'Orléans, near Québec City

flecting its appeal to families, Charlesbourg has 15 elementary and three secondary schools.

Île d'Orléans

If you imagine living in a small village, but still want to be within shopping or commuting distance of the city, consider Île d'Orléans. This rural island in the St. Lawrence is connected to the mainland by a bridge, but it feels worlds apart. Home to berry farmers, cider makers, and asparagus growers, it's both an agricultural district and a popular weekend getaway destination.

Fancy owning a B&B or making cheese or running a cycling outfitter? Explore Île d'Orléans. Just note that many island businesses are seasonal, reducing their hours or closing entirely between November and April.

DAILY LIFE

While it may not have Montréal's urban buzz, Québec City offers residents plenty to do. Its festival line-up includes the hugely popular Winter Carnival, a growing summer festival, and many special events in between.

Like many Canadian cities, family-oriented Québec City embraces its cold climate, with downhill skiing, snowboarding, cross-country skiing, and snowshoeing within an hour's drive or less. In summer, cyclists tool around town or day-trip over to Île d'Orléans.

Resources

If you can read French, the Québec City newcomer's housing guide
(www.ville.quebec.qc.ca) will be
useful. It describes various neighborhoods and explains common
housing terms.

Claiming to be North America's
oldest newspaper, the *Chronicle-
Telegraph* is the city's English-language weekly; it's been publishing
since 1764.

Schools

The majority of Québec City's schools
are francophone, administered by La
Commission Scolaire de la Capitale
(www.cscapitale.qc.ca), but many

© CAROLYN B. HELLER

A funicular links Québec City's Upper and
Lower Towns.

neighborhoods also have English-language schools. The Central Québec School
Board (www.cqsb.qc.ca) manages the English-language public schools.

If you don't already speak competent French when you relocate to Québec
City, learning the language should be one of your first priorities. Among the
locations offering adult French courses are Université Laval, Le Centre R.I.R.E.
2000, and Cégep de Sainte-Foy. Note that some language program websites
are in French only, which is obviously less useful for non-French speakers. If
you can't read French at all, try phoning for program details.

GETTING AROUND

Québec City's Jean-Lesage airport is west of the city center. There are direct
flights to Newark, Detroit, Toronto, Montréal, Ottawa, and a handful of other
destinations. Via Rail trains travel between Québec City and Montréal, with
connections to points farther afield.

Run by Réseau de Transport de la Capitale (www.rtcquebec.ca), Québec City's buses crisscross the city—a reasonable commuting option. A two-
minute funicular ride shuttles passengers—primarily tourists—between the
Upper and Lower Towns. Otherwise, walking is the best way to get around
the Old City. With narrow, winding streets and limited parking, driving can
be a challenge. Québec City motorists, like their Montréal counterparts, are
quite aggressive. Most traffic signs are in French only.

The Laurentians

Most Americans who've heard of the Laurentians know the area for Mont-Tremblant. The largest ski resort in eastern North America, Mont-Tremblant isn't only the playground of Montréalers, who can be on the slopes in less than two hours; it also attracts skiers from around the world.

Beyond Mont-Tremblant, though, the Laurentians offer everything from artsy villages to weekend getaways to the largest national park in Québec. The top outdoor recreation destination in the province, the Laurentians typically draw over two million visitors a year, making tourism the main source of jobs.

If you're looking to settle, buy a second home, or start a business in an active, outdoorsy region with plenty of services and amenities, all within an easy drive of Montréal, have a look at the Laurentians.

THE LAY OF THE LAND

The Laurentians region rises into the mountains northwest of Montréal. Although the Laurentians' year-round population is around 500,000, the area is dotted with small and mid-sized communities, including St.-Jérôme, St.-Saveur, Ste.-Adèle, Val-David, and Ste.-Agathe-des-Monts, as well as Mont-Tremblant.

Ville de Mont-Tremblant, as the town surrounding the ski area is known, is itself divided into three districts. Many people who work on the mountain live in the community of St.-Jovite, which also has most of the day-to-day services. The Village de Mont-Tremblant, the "old" village, feels like a classic European ski town, with homey bistros and old inns. The Station Mont-Tremblant is the ski village, with dozens of hotels and condos marching up the mountain and skier-friendly restaurants, pubs, and shops around the base. Ville de Mont-Tremblant has a permanent population of about 9,000, plus another 8,500 seasonal residents.

WHERE TO LIVE

To be in the heart of the Mont-Tremblant action, look for a condo in the Station Mont-Tremblant. From basic apartments to townhouses to full-service condo-hotels, there's a range of condominium options on and around the mountain.

You'll find more varied housing choices—and lower prices—off the mountain. St.-Jovite is just a few minutes' drive from the ski hill, but it's more of a year-round community with single-family homes, as well as condos and apartments.

About 30 kilometers (18 miles) south of Mont-Tremblant, the town of Ste.-Agathe-des-Monts is built around Lac des Sables, and many of its prettiest residences are along the lakeshore. Although it's long been a popular holiday

© CAROLYN B. HELLER

There's plenty to do at Mont-Tremblant, even in the summer.

destination, this community of 9,000 feels more "local" than Mont-Tremblant, and it's definitely more francophone.

Just south of Ste.-Agathe-des-Monts, Val-David is a small community of just under 4,000 that blends art and the outdoors. Artsy Val-David hosts North America's largest ceramics festival, "1001 Pots," for five weeks every summer. With mountains ringing the town, there are opportunities for all sorts of outdoor activities as well.

If you'd rather be closer to Montréal, and you enjoy conveniences like factory-outlet shopping, look at St. Saveur. There are several small but locally popular ski hills nearby, and the town, with about 8,500 residents, has the best gourmet shop between Montréal and Mont-Tremblant. After all, if you're embracing the francophone lifestyle, you'll need a place to purchase your local cheeses and freshly made pâté.

DAILY LIFE

In winter, daily life in the Laurentians revolves around the snow, whether you ski or run a business that serves winter tourists. The rest of the year, both locals and visitors head outdoors for hiking, cycling, and water sports. Several towns have artist communities, so gallery visits and arts festivals are also on the agenda. And if you need a big-city fix, Montréal is just a day-trip away.

Resources

The Ville de Mont-Tremblant (www.villedemont-tremblant.qc.ca) publishes a guide to living and working in town, with details about housing and city services. Unfortunately, it's in French only. For general information in English about the region, better sources are the ski area's website (www.tremblant.ca) or the local tourism agencies, including Tourism Mont-Tremblant (www.tourismemonttremblant.com) and Tourisme Laurentides (www.laurentians.com).

The *Tremblant Express* is a bilingual monthly newspaper covering Mont-Tremblant and vicinity. The daily Montréal *Gazette* is widely available in the Laurentians.

You'll find lots of English-speakers around Mont-Tremblant, but if you're looking for work on the mountain, you'll have an edge if you're bilingual. In any other town, speaking French will make your life easier. Intensive French courses for Laurentians newcomers are taught at Cégep de Saint-Jérôme. Part-time French classes are offered in the northern Montréal suburb of Laval.

Schools

The Sir Wilfrid Laurier School Board (www.swlauriersb.qc.ca) manages the Laurentians' English-language schools. Among the district's 11 elementary and five secondary schools are English-language programs in Arundel (serving Mont-Tremblant), Ste.-Agathe-des-Monts (also serving Val David), and Morin Heights (covering St. Saveur).

GETTING AROUND

Montréal is the major airport serving the Laurentians, although the small but grandly named Mont Tremblant International Airport has seasonal direct service to Toronto and Newark, New Jersey.

Highway 15 is the main auto route from Montréal to the Laurentians. Buses travel between Montréal and many Laurentian communities, although if you need to get from town to town, it's easier if you have your own car.

Within Ville de Mont-Tremblant, there's a free shuttle between the residential areas and the mountain. Many Laurentians towns are small enough to navigate on foot or by bicycle. Le Parc Linéaire Le P'tit Train du Nord is a former rail-line-turned-multiuse-path that extends roughly 200 kilometers (125 miles) through the Laurentians, drawing cyclists and hikers in summer and cross-country skiers in winter.

The Eastern Townships

When you drive over the border from Vermont, the rolling hills and green pastures of Québec's Eastern Townships look like the New England countryside you left behind. Yet suddenly, maple syrup has become *syrop d'érable,* and *poutine* has replaced French fries as the snack of choice.

"Life is good in Magog."

In the late 1700s, many English speakers settled in the Eastern Townships. Some were Loyalists who fled north during the American Revolution, others were New England farmers looking for new land, and still others were immigrants from England, Scotland, and Ireland. By the mid-1800s, more than half the Townships' residents were English speakers.

Today, however, like the rest of Québec, the bucolic and largely rural Eastern Townships have become predominantly French-speaking. Only about 10 percent of the Townships' population speaks English as a first language.

Why choose the Eastern Townships? If you're looking for small-town living, or if you enjoy outdoor activities, particularly winter sports, the Eastern Townships may appeal to you. Many Montréal residents—and some Americans—own second homes in the region.

If you're looking for work, about 30 percent of the jobs in the Eastern Townships are in manufacturing. The region has a small technology industry, primarily around the city of Sherbrooke, and there are jobs in agriculture and tourism. But the main reason to settle in the Townships may be to enjoy French-accented small-town life.

THE LAY OF THE LAND

The Eastern Townships' largest city is Sherbrooke, about 150 kilometers (95 miles) east of Montréal along Highway 10. Otherwise, the communities here, including Magog, Knowlton, and Sutton, are fairly small.

Several family-friendly ski areas—Mont Orford outside Magog, Mont Sutton and Bromont near the towns of the same names, and Owl's Head, close to the U.S. border—bring winter visitors. Summer activities center around the many lakes; the largest, Lake Memphrémagog, stretches from Magog south to Vermont.

WHERE TO LIVE

With a population of about 25,000, Magog is one of the Townships' larger towns, set on the shore of Lake Memphrémagog about 125 kilometers (75 miles) east of Montréal. Sawmills and textile factories previously employed many residents, but recently, tourism has become a major industry.

Magog is a popular weekend destination for Montréalers, who come in summer for boating, cycling, and hiking, and in winter to ski at Mont Orford. In the colder months, the city floods a lakeside path, creating an outdoor skating route.

Magog's main street, Rue Principale, is lined with bistros and boutiques. Many Victorian-era houses remain in the town center, and the lakeshore is dotted with vacation homes. Development at Mont Orford is restricted; while there are houses near the mountain, you won't find ski-in, ski-out condos. In 2007, the median price for a home in Magog was $215,000. Houses near Mont Orford were selling in the $300,000s, but the in-town Victorians and lakeshore homes go for much more.

Southwest of Magog, about 100 kilometers (60 miles) from Montréal is the lakeside community of Lac-Brome. With a permanent population of about 5,000, Lac-Brome is comprised of several villages, the largest of which is Knowlton. It's a cute little village, filled with antiques shops and boutiques, as well as outlets for upscale brands like Jones New York and Nine West. Many homes here date to the late 1800s and early 1900s.

You may hear a bit more English in Knowlton than in other parts of the Townships. The other thing you'll notice is the number of ducks—Brome Lake Ducks is one of Canada's largest duck-breeding businesses. Not only do ducks appear on restaurant menus, but duck souvenirs fill the shops.

In the hills southwest of Knowlton, near the Vermont border, is the town of Sutton, with just under 4,000 year-round residents. Best known for the nearby Mont Sutton ski area, Sutton also has a good selection of galleries. Residents include a number of artists as well as outdoor enthusiasts.

DAILY LIFE
Resources

A useful resource for English speakers is the Townshippers' Association. Their website (www.townshippers.qc.ca) has links to a wide range of English-language information and services across the Eastern Townships. The Sherbrooke-based Job Links program (www.etsb.qc.ca/joblinks) provides resources for English speakers looking for work in the Townships.

Ministry-sponsored French-language courses for newcomers are offered through Cégep de Sherbrooke, and through Solidarité Ethnique Régionale de la Yamaska (SERY-Granby) and Cégep de Granby-Haute-Yamaska, both in the town of Granby. There are also numerous programs available in Montréal.

Many English-speaking Township residents read the Montréal *Gazette*, but the Sherbrooke *Record* (www.sherbrookerecord.com) is also an English-language daily newspaper. Other community papers publishing in English include the weekly *Stanstead Journal* (www.stanstead-journal.com) and Magog's monthly *Outlet* (www.outletjournal.com).

Schools

While the majority of Townships schools provide education in French, many communities, including Magog, Knowlton, and Sutton, also have an English-language elementary school, and the region has three English-language high schools. The Eastern Townships School Board (www.etsb.qc.ca) administers the anglophone schools. Independent schools that provide instruction in English include Bishop's College School in Sherbrooke and Stanstead College in Stanstead.

GETTING AROUND

Getting to the Eastern Townships by air means flying either to Montréal or to Burlington, Vermont. By car, Highway 10 from Montréal is the main east–west route across the region. Highway 55 runs north–south from the U.S. border, past Magog and Sherbrooke. Off these main highways, many roads meander through the countryside, so allow more time than you might anticipate to drive from town to town.

In this largely rural region, there's not much public transportation. You really need a car to get around—unless you're an avid cyclist, that is. Kilometers of bicycling paths, part of the province-wide Route Verte (Green Route), link many communities in the Eastern Townships.

ALBERTA

With the towering Rocky Mountains along its western border and miles of wide-open prairie to the east, Alberta has historically been Canada's "wild west." Some of the country's most dramatic territory is here—in the snow-capped mountains of Banff National Park, the startlingly clear water of Lake Louise, and the glacier-lined Icefields Parkway that leads to Jasper National Park. There are still places where the bison roam and where there really are more moose than people.

These days, though, Alberta residents are more likely to be riding a bus than a horse. About one-third of Alberta's population lives in Calgary—the largest city—and nearly one-third in the Edmonton metropolitan region, with the balance in smaller towns. Yet despite recent rapid population growth, even the cities have plenty of open space. If you're seeking a laid-back, outdoorsy lifestyle and don't mind long snowy winters, you might want to consider Alberta.

These days, too, if you're looking for work, Alberta is a good place to be. Thanks largely to the province's booming oil industry, jobs are plentiful, and Alberta has the lowest unemployment rate in Canada.

© CAROLYN B. HELLER

GETTING SETTLED IN ALBERTA

If you're thinking about settling in Alberta, Canada's main oil-producing region, you've got to know something about oil. Almost one in every six Alberta workers is employed in an energy-related business.

The province's "oil sands," as its deposits of bitumen—a thick, sticky form of crude oil—are known, are the second-largest reserves in the world; only those in Saudi Arabia are larger. Alberta's oil reserves are almost 30 times the size of those in Texas and 40 times bigger than those in Alaska, the two largest oil-producing states in the United States. A "black gold rush" is luring investors, managers, and workers from around the world for jobs in mining, processing, and refining.

Alberta produces not only nearly 70 percent of Canada's crude oil but also more than 80 percent of its natural gas. Construction, manufacturing, and a variety of services support the province's energy-based businesses.

Working in Alberta

Beyond the oil industry, agriculture has long been a driver of Alberta's economy, with wheat and barley the major crops. Alberta beef is renowned across North America, and provincial farms raise poultry, hogs, and sheep as well.

Alberta has plenty of jobs in financial services and real estate, and the provincial government is encouraging technology entrepreneurs to set up shop here. Alberta's government is among Canada's most pro-business. Alberta is the only province without a provincial sales tax, there are no payroll taxes, and its corporate tax rates are the country's lowest.

Taxes are lower for individuals, too, than elsewhere in Canada. According to Alberta Finance, a two-income family of four earning $125,000 per year would pay about $1,178 less in total provincial taxes than a similar family in British Columbia, about $2,873 less than in Ontario, and nearly $8,877 less than in Québec.

What else do Albertans do? Many tend to the roughly eight million tourists who visit Alberta's mountains and parks every year. In and around Banff, Lake Louise, and Jasper, tourism jobs are especially plentiful during the summer high season, and when the snow begins to fall, the winter brings skiers—and ski-related jobs.

Immigration and Social Issues

In the late 1800s and early 1900s, Alberta attracted immigrants from the United Kingdom, the Ukraine, and Germany looking for opportunity in the wide-open West. Since the 1970s, however, many immigrants have arrived

PRIME LIVING LOCATIONS

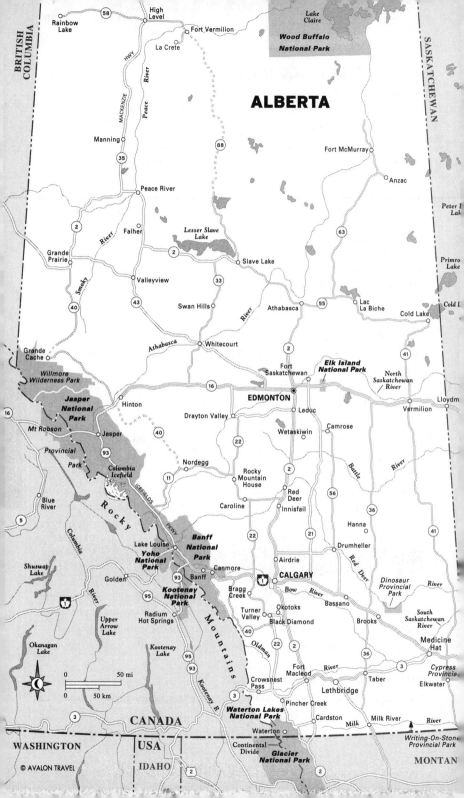

from Asia and the Middle East. Employees of oil-related businesses in the United States and abroad continue to flow into Alberta.

Not only is Alberta Canada's most business-friendly province, it has historically been one of the most socially conservative. The Alberta government was a major opponent of Canada's same-sex marriage legislation, passing a 2002 bill outlawing marriage between same-sex couples that was overruled in 2005, when Canada passed national legislation legalizing same-sex marriage. Today, Calgary has a gay scene, but many less urban areas remain more conservative.

Health Care

Newcomers to Alberta are generally eligible for health coverage on the date you arrive in the province. All Alberta residents must register with the Alberta Health Care Insurance Plan. You need to provide proof of your immigration status (e.g., work or study permit, permanent residence card), a government-issued photo ID (such as a passport), and proof of your Alberta address. More information and application forms are available from the Alberta Health and Wellness Ministry (www.health.gov.ab.ca).

Alberta has a government-sponsored supplemental health care insurance program for services not covered under the basic plan, including prescription drugs, ambulance services, and partial payment for services such as psychologist visits or home nursing care. Alberta Blue Cross runs the supplemental coverage program; get more information from the Health and Wellness Ministry.

Inform Alberta has an extensive list of health care-related resources online (www.informalberta.ca). To find a doctor who's accepting new patients, search the College of Physicians and Surgeons of Alberta's database (www.cpsa.ab.ca), and for a dentist, check the Alberta Dental Association and College (www.abda.ab.ca).

PRIME LIVING LOCATIONS

Calgary

If you wander amidst the glass-and-steel towers that dominate downtown Calgary, you'll likely see some familiar names—at least if you're familiar with major international oil companies. Companies like Shell, Esso, BP, Imperial Oil, and Petro-Canada all have a significant presence in Calgary, and energy-based businesses account for a considerable percentage of Calgary's jobs.

Beyond the oil industry, Calgary has a developing high-technology sector, reporting the largest number of technology start-ups per capita in Canada. Calgary's construction and real estate industries are booming, and the region is a Western transportation hub, home to more than 4,000 transportation and logistics companies. The University of Calgary is a major employer, with over 5,000 staff to support its 28,000 students. Calgary's edge-of-the-prairies location means that agricultural businesses have long been based here, while its near-the-mountains setting has made it a starting point for Rockies tourism.

Why settle in Calgary? A clerk in a downtown outdoor-gear store put it this way: From Monday through Friday, Calgary works hard. But by Friday afternoon, it's time to play. And whether that play involves heading for the mountains to ski, snowboard, bike, or hike, or staying in the city to jog in the park or meet your pals for drinks, Calgary plays hard. From hip eateries and sidewalk cafés to riverfront paths filled with skaters and cyclists, Calgary bristles with energy—and it doesn't all come out of the ground.

Calgary feels something like Denver, Salt Lake City, or other active mountain metropolises. It isn't actually in the mountains, but the Rockies begin just 120 kilometers (75 miles) to the west. You can drive from downtown Calgary to Banff National Park in about 90 minutes, or be on the ski slopes at Lake Louise within a couple of hours.

THE LAY OF THE LAND

The Bow River runs through the center of Calgary, and downtown developed along the river's south bank. The Elbow River meanders into the city center from the southwest and joins the Bow east of downtown. Many of Calgary's nicest homes overlook one of the rivers, and the banks of both are lined with parkland.

Calgary is divided into four quadrants: northwest, northeast, southwest, and southeast. Numbered avenues run east–west, while numbered streets go north–south, and both begin downtown. The corner of 4th Avenue S.W. and 4th Street S.W. is downtown, an address on 14th Avenue N.W. is in the northwest quadrant not far from the city center, while 90th Street S.E. is in the southeastern suburbs.

Calgary is a city of neighborhoods, and locals identify where they live by neighborhood name. The districts ringing the downtown core are undergoing a renaissance as younger residents move in, drawn by new development, condo conversions, and opportunities to refurbish older homes. Another ring of more established neighborhoods surrounds the revitalizing central areas, and farther out, you'll find suburban developments everywhere.

Climate

Of Canada's 10 largest cities, Calgary boasts the greatest number of sunny days. Summers are mild, with more than 16 hours of daylight in June. The sun often shines even mid-winter, but winters are cold, and the city averages 130 centimeters (about 50 inches) of snow annually. Spring can be volatile, warm and sunny one day, windy and grey the next. Fall is pleasant and crisp, with the leaves turning color in September and October.

Fortunately, the city deals well with its variable weather. A network of enclosed passageways—the "+15 Walkways"—connects the downtown buildings, so you can walk for blocks without going outside. Look for the "+15" signs around downtown to find an entrance.

The "Chinook winds" are a weather phenomenon unique to southern Alberta. Warm, dry winds that blow

© CAROLYN B. HELLER

The "+15 Walkways" link buildings in downtown Calgary.

in from the west, Chinooks can cause temperatures to rise as much as 20 degrees Celsius in an hour or two. Chinooks are most frequent—and most welcome—in winter, when they trigger snow-melts and bring Calgarians outdoors to enjoy the unexpectedly mild weather.

Culture

Life in Calgary takes its cues from the outdoors, but the city does have a growing arts scene. Its longstanding arts institutions include the Calgary Philharmonic Orchestra, the Alberta Ballet (which splits its time between Calgary and Edmonton), the Calgary Opera, and a variety of local theater groups, and both established and new galleries feature local artists' work. Calgary's restaurants have begun to showcase regional ingredients and incorporate elements of various ethnicities into their cuisine.

WHERE TO LIVE

Calgary has a well-regarded public transit system, built around a light rail network, so if you can live near a light rail depot, it may simplify your commute. Like many growing cities, Calgary's highways and boulevards are becoming increasingly traffic-clogged. Although the many bridges that span the city's two rivers help reduce (but not eliminate) river-crossing

STAMPEDING TO CALGARY

Even as Calgary becomes increasingly urban, the biggest event of the year has its roots in cowboy culture – the annual Calgary Stampede. Taking over the city for 10 days every July, the Stampede bills itself as "The Greatest Outdoor Show on Earth." It's a rodeo, county fair, and crazy party rolled into one.

The Stampede, which began in 1912, was the vision of an American expat. Born in Rochester, New York, Guy Weadick became a vaudeville and rodeo performer who appeared across North America. In Calgary, he met H. C. McMullen, a livestock agent for the Canadian Pacific Railway, and they hatched a plan for a "wild west" show. They secured funding from several local businessmen, and the Stampede was launched.

The Stampede opens with a huge parade through downtown. Other attractions include chuck wagon races, calf roping, bull riding, horse shows, a carnival midway, and concerts by big-name entertainers. The Stampede typically draws more than 100,000 people per day, so pull on your boots and come on down!

bottlenecks, it's worth thinking about where you'd need to cross the river to get to work or school.

At the end of 2007, the average price for a single-family home in metro Calgary was $472,230, and the average condo was $316,370, but expect a big range between the highest and lowest prices.

Downtown

Downtown Calgary has traditionally been business-focused, with office towers lining the city-center streets. More recently, residential condo buildings have been going up, and older buildings are being rehabbed into residential communities.

Much of the downtown development is in the Eau Claire neighborhood bordering the riverfront. The median income of Eau Claire residents soared from $47,000 in 1995 to more than $80,000 by 2000, as increasingly well-heeled residents moved in. Development is also creeping into Chinatown, on downtown's east side, which was originally settled in the late 1800s and early 1900s.

Though it's not a residential area, downtown's liveliest district is along Stephen Avenue, where many historic stone and brick buildings have been converted to trendy restaurants, cafés, and shops. A pedestrian zone, Stephen Avenue is hopping at lunchtime and after work, though it can be quieter on weekends when many downtown office workers have decamped for the suburbs.

Around Downtown

Several neighborhoods surrounding the downtown core are also in the midst of a revival. Across the Bow River northwest of downtown, part-bohemian, part-yuppie Kensington is filled with eclectic shops, coffee houses, and ethnic restaurants. Housing options include restored (and to-be-restored) older homes, new condos, and "infill" houses—new homes built on subdivided lots.

East of downtown, Bridgeland and Inglewood are in earlier stages of gentrification. Young families are buying Bridgeland's bungalows, while new condos and apartments are drawing younger people to Centre Avenue. Housing in Inglewood is a bit of a hodgepodge, with restored bungalows on some streets and modest older homes on others. On Inglewood's main thoroughfare—9th Avenue S.E.—funky eateries and cafés, art galleries, and old-time businesses like Sprouse Fire & Safety (which sells fire-fighting gear) stand side-by-side.

South of downtown, in the trendy Mission and Cliff Bungalow neighborhoods, nearly 40 percent of the residents are between 20 and 35, and few have children. The predominance of apartments and condos—as well as hip restaurants and hopping bars—reflect this younger demographic.

The Southwest and the Southeast

One of Calgary most upscale, established neighborhoods, Mount Royal extends south from the 17th Avenue SW shopping strip. The lower (northern) section mixes apartment buildings and smaller houses, but as you climb into Upper Mount Royal, the winding tree-lined streets are filled with gracious older homes.

Mount Royal was originally known as "American Hill," since a number of American entrepreneurs settled there in the early 1900s. Mount Royal offers a quiet setting just a few minutes from downtown, but that convenience will cost you—it's among the city's most expensive communities.

Slightly farther south, Elbow Park is another family-friendly neighborhood of well-maintained older homes and bungalows. South of Elbow Park, built into a bend of the river, Britannia mixes older residences, 1960s contemporaries, and newer houses on large lots. Average incomes of the Upper Mount Royal, Elbow Park, and Britannia residents are over $100,000.

Continuing southwest, the neighborhoods become increasingly suburban, and the age of the homes changes from the 1960s to the present the farther south you go. Many upscale family communities surround the Glenmore Reservoir.

McKenzie Town, one of Calgary's largest developments, is in the far southeast. McKenzie Town includes single-family detached homes, townhouses, and condominiums, designed to appeal to a broad range of families. More than

10,000 people call this community home, and three-quarters of McKenzie Town residents have children under 14.

The Northwest and the Northeast

Calgary's northwest quadrant is also a popular residential area, with scores of suburban-style developments. Faculty and staff at the nearby University of Calgary tend to live in this area. Nose Hill Park, one of the largest urban parks in Canada, is here, and the northwest has easy access to the highways heading for the Rockies. The CTrain, Calgary's light rail system, serves many northwest neighborhoods.

The northeast quadrant, which includes the Calgary Airport, is more diverse—part industrial, part residential. Many northeast neighborhoods draw a higher percentage of new immigrants than other Calgary districts. For families, some of the more desirable northeast communities are on the north edge of town, in developments such as Panorama Hills. Although the CTrain goes to some northeast neighborhoods, public transit is less accessible on the north perimeter.

DAILY LIFE

You'll often find Calgary residents out-of-doors, whether skiing, bicycling, ice skating, or walking along the riverbank or in one of the many parks. Recreation centers, pools, and rinks offer a variety of fitness programs, which are good places to get acquainted with your new neighbors. For spectators, the most popular sport is hockey with the NHL Calgary Flames.

The city of Calgary claims that its residents volunteer for charitable causes more than any other city in Canada. Volunteer work is another way to get to know the community. Volunteer Calgary (www.volunteercalgary.ab.ca) can help you locate local volunteer opportunities.

Resources

The city of Calgary publishes demographic profiles of its many neighborhoods on its website (www.calgary.ca). The Calgary Real Estate Board has housing statistics and other useful information for potential homebuyers, and the city's Economic Development department has more helpful information about relocating to Calgary. For job-hunters, Alberta's Employment, Immigration, and Industry ministry publishes a monthly Labour Market News report on the Calgary area.

Calgary has two daily newspapers, the *Calgary Herald* and the *Calgary Sun,* plus the alternative *FFWD (Fast Forward Weekly)*. *Avenue* is a glossy monthly

CAROLYN B. HELLER

Active Calgary residents say, "Why take your bike to the shop when the shop can come to you?"

city magazine, and *City Palate* covers Calgary's food scene. Although designed for visitors, *Where* magazine's Calgary edition details urban happenings.

Schools

In Calgary, elementary schools span kindergarten through Grade 6, junior high covers Grades 7–9, and high school encompasses Grades 10–12. Calgary schools are neighborhood-based, so in general, where you live determines where your children will attend school. A Calgary Board of Education map shows which schools serve which neighborhoods. Calgary also has publicly funded Catholic schools, run by the Calgary Roman Catholic Separate School District.

Calgary has several private college preparatory schools and religious schools. You can get a full list from the Association of Independent Schools and Colleges in Alberta.

GETTING AROUND

The Calgary airport is in the city's northeast quadrant, about 15 kilometers (10 miles) from downtown.

The Calgary Transit System (CTS) runs a light rail system called the CTrain as well as an extensive bus network. One light rail line runs between downtown and the southern suburbs, while the other travels roughly east–west, from the northwest through downtown to the northeast. The CTrain is free within the downtown core. While some Calgary residents rely on their cars, some who live near a CTrain line or bus route take transit when they can.

PRIME LIVING LOCATIONS

The Trans-Canada Highway (Highway 1) crosses Calgary, and Highway 2 runs along Calgary's east side, passing the airport and continuing north to Edmonton. While the central city is laid out in a grid pattern, many diagonal roads feed into the grid, and other routes curve along the riverbanks and around the parks. A detailed street map will definitely help you find your way around.

For walkers and cyclists, Calgary has one of the most extensive urban pathway networks in North America, encompassing more than 600 kilometers (370 miles) of multiuse paths and nearly 300 kilometers (180 miles) of on-street bike routes. In winter, the city tries to keep snow cleared from the most heavily traveled paths.

Despite Calgary's increasing sprawl, plenty of people do commute by bike. There's bike parking at CTrain stations, as well as a "Park 'n' Bike" program, where you can drive partway into the city, park your car, and ride your bike the rest of the way.

Edmonton

Boomtown. That's what Edmonton residents call their city these days. This municipality of just over one million people may be smack in the middle of the province, but it looks north to oil patch towns like Fort McMurray and Grande Prairie. Many businesses that support the oil industry, including manufacturing, refining, and transportation, have operations in Edmonton.

Albertans say that while the bosses live in Calgary, the work gets done in Edmonton. The oil patch may dominate current headlines and provide many jobs, but as the provincial capital, Edmonton has long been a center of government and commerce. With over 35,000 employees, the provincial government is the largest employer in town.

The University of Alberta, with more than 30,000 students, employs roughly 8,000 people. The university has particular strengths in engineering and medicine, and Edmonton's hospitals draw patients from across the region. Finance, insurance, real estate, and construction are other important components of Edmonton's economy. The West Edmonton Mall, North America's largest, provides retail and tourism-related jobs.

Even though Edmonton has grown to be Canada's fifth-largest city, it can still feel a little like a small town. People are friendly, and the rush-rush of cities back East doesn't seem to have migrated here. While it's nearly as far west as Missoula and Boise, the vibe is more like Omaha or Des Moines, or—with the oil influence—like a wintery Texas.

© CAROLYN B. HELLER

Edmonton now has more than a million residents.

Yet Edmonton is rapidly changing, like many Canadian cities, through immigration. The region has a strong heritage of immigration from the Ukraine, Poland, Germany, and Eastern Europe, while more recent immigrants hail from the Middle East or Asia (primarily China). The city has a large Muslim community, estimated at about 30,000 people. Edmonton is also home to Canada's second-largest aboriginal community, after Winnipeg.

THE LAY OF THE LAND

The North Saskatchewan River bisects Edmonton, with downtown on the north bank and the University of Alberta on the south. Edmonton divides its streets into four quadrants—northwest, northeast, southwest, and southeast—and more than 100 different neighborhoods.

Numbered avenues begin in the south, so 23rd Avenue is on the south side, and 111th Avenue is in the north. Numbered streets begin in the east; 17th Street is near the eastern boundary, while 170th Street runs past the West Edmonton Mall on the west side.

Climate

Unless you love long, cold winters, don't choose Edmonton for its weather. The average high temperature in January is only -8°C (17°F), roughly the same as Moscow. At least it's often sunny, even in winter. Springs are short and changeable, but summers are sweet, with July highs a comfortable 22°C (72°F). It usually stays nice throughout September, but the first flurries may fall in October.

© CAROLYN B. HELLER

Railtown Park is one of several redeveloped neighborhoods in Edmonton's city center.

Culture

To make up for the long winters, Edmonton parties in the summers, hosting festivals nearly every week. The Edmonton International Fringe Theatre Festival is North America's largest fringe event, bringing dozens of avant-garde acts and plenty of good times to Edmonton for 10 days every August.

Sports are big in Edmonton, particularly hockey, and the local NHL team—the Edmonton Oilers—has legions of loyal fans. Calgary may boast of its Stampede, but every November, it's Edmonton that shows its cowboy colors as host of the Canadian Finals Rodeo, typically drawing more than 90,000 people.

Edmonton has a small but active cultural scene, with a symphony orchestra, opera company, the Alberta Ballet, and local theater troupes. Along 124th Street west of downtown, there's an emerging gallery district.

WHERE TO LIVE

Edmonton real estate prices have been highly volatile in recent years, with big increases in 2006, followed by ups and downs in 2007. Still, compared to Vancouver or even Calgary, housing prices in Edmonton remain moderate. As of late 2007, the average price for a single-family home was $382,022 and for a condo $253,270.

Locals recommend living and working on the same side of the river to avoid bridge bottlenecks and save yourself some commuting time.

Downtown and the Central City

Edmonton's downtown is entering a redevelopment stage as aging buildings are rehabilitated and new buildings constructed. While there isn't a large amount of housing stock yet, there are some condominiums and apartments, including communities such as Railtown built around a park, with more in the works.

Several of Edmonton's well-established residential neighborhoods, including Glenora, Crestwood, Parkview, West Jasper Place, and Laurier Heights, are just west of downtown. Many of the nicely maintained older homes here date to the early 1900s.

Riverdale, in a former brickyard and mill district northeast of downtown, is drawing younger families to its older cottages and newer infill housing. Also in the northeast, the Highlands has both older Victorians and newer homes, bordering a golf course and overlooking the river.

Strathcona and the University

Across the river south of downtown, Strathcona is one of Edmonton's oldest communities. Whyte Avenue is its commercial center, and with its proximity to the University of Alberta, many shops, restaurants, and bars cater to students. The popular Strathcona Farmer's Market is just off Whyte Ave. Low-rise apartments and rental homes are plentiful, and high-rise towers, most of which are condominiums, line the riverbank.

South and west of the university are comfortable residential neighborhoods. The closer to the river, the more posh the houses become. Belgravia is conveniently located just south of campus, and farther southwest are neighborhoods such as Bulyea Heights that house both university and business people.

The Suburbs

Much of Edmonton's new residential development is in the southwest. Many neighborhoods here are typical suburban communities: quiet cul-de-sacs of similar homes. One exception is Terwillegar Towne, a large development that has embraced the principles of "new urbanism"—traditionally styled homes with front porches built close to the street on smaller lots. Their designs are intended to foster a greater sense of community.

Outside the city proper are family-oriented towns that may appeal to those looking for a less urban environment. St. Albert to the northwest, Sherwood Park to the east, and Spruce Grove, Stony Plain, and Devon to the west, are all within reasonable commuting distance to many parts of Edmonton.

DAILY LIFE
Resources

Move to Edmonton (www.move-toedmonton.com), published by the Edmonton Economic Development Corporation, is a helpful guide for newcomers.

The *Edmonton Journal* and *Edmonton Sun* are the two daily newspapers. The city also has two arts and entertainment weeklies: *Vue Weekly* and *See Magazine.*

The Realtors Association of Edmonton (formerly the Edmonton Real Estate Board) publishes a useful book of maps showing every Edmonton neighborhood, with information about nearby schools, hospitals, libraries, shopping centers, and recreational opportunities.

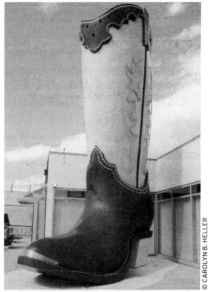

© CAROLYN B. HELLER

Alberta retains elements of its wild-west traditions, including this western-style boot that claims to be the world's largest.

Local real estate agents should be able to get you a copy, or you can purchase it from the association offices.

Job-seekers may want to check the monthly Labour Market News report from Alberta's Employment, Immigration, and Industry ministry.

Schools

The Edmonton Public School Board runs the city's "open boundary" school system, in which students can attend their neighborhood school or apply to any school in the city. Edmonton's elementary schools encompass kindergarten through Grade 6, junior high includes Grades 7–9, and high school covers Grades 10–12. The Edmonton Catholic School District administers the city's publicly funded Catholic schools.

The Edmonton Islamic Academy considers itself the largest Muslim academic school in North America. For a list of other Edmonton private schools, contact the Association of Independent Schools and Colleges in Alberta.

GETTING AROUND

Edmonton's airport is in Leduc, south of the city. Via Rail's passenger train between Vancouver and the east also stops in Edmonton.

NORTH AMERICA'S LARGEST MALL

You can surf the waves, take in a sea lion show or the latest Hollywood flick, climb aboard a pirate ship, or take a few spins around the ice rink. Oh, and you can do your shopping, too.

Edmonton's biggest tourist attraction is the gargantuan West Edmonton Mall, housing more than 800 stores and entertainment outlets. Until even more gigantic complexes went up in China, Edmonton's shopping center claimed the title of world's largest mall – now it has to settle for being the biggest in North America.

Not just a tourist attraction, the mall is a shopping destination for many Edmonton residents. It's home to North American and international chains, as well as Canadian-owned retailers – even a "Chinatown" anchored by the large T&T Supermarket. Tip: If hunger strikes and you're looking for something beyond food-court fare, pick up some sushi, pork buns, or other prepared foods at the T&T.

© CAROLYN B. HELLER

familiar chain restaurants at the West Edmonton Mall

The Edmonton Transit System operates a light rail network, known as the LRT, as well as a citywide bus system. The LRT line begins in the northeast, heads downtown, then crosses the river to the University of Alberta. At this writing, an extension to the south was under construction. Residents suggest that if you live near a light rail station and work downtown, it's a convenient commuting option. You can get around by bus if you have to, although Edmonton remains firmly steeped in the car culture.

Highway 2 is the main road north from Calgary to Edmonton. Highway 16 traverses the city's north side, Anthony Henday Drive circles the south and west sides of town, and Highway 216 runs along the eastern edge. As in most cities, locals complain about the traffic, and Edmonton's growth is fueling car commuters' gripes.

In spread-out Edmonton, walking is feasible within particular districts but not to get across town. Bicycling is a better option—at least when the ground isn't snow-covered—on the many paths, trails, and bike lanes designed for cyclists. You can get detailed cycling maps on the City of Edmonton's website.

Banff and the Rocky Mountains

It's hard not to gush about the Canadian Rockies. Even when you've seen photos of the snow-capped peaks, crystal-blue lakes, and towering evergreens, it still doesn't prepare you for being up close and personal with these iconic mountains. If you're lucky enough to live in the Rocky Mountains, keep a second home here, or just come for an extended visit, you're, well, lucky.

THE LAY OF THE LAND

Hugging the provincial border between Alberta and British Columbia are Banff and Jasper National Parks. Three towns lie inside the parks themselves: Banff, Lake Louise, and Jasper. Banff is the largest, with about 7,500 year-round residents, more than half of whom work in a tourism-related occupation. Banff Avenue is the town's main street, lined with hotels, restaurants, and shops. Two downhill ski areas are just outside town: Mount Norquay and Sunshine Village.

The town of Lake Louise is more a service center than a town, with a minimall, some cafés and restaurants, and a few hotels. The lake itself is several kilometers above the village, and Lake Louise Ski Area sits above town in the opposite direction.

Located about 280 kilometers (175 miles) north of Banff, Jasper is at the end of the dramatic Icefields Parkway that begins at Lake Louise. Jasper's year-round population of just under 5,000 can swell to more than 20,000 on a busy summer day. As in Banff, the majority of Jasper's residents work in tourism.

About 25 kilometers (15 miles) southeast of the Banff National Park boundary is the town of Canmore. Because housing within the town of Banff is restricted, many people working in, or regularly visiting, the Banff area are choosing Canmore as their base. Canmore has approximately 12,000 permanent denizens, plus nearly 5,000 part-time residents.

© CAROLYN B. HELLER

Banff residents live close to the mountains.

Climate

Mountain weather can be quite changeable, with temperatures varying significantly within a single day. Summer days are warm, averaging 21°C (70°F), and nights are crisp, dipping down to 7°C (45°F). Fall remains pleasant, although cooler, and snows generally start by October or November. Expect lots of snow, too, and winter temperatures averaging only -12°C (6°F). Spring doesn't begin till at least April, and snow remains on the ground at higher elevations till summer rolls around again.

Culture

Most activities in these Rocky Mountain towns revolve around the outdoors: skiing, boarding, hiking, mountain biking, and camping. The many bars get busy when it's time to come inside.

The Banff Centre is a well-regarded arts training facility that runs educational programs for musicians, actors, dancers, artists, and writers. Year-round, it also hosts recitals, plays, lectures, and other events open to the public. Otherwise, Banff and Canmore are close enough to Calgary that you can head to the big city for a dose of urban culture.

WHERE TO LIVE

Because the towns of Banff and Jasper lie within the park boundaries and housing stock is limited, there are special restrictions on living and buying property here. You must demonstrate that you have a "need to reside" in town by showing that you have a job or that you own a local business that's your principal source of income, not just a hobby venture.

The "need to reside" requirement applies only if you actually want to live in town. You can buy residential property for investment purposes and rent it out to locals, rather than using it yourself.

When you buy a home in Banff or Jasper, you're buying the structure but not the land. You lease the land, which belongs to the national park, from Parks Canada.

Few properties are available for sale at any given time in Banff or Jasper. In Banff, less than 15 percent of the housing stock is single-family

© CAROLYN B. HELLER

Because of residence restrictions in Banff, many homebuyers are looking to nearby Canmore.

detached homes. Nearly half are apartments, with townhouses, duplexes, and other multi-unit buildings making up the balance. Townhouses and duplex units start in the $500,000–750,000 range, but single-family homes go much higher. In Jasper, properties rarely come on the market for less than $500,000.

Rental vacancies are limited in both Banff and Jasper, too. Rentals start at about $500–600 per month for a studio or one-bedroom and $800–900 for a two-bedroom. Some employers provide housing for their employees, generally dormitory-style accommodations with shared facilities.

An alternative to living in the parks is to look at towns outside the park boundaries. The town of Canmore has a desirable location just outside of Banff National Park and within a 90-minute drive of Calgary. Rising housing prices reflect Canmore's popularity with both permanent and part-time residents. The *Rocky Mountain Outlook,* a local weekly, reported that, in 2007, an average single family house in Canmore was priced above $900,000, while the average condo topped $500,000.

DAILY LIFE

Many jobs in the Rockies are seasonal, from April or May through the fall. Tourism peaks in July and August, although winter draws skiers and boarders (and mountain staff), too. The quietest times are early spring and late fall.

Resources

Several weekly newspapers serve Banff/Canmore including the *Banff Crag & Canyon, Canmore Leader,* and *Rocky Mountain Outlook.* Jasper's weeklies are the *Fitzhugh* and the *Jasper Booster.*

The town of Banff's website (www.banff.ca) has lots of valuable tips for living and working in the area. The town of Jasper (www.jasper-alberta.com) publishes a Jasper Survival Guide that's designed for seasonal workers but may be useful for all newcomers.

If you're looking for work, try the BanffLIFE Job Board (from www.banff. ca, choose "Working"), the Job Resource Centre (www.jobresourcecentre.com) with offices in Banff and Canmore, and the Jasper Employment Centre (with job postings online at www.ability.ab.ca).

Schools

Both Banff and Jasper have elementary schools that run through Grade 6, and combined junior/senior highs for Grades 7–12. In Canmore, kindergarten–Grade 4 students attend the elementary school, Grades 5–8 attend the middle school, and Grades 9–12 go to the high school.

GETTING AROUND

The closest major airport to Banff and Canmore is in Calgary. Edmonton has the nearest major airport to Jasper, although it's more than 350 kilometers (220 miles) east of the park. Via Rail trains stop in Jasper en route between Vancouver and Edmonton.

Banff has a local bus system that runs three routes through town in summer and two in winter. Banff and Jasper are both small enough that you can get around on foot or by bike. In Canmore, the center of town is walkable, but if you're going to destinations beyond the town core or into the park, it would help to have a car.

RESOURCES

© CAROLYN B. HELLER

Consulates and Embassies

IN THE UNITED STATES

The Buffalo (NY) office of the Consulate General of Canada handles all applications from U.S. citizens for Canadian permanent residence, regardless of where you reside. If you're applying for a work permit or study permit, contact the Canadian Consulate office in the U.S. region that's closest to where you live. While Canada has consulates in many U.S. cities, only the consular offices in Buffalo, Detroit, Los Angeles, New York, and Seattle deal with immigration and visa issues.

CANADIAN EMBASSY
501 Pennsylvania Ave., NW
Washington, D.C.
tel. 202/682-1760
fax 202/682-7689
http://geo.international.gc.ca/can-am/washington

CONSULATE GENERAL OF CANADA - IMMIGRATION SECTION
3000 HSBC Center, 30th Floor
Buffalo, NY 14203-2884
tel. 716/858-9501
fax 716/852-2477
http://geo.international.gc.ca/can-am/buffalo
This office processes all applications from U.S. citizens for permanent residence in Canada.

CONSULATE GENERAL OF CANADA - DETROIT
600 Renaissance Centre, Suite 1100
Detroit, MI 48243-1798
tel. 313/567-2340
fax 313/567-2164
www.detroit.gc.ca

CONSULATE GENERAL OF CANADA - LOS ANGELES
550 S. Hope St., 9th Floor
Los Angeles, CA 90071
tel. 213/346-2700
fax 213/620-8827
www.dfait-maeci.gc.ca/los_angeles

CONSULATE GENERAL OF CANADA - NEW YORK
1251 Avenue of the Americas
New York, NY 10020-1175
tel. 212/596-1628
fax 212/596-1790
www.dfait-maeci.gc.ca/new_york

CONSULATE GENERAL OF CANADA - SEATTLE
1501 4th Ave., Suite 600
Seattle, WA 98101
tel. 206/443-1777
fax 206/443-9662
www.dfait-maeci.gc.ca/seattle

IN CANADA

A useful source of information for Americans living in Canada is the American Consular Services website: www.amcits.com.

U.S. EMBASSY
490 Sussex Dr.
Ottawa, ON K1N 1G8
tel. 613/688-5335
fax 613/688-3082
http://canada.usembassy.gov

U.S. CONSULATE GENERAL VANCOUVER
1075 W. Pender St.
Vancouver, BC V6E 2M6
tel. 604/685-4311
fax 604/685-7175
http://vancouver.usconsulate.gov

U.S. CONSULATE GENERAL TORONTO
360 University Ave.
Toronto, ON M5G 1S4
tel. 416/595-1700
fax 416/595-1090
http://toronto.usconsulate.gov

U.S. CONSULATE GENERAL MONTRÉAL
1155 rue Saint-Alexandre
Montréal, QC H3B 3Z1
tel. 514/398-9695
fax 514/398-0973
http://montreal.usconsulate.gov

**U.S. CONSULATE GENERAL
QUÉBEC CITY**
2 rue de la Terrasse-Dufferin
Québec, QC G1R 4T9
tel. 418/692-2095
fax 418/692-4640
http://quebec.usconsulate.gov

**U.S. CONSULATE
GENERAL CALGARY**
615 Macleod Trail, S.E., Suite 1000
Calgary, AB T2G 4T8
tel. 403/266-8962
fax 403/264-6630
http://calgary.usconsulate.gov

Planning Your Fact-Finding Trip

TRAVEL AND TOURISM INFORMATION
CANADIAN TOURISM COMMISSION
www.canada.travel

TOURISM BRITISH COLUMBIA
www.hellobc.com

ONTARIO TOURISM
www.ontariotravel.net

TOURISME QUÉBEC
www.bonjourquebec.com

TRAVEL ALBERTA
www.travelalberta.com

ACCOMMODATIONS OPTIONS

Short-Term Rentals
VACATION RENTALS BY OWNER
www.vrbo.com

HOME AWAY
www.homeaway.com

CRAIGSLIST
www.craigslist.org

KIJIJI
www.kijiji.ca

Making the Move

IMMIGRATION AND VISAS
Citizenship and Immigration Canada (CIC) has all the information you need about entering Canada as a visitor, worker, or student, or about applying for permanent resident status. They also publish a variety of useful publications about immigration-related topics; check their website for details.

**CITIZENSHIP AND IMMIGRATION
CANADA (CIC)**
www.cic.gc.ca

Work Permits
**WORKING TEMPORARILY
IN CANADA**
www.cic.gc.ca/english/work/index.asp
General information about working in Canada and applying for a work permit.

**WORKING IN CANADA:
APPLYING FOR A WORK PERMIT**
www.cic.gc.ca/english/pdf/kits/guides/5487E.PDF
Detailed instructions about how to apply for a Canadian work permit.

Study Permits
STUDYING IN CANADA
www.cic.gc.ca/english/study/index.asp
General information about going to school or university in Canada and applying for a study permit.

STUDYING IN CANADA: APPLYING FOR A STUDY PERMIT
www.cic.gc.ca/english/pdf/kits/guides/5269E.PDF
Detailed instructions about how to apply for a Canadian study permit.

Permanent Residence Applications
IMMIGRATING TO CANADA
www.cic.gc.ca/english/immigrate/index.asp
General information about immigrating to Canada and applying for permanent residence.

CANADIAN NATIONAL OCCUPATIONAL CLASSIFICATION LIST
www.cic.gc.ca/english/work/noc.asp
Look up your occupation here to find out whether you qualify to apply for permanent resident status in the "Skilled Workers and Professionals" class.

FEDERAL BUREAU OF INVESTIGATION (F.B.I.)
www.fbi.gov/hq/cjisd/fprequest.htm
For information about arranging for security checks for permanent resident applications.

Provincial Immigration Offices
BRITISH COLUMBIA IMMIGRATION
www.ag.gov.bc.ca/immigration

ONTARIO IMMIGRATION
www.ontarioimmigration.ca

QUÉBEC IMMIGRATION
www.immigration-quebec.gouv.qc.ca

ALBERTA IMMIGRATION
www.alberta-canada.com/immigration

CUSTOMS
CANADA BORDER SERVICES AGENCY
www.cbsa.gc.ca
General information about Canadian Customs and border regulations.

REGISTRAR OF IMPORTED VEHICLES (RIV)
www.riv.ca
Provides information to determine whether your car can be brought into Canada.

WHEN YOU ARRIVE
SERVICE CANADA CENTRE
www.servicecanada.gc.ca
To apply for a Social Insurance Number (SIN).

INSURANCE BUREAU OF CANADA
www.ibc.ca
Industry trade association that provides general information about insurance in Canada.

INSURANCE CORPORATION OF BRITISH COLUMBIA (ICBC)
www.icbc.com
Responsible for auto insurance, drivers' licenses, and vehicle registration in B.C.

ONTARIO MINISTRY OF TRANSPORTATION
www.mto.gov.on.ca
For instructions about applying for a driver's license in Ontario.

FINANCIAL SERVICES COMMISSION OF ONTARIO
www.ontarioinsurance.com
The provincial agency that regulates auto insurance in Ontario.

SOCIÉTÉ DE L'ASSURANCE AUTOMOBILE DU QUÉBEC (QUÉBEC AUTOMOBILE INSURANCE SOCIETY)
www.saaq.qc.ca
Responsible for auto insurance, drivers' licenses, and vehicle registration in Québec.

SERVICE ALBERTA
www.servicealberta.gov.ab.ca
Provides information about drivers' licenses and vehicle registration in Alberta.

ALBERTA SUPERINTENDENT OF INSURANCE
www.finance.alberta.ca/business/insurance
The provincial agency that regulates auto insurance in Alberta.

Housing Considerations

CANADA'S OFFICE OF CONSUMER AFFAIRS
www.ic.gc.ca
Includes a "Rent or Buy" calculator that identifies factors to consider in deciding whether to rent or buy a home.

RENTING A HOME
The following agencies provide information about tenants' rights and responsibilities in each province.

BRITISH COLUMBIA OFFICE OF HOUSING/RESIDENTIAL TENANCY BRANCH
www.rto.gov.bc.ca

ONTARIO LANDLORD AND TENANT BOARD
www.ltb.gov.on.ca

QUÉBEC RÉGIE DU LOGEMENT
www.rdl.gouv.qc.ca

ALBERTA MINISTRY OF SERVICE
www.servicealberta.gov.ab.ca

BUYING A HOME
CANADA MORTGAGE AND HOUSING CORPORATION
www.cmhc-schl.gc.ca
Publishes "Home Buying Step By Step," a helpful guide to the home-buying process in Canada. Also reports numerous statistics about the housing market in Canadian cities.

MULTIPLE LISTING SERVICE (MLS)
www.mls.ca
Lists properties for sale in most Canadian provinces.

REALTY LINK (BRITISH COLUMBIA)
www.realtylink.org
British Columbia's local version of the MLS listings.

CANADIAN BAR ASSOCIATION
www.cba.org
Provides referrals to real estate lawyers.

Vancouver
REAL ESTATE BOARD OF GREATER VANCOUVER
2433 Spruce St.
Vancouver, BC V6H 4C8
tel. 604/730-3000
www.rebgv.org

British Columbia
TRAVEL WITH TASTE
Kathy McAree
tel. 250/385-1527
www.travelwithtaste.com
McAree plans "Relocation Vacations" and neighborhood tours for those considering a move to Greater Victoria.

VICTORIA REAL ESTATE BOARD
3035 Nanaimo St.
Victoria, BC V8T 4W2
tel. 250/385-7766
www.vreb.org

VANCOUVER ISLAND REAL ESTATE BOARD
6374 Metral Dr.
Nanaimo, BC V9T 2L8
tel. 250/390-4212
www.vireb.com

WHISTLER LISTING SERVICES
www.whistlerlistings.com

**OKANAGAN MAINLINE
REAL ESTATE BOARD**
#112 - 140 Commercial Dr.
Kelowna, BC V1X 7X6
tel. 250/491-4560
www.omreb.com
Real estate information and listings for Kelowna and the Central Okanagan.

**SOUTH OKANAGAN
REAL ESTATE BOARD**
#3 - 212 Main St.
Penticton, BC V2A 5B2
tel. 250/492-0626
www.soreb.org
Real estate information and listings for Penticton and the South Okanagan.

Toronto
TORONTO REAL ESTATE BOARD
1400 Don Mills Rd.
Toronto, ON M3B 3N1
tel. 416/443-8100
www.torontorealestateboard.com

PATRICE GALE
Sales Representative and Relocation Specialist
Royal LePage Real Estate Services Ltd., Brokerage
tel. 416/487-4311
www.settleintoronto.com
www.patricegale.com
Real estate agent who specializes in relocation to Toronto.

HEIDI NELSON
Sales Representative
Harvey Kalles Real Estate Ltd., Brokerage
tel. 416/441-2888, ext. 400
www.torontohomesandhouses.com
Real estate agent who specializes in relocation to Toronto.

Ontario
OTTAWA REAL ESTATE BOARD
1826 Woodward Dr.
Ottawa, ON K2C 0P7
tel. 613/225-2240
www.oreb.ca

**REALTORS ASSOCIATION OF
HAMILTON-BURLINGTON**
505 York Blvd.
Hamilton, ON L8R 3K4
tel. 905/529-8101
www.rahb.ca

**LONDON AND ST. THOMAS
ASSOCIATION OF REALTORS**
342 Commissioners Rd. W.
London, ON N6J 1Y3
tel. 519/641-1400
www.lstreb.com

**KITCHENER-WATERLOO REAL
ESTATE BOARD**
540 Riverbend Dr.
Kitchener, ON N2K 3S2
tel. 519/576-1400
http://boards.mls.ca/kwreb

**NIAGARA ASSOCIATION
OF REALTORS**
116 Niagara St.
St. Catharines, ON L2R 4L4
tel. 905/684-9459
www.mls-niagara.com

Québec
**GREATER MONTRÉAL
REAL ESTATE BOARD**
600 chemin du Golf
Île-des-Soeurs, QC H3E 1A8
tel. 514/762-2440
www.cigm.qc.ca

**CHAMBRE IMMOBILIÈRE
DE QUÉBEC**
990 avenue Holland
Québec, QC G1S 3T1
tel. 418/688-3362
www.ciq.qc.ca

**QUÉBEC FEDERATION OF
REAL ESTATE BOARDS**
www.fciq.ca

Alberta
CALGARY REAL ESTATE BOARD
300 Manning Rd. NE
Calgary, AB T2E 8K4
tel. 403/263-0530
www.creb.com
Provides market statistics and information about area real estate agents.

**CALGARY ECONOMIC
DEVELOPMENT DEPARTMENT**
www.calgaryeconomicdevelopment.com
Provides information about relocating to the city of Calgary.

**REALTORS ASSOCIATION OF
EDMONTON (FORMERLY THE
EDMONTON REAL ESTATE BOARD)**
14220 112 Ave.
Edmonton, AB T5M 2T8
tel. 780/451-6666 or 888/674-7479
www.ereb.com
Provides market statistics and information about Edmonton-area real estate agents.

COMMUNITY COMPASS, INC.
Daphne Bezovie and Sandra Green, Principals
tel. 780/974-1429
www.communitycompassinc.com
Edmonton relocation firm that provides a wealth of information and services for individuals, families, and corporations.

Language and Education

**CITIZENSHIP AND IMMIGRATION
CANADA: STUDYING IN CANADA**
www.cic.gc.ca/english/study/index.asp
General information about education in Canada and about Canadian study permits.

**CANADIAN ASSOCIATION OF
INDEPENDENT SCHOOLS**
www.cais.ca

**ASSOCIATION OF UNIVERSITIES
AND COLLEGES OF CANADA**
www.aucc.ca
General information about Canadian colleges and universities.

COLLEGES AND UNIVERSITIES

Vancouver
**UNIVERSITY OF BRITISH
COLUMBIA**
2329 West Mall
Vancouver, BC V6T 1Z4
tel. 604/822-2211
www.ubc.ca

SIMON FRASER UNIVERSITY
8888 University Dr.
Burnaby, BC V5A 1S6
tel. 778/782-3111
www.sfu.ca

**EMILY CARR INSTITUTE
OF ART + DESIGN**
1399 Johnston St.
Granville Island
Vancouver, BC V6H 3R9
tel. 604/844-3800
www.eciad.ca

British Columbia
UNIVERSITY OF VICTORIA
3800 Finnerty Rd.
Victoria, BC V8P 5C2
tel. 250/721-7211
www.uvic.ca

QUEST UNIVERSITY CANADA
3200 University Blvd.
Squamish, BC V8B 0N8
tel. 604/898-8000
www.questu.ca

Toronto
RYERSON UNIVERSITY
350 Victoria St.
Toronto, ON M5B 2K3
tel. 416/979-5000
www.ryerson.ca

UNIVERSITY OF TORONTO
27 King's College Circle
Toronto, ON M5S 1A1
tel. 416/978-2011
www.utoronto.ca

YORK UNIVERSITY
4700 Keele St.
Toronto, ON M3J 1P3
tel. 416/736-2100
www.yorku.ca

Ontario
CARLETON UNIVERSITY
1125 Colonel By Dr.
Ottawa, ON K1S 5B6
tel. 613/520-7400
www.carleton.ca

MCMASTER UNIVERSITY
1280 Main St. W.
Hamilton, ON L8S 4L8
tel. 905/525-9140
www.mcmaster.ca

QUEEN'S UNIVERSITY
99 University Ave.
Kingston, ON K7L 3N6
tel. 613/533-2000
www.queensu.ca

WILFRID LAURIER UNIVERSITY
75 University Ave. W.
Waterloo, ON N2L 3C5
tel. 519/884-1970
www.wlu.ca

UNIVERSITY OF GUELPH
50 Stone Rd. E.
Guelph, ON N1G 2W1
tel. 519/824-4120
www.uoguelph.ca

UNIVERSITY OF OTTAWA
75 Laurier Ave. E.
Ottawa, ON K1N 6N5
tel. 613/562-5700
www.uottawa.ca

UNIVERSITY OF WATERLOO
200 University Ave. W.
Waterloo, ON N2L 3G1
tel. 519/888-4567
www.uwaterloo.ca

UNIVERSITY OF WESTERN ONTARIO
1151 Richmond St.
London, ON N6A 5B8
tel. 519/661-2111
www.uwo.ca

UNIVERSITY OF WINDSOR
401 Sunset Ave.
Windsor, ON N9B 3P4
tel. 519/253-3000
www.uwindsor.ca

Québec
CONCORDIA UNIVERSITY
1455 De Maisonneuve Blvd. W.
Montréal, QC H3G 1M8
tel. 514/848-2424
www.concordia.ca

MCGILL UNIVERSITY
845 Sherbrooke St. W.
Montréal, QC H3A 2T5
tel. 514/398-4455
www.mcgill.ca

UNIVERSITÉ DE MONTRÉAL
PO Box 6128, Station Centre-ville
Montréal, QC H3C 3J7
tel. 514/343-6111
www.umontreal.ca

UNIVERSITÉ DU QUÉBEC À MONTRÉAL (UQAM)
405 Sainte-Catherine St. E.
Montréal, QC H2L 2C4
tel. 514/987-3000
www.uqam.ca

Alberta
UNIVERSITY OF ALBERTA
Administration Building
Edmonton, AB T6G 2M7
tel. 780/492-3111
www.ualberta.ca

UNIVERSITY OF CALGARY
2500 University Dr. NW
Calgary, AB T2N 1N4
tel. 403/220-5110
www.ucalgary.ca

Health

PROVINCIAL HEALTH AGENCIES AND LOCAL RESOURCES

British Columbia
HEALTH INSURANCE BC
Medical Services Plan
PO Box 9035 Stn Prov Govt
Victoria, BC V8W 9E3
tel. 800/663-7100 or 604/683-7151 (in Vancouver)
www.health.gov.bc.ca/insurance

COLLEGE OF PHYSICIANS AND SURGEONS OF BRITISH COLUMBIA
www.cpsbc.ca/cps/physician_directory/search
Physician search function helps find B.C. doctors who are accepting new patients.

Ontario
ONTARIO HEALTH INSURANCE PLAN
Client Services Unit
Ministry of Health and Long-Term Care
Suite M1-57, Macdonald Block
900 Bay St.
Toronto ON M7A 1R3
tel. 866/532-3161
www.health.gov.on.ca

COLLEGE OF PHYSICIANS AND SURGEONS OF ONTARIO
www.cpso.on.ca
"Doctor Search" function helps locate Ontario-based physicians.

Québec
RÉGIE DE L'ASSURANCE MALADIE DU QUÉBEC (MONTRÉAL OFFICE)
425 boulevard De Maisonneuve Ouest
3rd Fl, Bureau 300
Montréal, QC H3A 3G5
tel. 514/864-3411
www.ramq.gouv.qc.ca
Québec's health insurance agency.

RÉGIE DE L'ASSURANCE MALADIE DU QUÉBEC (QUÉBEC CITY OFFICE)
1125 Grande Allée Ouest
Québec, QC G1S 1E7
tel. 418/646-4636

Alberta
ALBERTA HEALTH CARE INSURANCE PLAN (AHCIP)
PO Box 1360, Station Main
Edmonton, AB T5J 2N3
tel. 780/427-1432
www.health.gov.ab.ca

COLLEGE OF PHYSICIANS AND SURGEONS OF ALBERTA
www.cpsa.ab.ca
To find doctors in Alberta who are accepting new patients.

SUPPLEMENTAL MEDICAL INSURANCE
CANADIAN LIFE AND HEALTH INSURANCE ASSOCIATION
tel. 800/268-8099 or 416/777-2221
www.clhia.ca
Provides information about companies that offer temporary medical insurance.

Private Health Insurance Companies
The following is a partial list of companies that provide temporary insurance when you arrive in Canada, travel insurance, or supplemental coverage beyond standard provincial insurance.

CANADIAN AUTOMOBILE ASSOCIATION
www.caa.ca

ETFS
www.etfsinc.com

HEALTHQUOTES.CA
www.healthquotes.ca

MANULIFE FINANCIAL
www.manulife.ca

ONTARIO BLUE CROSS
www.useblue.com

DISABLED ACCESS
**PERSONS WITH
DISABILITIES ONLINE**
www.pwd-online.ca
Canadian government umbrella website offering resources for people with disabilities.

ACCESS TO TRAVEL
www.accesstotravel.gc.ca
Information about accessible travel to and around Canada.

CANADIAN ABILITIES FOUNDATION
www.abilities.ca
Publishes *Abilities* magazine.

ACCESS GUIDE CANADA
www.enablelink.org/agc
Guide to accessible places in Canada.

KÉROUL
www.keroul.qc.ca
Québec-based organization whose mission is to make tourism and culture accessible to people with limited physical ability.

Employment

RESOURCES FOR STARTING A BUSINESS

Nationwide
CANADA'S INVESTMENT, SCIENCE, & TECHNOLOGY BRANCH
www.investincanada.gc.ca

CANADA BUSINESS
www.canadabusiness.ca
Government resources for entrepreneurs.

INDUSTRY CANADA
www.ic.gc.ca

LOCATION CANADA
www.locationcanada.com

BUSINESS DEVELOPMENT BANK OF CANADA
www.bdc.ca

British Columbia
BRITISH COLUMBIA MINISTRY OF ECONOMIC DEVELOPMENT
www.gov.bc.ca/ecdev

INVEST BRITISH COLUMBIA
www.investbc.com

B.C. ONE STOP BUSINESS REGISTRY
www.bcbusinessregistry.ca

VANCOUVER ECONOMIC DEVELOPMENT COMMISSION
www.vancouvereconomic.com

GREATER VICTORIA ECONOMIC DEVELOPMENT COMMISSION
www.businessvictoria.net

INVEST KELOWNA/OKANAGAN ECONOMIC DEVELOPMENT COMMISSION
www.edccord.com

Ontario
ONTARIO MINISTRY OF ECONOMIC DEVELOPMENT AND TRADE
www.2ontario.com

TORONTO ECONOMIC DEVELOPMENT CORPORATION
www.tedco.ca

OCRI GLOBAL MARKETING
www.ottawaregion.com
Economic development organization promoting business and entrepreneurship in the Ottawa region.

HAMILTON ECONOMIC DEVELOPMENT
www.investinhamilton.ca

LONDON ECONOMIC DEVELOPMENT CORPORATION
www.ledc.com

CANADA'S TECHNOLOGY TRIANGLE
www.techtriangle.com
Economic development organization promoting business and entrepreneurship in the Kitchener-Waterloo region.

Québec
GOVERNMENT OF QUÉBEC
www.gouv.qc.ca
Click on "Services Québec - Business," then "Invest in Québec."

INVESTISSEMENT QUÉBEC
www.investquebec.com

QUÉBEC MINISTRY OF ECONOMIC DEVELOPMENT, INNOVATION AND EXPORT TRADE
www.mdeie.gouv.qc.ca

MONTRÉAL INTERNATIONAL
www.montrealinternational.com

Alberta
ALBERTA MINISTRY OF EMPLOYMENT, IMMIGRATION, AND INDUSTRY
www.employment.alberta.ca
Publishes a monthly Labour Market News report outlining trends and opportunities in various Alberta cities.

CALGARY ECONOMIC DEVELOPMENT
www.calgaryeconomicdevelopment.com

EDMONTON ECONOMIC DEVELOPMENT CORPORATION
www.edmonton.com/eedc

RESOURCES FOR JOB HUNTING
CANADIAN LABOR MARKET INFORMATION
www.labourmarketinformation.ca

National Job Sites
JOB BANK
www.jobbank.gc.ca

WORKING IN CANADA
www.workingincanada.gc.ca

WORKOPOLIS
www.workopolis.com

CAREERBUILDER CANADA
www.careerbuilder.ca

ALLSTARJOBS CANADA
www.allstarjobs.ca

BRAINHUNTER
www.brainhunter.com

ELUTA CANADA
www.eluta.ca

JOBBOOM
www.jobboom.com

CAREERCLICK
www.careerclick.com
Links to newspaper classified ads nationwide.

MONSTER
www.monster.ca

HOTJOBS
www.hotjobs.ca

WORKRIGHTS.CA
www.workrights.ca
Links to a variety of industry-specific job posting sites.

Volunteering
VOLUNTEER CANADA
www.volunteer.ca

VOLUNTEER VANCOUVER
www.govolunteer.ca
Volunteer opportunities in Vancouver and British Columbia.

TORONTO VOLUNTEER BRIDGE
www.volunteerbridge.ca
Encourages young professionals in Toronto to volunteer.

VOLUNTEER TORONTO
www.volunteertoronto.on.ca
Toronto-area volunteer opportunities.

SECRÉTARIAT À L'ACTION COMMUNAUTAIRE AUTONOME ET AUX INITIATIVES SOCIALES
www.benevolat.gouv.qc.ca
Information about volunteering in Québec.

VOLUNTEER ALBERTA
www.volunteeralberta.ab.ca
Links to volunteer opportunities in Alberta communities.

Finance

CANADA REVENUE AGENCY
www.cra-arc.gc.ca
Canada's tax agency publishes an online tax guide for newcomers to Canada.

INTERNATIONAL TAX SERVICES OFFICE
Canada Revenue Agency
2204 Walkley Rd.
Ottawa ON K1A 1A8
tel. 800/267-5177

This Canada Revenue Agency office deals with international tax issues and questions.

STEPHEN KATZ LTD.
#224 - 2211 West 4th Ave.
Vancouver, BC V6K 4S2
tel. 604/732-1515
www.stephenkatzltd.com
Specializes in U.S. and Canadian tax preparation.

Communications

PHONE COMPANIES
BELL CANADA
www.bell.ca

FIDO WIRELESS
www.fido.ca

ROGERS COMMUNICATIONS
www.rogers.com

SHAW COMMUNICATIONS
www.shaw.ca

7-ELEVEN SPEAKOUT WIRELESS
www.7-eleven.com

TELUS
www.telus.com

VIRGIN MOBILE
www.virginmobile.ca

POSTAL SERVICE
CANADA POST
www.canadapost.ca

MEDIA
CANADIAN NEWSPAPER ASSOCIATION
www.cna-acj.ca
Links to major newspapers across Canada.

CANADIAN MAGAZINE PUBLISHERS ASSOCIATION
www.cmpa.ca
Links to magazines published in Canada.

CANADIAN BROADCASTING CORPORATION
www.cbc.ca

Travel and Transportation

AIRLINES

AIR CANADA
tel. 888/247-2262 or 514/393-3333
www.aircanada.ca

WESTJET
tel. 888/937-8538 or 403/444-2586
www.westjet.com

ZOOM AIRLINES
tel. 866/359-9666 or 613/235-9666
www.flyzoom.com

AIR TRANSAT
tel. 877/872-6728 or 514/636-3630
www.airtransat.ca

PORTER AIRLINES
tel. 888/619-8622 or 416/619-8622
www.flyporter.com

CANADIAN ONLINE TRAVEL BOOKING SITES

TRAVELOCITY
www.travelocity.ca

EXPEDIA
www.expedia.ca

FLIGHT CENTRE
www.flightcentre.ca

FLIGHT NETWORK
www.flightnetwork.com

SECURITY AND CUSTOMS REGULATIONS

CANADA BORDER SERVICES AGENCY
www.cbsa.gc.ca

TRAIN TRAVEL

VIA RAIL
tel. 888/842-7245 or 514/989-2626
www.viarail.ca

BUS TRAVEL

GREYHOUND CANADA (NATIONWIDE)
tel. 800/661-8747
www.greyhound.ca

Ontario

COACH CANADA
tel. 800/461-7661 or 705/748-6411
www.coachcanada.com

ONTARIO NORTHLAND
tel. 800/363-7512 or 705/472-4500
www.ontarionorthland.ca

Québec

ORLÉANS EXPRESS
tel. 888/999-3977 or 514/395-4000
www.orleansexpress.com

AUTOBUS GALLAND
tel. 450/687-8666
www.galland-bus.com

LIMOCAR
tel. 514/842-2281
www.limocar.ca

PUBLIC TRANSPORTATION

British Columbia

VANCOUVER TRANSIT AUTHORITY
tel. 604/953-3333
www.translink.bc.ca

BC TRANSIT
tel. 250/385-2551
www.bctransit.com
Details about public transportation in Victoria, Nanaimo, Whistler, Squamish, Kelowna, and other British Columbia communities.

VICTORIA REGIONAL TRANSIT SYSTEM
tel. 250/382-6161
www.bctransit.com

NANAIMO REGIONAL TRANSIT SYSTEM
tel. 250/390-4531
www.bctransit.com

WHISTLER TRANSIT
tel. 604/932-4020
www.bctransit.com

SQUAMISH TRANSIT
tel. 604/892-5559
www.bctransit.com

KELOWNA REGIONAL TRANSIT SYSTEM
tel. 250/860-8121
www.bctransit.com

SALT SPRING TRANSIT
tel. 250/ 537-6758
www.busonline.ca

Ontario
TORONTO TRANSIT COMMISSION
tel. 416-393-4636
www.toronto.ca/ttc

GREATER TORONTO TRANSIT AUTHORITY
tel. 888/438-6646 or 416/869-3200
www.gotransit.com

OC TRANSPO (OTTAWA)
tel. 613/741-4390
www.octranspo.com

HAMILTON STREET RAILWAY COMPANY
tel. 905/527-4441
www.myhamilton.ca/myhamilton/CityandGovernment/CityServices/Transit

LONDON TRANSIT COMPANY
tel. 519/451-1347
www.londontransit.ca

GRAND RIVER TRANSIT (KITCHENER-WATERLOO)
tel. 519/585-7555
www.grt.ca

NIAGARA TRANSIT
tel. 905/356-1179
www.niagarafalls.ca/services/transit

ST. CATHARINES TRANSIT COMMISSION
tel. 905/687-5555
www.yourbus.com

Québec
SOCIÉTÉ DE TRANSPORT DE MONTRÉAL
tel. 514/786-4636
www.stm.info

AGENCE MÉTROPOLITAINE DE TRANSPORT
tel. 514/287-8726
www.amt.qc.ca
Operates commuter train services in Greater Montréal.

RÉSEAU DE TRANSPORT DE LA CAPITALE (QUÉBEC CITY)
tel. 418/627-2511
www.rtcquebec.ca

Alberta
CALGARY TRANSIT
tel. 403/262-1000
www.calgarytransit.com

EDMONTON TRANSIT AUTHORITY
tel. 780/496-1600
www.takeets.com

CAR TRAVEL
CANADIAN AUTOMOBILE ASSOCIATION
www.caa.ca

Car-Sharing Networks
CAR-SHARING IN CANADA
www.carsharing.net
General information about car-sharing in Canada.

CO-OPERATIVE AUTO NETWORK, VANCOUVER
tel. 604/685-1393
www.cooperativeauto.net

AUTOSHARE, TORONTO
tel. 416/340-7888
www.autoshare.com

ZIPCAR
tel. 416/977-9008 (Toronto)
tel. 604/697-0550 (Vancouver)
www.zipcar.com

VRTUCAR, OTTAWA
tel. 613/798-1900
www.vrtucar.com

COMMUNAUTO
tel. 514/842-4545 (Montréal)
tel. 418/523-1788 (Québec City)
tel. 819/595-5181 (Gatineau)
www.communauto.com

CALGARY ALTERNATIVE TRANSPORTATION CO-OPERATIVE
tel. 403/264-2422
www.catco-op.org

Prime Living Locations

VANCOUVER

General
CITY OF VANCOUVER
www.vancouver.ca

THE NEWCOMER'S GUIDE TO THE CITY OF VANCOUVER
www.vancouver.ca/commsvcs/socialplanning/newtovancouver
A city publication packed with details about everything from Vancouver neighborhoods to child care to garbage collection.

INFORMATION SERVICES VANCOUVER
tel. 604/875-6381
www.vcn.bc.ca/isv/infrm.htm
Operates a 24/7 information line about Vancouver-area social and community services.

TOURISM VANCOUVER
www.tourismvancouver.com

Media
VANCOUVER SUN
www.vancouversun.com

VANCOUVER PROVINCE
www.vancouverprovince.com

GEORGIA STRAIGHT
www.straight.com

VANCOUVER COURIER
www.canada.com/vancouvercourier

WEST ENDER
www.westender.com

VANCOUVER MAGAZINE
www.vancouvermagazine.com

Schools
VANCOUVER SCHOOL BOARD
tel. 604/713-5000
www.vsb.bc.ca

B.C. FEDERATION OF INDEPENDENT SCHOOL ASSOCIATIONS
tel. 604/684-6023
www.fisabc.ca
Provides a directory of independent schools in Vancouver and elsewhere in B.C.

BRITISH COLUMBIA

General
BRITISH COLUMBIA NEWCOMERS' GUIDE
www.ag.gov.bc.ca/immigration/sam/newcomers_guide.htm

OPPORTUNITIES AT THE UNIVERSITY OF VICTORIA
www.opportunities.uvic.ca
Although designed for prospective new faculty, this guide is useful for anyone considering relocation to the Victoria area.

TOURISM VICTORIA
www.tourismvictoria.com

TOURISM VANCOUVER ISLAND
www.vancouverisland.travel

SQUAMISH ADVENTURE CENTRE
38551 Loggers Ln.
Squamish, BC V8B 0H2
604/815-4994 or 866/333-2010
www.adventurecentre.ca
Houses the town's visitor center, tourism offices, and business development department.

TOURISM WHISTLER
www.tourismwhistler.com

WHISTLER CHAMBER OF COMMERCE
www.whistlerchamber.com

WHISTLER EMPLOYMENT RESOURCE CENTRE
#201 - 4230 Gateway Dr.
Whistler, BC V0N 1B4
tel. 604/932-5922, ext. 23
www.whistlerchamber.com

THOMPSON OKANAGAN TOURISM ASSOCIATION
www.totabc.com

CITY OF KELOWNA
www.kelowna.ca

CITY OF PENTICTON
www.penticton.ca

BRITISH COLUMBIA WINE INSTITUTE
www.winebc.com
Information about the wine industry in the Okanagan and elsewhere in B.C.

Media
VICTORIA TIMES-COLONIST
www.canada.com/victoriatimescolonist

MONDAY MAGAZINE
www.mondaymag.com

SQUAMISH TODAY
www.canwestglobal.com

PIQUE NEWSMAGAZINE (WHISTLER)
www.piquenewsmagazine.com

WHISTLER QUESTION
www.whistlerquestion.com

KELOWNA DAILY COURIER
www.kelownadailycourier.ca

Schools
GREATER VICTORIA SCHOOL DISTRICT #61
tel. 250/475-3212
www.sd61.bc.ca

SOUTHERN GULF ISLANDS SCHOOL DISTRICT #64
tel. 250/537-5548
www.sd64.bc.ca

NANAIMO SCHOOL DISTRICT #68
tel. 250/754-5521
www.sd68.bc.ca

COMOX VALLEY SCHOOL DISTRICT #71
tel. 250/334-5500
www.sd71.bc.ca

CAMPBELL RIVER SCHOOL DISTRICT #72
tel. 250/830-2300
www.sd72.bc.ca

TOFINO AND UCLUELET SCHOOL DISTRICT #70
tel. 250/723-3565
www.sd70.bc.ca

HOWE SOUND SCHOOL DISTRICT #48 (SQUAMISH/WHISTLER)
tel. 604/892-5228
www.sd48.bc.ca

CENTRAL OKANAGAN SCHOOL DISTRICT #23 (KELOWNA AREA)
tel. 250/860-8888
www.sd23.bc.ca

PENTICTON/NARAMATA SCHOOL DISTRICT #67
tel. 250/770-7700
www.sd67.bc.ca

OKANAGAN SIMILKAMEEN SCHOOL DISTRICT (OLIVER, OSOYOOS)
tel. 250/498-3481
www.sd53.bc.ca

Transportation (Vancouver Island and the Gulf Islands)
B.C. FERRIES
tel. 888/223-3779
www.bcferries.bc.ca

CLIPPER FERRY (SEATTLE, WA TO VICTORIA)
tel. 800/888-2535 or 206/448-5000 (Seattle)
tel. 250/382-8100 (Victoria)
www.clippervacations.com/ferry

COHO FERRY (PORT ANGELES, WA TO VICTORIA)
tel. 360/457-4491 (Port Angeles)
tel. 250/386-2202 (Victoria)
www.cohoferry.com

VICTORIA EXPRESS FERRY (PORT ANGELES, WA TO VICTORIA)
tel. 360/452-8088 (Port Angeles)
tel. 250/361-9144 (Victoria)
www.victoriaexpress.com

HARBOUR AIR
tel. 800/665-0212 or 604/274-1277
www.harbour-air.com

KENMORE AIR
tel. 866/435-9524 or 425/486-1257
www.kenmoreair.com

WEST COAST AIR
tel. 800/347-2222 or 604/606-6888
www.westcoastair.com

TORONTO

General
CITY OF TORONTO
www.toronto.ca
The immigration section of the city's website has a wealth of information for newcomers.

TORONTO REAL ESTATE BOARD
www.torontorealestateboard.com
Provides a useful map with profiles of many Toronto neighborhoods.

TORONTO CONVENTION & VISITORS ASSOCIATION
www.torontotourism.com

UNIVERSITY OF TORONTO FACULTY RELOCATION SERVICE
www.facultyrelocation.utoronto.ca
Although designed for prospective new faculty, this website includes resources helpful for anyone considering relocation to Toronto.

TORONTO AMBASSADOR PROGRAM
www.toronto.ca/tapto
Free walking tours of Toronto neighborhoods led by enthusiastic volunteer "greeters."

TORONTO INFORMATION SERVICE
www.211toronto.ca
Information about community, social,

health, and government services. Also available by phone; dial 211.

ENTERPRISE TORONTO
www.enterprisetoronto.com
Networking events and other resources for entrepreneurs and small-business owners.

Media
GLOBE AND MAIL
www.theglobeandmail.com

NATIONAL POST
www.nationalpost.com

TORONTO STAR
www.thestar.com

TORONTO SUN
www.torontosun.com

NOW
www.nowtoronto.com

EYE WEEKLY
www.eyeweekly.com

TORONTO LIFE
www.torontolife.com

Schools
TORONTO DISTRICT SCHOOL BOARD
tel. 416/397-3000
www.tdsb.on.ca

TORONTO CATHOLIC DISTRICT SCHOOL BOARD
tel. 416/222-8282
www.tcdsb.org

ONTARIO MINISTRY OF EDUCATION
tel. 416/325-2929
www.edu.gov.on.ca/eng/general/elemsec/privsch/index.html
Lists private schools in Toronto and elsewhere in Ontario.

ONTARIO

General
ONTARIO TOURISM
www.ontariotravel.net

SETTLEMENT.ORG
www.settlement.org
Resources for newcomers to Toronto and other Ontario communities.

LIVE IN OTTAWA
www.ottawa.com
The City of Ottawa produces this guide to living and working in the capital region.

OTTAWA TOURISM
www.ottawatourism.ca

CITY OF HAMILTON
www.myhamilton.ca

CITY OF LONDON
www.london.ca

CITY OF KITCHENER
www.kitchener.ca

CITY OF WATERLOO
www.city.waterloo.on.ca

THE REGIONAL MUNICIPALITY OF NIAGARA
www.regional.niagara.on.ca

TOURISM NIAGARA
www.tourismniagara.com

WINE COUNCIL OF ONTARIO
www.winesofontario.org
Information about the wine industry in the Niagara region and elsewhere in Ontario.

Media
OTTAWA CITIZEN
www.ottawacitizen.com

OTTAWA SUN
www.ottawasun.com

OTTAWA XPRESS
www.ottawaxpress.ca

OTTAWA MAGAZINE
www.ottawamagazine.com

HAMILTON SPECTATOR
www.thespec.com

LONDON FREE PRESS
www.lfpress.ca

THE RECORD
(KITCHENER-WATERLOO)
www.therecord.com

NIAGARA FALLS REVIEW
www.niagarafallsreview.ca

ST. CATHARINES STANDARD
www.stcatharinesstandard.ca

Schools
**ONTARIO MINISTRY OF EDUCATION
SCHOOL AND SCHOOL BOARD
FINDER**
www.edu.gov.on.ca/eng/sbinfo

**OTTAWA-CARLETON DISTRICT
SCHOOL BOARD**
tel. 613/721-1820
www.ocdsb.edu.on.ca

**OTTAWA-CARLETON CATHOLIC
SCHOOL BOARD**
tel. 613/224-2222
www.occdsb.on.ca

**WESTERN QUÉBEC SCHOOL BOARD
(GATINEAU AREA)**
tel. 819/684-2336
www.wqsb.qc.ca

**HAMILTON-WENTWORTH DISTRICT
SCHOOL BOARD**
tel. 905/527-5092
www.hwdsb.on.ca

**HAMILTON-WENTWORTH CATHOLIC
DISTRICT SCHOOL BOARD**
tel. 905/525-2930
www.hwcdsb.edu.on.ca

**WATERLOO REGION DISTRICT
SCHOOL BOARD (KITCHENER-
WATERLOO)**
tel. 519/570-0003
www.wrdsb.on.ca

**WATERLOO CATHOLIC DISTRICT
SCHOOL BOARD (KITCHENER-
WATERLOO)**
tel. 519/578-3660
www.wcdsb.edu.on.ca

**THAMES VALLEY DISTRICT
SCHOOL BOARD (LONDON)**
tel. 519/452-2000
www.tvdsb.on.ca

**LONDON DISTRICT
CATHOLIC SCHOOL BOARD**
tel. 519/663-2088
www.ldcsb.on.ca

**DISTRICT SCHOOL
BOARD OF NIAGARA**
tel. 905/641-1550
www.dsbn.edu.on.ca

**NIAGARA CATHOLIC
DISTRICT SCHOOL BOARD**
tel. 905/735-0240
www.niagararc.com

QUÉBEC
General
LEARNING ABOUT QUÉBEC
www.immigration-quebec.gouv.qc.ca
A guide for newcomers to Québec published by Québec Immigration.

SERVICES QUÉBEC
www.gouv.qc.ca
Québec government portal with links to a variety of resources.

CITY OF MONTRÉAL
www.ville.montreal.qc.ca
On this website, look for "Accèss Montréal" for all kinds of useful details about living and working in the city.

TOURISM MONTRÉAL
www.tourisme-montreal.org

CITY OF QUÉBEC
www.ville.quebec.qc.ca

QUÉBEC CITY TOURISM
www.quebecregion.com

VILLE DE MONT-TREMBLANT
www.villedemont-tremblant.qc.ca

SKI MONT-TREMBLANT
www.tremblant.ca

TOURISM MONT-TREMBLANT
www.tourismemonttremblant.com

TOURISME LAURENTIDES
www.laurentians.com

TOWNSHIPPERS' ASSOCIATION
www.townshippers.qc.ca
Provides links to a wide range of English-language information and services across the Eastern Townships.

JOB LINKS
www.etsb.qc.ca/joblinks
Resources for English speakers looking for work in the Eastern Townships.

EASTERN TOWNSHIPS TOURISM ASSOCIATION
www.cantonsdelest.com

TOURISM MEMPHRÉMAGOG
www.tourisme-memphremagog.com

Media
MONTRÉAL GAZETTE
www.montrealgazette.com

MONTRÉAL MIRROR
www.montrealmirror.com

HOUR (MONTRÉAL)
www.hour.ca

CHRONICLE-TELEGRAPH (QUÉBEC CITY)
www.qctonline.com

TREMBLANT EXPRESS
www.tremblantexpress.com

SHERBROOKE RECORD
www.sherbrookerecord.com

Schools
QUÉBEC MINISTRY OF EDUCATION, LEISURE, AND SPORTS
tel. 866/747-6626 or 418/643-7095
www.meq.gouv.qc.ca
Provides information about Québec's educational system and details about who qualifies for English-language instruction.

FÉDÉRATION DES CÉGEPS
tel. 514/381-8631
www.fedecegeps.qc.ca
Information about Québec's CÉGEP post-secondary programs.

ENGLISH MONTRÉAL SCHOOL BOARD
tel. 514/483-7200
www.emsb.qc.ca
Administers English-language schools in central Montréal.

LESTER B. PEARSON SCHOOL BOARD
tel. 514/422-3000
www.lbpsb.qc.ca
Administers English-language schools in Montréal's western suburbs.

CENTRAL QUÉBEC SCHOOL BOARD
tel. 418/688-8730
www.cqsb.qc.ca
Administers English-language schools in Québec City.

SIR WILFRID LAURIER SCHOOL BOARD
tel. 450/621-5600
www.swlauriersb.qc.ca
Manages English-language schools in the Laurentians region.

EASTERN TOWNSHIPS SCHOOL BOARD
tel. 819/868-3100
www.etsb.qc.ca
Manages English-language schools in the Eastern Townships.

QUÉBEC ASSOCIATION OF INDEPENDENT SCHOOLS
tel. 514/483-6111
www.qais.qc.ca
Lists private schools throughout Québec.

ALBERTA

General
CITY OF CALGARY
www.calgary.ca
Publishes demographic profiles of the city's neighborhoods.

CALGARY ECONOMIC DEVELOPMENT
www.calgaryeconomicdevelopment.com
Includes resources for relocating to Calgary.

CALGARY INFORMATION SERVICE
www.211calgary.ca
Information about community, social, health, and government services. Also available by phone; dial 211.

MOVE TO EDMONTON
www.movetoedmonton.com
A newcomers' guide published by the Edmonton Economic Development Corporation.

EDMONTON INFORMATION SERVICE
www.211edmonton.info
Information about community, social, health, and government services. Also available by phone; dial 211.

TOWN OF BANFF
www.banff.ca

BANFF JOB RESOURCE CENTRE
www.jobresourcecentre.com

BANFFLIFE JOB BOARD
www.banff.ca (choose "Working")

CANMORE JOB RESOURCE CENTRE
www.jobresourcecentre.com

TOWN OF JASPER
www.jasper-alberta.com

JASPER EMPLOYMENT CENTRE
www.ability.ab.ca

Media
CALGARY HERALD
www.calgaryherald.com

CALGARY SUN
www.calgarysun.com

FFWD (FAST FORWARD WEEKLY)
www.ffwdweekly.com

AVENUE MAGAZINE
www.avenuemagazine.ca

EDMONTON JOURNAL
www.edmontonjournal.com

EDMONTON SUN
www.edmontonsun.com

VUE WEEKLY (EDMONTON)
www.vueweekly.com

SEE MAGAZINE (EDMONTON)
www.seemagazine.com

BANFF CRAG & CANYON
www.banffcragandcanyon.com

CANMORE LEADER
www.canmoreleader.com

ROCKY MOUNTAIN OUTLOOK (BANFF, CANMORE)
www.rockymountainoutlook.ca

FITZHUGH (JASPER)
www.fitzhugh.ca

JASPER BOOSTER
www.jasperbooster.com

Schools
CALGARY BOARD OF EDUCATION
tel. 403/294-8211
www.cbe.ab.ca

CALGARY ROMAN CATHOLIC SEPARATE SCHOOL DISTRICT
tel. 403/298-1411
www.cssd.ab.ca

EDMONTON PUBLIC SCHOOLS
tel. 780/429-8000
www.epsb.ca

EDMONTON CATHOLIC SCHOOLS
tel. 780/441-6000
www.ecsd.net

ASSOCIATION OF INDEPENDENT SCHOOLS AND COLLEGES IN ALBERTA
tel. 780/469-9868
www.aisca.ab.ca
Lists private schools throughout Alberta.

French Phrasebook

If you learned to speak French in Paris, or from a France-born instructor, you'll be able to make yourself understood in Québec. Québec denizens have a somewhat different accent and some uniquely Québecois pronunciations, but the basic language is the same.

USEFUL WORDS AND PHRASES

In Québec, people are fairly formal in their speech, at least when you first meet. When you enter a store or other business, greet the shopkeeper or clerk with *"Bonjour, Monsieur"* or *"Bonjour, Madame."* And when you're ready to go, say *"Bonne journée!" (Have a good day!)*.

Hello. *Bonjour.*
Hi. *Salut.*
How are you? *Comment ça va?*
Fine. *Ça va.*
I'm fine, thanks. *Ça va bien, merci.*
not bad *pas mal*
please *s'il vous plaît*
Thank you. *Merci.*
Thank you very much. *Merci beaucoup.*
You're welcome. *De rien.*
yes *oui*
no *non*
OK *d'accord*
I don't know. *Je ne sais pas.*
I don't understand. *Je ne comprends pas.*
Excuse me. *Excusez-moi.*
Pardon me. *Pardon.*
What? *Comment?*
I'm sorry. *Désolé(e)/Je suis désolé(e).*
See you later! *À bientôt!*
Goodbye. *Au revoir.*

TERMS OF ADDRESS

I *je*
you *tu* (familiar)
you *vous* (formal and plural)
he *il*
she *elle*
we/us *nous*
they *ils* (masculine)/*elles* (feminine)
Mr./Sir *Monsieur*
Mrs./Madam *Madame*
Miss *Mademoiselle*

NUMBERS

0 *zéro*
1 *un* (masculine)/*une* (feminine)
2 *deux*
3 *trois*
4 *quatre*
5 *cinq*
6 *six*
7 *sept*
8 *huit*
9 *neuf*
10 *dix*
11 *onze*
12 *douze*
13 *treize*
14 *quatorze*
15 *quinze*
16 *seize*
17 *dix-sept*
18 *dix-huit*
19 *dix-neuf*
20 *vingt*
21 *vingt-et-un*
22 *vingt-deux*
30 *trente*
40 *quarante*
50 *cinquante*
60 *soixante*
70 *soixante-dix*
80 *quatre-vingts*
90 *quatre-vingt-dix*
100 *cent*
200 *deux cents*
1,000 *mille*
1 million *un million*

DAYS OF THE WEEK

Monday *lundi*
Tuesday *mardi*
Wednesday *mercredi*
Thursday *jeudi*

Friday *vendredi*
Saturday *samedi*
Sunday *dimanche*

TIME

What time is it? *Quelle heure est-il?*
It's one o'clock. *Il est une heure.*
It's 2:15. *Il est deux heures et quart./ deux heures quinze.*
It's 2:30. *Il est deux heures et demie./ deux heures trente.*
It's 2:45. *Il est deux heures moins le quart./deux heures quarante-cinq.*
It's 6 A.M. *Il est six heures du matin.*
It's 6 P.M. *Il est six heures du soir.*
noon *midi*
midnight *minuit*
today *aujourd'hui*
tomorrow *demain*
tomorrow morning *demain matin*
yesterday *hier*
last night *hier soir*
the next day *le prochaine jour*

GETTING AROUND

Where is...? *Où est.?/Où se trouve...?*
from...to... *de...à/au...*
street *la rue*
highway *l'autoroute*
kilometer *kilomètre*
to the right *à droite*
to the left *à gauche*
straight ahead *tout droit*
exit *sortie*
north *nord*
south *sud*
east *est*
west *ouest*

ACCOMMODATIONS

I would like a room... *Je voudrais une chambre...*
for one night/two nights *pour une nuit/deux nuits*
for one person/two people *pour une personne/deux personnes*
What is the rate? *Quel est le prix?*
1st floor (ground floor) *le rez-de-chaussée*

2nd floor (1st floor in Québec) *le premier étage*
key *le clef*
bathroom *la toilette/la salle de bain/W.C.*
shower *la douche*
towel *la serviette*
soap *le savon*
toilet paper *le papier de toilette*
air conditioning *air climatisé*
blanket *une couverture*
No vacancy *Complet*

FOOD

I would like... *Je voudrais...*
breakfast *petit déjeuner*
lunch *déjeuner*
dinner *dîner, souper*
menu *la carte*
fork *une forchette*
knife *un couteau*
spoon *une cuillière*
glass *une verre*
napkin *une serviette*
coffee *le café*
tea *le thé*
milk *le lait*
cream *la crème*
sugar *le sucre*
a coffee with milk *un café au lait*
water *l'eau*
mineral water *l'eau minerale*
wine *le vin*
beer *la bière*
juice *le jus*
bread *le pain*
butter *la beurre*
jam *la confiture*
eggs *les oeufs*
pancakes *les crêpes*
"French toast" *le pain doré*
vegetarian *végétarien*
meat *la viande*
steak *le biftek*
steak with fries *steak frites*
chicken *le poulet*
fish *le poisson*
salad *la salade*
fries *les frites*
fries with gravy and cheese *la poutine*

meat pie *la tourtière*
baked beans *les fèves au lard*
maple syrup *le syrop d'érable*
the check, the bill *l'addition*
tip *le pourboire*

SHOPPING
I need... *J'ai besoin du/de/de la...*
I would like... *Je voudrais...*
Do you have...? *Avez-vous...?*
How much does...cost? *Combien côute...?*
How much is it? *Ça fait combien?*
Sale! *Soldes!*
store *le magasin*
convenience store *le dépanneur*
bakery *la boulangerie*
bookstore *la librairie*
library *la bibliothèque*
money *l'argent*
credit card *la carte de crédit*
cashier, checkout *la caisse*

TRANSPORTATION
airport *l'aéroport*
subway *le métro*
bus *l'autobus*
train *le train*
train station *la gare*

ticket *le billet*
round-trip ticket *un billet aller-retour*
one-way ticket *un billet simple*
parking *stationnement*
prohibited *interdit/défense de*
no parking *stationnement interdit/ défense de stationner*
slow down *ralentissez*
slowly *lentement*
exit *sortie*
lane *voie*
right *droit(e)*
left *gauche*
Caution! *Attention!*

HEALTH
Help me please. *Aidez-moi, s'il vous plaît.*
I'm sick. *Je suis malade, Je me sens malade.*
I need a doctor. *J'ai besoin d'un médecin.*
medicine *le médicament*
I have a stomachache. *J'ai mal à l'estomac.*
I have a headache. *J'ai mal à la tête.*
fever *la fièvre*
diarrhea *la diarrhée*
cough *la toux*

Suggested Reading

HISTORY, POLITICS, AND CULTURE

Colburn, Kerry and Rob Sorensen. *So, You Want to Be Canadian: All About the Most Fascinating People in the World and the Magical Place We Call Home.* San Francisco: Chronicle Books, 2004. A humorous look at Canada and all things Canadian.

Colombo, John Robert. *1000 Questions About Canada.* Toronto: Dundurn Press, 2001. A wealth of facts and trivia about Canadian history and culture.

Coupland, Douglas. *Souvenir of Canada.* Vancouver: Douglas & McIntyre, 2002. Canadian culture dissected in a series of quirky essays and photos.

Coupland, Douglas. *Souvenir of Canada 2.* Vancouver: Douglas & McIntyre, 2004. More quirky essays and photos about Canadian culture.

Douglas, Ann. *Canuck Chicks and Maple Leaf Mamas: Women of the Great White North.* Toronto: McArthur & Company, 2002. A light-hearted chronicle of notable Canadian women from the worlds of entertainment, politics, sports, and more.

Ferguson, Will. *Canadian History for Dummies.* Toronto: John Wiley & Sons (Canada), 2005. The essentials of Canadian history distilled into an easy-to-read guide.

Ferguson, Will and Ian Ferguson. *How to Be a Canadian.* Vancouver: Douglas & McIntyre, 2003. An entertaining, satirical look at Canadian society.

Olive, David. *Canada Inside Out: How We See Ourselves, How Others See Us.* Toronto: Doubleday Canada Ltd., 1996. Quotations about Canada from notable people within the country and abroad.

Pevere, Geoff and Greig Dymond. *Mondo Canuck: A Canadian Pop Culture Odyssey.* Scarborough (ON): Prentice Hall Canada, 1996. A guide to Canadian popular culture.

See, Scott W. *The History of Canada.* Westport (CT): Greenwood Press, 2001. A useful overview of Canadian history.

Wong, Jan. *Lunch with Jan Wong.* Toronto: Anchor Canada, 2001. A Toronto journalist dishes the dirt she uncovered during lunches with various celebrities.

FICTION AND MEMOIR

Brand, Dionne. *What We All Long For.* Toronto: A. A. Knopf Canada, 2005. A novel about a young Toronto artist from a Vietnamese immigrant family and several of her friends.

Choy, Wayson. *The Jade Peony.* Vancouver: Douglas & McIntyre, 1995. A portrait of life in Vancouver's Chinatown in the early 20th century.

Kogawa, Joy. *Obasan.* Toronto: Penguin Canada, 2003 (© 1981). The internment and forced relocation of Japanese-Canadians in Western Canada during World War II, depicted through the eyes of a young girl.

McLean, Stuart. *Stories from the Vinyl Cafe.* Toronto: Penguin Canada, 2005. Based on the long-running CBC Radio program, "The Vinyl Cafe," stories from a beloved Canadian humorist and storyteller.

Munro, Alice. *Lives of Girls and Women.* New York: McGraw-Hill, 1973. A collection of linked stories chronicling a young woman's coming-of-age in small-town Ontario.

Proulx, Monique. *Aurora Montrealis.* Vancouver: Douglas & McIntyre, 2005. Short stories about life in 1990s Montréal.

Richler, Mordecai. *The Apprenticeship of Duddy Kravitz.* Toronto: McClelland & Stewart Ltd., 1989 (© 1959). A classic novel about an ambitious young Jewish man growing up in post-war Montréal.

Roy, Gabrielle. *Street of Riches.* Toronto: McClelland & Stewart Ltd., 1957. Stories set in the francophone community of St. Boniface, Manitoba.

Shields, Carol. *The Stone Diaries.* Toronto: Random House Canada, 1993. The Pulitzer Prize-winning fictional autobiography chronicling the life and times of an 80-year-old Canadian woman.

Shields, Carol. *Unless.* Toronto: Random House Canada, 2002. The eldest daughter of an Ontario novelist becomes a mute panhandler in downtown Toronto.

Taylor, Timothy. *Stanley Park.* Toronto: Vintage Canada, 2001. Locavore chefs, coffee magnates, and the homeless cross paths in this thriller set in and around Vancouver's largest green space.

GOVERNMENT PUBLICATIONS

Citizenship and Immigration Canada. *A Newcomer's Introduction to Canada.* Ottawa: Government Services Canada, 2002, www.cic.gc.ca/english/resources/publications/guide/index.asp. A government publication that provides a useful overview of the Canadian immigration process.

Citizenship and Immigration Canada. *Coming to Canada as a Business Immigrant.* Ottawa: Government Services Canada, 2004, www.cic.gc.ca/english/resources/publications/busimm.asp. A description of Canada's business immigration program, offering permanent resident status to investors, entrepreneurs, and the self-employed.

Citizenship and Immigration Canada. *You Asked About...Immigration and Citizenship.* Ottawa: Government Services Canada, 2002, www.cic.gc.ca/english/resources/publications/you-asked/index.asp. A guide to Canada's immigration policies with details about various immigration options.

Citizenship and Immigration Canada. *Working Temporarily in Canada.* Ottawa: Government Services Canada, 2005, www.cic.gc.ca/english/resources/publications/work-temp.asp. Guidelines for applying for a work permit in Canada.

Department of Canadian Heritage. *Official Languages: Myths and Realities.* Hull (QU): Government Services Canada, 1999. What it means to be a bilingual country.

NONFICTION

Brody, Leonard, and David Raffa. *Everything I Needed to Know About Business...I Learned from a Canadian.* Toronto: John Wiley & Sons Canada Ltd., 2005. Essays about business with commentary from Canadian entrepreneurs.

Laxer, James. *The Border: Canada, the US and Dispatches from the 49th Parallel.* Toronto: Random House Canada, 2003. A political science professor looks at U.S.-Canadian relations.

Ferguson, Will. *Beauty Tips from Moose Jaw.* Toronto: Knopf Canada, 2004. A satirical Canadian travelogue.

McLean, Stuart. *Welcome Home: Travels in Smalltown Canada.* Toronto: Penguin Books Canada, 2002 (© 1992). Tales from small communities across Canada.

Stackhouse, John. *Timbit Nation: A Hitchhiker's View of Canada.* Toronto: Random House Canada, 2003. A *Globe and Mail* reporter explores the Trans-Canada Highway, and the people and culture he discovers along the way.

Vaillant, John H. *The Golden Spruce: A True Story of Myth, Madness, and Greed.* Toronto: Alfred A. Knopf Canada, 2005. Environmentalism, native rights, and the logging industry clash after a sacred 300-year-old tree is cut down in British Columbia's Queen Charlotte Islands.

Yerema, Richard W., ed. *Canada's Top 100 Employers: The Nation's Best Places to Work.* Toronto: Mediacorp Canada, 2007. An annual guide profiling the best companies to work for in Canada.

TRAVEL GUIDES

Edwards, Jennifer. *Moon Montréal & Québec City.* Berkeley (CA): Avalon Travel, 2007.

Hempstead, Andrew. *Moon Alberta.* Berkeley (CA): Avalon Travel, 2007.

Hempstead, Andrew. *Moon Vancouver & Victoria.* Berkeley (CA): Avalon Travel, 2008.

Hempstead, Andrew. *Moon Western Canada.* Berkeley (CA): Avalon Travel, 2007.

Moon Metro Montréal. Berkeley (CA): Avalon Travel, 2007.

Moon Metro Vancouver. Berkeley (CA): Avalon Travel, 2008.

CHILDREN'S BOOKS

Chan, Gillian. *An Ocean Apart: The Gold Mountain Diary of Chin Mei-ling, Vancouver, British Columbia, 1922.* Markham (ON): Scholastic Canada, 2004. Part of the *Dear Canada* series of historical fiction.

Little, Jean. *Orphan at My Door: The Home Child Diary of Victoria Cope, Guelph, Ontario, 1897.* Markham (ON): Scholastic Canada, 2001. Part of the *Dear Canada* series of historical fiction.

Montgomery, L. M. *Anne of Green Gables.* Boston: L. C. Page, 1908. The Canadian classic about a spunky red-haired orphan living on Prince Edward Island.

Pearson, Kit. *Whispers of War: The War of 1812 Diary of Susanna Merritt, Niagara, Upper Canada, 1812.* Markham (ON): Scholastic Canada, 2002. Part of the *Dear Canada* series of historical fiction.

Spencer, Bev. *You Can't Do That in Canada: Crazy Laws from Coast to Coast.* Richmond Hill (ON): Scholastic Canada, 2000. A humorous look at what's legal and illegal across Canada.

Index

Acknowledgments

Without the help, support, and hospitality of many people and organizations across Canada and elsewhere, this book could not have been written.

For information and travel assistance in British Columbia, my thanks to Heather Kirk and Laura Serena, Immedia PR; Deirdre Campbell, Melinda Jolley, and Trisha Lees, Tartan Public Relations; Jessica Harcombe, Bellstar Hotels & Resorts; Bellasera Tuscan Villas, Kelowna; Predator Ridge Golf Resort, Vernon; Westin Bear Mountain, Victoria; and Debora Annan, Sheerwater, Kelowna. In the Victoria area, thanks also to Peter Daniel, Aquattro; the staff at Dockside Green; Richard Lovett, Bayview Properties; Dale Sproule, Bear Mountain Resort; Ross Tennant, Three Point Properties; Kevin Walker, Oak Bay Beach Hotel; and fellow foodie Kathy McAree of Travel with Taste.

In Ontario, many thanks to the Ottawa Tourism team, especially Jantine Van Kregten and Misty Wade Hovey; Teresa Spagnuolo at Toronto Tourism; Alex Busetti, TD Canada Trust; relocation specialist Patrice Gale, Royal LePage Real Estate Services Ltd. Brokerage; relocation specialist Heidi Nelson, Harvey Kalles Real Estate Ltd. Brokerage; Caroline Risi, Extended Stay Deluxe Hotel, Ottawa; Jerry Ross, Lowther Suites, Toronto; Annex Quest House, Toronto; Ted Genova; Sheila Hayes; Josh Lawson; Julia McKinnell; Melanie Scott; and the Toronto Serial Diners.

In Alberta, my appreciation to the staff at Travel Alberta, especially Elise Stephenson; Kelly Bertoncini and the Edmonton Tourism team; Jon Hall, Realtors Association of Edmonton; Kelly James Lewis, Tourism Calgary; Scott Logan, Edmonton Economic Development Corporation; Regency Suites Hotel Calgary; Ron Stanners, Calgary Real Estate Board; and Sherril Will, Chateau Nova Edmonton. Special thanks to relocation specialists Sandra Green and Daphne Bezovie at Community Compass, who know everything there is to know about moving to Edmonton.

Heaps of thanks to the team at Avalon Travel, including acquisitions manager Grace Fujimoto, editor extraordinaire Elizabeth McCue, production coordinator Domini Dragoone, cartographic editor Brice Ticen, and everyone else behind the scenes. For taking the time to offer helpful suggestions, thank you to Moon authors Andrew Hempstead and Erin Van Rheenen.

For sharing their stories and their friendship, a toast to fellow expats Pat Baird, Audrey Brashich, Ara Cusack, Joe Herron, Thibault Mayor, Celeste Moure, Chris Sjoholm, and Vanessa Warheit. For helping introduce us to Vancouver way back when, thank you to Dave and Kim Fujisawa, and for sharing her contacts (and coaxing me out for many a run), thanks to Karen Taylor.

Many thanks to Andy Pickar for making sure we could still get the *New York Times*, to Judy Levine for marketing advice, and to Keith Behnke and Vicki Arbitrio for letting me write at your dining room table.

Thank you to Ellie Siden and Hannah Siden for being good sports about dinner in Montréal and Québec City. A thousand thanks to Anne Gorsuch and Hal Siden, for offering all sorts of information and advice, feeding the kids, and just being there. It takes a village...

And finally, my gratitude to my family: to Michaela and Talia, for cheerfully and enthusiastically settling into our new Canadian life, and to Alan, for launching us on our Canadian adventure and providing companionship, humor, and love along the way.

www.moon.com

For helpful advice on planning a trip, visit www.moon.com for the **TRAVEL PLANNER** and get access to useful travel strategies and valuable information about great places to visit. When you travel with Moon, expect an experience that is uncommon and truly unique.

HANDBOOKS • OUTDOORS • METRO • LIVING ABRO

MAP SYMBOLS

▰▰▰▰ Expressway	○ City/Town	✗ Airfield	▰ Archaeological Site
══════ Primary Road	◉ State Capital	✈ Airport	⚑ Church
▱▱▱▱ Secondary Road	❂ National Capital	▲ Mountain	⛽ Gas Station
▪ ▪ ▪ ▪ Unpaved Road			Mangrove
⋯⋯⋯ Ferry	★ Point of Interest	♠ Park	Reef
━▪━▪━ Railroad	▪ Other Location	🎿 Skiing Area	Swamp

CONVERSION TABLES

°C = (°F − 32) / 1.8
°F = (°C x 1.8) + 32
1 inch = 2.54 centimeters (cm)
1 foot = 0.304 meters (m)
1 yard = 0.914 meters
1 mile = 1.6093 kilometers (km)
1 km = 0.6214 miles
1 fathom = 1.8288 m
1 chain = 20.1168 m
1 furlong = 201.168 m
1 acre = 0.4047 hectares
1 sq km = 100 hectares
1 sq mile = 2.59 square km
1 ounce = 28.35 grams
1 pound = 0.4536 kilograms
1 short ton = 0.90718 metric ton
1 short ton = 2,000 pounds
1 long ton = 1.016 metric tons
1 long ton = 2,240 pounds
1 metric ton = 1,000 kilograms
1 quart = 0.94635 liters
1 US gallon = 3.7854 liters
1 Imperial gallon = 4.5459 liters
1 nautical mile = 1.852 km

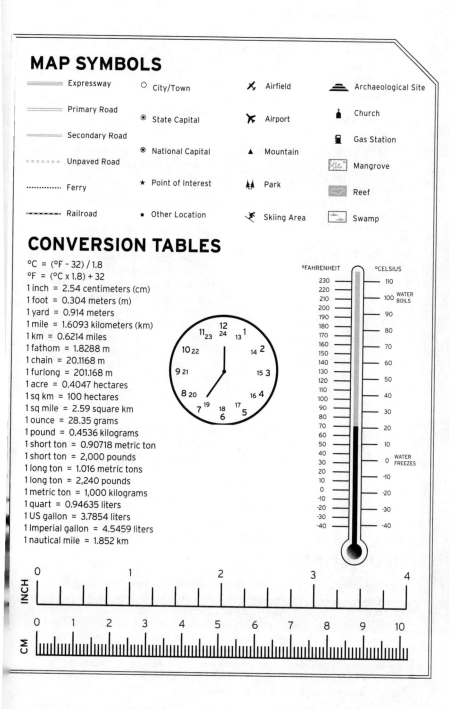

MOON LIVING ABROAD IN CANADA

Avalon Travel
a member of the Perseus Books Group
1700 Fourth Street
Berkeley, CA 94710, USA
www.moon.com

Editor and Series Manager: Elizabeth McCue
Copy Editor: Ellie Behrstock
Graphics and Production Coordinator: Domini
Dragoone
Layout: Amber Pirker
Cover Designer: Domini Dragoone
Map Editor: Brice Ticen
Cartographers: Kat Bennett, Mike Morgenfeld
Indexer: Judy Hunt

ISBN-10: 1-59880-046-9
ISBN-13: 978-1-59880-046-3
ISSN: 1942-5996

Printing History
1st Edition – September 2008
5 4 3 2 1

Some photos and illustrations are used by
permission and are the property of the original
copyright owners.

Front cover photo: Pedestrians Walking in the
Rain on Rue de Petit Champlain, © Richard T.
Nowitz/Corbis

Title page photo: Flags wave near Toronto's Old
City Hall, © Carolyn B. Heller

Interior photos: © Carolyn B. Heller except: pg.
6, 7 (top left) and 8 (top left and bottom) ©
Alan Albert.

Printed in the United States by RR Donnelley

KEEPING CURRENT

Although we strive to produce the most up-to-date guidebook that we possibly can, change
is unavoidable. Between the time this book goes to print and the time you read it, the
cost of goods and services may have increased, and a handful of the businesses noted
in these pages will undoubtedly move, alter their prices, or close their doors forever.
Exchange rates fluctuate – sometimes dramatically – on a daily basis. Federal and local
legal requirements and restrictions are also subject to change, so be sure to check with
the appropriate authorities before making the move. If you see anything in this book that
needs updating, clarification, or correction, please drop us a line. Send your comments via
email to feedback@moon.com, or use the address above.